AF478194

THE CULTURE OF REGIONALISM

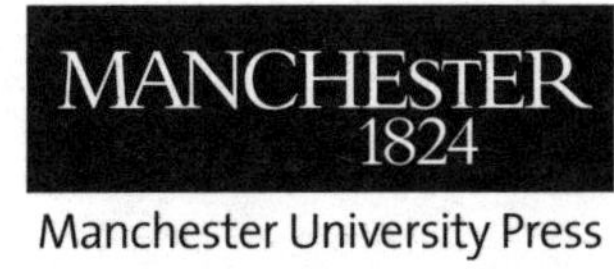

Manchester University Press

THE CULTURE OF REGIONALISM

Art, architecture and international exhibitions in France, Germany and Spain, 1890–1939

Eric Storm

Manchester University Press

Manchester and New York

distributed in the United States exclusively
by Palgrave Macmillan

Published by Manchester University Press
Oxford Road, Manchester M13 9NR, UK
and Room 400, 175 Fifth Avenue, New York, NY 10010, USA
www.manchesteruniversitypress.co.uk

Distributed in the United States exclusively by
Palgrave Macmillan, 175 Fifth Avenue, New York,
NY 10010, USA

Distributed in Canada exclusively by
UBC Press, University of British Columbia, 2029 West Mall,
Vancouver, BC, Canada V6T 1Z2

British Library Cataloguing-in-Publication Data
A catalogue record for this book is available from the British Library

Library of Congress Cataloging-in-Publication Data applied for

ISBN   978 0 7190 8147 7   hardback

First published 2010

The publisher has no responsibility for the persistence or accuracy of URLs for any external or third-party internet websites referred to in this book, and does not guarantee that any content on such websites is, or will remain, accurate or appropriate.

Designed and typeset
by Carnegie Book Production, Lancaster
Printed in Great Britain
by the MPG Books Group, UK

Contents

Plates and figures

Plates

Figures

Acknowledgements

This study of the culture of regionalism in France, Germany and Spain has been made possible by the generous support of various institutions. The funding for this post-doctoral research project was provided in 2002 by the Innovational Research Incentives Scheme of the Netherlands Organisation for Scientific Research (NWO). It has been matched, first, by the Faculty of Humanities of the University of Amsterdam and, from 2004 onwards, by the Faculty of Arts of Leiden University. A fellowship for 2007–8 from the Netherlands Institute for Advanced Study in the Humanities and Social Sciences (NIAS), idyllically located in the dunes of Wassenaar, enormously helped me to finish my manuscript. I am also grateful for a grant from the Van Eesteren-Fluck and Van Lohuizen Stichting, which funded the reproduction of the illustrations in this book. Finally, I thank Sage Publications for allowing me to republish various portions of my article 'Painting regional identities: nationalism in the arts, France, Germany and Spain, 1890–1914', from *European History Quarterly* (2009–4) in part I.

It is a pleasure to thank those who have supported this project in its various stages. They include Niek van Sas, Wim van der Doel, José Álvarez Junco, Juan Pablo Fusi, Xosé Manoel Núñez Seixas, Gerard Rooijakkers, Joep Leerssen, Dario Gamboni, Anne-Marie Thiesse and Karl Ditt. Neil McWilliam and Koos Bosma both supported my project and provided valuable suggestions and comments on some of my writing. They also helped me in their respective fields of art history and architectural history, which as a cultural historian were quite new for me. In this aspect I was also helped by various specialists of regionalist art and architecture, among whom I should mention Pedro Navascués Palacio, Alberto Villar Movellán, Javier González de Durana, Mariano Gómez de Caso, Wolfgang Voigt, Winfried Nerdinger, Hartmut Frank, Bernd Küster, François Loyer and André Cariou. Javier Moreno Luzón, Fernando Molina and José Luis de la Granja also provided me with valuable information on Spanish developments. Finally, I would like to thank my colleagues at the history departments of Amsterdam and Leiden and the fellows and staff of the NIAS for providing a stimulating environment. The support and assistance of all these people, and – last but not least – of my family and friends, have made this book possible, while any remaining shortcomings are my own.

Introduction

In 1904 the Provençal poet Frédéric Mistral was awarded the Nobel Prize
in Literature. Mistral decided to use the prize money to find a place to
exhibit a recently created collection in a proper museum in the nearby town
of Arles. Instead of showing paintings, sculptures, archaeological findings,
historical objects and other elements from high culture, the Museon Arlaten
put on display traditional costumes, local artisanal tools, old furniture and
even outdated cooking utensils. At about the same time, another French
writer, Edmond Rostand, decided to use the royalties from *Cyrano de
Bergerac*, the play which had brought him world fame, to construct a villa
in Cambo-les-Bains modelled after local Basque farmsteads. Why did these
famous authors refrain from collecting high art and building a palace or a
chateau as other nouveau riches would have done? Why did they instead
look for inspiration to vernacular buildings and were attracted to the
primitive folk culture of the countryside, going even to the extreme of
living in a villa that looked like a farm house and filling a museum with
rusty utensils and tools?

In the years after the turn of the twentieth century they were not
the only ones that showed a great interest in the popular culture of the
countryside. One could even speak of a widespread international trend
that could be labelled as 'regionalism'. But how should we understand
regionalism? Should regionalism, as many experts suggest, be interpreted
as a kind of 'awakening of the regions', brought about by a process of
growing collective self-awareness. This interpretation applies perfectly to
Mistral, who was the central figure in the Félibrige movement which aimed
to 'revive' and promote the language and literature of the Provence. With
his museum, Mistral hoped to increase the knowledge and awareness of
the region's identity. However, with Rostand the situation is different. He
came from a bourgeois family from Marseilles and later moved to Paris.
He only went to Cambo-les-Bains on the advice of his doctor to recover

from an attack of pleurisy. He liked it so much that he asked the Parisian architect Albert Tournaire to design a neo-Basque villa for him (see figure 10, p.117).[1] One might argue that his interest in local folk culture was rather superficial, since for instance the interior of the villa was a very eclectic mixture with an English hall, Louis XVI and Empire furniture and even a Chinese smoking room. But it is undeniable that Rostand and his architect contributed to the (re-)definition of the regional identity of this South-Western part of France by helping to create a neo-Basque architectural style, which would become quite popular in subsequent years. As will become clear in this study on the culture of regionalism in France, Germany and Spain between 1890 and 1939, 'outsiders' were probably more influential in (further) outlining regional identities than 'natives'.

A further problem with the accepted view is that the word 'awakening' suggests that the regional identity is already there, waiting to be discovered. This is an essentialist interpretation, which is also dear to nationalists who see the nation as a given, as something that was already there from time immemorial. Recent research on nationalism, however, has shown that this was not the case; nations are constructions and not very old. Does this imply that regions, or at least a widespread awareness of clearly circumscribed regional identities, have all been also established recently? In any case, to be fruitful, an analysis of regionalism should incorporate the new scholarship on nationalism, particularly because over the last few decades our understanding of nationalism has changed drastically. Hence, before further exploring and defining regionalism, we should first briefly review some of the most influential new interpretations of nationalism.

Path-breaking studies by Ernest Gellner, Eric Hobsbawm and Benedict Anderson, all published in 1983, have made it clear that nationalism was essentially a modern phenomenon and that national identities had been mostly invented deliberately. Anderson pointed out that nationalism could have only come into existence after the emergence of a modern secular world view and the creation of standard languages which was brought about by the rapid development of print capitalism. He also argued that nations, as 'imagined communities', were in fact cultural constructs. Gellner added that nations and nationalism were inconceivable in agrarian societies. A modern, capitalistic and industrialised society, on the contrary, presupposed a homogeneous national culture and the widespread knowledge of a standard language. Whereas craftsmen and farmers learned their trade in

---

[1] See, for example: Claude Mauron, *Frédéric Mistral* (Paris 1993), Sue Lloyd, *The Man Who Was Cyrano: A Life of Edmond Rostand, Creator of Cyrano de Bergerac* (Bloomington 2002) and Michel Forrier, *Petite Histoire d'Arnaga* (Pau 2006).

practice, industrial workers should be able to read manuals of different machines, change jobs and be able to communicate in the national language. Hobsbawm, in turn, argued that the nation-building process, which really started after the transition to modernity, required a great amount of invented traditions and he thus emphasised the largely artificial nature of national identities.[2]

In general there is a broad agreement that the French Revolution was the main watershed. Before 1789 identity was essentially defined by social position, profession and religion. Thus members of the clergy, nobility, bourgeoisie, the guilds, farmers and urban and rural poor generally related, socialised and married within their own social class. People from the various social groups generally dressed and behaved differently, had a different culture and used their own language or dialect. At the same time, frontiers between principalities and languages were porous and diffuse and in times of peace had little effect on the way people identified themselves. This changed radically when in 1789 all legal differences between the various estates, social groups, provinces, towns and guilds were abolished and consequently all subjects of the king became equal citizens of the French nation. Moreover, nationality not only became the main legal difference, distinguishing the citizens of France from foreigners, but it also had a political dimension, namely, royal absolutism was replaced by the sovereignty of the nation. As a result every adult (male) citizen had the right to participate in politics and co-determine the future of the nation.[3] In the following years and during the subsequent Napoleonic Wars, the ideals of the French Revolution and many of its reforms were exported to most parts of Europe.

This modernist interpretation has been seriously contested and criticised, particularly by Anthony Smith. In various studies he has underlined the continuity between ethnic and national identities and the relevance of common elements and patterns that could be found in both modern and pre-modern collective identities. Nonetheless, even Smith recognises the fundamental shift caused by the rise of modernity and the French Revolution and the fact that national identities became much more pervasive and

---

[2] Ernest Gellner, *Nations and Nationalism* (Ithaca 1983), Benedict Anderson, *Imagined Communities: Reflections on the Origin and Spread of Nationalism* (1983, revised edn., London and New York 1991), Eric Hobsbawm and Terence Ranger eds., *The Invention of Tradition* (Cambridge 1983) and Eric Hobsbawm, *Nations and Nationalism since 1780: Programme, Myth, Reality* (Cambridge 1990).

[3] See for a detailed study on this topic: David A. Bell, *The Cult of the Nation in France: Inventing Nationalism, 1680–1800* (Cambridge and London 2001).

paramount than ethnic identities had ever been.[4] Although other scholars have also been critical of Anderson, Gellner and Hobsbawm and revised or nuanced several aspects of their work, their main arguments have been largely accepted. Stimulated both by their view and the renewed actuality of nationalism since the 1980s – particularly after the fall of the Berlin Wall – a great number of studies have emerged which have enormously improved our knowledge of the rise of nationalism, the process of nation-building and the creation of national identities in almost all areas of the globe.[5]

Due to this body of knowledge, it has also become clear that during the nineteenth century a great part of the population, even in such modern nation-states as France, did not identify with the nation nor were even aware of their national identity. Already in 1976 Eugen Weber showed that peasants had to be transformed into Frenchmen and this, according to him, was largely done by an active policy of nation-building by the central State. In a recent book Graham Robb even raises doubts about whether this process was complete at the beginning of the twentieth century. Nevertheless, many historians have criticised Weber's view that a national elite imposed a process of nationalisation upon the periphery by means of education, military service, improved communications, a growing State bureaucracy and political propaganda. Authors such as Sahlins, Ford and Baycroft have persuasively argued that the regions were not passive recipients of a modern nation-building policy imposed by Parisian elites. In many cases, inhabitants of the periphery actively urged the central State to play a more active and interventionist role by invoking their national identity.[6]

A further result of these investigations has been that the strict dichotomy between a civic or political nationalism and an ethnic or

---

[4] Anthony D. Smith, *The Ethnic Origins of Nations* (Oxford 1986). He has written many other books and articles in which he continues to defend his position, such as Anthony D. Smith, *Nationalism and Modernism: A Critical Survey of Recent Theories of Nations and Nationalism* (London and New York 1998).

[5] See for a recent overview on the role of nationalism in Europe: Anne-Marie Thiesse, *La Création des identités nationales: Europe XVIIIe-XXe siècle* (Paris 1999) and Joep Leerssen, *National Thought in Europe: A Cultural History* (Amsterdam 2006).

[6] Eugen Weber, *Peasants into Frenchmen: The Modernization of Rural France* (Stanford 1976), Graham Robb, *The Discovery of France: Historical Geography from the Revolution to the First World War* (New York and London 2007), Peter Sahlins, *Boundaries: The Making of France and Spain in the Pyrenees* (Berkeley 1989), Caroline Ford, *Creating the Nation in Provincial France: Religion and Political Identity in Brittany* (Princeton 1993) and Timothy Baycroft, *Culture, Identity and Nationalism: French Flanders in the Nineteenth and Twentieth Century* (Woodbridge 2004). See also: Miguel Cabo and Fernando Molina, 'The Long and Winding Road of Nationalization: Eugen Weber's Peasants into Frenchmen in Modern European History (1976–2006)', *European History Quarterly* (2009) 264–86.

cultural nationalism – respectively associated especially with the French and German case – has been called into question. Political nationalism accordingly strove essentially for political rights of the citizens, who were merely defined as those who resided (for a minimum of years) in the country. Cultural nationalism, in turn, emphasized the shared language, history, ethnic descent, traditions and culture, and thus more or less explicitly excluded from the national community those inhabitants who had a different language or were from a different ethnic or cultural background. Many authors have already stressed that both variants were present in almost all cases and intermingled easily. Moreover, as Charlotte Tacke has pointed out, these presumed different national paths have heavily influenced later historiography. Most research on nationalism is embedded within national historiographic traditions and this way all kinds of supposed collective characteristics, which were highlighted by nationalists, still guide historical research. Thus German scholars have focused essentially on cultural forms of nationalism, whereas French historians preferred topics concerned with political nationalism.[7] Although there is still a certain disproportion, this situation has significantly changed during the last few years.

These new perspectives also influenced the study of regionalism, which had been largely disregarded in the decades after 1945. This disinterest was directly related to the dominant role of modernisation theory in the historical discourse of the post-war era, which assumed that separate regional economies, politics and cultures were doomed to be swallowed up by the nation. As Celia Applegate has argued, it was only in the 1970s, when historical sociologists such as Wallerstein and Rokkan developed their centre–periphery model, that the region received new attention. Research concentrated on the economic marginalisation and political oppression of certain areas by the centre. A relatively recent example of this focus is offered by the 1994 special issue of *Geschichte und Gesellschaft*, dedicated to 'Nationalism and Regionalism in Western Europe', which deals with Northern Ireland, Catalonia, the Basque Country and various 'underprivileged' regions within France.[8]

---

[7] See for example Timothy Baycroft and Mark Hewitson eds., *What is a Nation? Europe 1789–1914* (Oxford 2006) and Charlotte Tacke, 'National Symbols in France and Germany in the Nineteenth Century' in: Heinz-Gerhard Haupt, Michael Müller and Stuart Woolf eds., *Regional and National Identities in Europe in the XIXth and XXth Centuries* (The Hague 1998) 411–36.

[8] Celia Applegate, 'A Europe of Regions: Reflections on the Historiography of Sub-National Places in Modern Times', *American Historical Review* (1999) 1157–83. *Geschichte und Gesellschaft* XX (1994) Heft 3.

Since the early 1990s, however, regional identities and regionalism have been very fruitfully studied by integrating the new methods and the results of the research on nationalism, nation-building and national identities. This has the advantage that now all regions are of interest, rather than only the 'unhappy regions' in which the national identity was contested.[9] Thus, whereas it was previously assumed that national identities replaced older, traditional regional identities, it now has become clear that this was not the case. Regional identities, in fact, were more precisely defined or even invented after 1890 when the corresponding national identity had already largely crystallised.[10] Therefore, we could define regionalism in a more neutral way as the movement that promoted the study, construction and reinforcement of regional identity. To understand the rise of regionalism, however, we should first briefly sketch the development of the nation-building process in Western Europe.

During the first part of the nineteenth century, the process of nation-building had been directed principally towards defeating the forces of the *Ancien Régime* by legitimising a more or less constitutional liberal government or at least creating the basis for one, and if necessary creating a national State where there was none before. The driving forces were the bourgeois elites and the upper-middle class. Around 1870, when a more or less liberal regime had been installed in most West-European countries, the nation-building process had to be adapted to the new situation. During the first half of the nineteenth century nationalists still generally thought that a bright future of peaceful coexisting nation-states awaited humankind if every people would have their own State in which the citizens would effectively control the political institutions. At the end of the century, however, these optimistic hopes slowly faded as people from both the left and the right increasingly refused to accept the nation as the highest ideal. Socialists and anarchists preferred the international solidarity of the

---

9   Applegate, 'A Europe of Regions' and Eric Storm, 'Regionalism in History, 1890–1945: The Cultural Approach', *European History Quarterly* (2003) 251–65.
10   Celia Applegate, *A Nation of Provincials: The German Idea of Heimat* (Berkeley 1990), Alon Confino, 'The Nation as a Local Metaphor: Heimat, National Memory and the German Empire, 1871–1918', *History & Memory* (1993) 42–86, Thomas Kühne, 'Die Region als Konstrukt: Regionalgeschichte als Kulturgeschichte' in: James Retallack ed., *Sachsen in Deutschland: Politik, Kultur und Gesellschaft 1830–1918* (Bielefeld 2000) 253–64, Jean-Clément Martin, 'La Construction culturelle d'une région, la Vendée' in: Heinz-Gerhard Haupt, Michael Müller and Stuart Woolf eds., *Regional and National Identities in Europe in the XIXth and XXth Centuries* (The Hague 1998) 437–65, Manuel Suárez-Cortina, *Casonas, hidalgos y linajes: La invención de la tradición cántabra* (Santander 1994).

workers, whereas confessional parties primarily seemed to observe their religion and the guidelines set by their leaders which did not necessarily stop at national frontiers. Thus, in the eyes of most more or less liberal nationalists it became necessary to socialise the new voters from the lower classes and make them aware of their national identity in order to safeguard the existing political order.

At the same time, international co-operation and free trade suffered as the colonial race and the introduction of tariff barriers increased the political and economic rivalry between the European powers. This led to a more aggressive foreign policy, not only of the major colonial powers, which protected and extended their existing colonies, but also of late-comers like the German Empire, which claimed or annexed areas with a German-speaking population such as Alsace-Lorraine. In most European countries, these escalating international tensions contributed to the rise of a new nationalism, as they fuelled the need to nationalise the masses in order to overcome internal discord and stimulate national unity. As a result, conscious attempts to stimulate national feeling were no longer directed toward clubs, academies and learned societies, where the upper classes gathered, but had to be visible to wider audiences. Nationalism now conquered the streets in the form of national holidays, parades, festivals, statues, and large-scale commemorations. This process had already begun around 1870 but clearly gained momentum during the last decade of the nineteenth century.[11]

Not only the political climate deteriorated, dampening optimism, but the same was also true for the cultural sphere. Belief in progress, sustained by new scientific discoveries in a better and more rational organisation of society, economic growth and the possibility of an increased general well-being that would reach all strata of the population, gradually faded. Many intellectuals now began to fear that society, instead of producing better and more sensible citizens, was disintegrating, and had entered a phase of decadence. They felt that the moral and physical degeneration of broad layers of the population constituted a serious threat to political stability. The rationalist and positivistic views and perspectives of scientists and sociologists, which had also been adopted by many progressive politicians and intellectuals, were increasingly criticised as being too rigid and limited. Reality could not be fully understood with rational methods, nor could science solve all human and social problems. After all, man was not only

---

11 See for example: Hobsbawm, *Nations and Nationalism since 1780*, Thiesse, *La Création des identités nationales*, and Oliver Zimmer, *Nationalism in Europe, 1890–1940* (Basingstoke and New York 2003).

a rational being, but also had irrational feelings, subjective fears, instincts and dreams that were as real as the objective world, the domain of science and rationality.

Both the more difficult political situation and the subjectivist cultural turn heavily influenced young intellectuals across Europe. Some, like Julius Langbehn, Maurice Barrès and Ángel Ganivet, began to revise existing nationalist ideologies. They were deeply influenced by the French historian Hippolyte Taine, who had tried to develop a scientific method to study the cultural past. According to Taine, every cultural expression was determined by *race, milieu et moment* (race, environment and moment). Every work of art, literature, or music could be explained by studying the national traditions, the natural environment and the specific historical situation in which it was produced. This view implied that every cultural expression was almost completely determined by its context. Whereas Taine used race, environment and moment as analytical concepts to study the past, these young intellectuals converted them into present-day moral categories. Meaningful cultural expressions had to be rooted in the national past and the natural environment, and they had to reflect current needs. In this way they converted an 'objective' method of historical study into a subjective, present-day obligation to create a truly national culture.[12]

Their idealist outlook also manifested itself in their endeavour to revive the romantic idea of *Volksgeist* (spirit/genius of the people/nation). Since they accepted the influence of physical environment on cultural expression, they expanded *Volksgeist*'s meaning to include regions as well as nations. Mountainous areas, for example, required different cultural adaptations than living on plains or along a coast. They consequently concluded that each region had its own 'genius' and that all regions combined constituted the national spirit. This mode of thinking became entwined with biological terminology, which had become popular thanks to Darwin. The nation was seen as a body and the regions as its organs. If one part was missing or had been amputated, then the whole organism suffered. Such a loss could even threaten its existence. The health of the whole could only be guaranteed by the well-being of its parts; and health, in the vocabulary of *Volksgeist*, meant being faithful to one's unique personality.

---

[12] See, for example: Julius Langbehn, *Rembrandt als Erzieher: Von einem Deutschen* (Leipzig 1890), Maurice Barrès, *Les Déracinés* (Paris 1897), Maurice Barrès, *Scènes et doctrines du nationalisme* (Paris 1902), and Ángel Ganivet, *Idearium español* (Madrid 1897). See also: Fritz Stern, *The Politics of Cultural Despair: A Study in the Rise of the Germanic Ideology* (Berkeley 1961), Zeev Sternhell, *Maurice Barrès et le nationalisme français* (Paris 1972) and Eric Storm, *La perspectiva del progreso: Pensamiento político en la España del cambio de siglo (1890–1914)* (Madrid 2001).

This kind of reasoning did not necessarily lead to a reactionary or extremely conservative attitude. A 'popular spirit' could, after all, be seen as the historical product of a people living in a certain area. Within the natural and climatic limits set by the environment, people adapted themselves to circumstances. At the same time they also exploited nature to meet their needs. The result of this historical process of adaptation to and dominance of nature constituted a particular area's specific cultural form. Crucially, however, these intellectuals believed that this process should not be halted or undone. It should only be rectified if necessary and then only in accordance with the voice of the 'collective soul' in order to regain its true course.

There were some developments around 1890 which led not only to changes in the national sphere, but also occasioned a fundamental shift at the local level. Until that point the study of regional identities appealed only to a small group of provincial notables and as a consequence had been a quite limited phenomenon. The historical, archaeological and geographic backgrounds of a region were analysed within a wider context and as an indispensable – if not always fully recognised – contribution to national greatness. The results of these erudite studies were generally presented to the members of learned societies or to the local elite.[13] Nonetheless, it is doubtful whether the term regionalism is appropriate for describing the activities of these scholars, as they were not so much interested in the idiosyncratic identity that distinguished their region from the rest of the nation as in those elements that made it an irreplaceable part of the whole.

During the last decade of the nineteenth century this situation changed as young, well-educated members of the local elite attempted to mingle with a broader public. This meant they had to develop other forms of sociability and expression. In order to mobilise the middle and lower classes, they founded new regional associations that were essentially oriented towards recreational activities. Instead of giving lectures, organising banquets and publishing erudite studies, they now undertook excursions, staged festivals and opened local museums. They also began to appreciate local dialects or vernacular languages, not only as an object of study but also as a vehicle for publication. At the same time, probably influenced by the

---

13 See, for example: Stéphane Gerson, *The Pride of Place: Local Memories and Political Culture in Nineteenth-Century France* (Ithaca and London 2003), Applegate, *A Nation of Provincials* 31–68, Georg Kunz, *Verortete Geschichte: Regionales Geschichtsbewusstsein in den deutschen Historischen Vereinen des 19. Jahrhunderts* (Göttingen 2000), Josep M. Fradera, 'La política liberal y el descubrimiento de una identidad distinctiva en Cataluña (1835–1865)', *Hispania* (2000) 673–702, and Sören Brinkmann, *Der Stolz der Provinzen, Regionalbewußtein und Nationalstaatsbau im Spanien des 19. Jahrhunderts* (Frankfurt 2005).

new interpretations of the *Volksgeist* concept, their attention shifted from a distant past, in which the roots of regional and national identity were to be found, to the current cultural and natural patrimony that distinguished their region from the rest of the nation. Thus excursions were taken to peculiar landscapes, historical and natural sights, and to typical villages, small towns and buildings. Regional museums, such as the one in Arles, began to display local handicrafts, old tools, traditional costumes, and other folk items; vernacular art, architecture, literature and other expressions of traditional popular culture became the focus of attention.[14] Although they stressed the idiosyncratic identity of their homeland, in general they continued to underscore that their region was organically connected to the broader fatherland. Regionalism, as a consequence, has been interpreted as a new phase in the nation-building process as most 'new' regional identities supplemented the existing national identities by vastly broadening the national heritage and by providing it with local roots.[15]

The rise of both the new regional movements and a more activist nationalism – in which ample space was accorded to individual regional identities, as long as they continued to form an integral part of the national body – had an enormous impact upon the various European countries. The new appreciation of folklore, historical monuments, traditional buildings, customs, crafts, typical landscapes and natural sights led to attempts to protect the highlights of the regional and national heritage. As a result, the preservation of natural and historical sites received massive support, and all kinds of traditional artefacts were collected by both individuals and museums. Even high culture was affected as ethnology became a new branch of science and as composers, writers, architects and sculptors increasingly included popular motifs in their works. While this was not completely new, its scale was now much greater. In this way, a few isolated precursors became part of a broad movement and a highly influential public discourse.

---

[14] Applegate, *A Nation of Provincials* 60–107, Alon Confino, *The Nation as a Local Metaphor: Württemberg, Imperial Germany, and National Memory, 1871–1918* (Chapel Hill 1997), Karl Ditt, 'Die deutsche Heimatbewegung 1871–1945': in Will Cremer and Ansgar Klein eds., *Heimat: Analysen, Themen, Perspektiven* (Bielefeld 1990) 135–55, Joan-Lluis Marfany, *La cultura del catalanisme en els seus inicis* (Barcelona 1995), Anne-Marie Thiesse, *Écrire la France: Le Mouvement littéraire régionaliste de langue française entre la Belle Epoque et la Libération* (Paris 1991), and Julian Wright, *The Regionalist Movement in France 1890–1914: Jean Charles-Brun and French Political Thought* (Oxford 2003).

[15] Applegate, *A Nation of Provincials*, Confino, *The Nation as a Local Metaphor*, Thiesse, *Écrire la France* and Xosé-Manoel Núñez, 'The Region as Essence of the Fatherland: Regionalist Variants of Spanish Nationalism (1840–1936)', *European History Quarterly* XXXI (2001) 483–518.

Karl Ditt, a specialist on the German regional movement, even calls regionalist culture – for which he uses the German terms *Heimat-* and *Volkstumskultur* – one of the five important cultural forms of the period between the end of the nineteenth and the middle of the twentieth century. He also mentions high culture, avant-garde culture, working-class culture and mass culture. According to him, the last two forms created their own separate sphere, whereas the regionalist culture and the avant-garde started to compete with the existing high culture. The avant-garde attacked the outdated esthetical norms which hampered artistic freedom and creativity. The regionalists in turn, criticised the elitist and cosmopolitan character of high culture. Instead of an international genius-driven cultural progress, its representatives tried to stimulate the organic growth of a popular culture that had its roots in the *Volksgeist*. The individual was not free, but bound by nature, the past and tradition. All cultural expressions had to be oriented on this common background. If they were not, the result would be collective degeneration.[16]

Ditt's characterisation of German regionalism – together with the avant-garde – as the main challenger of the existing high culture can easily be transported to most other European countries. Regionalism, in fact, was an extremely important cultural trend that started around 1890 as an innovative tendency. Like other reform movements at the end of the century, regionalists criticised classical laissez-faire liberalism for ignoring local differences and refraining from any state intervention. Furthermore, regionalism with its stress on participation and its anti-elitism also had a clear democratic component. About a decade later it became a mainstream movement. It was thought that every region had its own 'soul' and, as an organic part of the nation, its particular character should be studied and reinforced. As a result the period between roughly 1890 and 1939 became the golden age of regionalist popular culture. Local museums, regionalist periodicals, folkloric festivals, plays in provincial dialect and regional novels, flowered as never before, and the preservation of typical natural scenery, vernacular architecture and popular arts and handicrafts were seen as a vital necessity.

The ascendancy of the various European Fascist parties constituted an important turning point in the history of regionalism. Many of their activists accepted or even supported the new Fascist regimes, as they hoped to realise their ideal of a harmonious society in line with national and regional

---

[16] Karl Ditt, 'Konservative Kulturvorstellungen und Kulturpolitik vom Kaiserreich bis zum Dritten Reich', *Neue Politische Literatur* XLI (1996) 230–60, especially 230–2.

traditions within the new State. In general, the Fascist parties supported parts of the regionalist programme, like the idyllic notion of an untouched countryside as the heartland of the nation. Nevertheless, other aspects of their ideology clashed with regionalist thought and practice. The strong centralism of the new regimes, their cult of violence, modernism, brutality, totalitarian character, and (particularly in the German case) racism were incompatible with the mostly peaceful and multiform regionalist culture. Contrary to the expectations of many regionalists, regionalism did not really prosper in the new States. Some of its projects were realised, but in general regionalist associations were purged of undesirable elements, had to follow the instructions of the new leaders and finally were openly deployed to realise the rather different goals of the Fascist regimes.[17]

The collaborative attitude of many regionalists and the appropriation of regionalism by Fascism determined the historiographic fate of the movement. After 1945 regionalism – like the region in general – was generally viewed negatively as a backward-looking force and an ideological forerunner of Fascism.[18]

Although regionalism is now studied in its own right, there are still many questions to be answered about it and the more general process of regional identity formation. Why did regionalism arise? Was regionalism essentially produced by 'natives' like Mistral or did 'outsiders' like Rostand also play a role? Should regionalism therefore be interpreted principally as an 'awakening of the regions' or did it originate from the centre? Did it spring from a kind of nostalgia about an orderly and stable world that seemed to be disappearing, as has been often said, or should it be seen in the first place as an innovative movement that was intimately connected with modernity? Was it principally concerned with a cultural definition of the region, or did it also have political implications? In what way was it connected to the nation-building process and how and why did this relationship change? What was its impact on the existing high culture? Are there significant differences between the various regional movements

---

[17] Rudy Koshar, *Germany's Transient Pasts: Preservation and National Memory in the Twentieth Century* (Chapel Hill 1998), 151–99, Karl Ditt, '"Mit Westfalengruß und Heil Hitler": Die Westfälische Heimatbewegung 1918–1945' in: Edeltraud Klueting ed., *Antimodernismus und Reform: Zur Geschichte der deutschen Heimatbewegung* (Darmstadt 1991) 191–215, Thiesse, *Écrire la France* 261–86, Christian Faure, *Le Projet culturel de Vichy* (Paris 1989), Xosé-Manoel Núñez and Maiken Umbach, 'Hijacked Heimats: National Appropriations of Local and Regional Identities in Germany and Spain, 1930–1945', *European Review of History* XV (2008) 295–316.

[18] See for Germany Klaus Bergmann, *Agrarromantik und Großstadtfeindlichkeit* (Meisenheim am Glan 1970) and Werner Hartung, *Konservative Zivilisationskritik und regionale Identität am Beispiel der niedersächsischen Heimatbewegung 1895 bis 1919* (Hanover 1991).

and between regionalism in various countries? And how could we explain these differences?

Instead of comparing various regional movements within different countries, with all the accompanying methodological problems,[19] I have chosen a very different approach: the analysis of the culture of regionalism in different national contexts. Hence, I will not study certain specific regions, but the role of regionalism in three different nation-states. However, this is only possible with a clear focus. As in the new self-definition of regions, painters, architects and exhibitions played a foremost role, their contributions will be analysed in this book. As will be shown, after 1890 a new regionalist artistic current was produced by painters that specialised in regional topics and architects that developed a neo-vernacular style. They visualised what they considered to be essential or typical for a certain region and their work attracted a lot of attention and debate. The discussions on this new regionalist artistic and architectural trend were generally national debates and by particularly studying the writings of authors that were favourable to the new tendency, one could extract and outline, in the first place, a core of arguments and ideas that could be found in all countries under review, secondly, particularities that could be explained by reference to the various national contexts and, finally, the regional differences within each country. Consequently, the principal sources for this research are not individual paintings, buildings, or pavilions, nor specific artists or architects, but the interpretations of their works by contemporary critics as published in the main artistic and architectural periodicals of each country. How did these authors – many of whom were artists or architects as well – 'recognise' the characteristic elements of a specific region? How could one 'find' the 'true identity' of a certain area? And how should these identities become visible in paintings, buildings and pavilions?

This approach will provide a comprehensive examination of regionalism's ideological core, its development over the years, and the various national and regional differences and peculiarities. However, a weakness of this type of discourse analysis is that it is rather difficult to get any relevant insight into regionalism's more structural causes. Why was it important to define regional identities? What were the main causes of its later development?

---

[19]   It would be very difficult to select representative regions that show enough similarities for a fruitful comparison. Moreover, it would be complicated to ascertain if possible differences between these movements should be explained from the specific regional or national level, and if changes were induced from the national cultural and political centre(s) or from the regions themselves.

And why did it decline? In order to get some clues to these questions, a detailed study of the textual sources will also be combined, as far as possible and feasible, with a survey of the political sympathies of the main figures and periodicals, and an analysis of the political and social implications of the regionalist ideology, which often were left implicit. Moreover, in order to capture the political dimension, the appropriation of regionalism by the various authorities, which started around 1910, is given special attention in part III by analysing the role of regionalism at various major exhibitions. This way, I also hope to shed new light on the more general questions about the causes, the nature and the impact of regionalism at large.

To assure a sufficient level of analytical depth, this research project is limited to the debates on the representation of the region in three major European countries: France, Germany and Spain. France and Germany were the two major cultural centres of Europe and are traditionally seen as embodying political and cultural nationalism, respectively. Furthermore, France is one of the oldest nation-states with a long history of centralisation, whereas in the recently unified German Empire the regions still had a considerable political and cultural autonomy. Spain, in turn, was culturally oriented towards France, although at the turn of the century German influence grew rapidly. Politically, Spain resembled France in that it was an old nation-state with a centralised administration. Nevertheless, as some Spanish regions not only tried to strengthen their cultural identity but also claimed political autonomy, there are also substantial differences. Consequently, Spain is a fitting addition to a comparative study of the French and the German case.

An international comparative approach is of paramount importance, as the vast majority of studies on regionalism still focus either on one region, or one aspect of regionalism within one country (such as the rise of historical preservation, environmental protection, ethnography, folklore, or regional literature).[20] Moreover, although most scholars now acknowledge that

---

[20] For Germany see for example: Hannjost Lixfeld, *Folklore and Fascism: The Reich Institute for German Volkskunde* (Bloomington 1994), Willi Oberkrone, *Volksgeschichte: Methodische Innovation und völkische Ideologisierung in der deutschen Geschichtswissenschaft, 1918–1945* (Göttingen 1993), Elizabeth Boa and Rachel Palfreyman, *Heimat: A German Dream. Regional Loyalties and National Identity in German Culture, 1890–1990* (Oxford 2000), William H. Rollins, *A Greener Vision of Home: Cultural Politics and Environmental Reform in the German Heimatschutz Movement 1904–1918* (Ann Arbor 1997), Thomas M. Lekan, *Imagining the Nation in Nature: Landscape Preservation and German Identity, 1885–1945* (Cambridge 2004), Winfried Speitkamp, *Die Verwaltung der Geschichte: Denkmalpflege und Staat in Deutschland 1871–1933* (Göttingen 1996) and Koshar, *Germany's Transient Pasts*. For a historiographical overview see also: Alon Confino, *Germany as a Culture of Remembrance: Promises and Limits of Writing History* (Chapel Hill 2006) 23–9.

regionalism was an international phenomenon, even in recent years they still largely explain it from the national context which forms the framework of their research. As a result, explanations have been brought forward which almost completely contradict each other. Thus, it is argued that in Germany regionalism was caused by the fast process of urbanisation and industrialisation that weakened traditional bonds of loyalty, by the unsteady political position of the *Bildungsbürgertum* (educated middle class), and by the late national unification, which meant that the nation-building process still showed fundamental weaknesses. In France regionalism was brought about by the defeat in the war of 1870 and the relatively lagging international position of the country. The strongly centralised State bureaucracy also led to dissent and opposition from the provinces. Thus, while in Germany regionalism was caused by an overabundant change, in France it was stagnation that seemed to stimulate regionalism, and while in Germany the lack of national unity encouraged regionalism, in France this was supposedly instigated by too much centralisation. In Spain there were yet other contributing factors. There, the loss of the main colonies in 1898 and the need to regenerate the country led to a profound malaise and identity crises. Moreover, unlike the situation in France, the Spanish government was centralised but inefficient, so it failed to impose a coherent national culture.[21]

This lack of connection between various national debates and interpretations is also caused by the absence of a generally accepted common terminology. In Germany the central concept in regard to regionalism is *Heimat*, a complex term which can be translated as 'home', 'homeland', 'region' and 'fatherland'. This term turns up in *Heimatbewegung* (regional movement), *Heimatschutz* (preservation), *Heimatkunst* (regionalist art) and *Heimatarchitektur* (regionalist architecture). As it will become clear, the ideas, arguments, rhetoric and forms in which regionalism expressed itself in the three countries are very similar; as a consequence, I shall use the more neutral term 'regionalism' to refer to both the new interest in rural popular culture and folklore, and the efforts towards 'region-building' undertaken in the period between about 1890 and 1945. Regionalist architecture anyhow is an accepted term in both France and Spain, whereas in Spain regionalist painting is a widely recognised artistic current.

---

[21] See for example: Applegate, *A Nation of Provincials* 12–17 and 60, Hermann Bausinger, 'Heimat in einer offenen Gesellschaft: Begriffsgeschichte als Problemgeschichte' in: Will Cremer and Ansgar Klein eds., *Heimat, Analysen, Themen, Perspektiven* (Bielefeld 1990) 76–91, Confino, *The Nation as a Local Metaphor* 14–15, 134, 149 and 188–9, Thiesse, *Écrire la France* 12–13, Borja de Riquer, 'La débil nacionalización española en el siglo XIX', *Historia Social* 20 (1994) 97–114, and Núñez, 'The Region as Essence'.

As with nationalism, the study of regionalism until very recently generally followed the patterns that had already been developed by nineteenth-century nationalist historians. Thus, in Germany, where nationalism was essentially seen as a cultural phenomenon, the various regional movements were mainly studied from a cultural perspective.[22] However, in the last few years political regionalism and especially the role of the (former) States and the federal nature of the new Empire has been given more attention.[23] In France, on the contrary, a political interpretation of the nation was dominant and as a result most studies focused on the role of the State in the creation of both national and regional identities.[24] Recently, nonetheless, a more cultural approach has also emerged in some interesting studies.[25] In Spain, on the other hand, the rise of the political regionalism of the so-called peripheral nationalisms and the apparent weakness of the Spanish nation-building process (in comparison with France) attracted almost all scholarly attention.[26] This has changed considerably during the last few years, as other regions (where claims for home rule were rare or even totally absent) are also being currently studied and the focus is more on regional identity construction.[27] Nonetheless, thorough comparative studies are still extremely rare.

[22] Apart from the many studies on folklore, preservation and conservation, the cultural focus predominates among others in: Applegate, *A Nation of Provincials*, Confino, *The Nation as a Local Metaphor* and Jeffrey K. Wilson, 'Imagining a Homeland: Constructing Heimat in the German East, 1871–1914', *National Identities* (2007) 331–49.

[23] Abigail Green, *Fatherlands: State-Building and Nationhood in Nineteenth-Century Germany* (Cambridge 2001), Abigail Green, 'The Federal Alternative? A New View of Modern German History', *Historical Journal* (2003) 187–202, Maiken Umbach, 'Nation and Region: Regionalism in Modern European Nation-States' in: Timothy Baycroft and Mark Hewitson eds., *What is a Nation? Europe 1789–1914* (Oxford 2006) 63–81, and Siegfried Weichlein, *Nation und Region: Integrationsprozesse im Bismarckreich* (Düsseldorf 2004). A cultural and political approach are combined in: Jennifer Jenkins, *Provincial Modernity: Local Culture and Liberal Politics in Fin-de-Siècle Hamburg* (Ithaca 2003).

[24] Many studies were written as a response to Weber's *Peasants into Frenchmen*: Jean-François Chanet, *L'École républicaine et les petites patries* (Paris 1996), Anne-Marie Thiesse, *Ils apprenait la France: L'Exaltation des regions dans le discourse patriotique* (Paris 1997), Ford, *Creating the Nation in Provincial France*, Baycroft, *Culture, Identity and Nationalism* and Wright, *The Regionalist Movement in France*.

[25] Thiesse, *Écrire la France*, Benoît Mihail, *Une Flandre à la française: L'identité régionale à l'épreuve du modèle républicain* (Saintes 2006) and Kolleen M. Guy, *When Champagne became French: Wine and the Making of National Identity* (Baltimore 2007).

[26] See for an exhaustive historiographical overview: José Luis de la Granja, Justo Beramendi and Pere Anguera, *La España de los nacionalismos y las autonomías* (Madrid 2003) 265–93, and for an overview of the debate on the weakness of Spanish nationalism: Fernando Molina Aparicio, 'Modernidad e identidad nacional: El nacionalismo español del siglo XIX y su historiografía', *Historia Social* (2005) 147–72.

[27] See for example Ferran Archilés and Manuel Martí, 'Ethnicity, Region and Nation: Valencian Identity and the Spanish Nation-State', *Ethnic and Racial Studies* (2001) 779–97,

The rapidly growing body of literature on regionalism within different countries, nevertheless, clearly shows that the rise, flowering and demise of regionalism occurred at about the same time all over Europe, and that its forms, arguments and rhetoric were very similar everywhere. This means that the main rationale for this process must be common to the whole of Europe, and maybe even to a great part of the entire Western world, as expressions of regionalism can be found in the United States and South-America as well.[28] Thus, only an international comparative study can reveal how regionalism developed and why it did so. In order to improve our insight in the transnational development of the regionalist ideology in the period 1890–1939, I shall focus on the way regional identities were defined by painters and architects in France, Germany and Spain. This does not mean that I will try to give a comprehensive overview of the rise, heyday and demise of the culture of regionalism in these three countries. The focus here is the process of defining more specific regional identities, not the various identities that were formulated, nor their diffusion.

A secondary objective of this study will be to revise the interpretation of the painters and architects under review, and to present them as a clearly recognisable international current that was closely linked to both regionalism and the nation-building process. The regionalist painters had been largely disregarded after 1914 and almost disappeared from view, when, after the Second World War, art historians almost exclusively concentrated on the rise of the avant-garde. Only recently they have received more scholarly attention. In France and Germany their works are mainly shown in the area where they were painted and consequently they are principally studied on a local level. In Spain, however, the regionalist painters are more prominently present in current debates as they are seen

Carlos Forcadell Álvarez and María Cruz Romeo Mateo eds., *Provincia y nación: Los territorios del liberalismo* (Saragossa 2006), Xosé M. Núñez Seixas ed., *Ayer*, 64, *La construcción de la identidad regional en Europa y España (siglos XIX and XX)* (2006), X. M. Núñez, 'Überlegungen zum Problem der territorialen Identitäten: Provinz, Region und Nation im Spanien des 19. und 20. Jahrhunderts' in: Sven-Oliver Müller, Jörg Requate und Charlotte Tacke eds., *Unterwegs in Europa: Beiträge zu einer pluralen europäischen Geschichte* (Frankfurt am Main and New York 2008) 115–36, and for a recent historiographical overview: Xosé M. Núñez Seixas, 'De impuras naciones: Historiografía reciente y cuestión nacional en España', *Alcores* (2007) 211–39.

[28] This will become apparent for example in the neo-vernacular pavilions of the various American countries that were constructed for the Ibero-American Exhibition in Seville in 1929, as discussed in chapter 7. See for regionalism in the United States: Robert L. Dorman, *Revolt of the Provinces: The Regionalist Movement in America, 1920–1945* (Chapel Hill 1993) and for Eastern Europe: Philipp Ther and Holm Sundhausen eds., *Regionale Bewegungen und Regionalismen in europäischen Zwischenräumen seit der Mitte des 19. Jahrhunderts* (Marburg 2003).

as part of the nationalist reaction to the loss of the last remaining colonies after the Hispano-American War, which is particularly associated with the famous literary generation of 1898 (to which Ganivet also belonged). Regionalist architecture was also largely disregarded after 1945 and only recently has more interest in this current developed. Moreover, the same applies to the role of regionalism at international exhibitions. Nonetheless, even these recent studies still adopt a national slant.

This book is divided into three parts, which successively deal with the role of regionalism in painting, in architecture and at major international exhibitions, in a loose chronological order. The relatively short part I discusses the interpretation of the work of the main regionalist painters as provided by the principal French, German and Spanish artistic journals from about 1890 to 1914. As regionalist art first came into vogue in France, I will start with the French debate and then continue with Germany and Spain. In regard to regionalist architecture, which is the topic of the larger part II, Germany was clearly in the lead and was followed by France and Spain. In this case the main architectural journals from these countries have been scanned for articles on regionalist buildings and architects, while the focus was on the one hand on country houses and villas which were built for the upper-middle classes and on the other on the garden cities which were built for the less affluent people. Regionalist influences in architecture were only visible after the turn of the century and remained important until the early 1920s. Whereas parts I and II deal with artists and architects working for themselves or for private clients, part III shows that various authorities also started to adopt regionalism for official representations at major exhibitions. Surprisingly the Spanish towns of Barcelona and Seville took the lead. After decades of preparations, the major international exhibitions in both towns were held simultaneously in 1929. France and Germany would follow only in the 1930s. Based on well-documented existing studies and contemporary reviews in the architectural press, part III will show that regionalism was adopted (although in different ways) by regimes of almost all political colours: the more or less democratic town councils of Barcelona and Seville, the military dictatorship of Primo de Rivera, progressive and more conservative French governments, the Popular Front administration of Léon Blum, and various Nazi authorities. The political appropriation of regionalism, nonetheless, would coincide with its demise.

I

Painting (1890–1914)

1

France

Introduction

Regionalism had a slighter and less visible impact on painting than on architecture. However, regionalist painting in France, Germany and Spain pre-dated regionalist architecture by almost a decade and around 1900 it had already developed into a major innovative artistic trend. Nonetheless, until recently, regionalist painting has been almost entirely overlooked by art historians, as it was generally seen as a backward-looking trend that did not substantially contribute to the rise of the avant-garde. This can probably also be explained by the fact that regionalist artists did not produce manifestos, nor presented themselves as formal movements with their own exhibitions or publications. Yet neither the public nor critics had any difficulty distinguishing them as coherent and influential groups. As they chose their subjects mostly from specific parts of their fatherland, they were known by different names in each country. In France, regionalist artists generally were named after the region where they preferred to work. Maybe the best-known group, which included Lucien Simon and Charles Cottet, was referred to as painters of 'Breton life and scenery'. In Germany similar artists were known as *Heimatkünstler* (regionalist artists), although some of them disliked this term's provincial undertone. Only in Spain the term *regionalista* was used to characterise the paintings by Ignacio Zuloaga and others.[1] Before discussing the reviews of the main regionalist painters

[1] Léonce Bénédite, 'Lucien Simon', *Art et Décoration*, Vol. 1 (1906) 25–37, Achille Segard, 'Charles Cottet, Painter of Breton Life and Scenes', *The Studio* (January 1912) 269–77, Octave Uzanne, 'Fernand Maillaud: A Painter of the Old French Province of Berry', *The Studio* (September 1912) 273–82, Bernd Küster and Jürgen Wittstock, *Carl Bantzer: Aufbruch und Tradition* (Frankfurt am Main 2002), Andreas Bantzer ed., *Carl Bantzer: Ein Leben in Briefen. Briefe – Berichte – Werksverzeichnis* (2nd edn. Willingshausen 1998) 514–18, Carlos Reyero and Mireia Freixa, *Pintura y escultura en España (1800–1910)* (Madrid 1999) 464–7, Javier Tusell, *Arte, historia y política en España (1890–1939)* (Madrid 1999) 73–155.

in France, Germany and Spain, it is useful to first give a brief sketch of the common elements.

Regionalist painters were not the first to let their art be inspired by nationalist motives. During the nineteenth century, art had been greatly influenced by nationalism, as were almost all areas of culture. During the French Revolution, the nation was recognised as sovereign for the first time. Even before this principle became a reality throughout Europe later on in the nineteenth century, nations – or those who saw themselves as their representatives – wanted to express this new idea in all types of art. In this way, European high culture became thoroughly nationalised. As part of this process, the common European past, mainly founded in Antiquity and Christianity, was redefined along national lines and art, literature and music increasingly operated within national contexts. Writers and novelists searched their national past for inspiration and appropriate subjects. The same applied to the visual arts: painters and sculptors gradually turned away from scenes of Classical history or the bible, in favour of themes from national history. Their grandiloquent depictions of battles, kings and heroes visualised the nation's greatest moments for a national public.[2] By showing the long and glorious history of the nation, the more or less liberal middle and upper classes in fact legitimised their political aspirations. Who would dare to withhold the nation its natural rights? This programme of cultural nationalism in fact was a more or less explicit plea for a national state with a constitution, equal rights for all citizens and a representative government.

Academic painting was not the only vehicle for nationalism, however. During the second half of the nineteenth century realists and impressionists also frequently resorted to a nationalist language, albeit more subtle. Although their paintings were not designed to tell a patriotic story, realist painters showed what the fatherland and its people looked like. Instead of idealised classical landscapes they preferred national scenery and the faithful representation of ordinary people in their native country, thus defining new, typical 'national landscapes', such as the Rhine valley in Germany. The impressionists also partook in the nation-building enterprise. By recording modern life in their own countries and thus giving their viewers a sense of belonging, they stimulated their fellow citizens' national awareness.[3] Thus,

---

2   Monika Flacke ed., *Mythen der Nationen: Ein europäisches Panorama* (Berlin 1998).

3   Greg M. Thomas, 'The Topographical Aesthetic in French Tourism and Landscape' (2002). Retrieved on 30 March 2004 from http://19th-artworldwide.org/spring_02/ articles/thom.html. Richard Thomson ed., *Framing France: The Representation of Landscape in France, 1870–1914* (Manchester and New York 1998) and Tricia Cusack, 'Bourgeois

whereas the academic painters focused on the nation's glorious history and heroes of its golden age, realists and impressionists were more concerned with defining the national landscape and character.

Recent studies have made clear that nationalism continued to have a huge impact, even on avant-garde artists, not only in countries with a strong independence movement, such as Finland and other 'oppressed' nations in Eastern Europe, but also in those that were long established nation states. Art Nouveau artists such as Akseli Gallén-Kallela, Alfons Mucha, Antoni Gaudí, Fidus, as well as Hector Guimard, Emile Gallé and Ferdinand Hodler were, at least during part of their career, strongly inspired by nationalism and often tried to develop a new national style. The same is true for some of the German expressionists and it has even been argued for Matisse and the fauves.[4]

This also applies to art criticism. The most cursory research shows that, at the start of the twentieth century, artistic debates were infected by the nationalist virus. Thus in France around 1905 in a dispute over the future of modern French art two groups could be discerned, each of which tried to present itself as the true embodiment of the national tradition. The critic Charles Morice defended Impressionism as the continuation of a long French colourist tradition which had found a first flowering during the Rococo, whereas Maurice Denis proposed a reorientation of French art based on the country's classicist tradition. According to this neo-conservative painter and critic, Cézanne's work had paved the way for a French Classical rebirth. In Germany in the spring of 1911 a similar debate arose on the occasion of the purchase of a Van Gogh by the Bremer Kunsthalle. The landscape painter Carl Vinnen led a protest movement against the preferential treatment of contemporary foreign art by critics, artists and gallery directors throughout Germany. At the same time, Spanish intellectuals compared the luminous, cheerful, Mediterranean pictures of Joaquín Sorolla with the gloomy, tragic representations of the Castilian countryside by Ignacio Zuloaga. They argued over which of these highly successful contemporary Spanish painters best captured the nation's character.[5]

Leisure on the Seine: Impressionism, Forgetting and National Identity in the French Third Republic', *National Identities* (2007) 163–82.

[4] Magdalena Bushart, *Der Geist der Gotik und die expressionistische Kunst: Kunstgeschichte und Kunsttheorie 1911–1912* (Munich 1990), James D. Herbert, *Fauve Painting: The Making of Cultural Politics* (New Haven and London 1992), Jeremy Howard, *Art Nouveau: International and National Styles in Europe* (Manchester 1996).

[5] Maurice Denis, 'Cézanne', *L'Occident* (September 1907), also in Idem, *Théories (1890–1910): Du symbolisme et de Gauguin vers un nouvel ordre classique* (Paris 1920) 245–62, Charles

Artistic regionalism rose to prominence all over Europe at the end of the nineteenth century, thus at about the same time as the various new regional movements and the new more exalted nationalism of Barrès, Langbehn and Ganivet. It seems probable that the Scandinavian – or more generally the northern and eastern European – countries took the lead. This might be explained by their lack of both an internationally recognised cultural or political Golden Age, functioning as an attractive source of nationalistic rhetoric,[6] and of a strong, State-supported art market. Painting folkloric themes for a dominantly bourgeois public, instead of creating increasingly out-of-date, historical paintings, became a good option. This way national identity was not located in the glorious past deeds of kings and heroes, but in the still existing popular culture of the countryside. In any case, around 1890, a new international generation of painters, most of them born between 1855 and 1875, began to translate regionalism into highly successful pictures. Some of the best-known painters who produced regionalist paintings for at least part of their career were: the Norwegian Erik Werenskiold (1855–1938), the Swede Anders Zorn (1860–1920), the Finn Akseli Gallén-Kallela (1865–1931) and the Czech Alfons Mucha (1860–1939). Other less-known regionalists were: the Pole Jacek Malczewski (1854–1929), the Czech Jozef Uprka (1861–1940), the Bulgarian Jean Mrkvitchka (1856–1938), the Belgian Victor Gilsoul (1867–1939) and the Italian Ettore Tito (1859–1941).

France, Germany and Spain also produced internationally renowned regionalist painters, such as: Lucien Simon (1861–1945), Charles Cottet (1862–1924), Carl Bantzer (1857–1941), Ludwig Dettmann (1865–1944), Otto Heinrich Engel (1866–1949), Fritz Mackensen (1866–1953), Ignacio Zuloaga (1870–1945) and, in some ways, Joaquín Sorolla (1863–1923). Some secondary figures were: Charles Milcendeau (1872–1919), Fernand Maillaud (1863–1948), Louis-Marie Désiré-Lucas (1864–1949), Pierre-Gaston Rigaud (1874–1949), Jean Roque (1880–1926), Julien Lemordant (1878–1968), Mahurin Méhuet (1882–1958), Felix Borchardt (1857–1936), Richard Hoelscher (1867–1943), Wilhelm Thielemann (1868–1924), Paul Schultze-Naumburg (1869–1949), Marceliano Santa María (1866–1952),

Morice, 'Art moderne: La sixième exposition du Salon d'Automne', *Mercure de France* (1 November 1908) 155–66, Michael Marlais, *Conservative Echoes in Fin-de-Siècle Parisian Art Criticism* (University Park 1992), Carl Vinnen ed., *Ein Protest deutscher Künstler* (Jena 1911), Peter Paret, *The Berlin Secession: Modernism and its Enemies in Imperial Germany* (Cambridge 1980), Tusell, *Arte, historia y política*.

[6] See for an inspiring view on the role of Golden Ages, periods of origin and typical landscapes in the formation of nationalist rhetoric: Anthony D. Smith, *The Ethnic Origins of Nations* (Oxford 1986) chapter 8.

Eduardo Chicharro (1873–1949), Manuel Benedito (1875–1963), Fernando Álvarez de Sotomayor (1875–1960) and the brothers Valentín (1879–1963) and Ramón de Zubiaurre (1882–1969). Looking at their dates of birth we could even distinguish two groups. The first consisted of painters born in the late 1850s and early 1860s. They slowly evolved towards regionalist themes, whereas a second, generally less prominent group, born mainly in the early 1870s, participated in a trend that already existed when they reached artistic maturity.

Most of the regionalist painters in the three countries under review were born into provincial middle-class families, received a good education and thus belonged to the same social strata as the leaders of the new, more populist regional movements. The main exception to this was Lucien Simon, who originated from a distinguished Parisian bourgeois family. Nevertheless, most of them were not involved in a regional movement and many even preferred to paint regions where they were not born. Thus Cottet – who was raised in the Savoy – and Simon mainly painted themes from Brittany. Engel and Mackensen originated from hilly central Germany, but favoured depicting the northern German coastal planes, whereas Zuloaga, who was native to the Basque Country, preferred to paint in Castile. Only minor artists like Maillaud, Lemordant, Méhuet, Schultze-Naumburg, Santa María and Sotomayor restricted themselves primarily to representing their own native region, and few of them became active in the local regional movement. Regionalist art, therefore, should not be seen as a mere branch of the regional movement, but as a new art form that largely found its inspiration in the same ideological sources.

The reformist intentions of regionalism at large would manifest itself in regionalist art as well. The innovative attitude of the regionalist painters became evident in their negative opinion of academic art and their adaptation of most of the innovative aspects of *plein air* Realism and Impressionism. Thus, all regionalist painters openly rejected academic art with its conventions and strict rules for composition and chiaroscuro, and its preference for dignified subjects and a finished surface. Its technique was considered too dogmatic, lifeless, unrealistic and lacking spontaneity, while its representations were found to be theatrical and lacking authenticity.[7] For this reason none of the important French regionalists visited the Parisian Académie des Beaux-Arts. Instead they learned their *métier* in small academies set up by well-known painters. Thus Simon and Cottet

---

[7] See for Academic painting: Albert Boime, *The Academy and French Painting in the Nineteenth Century* (London 1971).

studied at the Académie Julian. Cottet was for some time a pupil of Roll and Puvis de Chavannes, and Zuloaga, who also spent his formative years in the French capital, studied at the so-called Académie de la Palette. In Germany, however, nearly all painters visited one or several of the academies that existed throughout the country, and most went from one professor to another. However, none was very positive about the education they received. Cottet, Simon and Zuloaga did not consider themselves pupils of one particular master, nor did they recognise a serious debt to the education they had received. The German painters all abhorred the traditional academic training and many declared to have absorbed nothing worth mentioning.[8]

The regionalists liked the *pleinairism* as practised by the painters of the *École de Barbizon* (especially Millet) and other artists' colonies much better than academic art. They shared their love of nature and the simple country life, their aversion to academic conventions and their preference for direct observation, simple compositions and realistic subjects.[9] However, regionalist paintings were clearly distinguishable from these predecessors, as these painters mostly chose different places to live, other subjects to paint and employed a different technique.

Although the regionalist painters moved to the countryside, they generally went to more remote areas and avoided the main existing artists' colonies. Instead of establishing themselves in Pont-Aven or Concarneau, Simon bought a house outside a small village in the West of Cornouaille, whereas his friend Cottet preferred to stay in remote western outposts of Finistère. Rigaud went to live in a village in Les Landes, where no 'modern painter' had ever worked. Zuloaga avoided the more typical sights of Andalusia and the Sierra de Guadarrama and preferred the small provincial towns of Segovia and Pedraza on the Castilian plains. Most German regionalists, on the contrary, preferred the company of other artists. Bantzer, Dettmann and Engel mainly stayed in established artists' colonies such as Willingshausen, Ekensund and Nidden. Bantzer was also involved in the founding of a new colony in Göppeln near Dresden, while

---

8 Thiébault-Sisson, 'La Vie artistique: Un Peintre de la vie et de la réalité. Lucien Simon', *Le Temps* (3 March 1912), Jacques Copeau, 'Charles Cottet', *Art et Décoration* XV (September 1911) 265–77, especially 266, F. Deibel, *Ludwig Dettmann* (Bielefeld and Leipzig, s.a. [1910]) 3–4 and 33–4, Fritz Overbeck, 'Ein Brief aus Worpswede', *Kunst für Alle* (15 October 1895) 20–4, especially 23.

9 See for example: Karl Krummacher, 'Die Malerkolonie Worpswede', *Westermanns Illustrierte Deutsche Monatshefte* (April 1899) 17–22, especially 19–20 and Jean Chantavoine, 'Artistes contemporains: M. Charles Cottet', *La Gazette des Beaux-Arts* (August 1911) 103–22 especially 106.

Mackensen, accompanied by a few friends, discovered the discreet beauty of Worpswede, a village in the moors north of Bremen.[10]

Generally, the regionalist painters did not produce romantic, mountain or lakeside pictures, nor paint charming hills or woods. They seemed to prefer quite unimpressive, flat landscapes of coastal planes and arid plateaux. Further preconditions for their work were untouched villages and traditionally dressed people. More than the *pleinairistes* of the existing artists' colonies – who mainly produced landscapes – they depicted the inhabitants and buildings of the countryside. These had to be clearly recognisable as representing a specific area or region. Traditional costumes, vernacular architecture, typical landscapes and specific local types thereby functioned as indispensable signifiers. Thus, whereas the *pleinairistes* painted anonymous peasants, from an unspecified region, who were dressed in ordinary working clothes, the regionalists depicted clearly identifiable types – of whom we often even know the name and profession – dressed in the traditional costume of a specific village, which could often even be recognised in the background.

However, the regionalist painters distinguished themselves from their *pleinairiste* predecessors not only by their choice of subject but also by their technique, for they absorbed most of the innovations of the impressionists, who had been so influential in abolishing academic conventions. They adapted the impressionists' virtuoso use of colour and their way of representing effects of light and shade, techniques with which they were able to suggest a particular moment of the day, with its own fleeting atmosphere. They also used the unconventional compositions of the impressionists, which were especially meant to highlight a significant moment that seemed to form part of a sequence. In this way, the impressionists were able to suggest movement and thereby to transmit the sensation of directness and presence that made their pictures so realistic and full of life.[11]

The anti-academic stance of the regionalist painters also manifested itself in their participation in various secessionist movements that mostly occurred in the 1890s after dissatisfaction with the policies of the traditionalist artists'

[10] André Girodie, 'P.-G. Rigaud', *L'Art et les Artistes* IX (1909) 23–9, especially 24. See also: Claus Pese ed., *Künstlerkolonien in Europa: Im Zeichen der Ebene und des Himmels* (Nuremberg 2001) and Nina Lübbren, *Rural Artists' Colonies in Europe 1870–1910* (Manchester 2001).

[11] For the adaptation of impressionistic techniques see: Léon David (pseud. Max Jacob), 'Lucien Simon', *Le Moniteur des Arts* (30 December 1898) as published in: André Cariou, *Lucien Simon* (Paris 2002) 28–35, especially 32, André Saglio, 'Lucien Simon', *L'Art Décoratif* (December 1902) 353–62, especially 355, Léon Rosenthal, 'Jean Rocque', *L'Art et les Artistes* XIII (1913) 24–31, especially 28, and Deibel, *Ludwig Dettmann*, 4–5.

associations had led to a break. Simon, Cottet and Zuloaga did not present their works at the traditional salon, but instead participated, almost from the beginning, in the slightly more selective and innovating salon of the *Société Nationale des Beaux-Arts*, which existed since 1890. Dettmann and Mackensen maintained good contacts with various secessions, while Engel was a member of the Munich Sezession and in 1898 one of the founders of the Berlin Sezession. Bantzer was involved in the foundation of the secession in Dresden in 1894 and, during its most active years, was its president.[12]

Although regionalist painters adopted impressionistic painting techniques and compositions, they generally defined their own artistic point of view in opposition to that of the impressionists. They, and the critics sympathetic to them, especially criticised the impressionists as being superficial on a theoretical level. With their preference for depicting atmospheric effects, reflections of light and movement – often even only in a rapid, sketchy way – the impressionists were merely interested in representing superficial, external appearances. This fascination with the rendering of atmosphere also meant that the impressionists generally chose to depict a contingent, floating moment. In this way the subject became a vehicle for a particular incidence of light, converting the theme of the painting into a secondary affair. Any motif would do. This was clearly visible in their paintings, as they preferred simple motifs from their direct surroundings or people at leisure in and around Paris. However, these almost arbitrarily chosen 'snapshots' recorded only some outward aspects of nature or of modern urban life. As both moral lessons and implicit metaphysical references were banned from their work, art became a kind of senseless exercise in virtuosity, at least in the eyes of many regionalist painters and their supporters.[13]

For the regionalist painters, art was a serious matter. Therefore, subjects should be meaningful and the way of depicting them dignified. Regionalist painters could not content themselves with depicting outward reality in a sketchy way. They wanted to look behind the visual appearances and penetrate into the essence of things. Instead of mirroring nature, as the impressionists and realists had done, they wanted to interpret reality by distilling its essence – its inner truth. However, they did not want to lose

---

[12] See for the Sezession movement: Paret, *The Berlin Secession*.

[13] See for the differences with impressionism: Gabriel Mourey, 'Charles Cottet's "Au Pays de la Mer" and Other Works', *The Studio* (January 1899) 227–41, especially 240, Henri Marcel, 'Lucien Simon: Artistes contemporains', *La Revue de l'Art Ancien et Moderne* (1903) I 123–38, especially 123–5, Krummacher, 'Malerkolonie Worpswede' 20 and 24, and Ludwig Bartning, 'A Decorative Landscape Painter: Paul Schultze-Naumburg', *The Studio* (December 1904) 210–18, especially 210 and 212.

themselves in individual, dreamlike fantasies as did the Symbolists and the German *Phantasiemaler*. Because the regionalist painters were striving for the essence behind reality, their art has sometimes been called 'subjective realism' or 'synthetic realism'.[14] In philosophical terms, however, it could be defined as neo-idealism, as they understood that ideas were more important for comprehending reality than visual observations, which in any case, according to Kant, originated in the human mind as well. Instead of painting immediate appearances, as the impressionists did, Zuloaga, for example, according to some critics, succeeded in discerning the 'soul' through the outer forms, thus interpreting reality instead of copying it.[15]

However, a good picture not only required a meaningful method of depiction, but also a relevant subject. Depicting air or light could not be the highest aspiration of art. The impressionists' world of pleasure and vice and the landscapes devoid of any intrinsic metaphysical references seemed insignificant to the regionalist painters. They preferred the countryside to the cosmopolitan urban world depicted by most of the impressionists. Yet the mere outward representation of landscapes or village scenes could not satisfy them either. Like the regionalists generally, they saw the countryside as the essence of the nation. But this was no generic countryside. Every region had its particular characteristics and precisely through this uniqueness constituted an indispensable part of the greatness of the nation. Exploring the character of a particular region was thus considered to be a patriotic deed. But how did this work out in each of the three countries?

The French case

In France, many painters adopted regionalist motives in their work. However, most of them did not become very renowned. The two main exceptions were Lucien Simon and Charles Cottet, who also were good friends. They specialised in Breton subjects and their works were generally discussed together by art critics. Surprisingly, in the beginning they did not so much attract attention for their subject choice as for their stylistic innovations. Some critics even presented Simon and Cottet as two of the main representatives of a highly relevant innovative artistic trend that could

---

[14] Léonce Bénédite, 'Charles Cottet', *Art et Décoration* (April 1904) 101–18, especially 112, and *Carl Bantzer 1857–1941: Foto/Zeichnung/Gemälde: Synthetischer Realismus* (Marburg 1977).
[15] Camille Mauclair, 'Ignacio Zuloaga', *Kunst für Alle* XXVII (1 October 1911) 1–17, especially 9–12, see also: Charles Morice, 'Ignacio Zuloaga', *L'Art et les Artistes* X (1910–11) 14–28, especially 22–3, and Copeau, 'Charles Cottet' 268.

indicate a way out of the impressionist deadlock. At the end of the nineteenth century many art critics observed that Impressionism had become the dominant artistic tendency in France. By this they did not so much mean a general recognition of the art of the most important impressionist painters, but the widespread influence of their way of painting. Most paintings that were seen at the two rivalling salons showed the light palette and choppy brushwork of Impressionism and its emphasis on capturing the atmosphere and light of a fleeting moment. Not all progressive critics applauded these developments. They argued that Impressionism, while it had successfully eliminated the stale conventions of academic art, had itself degenerated into a superficial exercise in virtuosity. The almost exclusive concentration on the representation of objective reality was also increasingly criticised.[16]

Symbolist art was one possible alternative to Impressionism. However, the Symbolists' highly individualist paintings, based on dreams and fantasies, did not convince all observers that they were the answer to the call for a new art as they could only be appreciated by the initiated few.[17] Around 1895 another possible alternative was offered, at least according to some critics, by a group of young painters, who began to attract critical and public attention at the Salon de la Société Nationale des Beaux-Arts. These painters preferred full and dark colours and frequently even used black. Their compositions were well worked out and their technique was not sketchy. In addition to René Ménard, who specialised in landscapes, Charles Cottet and Lucien Simon were seen as the most important members of this informal group, which for some time was known as the 'Bande noir'.[18]

Cottet and Simon could not only be distinguished from the impressionists by their technique, compositions and colours, but also by their choice of subject. They preferred countryside to city, and although both worked and lived in Paris they almost never depicted the French capital. Both showed a clear preference for Brittany, but they steered clear of the many artists' colonies in the region. After discovering the beauty of the Breton coast in 1892, Simon spent most of his summers in a house his in-laws had bought in the small coastal village of Bénodet, south of Quimper. In 1902 he acquired his own summer residence just outside the same village.

---

[16] Marcel, 'Lucien Simon' 123–25, Raymond Bouyer, 'L'Oeuvre de Lucien Simon', *L'Art et les Artistes* VI (February 1908) 528, Mourey, 'Charles Cottet's Works' 240, and Clément-Janin, 'Charles Cottet', *Die Graphische Künste* XXXII (1909) 49–54, especially 49.

[17] Bouyer, 'L'Oeuvre de Lucien Simon' 531. See also: Octave Uzanne, 'Gaston Hochard: A Painter of French Types', *The Studio* (April 1907) 215–19, especially 219.

[18] Bénédite, 'Lucien Simon' 32–4, Bénédite, 'Charles Cottet' 102, and Walther Gensel, 'Eine neue Pariser Künstlergruppe (Lucien Simon – Charles Cottet – René Ménard)', *Zeitschrift für bildende Kunst* 10 (1899) 20–33.

Cottet also spent a great deal of time, sometimes even part of the winter, in isolated parts of the Finistère, such as the small fishing port of Camaret and the tiny islands of Sein and Ouessant.[19]

Although Simon and Cottet painted scenes from the countryside, their subject choice and painting mode differed from those of the realist *pleinairistes* of the many existing artists' colonies. They did not produce charming pictures of hills or forests, but preferred the barren, coastal plains. In contrast to these *pleinairistes* they also depicted the countryside's inhabitants and buildings. Like the symbolist painters Paul Gauguin and Emile Bernard, who had painted in Brittany some years before, they showed great interest in the local population's primitive and authentic way of life. Yet in contrast to the generic (Breton) peasants in Gauguin's paintings, the local inhabitants, their costumes, the buildings and the landscapes represented in their works were clearly recognisable as representing a specific area or part of Brittany. Simon usually even referred to the exact site of the picture in his titles.

Simon and Cottet, just like regionalist painters elsewhere, also employed a painting technique that differed from the more realist painters that still dominated the artists' colonies. Although they had assimilated many of Impressionism's innovations they clearly distanced themselves from some of its aspects. They adapted the impressionists' virtuoso use of colour and their way of representing effects of light and shade. They also used the unconventional and dynamic compositions of the impressionists.[20] Simon and Cottet did not return to academic conventions which had become obsolete. Precisely because their scenes were so lively, they could be easily distinguished from the more anecdotal, theatrical and slick representations by somewhat older, naturalistic painters of Breton subjects like Pascal Dagnan-Bouveret, whose paintings also referred to Brittany in general and were not clearly recognisable as depicting a specific part or village.[21]

In contrast to most impressionists, Simon and Cottet preferred to paint from memory. They did outdoor sketches in oil and watercolour, but their major works were painted in the atelier.[22] Another characteristic of Simon and Cottet's oeuvre was that they continued to paint for the salon. Their

---

[19]   See, for biographical information on these painters: André Cariou, *Charles Cottet et la Bretagne* (Raillé 1988) and André Cariou, *Lucien Simon* (Paris 2002).

[20]   For the adaptation of impressionistic techniques see: David, 'Lucien Simon' and Saglio, 'Lucien Simon' 355.

[21]   Louis Aubert, 'L'Oeuvre de Charles Cottet', *Revue de Paris*, (15 June 1911) 761–81 and Karl Eugen Schmidt, *Französische Malerei des 19. Jahrhunderts* (Leipzig 1903) 150–9.

[22]   Achille Segard, 'A French Painter: Lucien Simon', *The Studio* (July 1912), 96 and Aubert, 'L'Oeuvre de Charles Cottet' 777.

main works were rather large and were exhibited at the salon of the Société Nationale. Although they also produced watercolours and engravings, and had some exhibitions at commercial galleries, they continued to address themselves in a conventional way to a broad public of art lovers. Their highest aspiration was a gold medal and the purchase of their paintings by the State (which meant that they would be acquired by the Musée du Luxembourg, then the National Museum of Contemporary Art, located in the Palais du Luxembourg in Paris) – which occurred several times – as well as a commission to paint a major official building mural. After 1914 both would become a member of the highly influential Conseil Supérieur des Beaux-Arts and Simon in 1927 was even elected into the Académie des Beaux-Arts.[23]

Although their way of painting and their choice of subjects showed many similarities, neither Simon and Cottet's paintings nor their personalities were identical. Lucien Simon was born into an upper-class Parisian family and was well educated.[24] From 1892 onwards Simon would spend most of the summer in Bénodet, making sketches and looking for motifs in the surrounding areas. Until then he had especially painted intimate family portraits and he continued to do this while he slowly became famous for his paintings of Breton folk life. He succeeded in transferring some of the warmth and intimacy of his family portraits to Breton interior scenes, such as *Les Soeurs quêteuses* (The Collecting Sisters, 1902) and *Famille bigoudène en deuil* (Bigoudène Family in Mourning, 1912). Most of the scenes he painted were outside events, however, in which people and buildings were placed against the background of the local landscape. In *Cirque forain* (Fairground Circus, 1898) and *Les lutteurs, Penmarc'h* (The Wrestling Match, Penmarc'h, 1898, plate 1) he depicted local feasts. He also celebrated daily work in paintings such as *La récolte de pommes de terre* (The Potato Harvest, 1907) and *La sardinerie, Camaret* (The Sardinery, Camaret, 1911). Another often repeated subject was religion, such as in *La procession à Penmarc'h* (The Procession at Penmarc'h, 1900), *Le menhir* (The Menhir, 1900) and *Messe en Bretagne* (Mass in Brittany, 1904). These depictions seemed to reflect his personal preference for a stable order, harmony and security both within the family and, on a wider scale, in society.

Simon's choice of subjects was very specific. He did not just depict

---

[23] Marie-Claude Genet-Delacroix, *Art et État sous la IIIe République: Le système des Beaux-Arts 1870–1940* (Paris 1992).

[24] Instead of going to the Polytechnique, as his parents probably would have preferred, Simon embarked upon a career as a painter. He was not a bohemian, but loved family life.

a contingent moment, but always chose a meaningful event in which people, nature and tradition seemed to form a harmonious union. This was especially the case in the open-air scenes. Thus, in *Les lutteurs* (plate 1), the traditionally dressed villagers gather around the wrestlers who, stripped to the waist, defend the honour of their parish in a primitive game celebrating the local patron saint of Penmarc'h. A sheep visible on the right is the trophy. Some women are seated on the rocks in the left foreground, while a few men watch the spectacle from horseback. Although the scene looks like a faithful representation of the event, the background is, in fact, a composite scene. In the centre we see the tower of the ancient church of Saint-Guénolé, a small village not far from Simon's summer residence, and on its right a fortified farmhouse. In reality such a farmhouse was found several kilometres away, whereas some ordinary houses, eliminated by the painter, surrounded the tower.[25] It is clear that it was not Simon's goal to represent visual reality truthfully. And while some of his departures from reality may have been motivated by aesthetic considerations, it appears that the most conspicuous changes were made to give the picture a clearer meaning. Through Simon's manipulation of the background, both the solitude and desolation of the landscape and the central role of the church were underlined.

In *Le menhir* (plate 2), Simon depicted a small group of adolescents chatting and possibly flirting, seated on some stones next to a menhir. In the background we see a few houses, a chapel, the coastline and a small procession. Again, landscape, buildings and people are melding together as earth, sky, houses and faces all have the same brownish colour and the stones on which the young villagers sit are also used as the main construction material. In the bare, flat landscape, everything seems to be subject to the same forces of nature, such as the wind, which forces the people to bow, the processional banner to billow and the clouds to drift along the sky. The presence of the menhir and the seemingly holy megalithic circle of stones around it, the chapel and the procession, bear witness to the ancient and strong religiosity of these simple villagers. By placing the menhir in the centre and by adding the non-existent circle of stones around the menhir – which was not present at the actual site[26] – Simon appears to suggest the continuity in religious feeling between prehistoric times and the present.

Raised in Savoy, Charles Cottet was the son of a magistrate. He was a solitary figure and travelled a great deal.[27] Like Simon, he often recorded

---

[25] Cariou, *Lucien Simon* 33.
[26] Ibid., 78–9.
[27] Cottet specialised in Breton scenes, but he also painted in other parts of France as well

the ceremonial aspects of Breton life in pictures of processions, feasts and other activities, such as *Femmes de Plougastel au pardon de Sainte-Anne-la-Palud* (Women of Plougastel at the Pilgrimage of Saint Anne-la-Palud, 1903). But he generally focused on tragic events, painting mourning and farewell scenes, such as *Enterrement* (Burial, 1895), *Repas d'adieu* (Farewell Dinner, 1898) and *Douleur au pays de la mer* (Sorrow at the Land by the Sea, 1908, plate 4). Both *Enterrement* and *Douleur* treat the sorrow of mothers, wives and other family members over the death of a fisherman. *Repas d'Adieu* (plate 3) depicts a farewell dinner in which the women do not know if they will ever see their beloved again. The imminent threat of the sea was a lasting presence in these communities. The sea gives them their daily bread but at any time can take whomever it likes. Although the landscape is almost invisible in these pictures, Cottet indirectly shows that the dependence on nature was almost complete, and that this determined almost all aspects of human existence around these small harbours, leading its inhabitants to place their life in God's hands.

Like nature, religious feeling was only hinted at indirectly by Cottet as he stylised many of his pictures in a religious fashion. *Douleur* (plate 4) was clearly modelled on the Lamentation of Christ, with a group of women resembling the three Marys behind the almost Christ-like body of the dead fisherman. All the figures are viewed frontally against the background of the village harbour. *Repas d'Adieu* was even given the form of a triptych, depicting those who are to leave on a long fishing trip on the left panel, and those who stay behind on the right. The central scene was fashioned after the many representations of the Last Supper, although again no direct religious signs were visible.[28] Around a table, he depicted thirteen [*sic*] men and women – the *mater familias* taking the position of Christ – who were perhaps gathered for the last time.

Although he sometimes also painted colourful festive events such as *Femmes de Plougastel*, Cottet preferred sombre, tragic moments, immediately before or after a major drama. Compared to Simon his colour scheme generally was more restrained, the costumes of the villagers less exuberant and his compositions more austere. He often also omitted a clear reference to the exact location of his representations in the titles, as opposed to Simon, and used instead the generic subtitle: *Au pays de la mer* (At the land by the sea) for many of his works. Instead of a special local event, he represented a scene of more general significance, with which the observer

as in Egypt, Turkey, Venice and Spain.
[28]   See also: Aubert, 'L'Oeuvre de Charles Cottet' 778.

could easily identify. He seemed to be not so much interested in exotic images as in the visualisation of general human feelings. Probably he thought that these emotions could be found in a purer form among these humble people, who still lived in direct contact with nature. Thus it seems that from within a similar ideological framework, both painters followed their own personal preferences, Simon stressing the role of tradition, while Cottet underlined the bond with nature.

From about 1895 the works of Simon and Cottet were well received by the critics. Their paintings, which were mostly hung in a prominent place at the yearly salon of the Société Nationale, were reviewed in the press, received medals and were acquired by the French State and foreign museums. They participated in international exhibitions and later on would be honoured with monographic exhibitions in one of the major Parisian art galleries. From about the turn of the century their work was also discussed in monographic essays in most international art magazines. Simon and Cottet were thus considered to belong among the most important and influential French artists of their time.[29] In 1903, the German critic Karl Eugen Schmidt even ended his book on French nineteenth-century painting with a chapter on Brittany, which was mainly dedicated to Simon and Cottet, thus suggesting that they represented the most promising new current.[30] Other painters followed in their footsteps and regionalist painting became a clearly distinguishable artistic tendency. Nevertheless, as Paris was the international art centre where at the various salons and galleries thousands of French and foreign painters exhibited their work, French regionalism was only one of the many styles that vied for public attention. But how were Simon's and Cottet's pictures of Breton folk life interpreted?

Highly influential art critics, such as Gabriel Mourey, director of *L'Art décoratif* and the Parisian correspondent for the influential English art journal *The Studio* (which appeared with a French translation), and Léonce

[29] In 1902, Mourey, for example, called Simon 'one of the best painters of the age', whereas ten years later Thiébault-Sisson still called Cottet 'one of the most creative artists of his time'. Bénédite maintained that the *Procession at Penmarc'h* by Simon and the *Farewell Dinner* by Cottet figured among 'the most outstanding works of our generation' and Louis Aubert called a painting by Cottet 'one of the ten most beautiful French paintings from the last twenty-five years'. See respectively: Gabriel Mourey, 'The Art of M. Lucien Simon', *The Studio* (April 1902) 157–70, especially 170, Thiébault-Sisson, 'Un peintre de la Bretagne et de la mer, Charles Cottet: La Vie artistique. A propos de la Société Nouvelle', *Le Temps* (10 March 1912) 3, Bénédite, 'Lucien Simon' 36, and Aubert, 'L'Oeuvre de Charles Cottet' 771.
[30] Schmidt, *Französische Malerei des 19. Jahrhunderts* 150–9.

Bénédite, director of the Musée du Luxembourg from 1895 until 1923, who were well acquainted with Simon and Cottet, observed that both painters deliberately suppressed details in order to produce simplified images. Instead of copying reality, they sought to convey an idea. According to these critics they tried to penetrate the character of the scene by concentrating on its essence. Thus instead of literally representing the fleeting aspects of nature as the impressionists had done, they sought to unveil permanent forms and distil the 'essence of things'. Or as Raymond Bouyer defined the 'poetics' of Cottet: '[He] departs from nature in order to interpret and recompose it, to make it speak, by adding to its mute suggestions the answer of his heart.' For these reasons their compositions were seen as meaningful and morally significant.[31]

Most critics agreed that Simon's figures were the product of a sharp psychological insight. He succeeded in representing his sitters' individuality by closely observing their dominant traits. Other painters also profoundly studied their subjects by living among them for longer periods of time. They were no 'tourist painters', as so many of their predecessors.[32] Simon's pictures of Breton folk life, such as *La procession à Penmarc'h*, were consequently seen as powerful expressions of the Breton *Volksgeist*. Indeed, Henri Marcel, who between 1903 and 1905 would be the highest official for Fine Arts, saw these paintings as true portraits of the 'Breton race', whereas Bénédite believed that Simon provided a faithful expression 'of the environment, of the soil, and of the race'.[33] In Simon's pictures, simple peasants and fishermen of Brittany appeared to live in close contact with nature and to have been shaped by their 'milieu' – or, as Mourey said, 'humankind [was] in perfect accord with its surroundings'. Cottet's paintings inspired similar remarks. Mourey particularly praised the *Repas d'adieu* (which Bénédite acquired for the Luxembourg Museum), in which the people's austere melancholy and sadness were shown as the fatal consequence of nature's hardships. The people's silent, meditative demeanour was accompanied by

---

31 Mourey, 'Charles Cottet's "Au Pays de la Mer"' 228 and 240, Bénédite, 'Charles Cottet' 106 and 116, Bénédite, 'Lucien Simon' 28–9 and 32–3, Mourey, 'The Art of Simon' 157–8 and 170, Raymond Bouyer, 'Charles Cottet', *L'Art et les Artistes*, 12 (1910–11) 167, and Aubert, 'L'Oeuvre de Charles Cottet' 767.

32 Thiébault-Sisson, 'Charles Cottet', Aubert, 'L'Oeuvre de Charles Cottet' 765–7, Gabriel Nigond, 'Fernand Maillaud', *L'Art et les Artistes* XV (1912) 169–73, especially 170. The condescending term 'tourist painters' was used in Gustave Geffroy, 'The Modern French Pastellists: Charles Milcendeau', *The Studio* (15 February 1904) 24–9, especially 26.

33 Marcel, 'Lucien Simon' 134–5, and Léonce Bénédite, 'Lucien Simon, aquarelliste', *Art et Décoration*, Vol. 2 (1909) 70. The term 'race' was very often used in a very loose manner during this period and could also be translated as 'people'.

the indifference of the sky and sea in the background behind the windows of this triptych's central scene. This critic concluded that by depicting significant moments of Breton folk life in sombre colours Cottet succeeded in evoking the local *Volksgeist*:[34]

> how can M. Cottet be blamed if, in striving to render as impressive
> as possible a country such as Brittany, with all its old traditions, its
> primitive manners, its mysticism, its air of wildness and fatality, if,
> having to evoke the spirit of the soil and its people, he should choose
> its most impressive manifestations, those which have acted most strongly
> upon his own sensibility? The essential point is that his manner of
> realizing his work is in adequate accordance with the very spirit of its
> subject.[35]

According to most critics, Simon and Cottet depicted the harmony between the inhabitants, the sea, the land and the sky in Brittany. The sea generally constituted the dominant menacing presence, but it was the sky that foretold the weather and thus signalled whether it was wise to go out fishing. The harsh climate was reflected in rugged landscapes, sinister shores and treacherous bays in which only hard work could earn a man a living. The barren plains, which did not provide much shelter against the elements, seem to be reflected in the small granite houses, the low-built churches and the equally primitive people. These resigned, diligent, simple men and women lived in close contact with their surroundings. The change of seasons and the weather determined the rhythm of their lives. Their gestures were instinctive and only an almost superstitious religious belief could reconcile them with their destiny. Simon's pictures in particular testify to religion's central role. In almost all of his outdoor scenes a church is the most impressive building and in other pictures he showed pilgrimages and processions. Bénédite even argued that by depicting menhirs and other megalithic holy places he stressed continuity with prehistoric religious feeling.[36]

Thus by representing these traditionally dressed people engaged in typical activities against the background of a village in its natural surroundings, Simon and Cottet tried to penetrate the collective 'soul' of this part of

---

[34]   Mourey, 'The Art of Simon' 164 and 169, Mourey, 'Charles Cottet's "Au Pays de la Mer"' 235 and 239.

[35]   Mourey, 'Charles Cottet's "Au Pays de la Mer"' 239.

[36]   Chantavoine, 'M. Charles Cottet' 110–12, Segard, 'Charles Cottet, painter of Breton life and scenes' 273–4, and Bénédite, 'Lucien Simon' 34–6. Sometimes this provoked anti-clerical remarks. Bénédite, for example, associated religion and mysticism with 'domination and submission': Bénédite, 'Lucien Simon' 36. See also: Bouyer, 'L'Oeuvre de Lucien Simon' 528.

Brittany. This, at least, is what most critics saw in their pictures. They also agreed that Simon and Cottet's paintings should not only be judged on their high artistic qualities, but also on their significance. But what did these pictures mean? Did they merely record a somewhat picturesque part of France, thus stimulating knowledge and awareness of the beauty and variety of the fatherland, or did they convey a more profound message?

A first striking element was their clear preference for Breton subjects. There was general agreement in the nineteenth century that Brittany was one of the most primitive regions of France. Brittany was seen as one of the most backward and picturesque regions, with its prehistoric megalithic monuments, its peculiar, untouched landscape, its folklore, traditional costumes, processions and pilgrimages, and its ancient Celtic language. Already in the 1860s and 1870s Brittany had attracted many painters, mainly French, British and American, who established major artists' colonies in Pont-Aven and Concarneau.[37] Most French regionalists also specialised in Breton subjects. This was the case of Désiré-Lucas, Lemordant and Méhuet, who were native from Brittany, but also of Simon, Cottet, Milcendeau and Roque, who came from other, mostly distant parts of France.

This preference for Brittany may seem strange, as this westernmost part of the country could hardly be considered the centre of France. It did not play a fundamental role in French history, economically it was quite backward, and culturally it was completely peripheral. However, as the Bretons still spoke an ancient language that was not derived from Latin and they still cherished traditions that had disappeared elsewhere, Brittany was seen as one of the few authentic French regions where vestiges of a pre-Roman culture still survived. That Simon and Cottet subscribed to this interpretation seemed probable, as they consciously ignored the signs of modernisation which should also have been visible in many parts of the region. In fact, at the time Brittany was modernising rapidly and its agriculture, industry and commerce were increasingly integrated into the national economy.[38] In the villages they depicted, however, time seemed to have come to a halt, prehistoric and medieval elements persisted and modern civilisation, seemingly, had not yet arrived.

Not all critics appreciated the supposed primitiveness of the Breton

---

[37] Cathérine Puget, 'Die Künstlerkolonie von Pont-Aven und Le Pouldu im 19. und 20. Jahrhundert' and André Cariou, 'Die Künstlerkolonie von Concarneau' in: Claus Pese ed., *Künstlerkolonien in Europa: Im Zeichen der Ebene und des Himmels* (Nürnberg 2001) respectively 57–65 and 67–77, and Denise Delouche, *Peintres de la Bretagne: Découverte d'une province* (Paris 1977).

[38] Fred Orton and Griselda Pollock, 'Les Données bretonnantes: La prairie de répresentation', *Art History*, 3 (1980) 314–45.

countryside. Some, like Raymond Bouyer, openly rejected it as backward and an obstacle to progress. In Brittany, as painted by Simon and Cottet, he only saw ignorance, brutality, violence and superstition. Others thought that these brute, degenerated people, with their 'prominent cheek-bones, the narrow eyes' were from 'Tibetan and Mongolian descent'.[39] Mostly, however, the local population as depicted by Simon and Cottet was seen as authentic and pure. Living in close contact with nature and respecting ancestral traditions, they still preserved their ancient collective personality. Thus, when speaking of Cottet's pictures of the Breton fishing communities, Bénédite said that it was possible to deduce a more general and mythical meaning from them:

> [these representations] remove the distance between the people from today and their distant ancestors and show that across the times, across the religions, across the civilisations, across everything that passes, these maritime races have preserved their former character intact, and their moral unity entirely.

Their world, however, was threatened by modern civilisation, by trains and schooling on one hand and by alcohol, political strife, disbelief and degeneration on the other.[40]

The appreciation of the countryside, as backward and uncivilised on the one hand or close to nature and morally intact on the other, had not changed fundamentally compared to earlier decades in which, for example, the paintings of Jean-François Millet and Jules Breton had received similar comments.[41] However, the main difference was that now both critics and painters did not refer to the countryside and its inhabitants in a general sense, but were very specific in their references. The depicted countryside

---

[39] Bouyer, 'L'Oeuvre de Lucien Simon' 528 and Mourey, 'The Art of Simon' 158. See also: Marcel, 'Lucien Simon' 132 and Charles Géniaux, 'Mathurin Méheut: Peintre de la Bretagne', *Art et Décoration* (1921), I 117–28, especially 117. This negative image also dominated in Paris, where Breton immigrants were often viewed as primitive and uncivilised, and which is best symbolised in the cartoon character of Bécassine, which from 1905 onwards became very popular. See Leslie Moch, *The Pariahs of Yesterday: Bretons in Paris* (forthcoming).

[40] Quote from: Bénédite, 'Charles Cottet' 112. See also: Aubert, 'L'Oeuvre de Charles Cottet' 762–6, Thiébault-Sisson, 'Lucien Simon'. This article was shamelessly plagiarised by the prominent German art critic Wilhelm Michel. He even made some translation errors, maintaining that Simon had married a woman from Brittany: Wilhelm Michel, 'Lucien Simon', *Kunst für Alle* (15 May 1913) 361–4.

[41] See Christopher Parsons and Neil McWilliam, '"Le Paysan de Paris": Alfred Sensier and the Myth of Rural France', *Oxford Art Journal* (1983) 37–58 and Neil McWilliam, 'Le Paysan au salon: Critique d'art et construction d'une classe sous le Second Empire' in: Jean-Paul Bouillon ed., *La critique d'art en France 1850–1900* (Saint-Etienne 1989) 81–95.

did not so much embody a generic heartland of the nation, but represented the 'soul' of a specific region, and had to be represented with its own particular natural environment and cultural traditions.

Yet Brittany was a special case. It was not just a primitive region, like Tahiti or Morocco, but one of the most savage areas of France. Although contrary to most parts of the country Brittany had deep Celtic roots and few Roman traces, some critics saw it as one of the most typical of French regions. Cultural practices which had disappeared elsewhere in France supposedly still existed in Brittany. When Bénédite discussed some of Simon and Cottet's Breton scenes he spoke of 'ethnic' and 'antehistorical survivals'. Hence according to some, traces of the true, original character of France could still be studied in this remote part of the country.[42] To many nationalists this implied that Brittany might be able to provide guidelines for national regeneration. They did not want France to return to this primitive stage, but believed she should harmoniously fuse international modernity with her own historical character. This could not be done, explained Mourey, either by these primitive peasants or by the cosmopolitan upper classes whose 'characteristic traits' were effaced by international fashion, which led only to 'uniformity'; instead it was the task of the provincial and Parisian middle classes who still had a living bond with the nation's traditions, and among whom 'the cares of life have developed the will [and] education accentuates instead of obliterate[es] the knowledge of oneself'.[43]

The way paintings by Simon and Cottet were interpreted by most critics can be easily connected with the new type of more activist and subjectivist nationalism. Some critics made casual references to Maurice Barrès, the main propagator of this type of nationalism. One even argued that Désiré-Lucas, when studying in Paris, was what Barrès called a 'déraciné'; consequently the young 'uprooted' painter only recovered his creative powers when he returned to his native soil.[44] Simon and Cottet implicitly followed Barrès' maxim that contemporary culture should reflect geographic environment, organically grown traditions, and the needs of the present which together constituted the *Volksgeist*. The French popular spirit, according to many, could probably best be studied in its most primary form

---

[42] Léonce Bénédite, 'Charles Cottet', *L'Art Décoratif* (1911) 221–36, especially 226 and 232, and Bénédite, 'Charles Cottet' 112. The cartoon character of Asterix seems to embody this positive interpretation of Brittany as heartland of France, free of foreign influences.

[43] Mourey, 'The Art of Simon' 169–70.

[44] Yvanhoé Rambosson, 'Désiré-Lucas', *L'Art Décoratif* (March 1906) 101–9, especially 104–6. See also: Chantavoine, 'Charles Cottet' 117.

in some of the most remote areas of the country; this was exactly what Simon and Cottet did. At the same time, their stress on the idiosyncratic nature of Breton folk life contributed to the rise of regionalism. Although they were not born in Brittany, they made an important contribution to the definition of a distinct regional identity. Consequently they were a source of inspiration for young Breton painters such as Désiré-Lucas, Lemordant and Méhuet, some of whom eventually became involved in the Breton movement.

2

Germany

In the German Empire the relationship between artists who painted similar themes as Simon and Cottet and the new type of nationalism was more direct. They were all well acquainted with the ideas of Julius Langbehn, the most influential theorist of the new nationalist ideology and author of the 1890 bestseller *Rembrandt als Erzieher* (Rembrandt as Educator). Fritz Mackensen, for example, discussed the book extensively with his friends. He saw his decision to establish himself in the small village of Worpswede in the moors north of Bremen confirmed by Langbehn, whose book contained quite a few chapters on art. According to Langbehn, good art must be national art, which meant that it should have roots in the national artistic tradition and close contact with the folk culture of the German countryside. He maintained that individuality was characteristic of the Germanic peoples and that the most individual and therefore most 'German' artist had been Rembrandt, thereby implicitly including the Low Countries within the German cultural orbit. However, contemporary art followed international trends and was produced in major towns. So Langbehn advised German painters to move to the countryside and develop a new, original art form with strong local roots. He argued further that national character was best preserved in the northern German countryside where Roman and Slavonic influences were almost non-existent. This did not mean that he completely rejected contemporary foreign influences. He dismissed the existing 'biased German peasant painting' and maintained that Germany needed a 'healthy, clear and vigorous' modern art, which could come into existence by adopting some of the technical innovations of the impressionists. He even advised German painters to combine the impressionists' stress on the moment with the eternal character of the 'popular soul' in order to give a lively picture of contemporary local culture.[1]

---

[1] Julius Langbehn, *Rembrandt als Erzieher: Von einem Deutschen* (Leipzig 1890) 9–10, 15–19,

Some German painters followed Langbehn's advice, adopting at least some of the impressionists' lessons, staying for longer or shorter periods in isolated villages, and demonstrating a lively interest in local folk culture. In the German Empire, nevertheless, there was no clear preference for one specific region, although most regionalists adopted Langbehn's recommendation and preferred the northern and central areas. The coastal regions seem to be overrepresented as both Dettmann and Engel preferred the coastal villages, and Mackensen went to the northern moors of Worpswede. Thus, the Germanic part of the country prevailed over the Romanised (and mostly Catholic) southern areas as the heartland of the nation. There were also exceptions, such as, for example, the Berlin-born Borchardt, who painted many Bavarian scenes that he exhibited at the Parisian salon.[2] Although most regionalists seemed to follow Langbehn, trying to become truly German artists, their attitude showed a clear resemblance with that of similar painters from other countries.

Like their French counterparts, these German painters did not produce sublime mountain or sea paintings, nor did they depict virgin forest or river landscapes. Instead of wild and untouched nature, they preferred landscapes where the human presence was clear at first sight; not only by the actual presence of human beings, but also by their artefacts and buildings and by their intervention in nature. They generally showed villages surrounded with cultivated fields, meadows and gardens. However, as the earth in these isolated villages generally was not very fertile, the inhabitants had to work hard to till the soil. This became especially manifest in the case of the old village of Worpswede, which during the second half of the eighteenth century had become the centre of a moor colony. Most of the peat in the surrounding moors had already been mined by the end of the nineteenth century, and the landscape with straight canals lined with trees thus was in great part the product of more than a century of hard labour. It seemed that exactly the reciprocal influence between man and nature, which in Worpswede was clearly visible, was what most interested these painters.

In terms of both quantity and quality, German regionalist painting was not stronger than its French counterpart. Bantzer, Dettmann, Engel and Mackensen all had more national and international success than the secondary French regionalist painters, but none of them reached the level

26, 121–2 and 135. See for his influence on Mackensen, Engel and Dettmann: Ulrike Hamm and Bernd Küster, *Fritz Mackensen 1866–1953* (Lilienthal 1990) 44, and Jutta Müller, *Otto H. Engel: Ein Künstlerleben um 1900 zwischen Berlin und Schleswig-Holstein* (Flensburg 1990) 50 and 72.
2   Louis Vauxcelles, 'Félix Borchardt', *L'Art et les Artistes* XIII (1913) 113–19.

of Simon, Cottet, or the Spanish regionalist Zuloaga. Nor did they receive much attention in foreign art magazines. Maybe this was also due to their teaching activities at one of the various art academies that had started to reform their curriculum in the years before the turn of the century, and where, relatively early in their careers, most of them became professors. Thus, Bantzer obtained a teaching assignment at the Academy of Fine Arts in Dresden in 1896, whereas Dettmann became a professor in Berlin in that same year and in 1901 was asked to become the director at the Academy in Königsberg. Mackensen was offered a chair at the Art Academy of Weimar in 1904 and six years later would become its director. Only Engel declined a few such offers. However, in 1906 he was elected into the Royal Art Academy and for some time was in charge of the organisation of the yearly art exhibition in Berlin. All these activities would absorb much of their time and energy.

Nevertheless, regionalism and nationalism were almost omnipresent in the German artistic debates. As Germany was only recently united and did not possess the prestige or colonies of great powers like Great Britain and France, a kind of national unease was widespread. On a cultural level many Germans felt that their country did not hold the position it deserved, particularly when its relatively low artistic prestige was compared to its economic and military power. In the visual arts the international dominance of their arch-enemy France was generally recognised and many critics regretted the secondary place their country occupied in relation to the central position of Paris. This was one of the threads in many art reviews, even in those where nationalism or regionalism did not seem very relevant. Some critics went further and asserted that French painting was not suitable for German artists as there was a fundamental difference between the two nations, whereby they generally opposed German spiritualism and idealism to a more superficial and materialistic French culture. Thus, while French painting stayed on the material surface, German artists wanted to penetrate into the spiritual, into the realm of ideas. This position was most clearly formulated by the nationalist ideologue Arthur Moeller van den Bruck in an article in the nationalist cultural magazine *Kunstwart* (Guardian of Art). According to him this incompatibility could be explained by racial factors:

> The difference between both peoples, which has always existed and
> still continues today, is deeply founded in the race. Notwithstanding
> all transformations, the Germans have preserved their pure Germanic
> origins, whereas the French, who originally were a mixture of

Celts and Germanics, have let themselves bit by bit be overwhelmed completely by Latin culture.[3]

Although not many respected art critics openly expressed comparable views, some endorsed his distinction between a more superficial, visual French art and a more profound, idealistic German art. Thus the prominent Munich *Jugendstil* artist and critic Hermann Obrist made a similar comparison between the inner German art of Schultze-Naumburg and the impressionistic French art, although without explicitly referring to French art. Schultze-Naumburg 'painted German', which meant that he 'put his own soul into the landscape, revealing what he had innermost observed, and not just optically correct representing what he had taken in with the optical tool of the eye'.[4] However, this opposition between a superficial, materialist French and a more profound, idealist German art – which during the First World War would be cultivated and broadened into a fundamental opposition between the superficial French civilisation and the more idealistic German *Kultur* – in fact meant that an artistic disagreement was projected upon two different nations, whereas in France regionalist painters and those critics sympathetic to their cause used the same arguments against the dominance of Impressionism on the French art scene. Some critics even defined this same artistic trend as essentially French. Bénédite, for example, maintained that Cottet was part of a great French tradition, using almost the same terms as Obrist applied to Schultze-Naumburg.[5]

Thus, whereas regionalist painting was probably not more prominent in Germany than in France, the nationalistic discourse, with its regionalist variants, certainly was. For this reason more than their subject choice, which would be approved by most nationalists, critics commented upon the impressionistic technique of Dettmann and Bantzer. Although most authors did not condemn their adoption of these 'foreign' innovations, they almost always seized the opportunity to regret the existing artistic dependence on France.[6]

---

[3] Moeller van den Bruck, 'Die Ueberschätzung französischer Kunst in Deutschland', *Kunstwart* (15 August 1905) 501–9, especially 502–3.

[4] Hermann Obrist, 'Brief an einen Freund', *Dekorative Kunst* IV (January 1909) 129–40, especially 135. See also: Max Osborn, 'Otto Heinrich Engel', *Zeitschrift für bildende Kunst* 14 (1903) 159–65, especially 160–1.

[5] Léonce Bénédite, 'Charles Cottet', *Art et Décoration* (April 1904) 101–18, especially 116.

[6] See Peter Paret, *The Berlin Secession: Modernism and its Enemies in Imperial Germany* (Cambridge 1980), Barbara Paul, *Hugo von Tschudi und die moderne französische Kunst im deutschen Kaiserreich* (Mainz 1993), Karl Krummacher, 'Die Malerkolonie Worpswede',

Consequently, as with the *Bande noire*, some of these German painters were singled out for their painting technique, although this time not as an alternative to Impressionism but as an importation of it. However, Bantzer, Dettmann and Engel differed in many ways from the French impressionists. In some of his major paintings Carl Bantzer used an impressionistic technique to achieve a sense of directness and suggest movement, but he did so on huge, carefully composed canvasses upon which he sometimes worked for more than a year and which were meant to be shown at a salon. His *Abendmahl in einer hessischen Dorfkirche* (Communion at a Hessian Village Church, 1892), *Hessischer Erntearbeiter* (Hessian Harvester, 1907), which depicted a life-size harvester in traditional white shirt and white knee breeches, and *Abendruhe* (Evening Rest, 1912) all portrayed traditionally dressed people from the Schwalm region near Marburg. In *Schwälmer Tanz* (Dance from the Schwalm, 1898, plate 5) he gave a close-up of a group of young men and women in the local dress for special occasions engaged in a swirling traditional dance. Like Simon, instead of choosing modern urban themes he depicted important events in the rural calendar such as weddings, attending church, local feasts, harvesting and resting after work. In his large paintings he gave a monumental picture of these simple, but honest country folk.[7]

Ludwig Dettmann applied impressionistic techniques to traditional genres, such as religious and historical painting and genre scenes. Thus in his *Überführung der Leiche Kaiser Wilhelms I. vom Palais zum Dom* (1895) he took a kind of monumental 'snapshot' of a contemporary historical event: the icy-cold winter night when the coffin of the old Emperor William I was conveyed from his palace to the cathedral. Works like *Die Heilige Nacht* (Holy Night, 1892), *Arbeit* (Work, 1894) and *Das deutsche Volkslied* (German Folk Song, 1895) were executed as triptychs, in which, in a way similar to Cottet, simple folk scenes were presented with an almost religious aura. He often worked in artists' colonies on the north German coast such as Ahrenshoop, Ekensund and Nidden where he produced many paintings, such as *Heimfahrt vom Kirchdorf* (Return Home from Kirchdorf, 1895, plate 6) and *Fischerkirchhof* (Fishermen's Cemetery 1895), depicting the simple and authentic life of these relatively isolated communities.[8]

His friend Otto Heinrich Engel painted many of the same motifs using

Westermanns Illustrierte Deutsche Monatshefte (April 1899) 17–22, especially 17–18, Max Osborn, 'Ludwig Dettmann', *The Studio* (September 1905) 279–89, especially 279–80, and Karl Eugen Schmidt, *Französische Malerei des 19. Jahrhunderts* (Leipzig 1903) 159–60.

[7] Bernd Küster, *Carl Bantzer* (Marburg 1993) and Bernd Küster and Jürgen Wittstock, *Carl Bantzer: Aufbruch und Tradition* (Frankfurt am Main 2002).

[8] F. Deibel, *Ludwig Dettmann* (Bielefeld and Leipzig, s.a. [1910]).

a similar style and technique. Often accompanied by Dettmann, he stayed for longer periods in Ekensund and on the Nord-Frisian island Föhr. Some of his best-known paintings are the triptych *Von de Waterkant* (From the 'Waterkant', 1898), *Arm in Arm zum Fest (Friesische Mädchen)* (Arm in Arm to the Feast; Frisian Girls, 1902) and *Trauerfeier in Friesland – Begräbnis auf Föhr* (Memorial Service in Frisia – Funeral on Föhr, 1904, plate 7). He clearly preferred to paint wedding scenes, funerals, local feasts, people in traditional costumes and typical local activities such as fishing and rope making.[9]

Fritz Mackensen was an exception as he did not go to an existing artists' colony, but founded a new one with some friends – most of them specialised in landscape painting – in Worpswede. The influence of impressionist techniques was less clear in his work as he used more simplified forms and did not accentuate his virtuoso painting skills; and whereas most of his colleagues' pictures were quite similar to the cheerful images of Breton folk life by Lucien Simon, Mackensen's paintings were more closely related to Cottet's gloomy and sometimes almost religious images. Both shared a preference for the hardships and tragic moments faced by the villagers, whose lives they observed from close by. This manifests itself in some of Mackensen's huge salon paintings such as *Gottesdienst im Freien* (Open-Air Service, 1895, plate 8), in which the simple villagers of Worpswede assemble in the open air to attend a religious service, *Die trauernde Familie* (The Mourning Family, 1896) and *Die Scholle* (Native Soil, 1898). In the monumental *Mutter und Kind* (Mother and Child, 1892) Mackensen depicted a poor young woman with clogs who had recently given birth but had to return to work, cutting peat in the moors outside Worpswede. She is represented taking a rest from work on a barrow to nurse her baby. The painting is clearly inspired by religious images and was known as the Moormadonna.[10]

Although every painter put his own accents, all focused on the most salient moments of rural life – on the natural and traditional events that regulated human existence in these untouched villages. Birth, marriage, death, local festivities, sowing, harvesting, taking a rest from work and going to church on Sundays, were depicted time after time by these painters. A self-evident, intimate bond with the surrounding nature – which especially came to the fore in working the land – and existing secular and religious traditions gave these people something to hold onto. The warm intimacy of family life and the safe haven of a harmonious, well-

---

[9] Müller, *Otto H. Engel.*
[10] Hamm and Küster, *Fritz Mackensen.* See also the chapter on Worpswede in Nina Lübbren, *Rural Artists' Colonies in Europe 1870–1910* (Manchester 2001).

ordered community as well as an unshakeable belief protected these people from despair, faced as they were with the inevitable hardships of human existence. Gender roles were clearly distinguishable, although women also participated in the work on the land. Foreign intrusions, both by people – with the exception of an occasional travelling circus that seemed to form an organic part of those feasts that were the traditional highlight of the year – and by modern inventions, did not threaten the traditional way of life. Although the poverty of many of the villagers and their hardships were not hidden by the painters, their models always seemed to be resigned to their fate. Thus, what was shown was not a comfortable, modern bourgeois existence, but a harmonious, traditional, hard-working community.

As in France, many critics understood these pictures as convincing interpretations of the local *Volksgeist*. Most observers asserted that these painters should not be seen as mere realists. They did not offer an empty, 'soulless' representation of nature, but by simplifying and eliminating the unnecessary, they tried to reach the 'essence' and give a sensitive and poetic interpretation of visual reality.[11] From their pictures one could comprehend how the monotony of the plains, sky and sea determined local life. The peasants, fishermen and shepherds depicted still lived in close contact with nature.[12] Or as Friedrich Deibel commented upon the paintings of Dettmann:

> The farmers, fishers and shepherds of the coast of Schleswig-Holstein, these simple children of nature with their joys and sorrows, their toilsome struggle with the barren soil of the land and their struggle with the elements are painterly brought to live in Dettmann's art ...
> In piles of images the painter has found time and again new motifs to artistically vivify this people in the framework of its landscape ... [to conclude that] we can learn new things and peculiarities about the soul of this people and the soul of this landscape from his art.[13]

In order to fully understand the interpenetration of man and nature,

11 Paul Schultze-Naumburg, 'Die Worpsweder', *Kunst für Alle*, (15 January 1897) 116–19, especially 118, Krummacher, 'Die Malerkolonie Worpswede' 20–4, Osborn, 'Otto Heinrich Engel' 160–1, and Wilhelm Schölermann, 'Hessische Landes-Ausstellung für freie und angewandte Kunst – Darmstadt 1908', *Deutsche Kunst und Dekoration*, 22 (1908) 283–96, especially 284–7.
12 Fritz Overbeck, 'Ein Brief aus Worpswede', *Kunst für Alle*, (15 October 1895) 20–4, especially 21–2 and Deibel, *Ludwig Dettmann* 24–5.
13 Deibel, *Ludwig Dettmann* 24–5 and 34.

these painters stayed for longer periods of time among these simple folk. By observing life in these villages, interacting with their inhabitants, participating in their activities, and plunging into local nature, their paintings should ultimately be considered an organic product of the spirit of the land and its people. The young poet Rainer Maria Rilke, who stayed in Worpswede between 1900 and 1902, even maintained that the impressions that Mackensen had received throughout the years had been attached to his childhood memories. Consequently, he really had become profoundly rooted in his new chosen homeland.[14] Real national art, these critics argued, could only be produced by those who have an intimate bond with the earth, who are rooted in native soil. This did not necessarily mean that one had to be born in the place where one worked. An intimate feeling of personal affinity and identification was indispensable, however. Dettmann's biographer Deibel argued that his art was so strongly rooted in the soil of his native Schleswig-Holstein that his 'Lower German nerve' could be discerned even in his powerful brush technique.[15]

A few critical reviewers nevertheless remarked that the selection of motifs, especially by Mackensen and the other Worpswede painters was deliberately one-sided. They only showed the traditional, desolate parts of the village, not the comfortable new houses of a few rich farmers or Worpswede's modern economic activities. Nor did they paint the bicycle riders or elegant carriages that arrived with good weather from nearby Bremen.[16] Some critics, especially from *Deutsche Kunst und Dekoration*, the art magazine of the reformist Darmstadt artists' colony, even dismissed the current fashion of *Heimatkunst* as extremely one-sided, as if Germany was merely an 'agreeable, harmless agrarian State'. Although the author accepted the notion that the country possessed a specific national character, it was wrong to equate German with 'everything undeveloped, rustic, rural, obtuse and slow'.[17] Nonetheless, most critics reviewed the new trend positively and, contrary to some of their French colleagues, they did not define the inhabitants of the countryside as barbaric or superstitious.

[14] Rainer Maria Rilke, *Worpswede: Fritz Mackensen, Otto Modersohn, Fritz Overbeck, Hans am Ende, Heinrich Vogeler* (2nd edn., Bielefeld and Leipzig 1905) 44 and 50. See also: Schultze-Naumburg, 'Die Worpsweder' 116, Osborn, 'Otto Heinrich Engel' 161–2, and Deibel, *Ludwig Dettmann* 34.

[15] Paul Warncke, 'Worpswede', *Zeitschrift für bildende Kunst*, 11 (1900) 147–55 and 176–86, especially 150 and 185 and Deibel, *Ludwig Dettmann* 24.

[16] Andreas Gildemeister, 'Worpswede', *Kunst für Alle* (15 March 1900) 267–80, especially 276–8, see also: Warncke, 'Worpswede' 182.

[17] W. Michel, 'Das nationale Element in der Kunst', *Deutsche Kunst und Dekoration* XVII (1905–6) 152–64, especially 152–3. See for a more theoretical rejection also: Emil Utitz, 'Heimatkunst', *Deutsche Kunst und Dekoration* XXVII (1910–11) 354–73.

As in France, some observers were aware that the traditional world found in these isolated villages was threatened by modern civilisation. Traditional costumes, like other habits, were likely to disappear under the influence of towns, military service and the levelling advance of modernity.[18] But depicting these primitive communities did not only have an archaeological value. Some German critics used an argument left implicit by their French colleagues when they openly praised work as an 'elevating ethical force'. By this they meant primarily the labour of the fishermen and farmers seen in the paintings. These countrymen still went to work cheerfully; they accepted labour as an intrinsic part of life and did not complain or protest – as did many uprooted urban workers. Some, such as the nationalist ideologue Adolf Bartels and the painter Momme Nissen, a close friend of Langbehn, even openly condemned internationalism and the anti-traditionalist attitude of the German socialist movement.[19] Mostly, however, the authors preferred to emphasise the good example of the rural population. Thus Mackensen's monumental *Die Scholle*, which showed two traditionally dressed women hauling a harrow that is guided by a man, was called a 'hymn to work, which promises peace'. The artists also did their duty by working with unflagging zeal.[20]

The painters themselves also commented upon the moral value of the depicted rural scenes. Dettmann, who according to his biographer was not a social critic, asked himself in a letter cited by his biographer: 'which worker, which artisan still loves, like in former times, his own work and creations?' adding that he hoped that 'through my paintings, many may again enjoy work'. Bantzer – although writing some decades later – also presented the rural simplicity and zeal as an example to his fellow countrymen, and one would think especially to the dissatisfied workers of the city. In a longer essay on his native region of Hesse, he maintained that the impression he got from the farmers of the Schwalm area was that of 'proud, self-conscious and free' men. They formed a type of man, who:

---

[18] K. Raupp, 'Willingshausen: Ein Studienplatz deutscher Künstler', *Kunst für Alle* (1 October 1886) 11–14, especially 14 and Carl Bantzer, *Hessens Land und Leute in der deutschen Malerei: Mit Kunstchronik von Willingshausen. Erweiterter Sonderdruck aus Hessenland* (Marburg 1933–35) 40 and 75.
[19] Quote from Osborn, 'Ludwig Dettmann' 284, Adolf Bartels, *Heimatkunst: Ein Wort zur Verständigung* (München and Leipzig 1904) 19 and Momme Nissen, 'Berliner konservative Malerei (Grosse Ausstellung 1902)', *Kunst für Alle* XVII (15 August 1902) 505–7, especially 507.
[20] Deibel, *Ludwig Dettmann* 22–4, Bantzer, *Hessens Land und Leute* 40, and Warncke, 'Worpswede' 151 and 155.

in general was diligent and after sour weeks also knew joyful
feasts, feasts of cheerfulness and feasts of work. On Sundays the
busy churchgoing showed the faithful holding on to the Church ...
Everywhere the meaningful customs and traditions from the cradle to
the grave were still alive and enriched people's existence ... Life and
work was one ... Striking also was the modesty and contentment of the
poor.[21]

However, in reality Bantzer's idyllic and harmonious rural society was
hard to find in the Schwalm region. Thus, for his *Communion at a
Hessian Village Church*, Bantzer built a copy of a church interior in the
gardens of the manor house of Baron von Schwertzell, who had a serious
conflict with the local farmers and day labourers about the usufruct of
the forests and the redeeming of servitudes. After the minister chose
the side of the villagers, the baron even boycotted the village church
that lay next to his manor house. As the local farmers refused to sit as
models, Bantzer was forced to hire day labourers, who often were drunk
and who consequently could hardly live up to his 'proud, self-conscious
and free' men. Furthermore, in the Schwalm region the independent
farmers only constituted a small minority (about 5 per cent) and social
conflicts between the farmers and the large majority of landless labourers
occurred frequently. Also the relations with the authorities were far
from harmonious and between 1890 and 1912 the Schwalm even elected
a populist politician with a virulently anti-Semitic programme as its
representative in the Reichstag.[22]

Nevertheless, this was not the message conveyed by the painters, nor by
those who reported on their work. Both consciously created a very different
and idealised image of the countryside, overlooking the misery, hardship
and social and political conflicts. Most of the critics thus agreed that the
paintings of these presumably harmonious rural communities could have
a moral impact and cure the soul, conferring a sense of power, seriousness
and peace, and reinforcing a sense of belonging. Thus Paul Warncke,
speaking of the poetical images of Worpswede, maintained:

Like a fresh breath from the sea it blows towards us; its name speaks
of strength and health, of quiet seriousness and sustained, iron, patient

---

21 Deibel, *Ludwig Dettmann* 22–4 and Bantzer, *Hessens Land und Leute* 40.
22 Martin Scharfte, 'Hessisches Abendmahl: Exkurs zu Wissenschaft und Vergewisserung
in volkskundlichem und folkloristischem Tableau', *Hessische Blätter für Volks- und
Kulturforschung* (1990) 9–46 and Robert von Friedeburg, *Ländliche Gesellschaft und Obrigkeit:
Gemeindeprotest und politische Mobilisierung im 18. und 19. Jahrhundert* (Göttingen 1997) 13–14,
50 and 251–76.

work. An unparalleled national feeling comes over us: joy in German art and German soil, joy in the glowing colourful beauty of a plain, native landscape, and joy, proud joy about the men, who with open heart and clear eyes sought, found and revealed you … [He even concluded that these paintings] were sermons that should penetrate the ear and the heart of the people.[23]

Nevertheless, these idyllic rural pictures should not only be seen as a nationalist antidote against the social unrest of urban lower classes. These scenes could also be a medicine for other social groups in big towns where the bustle of the masses and the metropolitan noise made people nervous and irritable and where the longing for comfort and fashionable products had weakened the collective identity. Eugen Kalkschmidt, for example, explained that in the second half of the nineteenth century, with the rise of the 'machine epoch', a 'specific superficial big town culture' had come into existence. This way the naïve communion with nature, which existed at the countryside, was lost. The pressure to produce faster and the noise of the big city had led to great physical and psychic stress; 'the nerves do not bear the unremitting roar of labour; the lungs long for pure air, the eyes for fresh and tranquillising colours'. Thus the modern inhabitants of the big cities felt a new need to visit the countryside, and recover by reconstituting contact with nature. And artists, like those from Worpswede, could give nature and the original homeland (*Heimat*) back to the 'jumbled up people from the big cities'.[24] In a similar vein, also referring to Worpswede, Andreas Gildemeister claimed:

However, I would like to know which popular tribe bears the character of his taciturn being more plain, truthful and powerful on his countenance than ours. Without a doubt this silent, genuine Nature and these people with their taciturn confidence exert an impulse towards strength and seriousness and tranquillity upon strangers who observe them with open eyes. When this strength and seriousness now, by means of art also affect the observer, who lives far from this land and its character, – would that not be a worthy moral influence on our weak, absent-minded, nervous generation?[25]

[23] Warncke, 'Worpswede' 147 and 154. See also: Friedrich Back, 'Carl Bantzer', *Kunst für Alle* (1 May 1918) 266.
[24] Eugen Kalkschmidt, 'Die Groszstadt, das Naturgefühl und die Landschaftskunst', *Kunst für Alle* (15 August 1905) 524–9 and 548–53, especially 525–8 and 552. See also: Rilke, *Worpswede* 13 and 44.
[25] Gildemeister, 'Worpswede' 272.

Thus, as in France, both German critics and painters seemed to agree that a reorientation inspired by these traditional, rural communities could regenerate the nation and strengthen its threatened identity. Good art should be national art, and its sources of inspiration could best be found at the countryside, where nothing seemed to have changed since immemorial times. The Worpsweder painter Fritz Overbeck, for example, maintained that the harsh circumstances of the farm workers had not changed since the times of Tacitus, whose remark 'Frisia non cantat' could still be applied to the area.[26] Thus by immersing themselves in the countryside, where people still felt an innate bond with both nature and tradition, artists could return German culture to its own roots, and help it to restore its original character and strength. Furthermore, by returning a sense of homeland to the inhabitants, they would also develop more profound national feelings. Thus, as Adolf Bartels, one of the best-known propagandists of regionalist art, explained, this way the artists could stimulate 'unity through variety'. And according to him, art could even, by nourishing and strengthening the roots of the German people, 'increase the national power of resistance and expansion'.[27]

Whereas the regionalist artists, the critics that were sympathetic to them and the discourse they used to describe their works, were closely connected to the new *völkisch* nationalism of Langbehn, their relationship with the various regional movements seemed less obvious. These painters, as we have seen, were quite mobile, as probably was part of their clientele. Fritz Mackensen, thus, originated from Holzminden near Hannover, studied painting in Düsseldorf and Munich, and after a long stay in Worpswede became professor in Weimar. Dettmann was born in Flensburg but soon moved with his parents to Hamburg. He studied in Berlin and later on became the director of the Art Academy of Königsberg. Engel was born in the small Hessian town of Erbach, but moved with his parents to Berlin, where he also started his artistic education. He continued in Karlsruhe and lived for a while in Munich. Then he returned to Berlin, although he stayed for longer periods in various coastal villages. Bantzer was born in the Schwalm region he preferred in his paintings, but soon his family moved to nearby Marburg. He studied in Berlin and afterwards obtained a teaching assignment in Dresden, where he stayed until after the First World War when he returned to his native Hessen. Thus none of these painters entirely identified with one region, or with a specific regional art

---

[26] Overbeck, 'Brief aus Worspwede' 22.
[27] Bartels, *Heimatkunst* 18–19. See also: Harald Grävell van Jostenoode, 'Germanische Kunst', *Deutsche Kunst und Dekoration* II (1898–99) 175–83.

school. They all exposed their paintings in the yearly exhibitions in the towns where they worked, but also sent their work to the other major German art centres. Thus whereas their subject matter was often limited to a specific region, they clearly addressed themselves to a national audience and a national art market.

3

Spain

Regionalist painting was more important in Spain than in France or Germany, although it arrived somewhat later and its representatives were slightly younger. Whereas the quality of Spanish regionalist painting was at least equal to that of their French and German counterparts, quantitatively it was substantially more important. Compared to the relatively small scale of the Spanish art scene – limited to a national salon in Madrid only every two years – the number and importance of regionalist painters was very impressive. The artistic scene and the salon in Madrid were both still dominated by academic painting, but *regionalismo*, as it was called in Spain, became its main contestant. For some years around 1910 it probably was even the dominant artistic tendency. Margarita Nelken – who in the 1930s would become an influential Spanish socialist and communist politician – in a review of the work of Eduardo Chicharro for the French journal *L'Art et les Artistes* even spoke of a Spanish artistic renaissance that had begun in the late 1890s and had been the work of the regionalist painters.[1]

A further characteristic of Spanish regionalist painting was that the two best-known Spanish painters of the time could be seen as regionalists. This was clearly the case with Ignacio Zuloaga, who after about 1900 probably grew to become the most internationally famous regionalist painter. Zuloaga's paintings generally were hung in the entrance hall of the Salon of the Société National and already in 1904 in a major international exposition of contemporary art in Düsseldorf he was assigned a whole room to expose his work; an honour he only had to share with two older and widely recognised artists: Adolph Menzel and Auguste Rodin. Joaquín Sorolla was something of an exception as he only turned to regionalism

---

1 M. Nelken, 'Eduardo Chicharro', *L'Art et les Artistes* XVIII (1913–14) 171–8, especially 171–2. See also: José Luis Bernal Muñoz, *La mirada del 98: Arte y literatura en la Edad de Plata* (Madrid 1998) and Javier Tusell, *Arte, historia y política en España (1890–1939)* (Madrid 1999).

after already having had a very successful career. He was internationally appreciated for his luminous images, especially from his native region of Valencia. He was a supporter of pictorial realism and was deeply influenced by Impressionism. His work showed many similarities to that of foreign impressionists of a second generation like Sargent, Liebermann, Krøyer and Serov. Around 1911, however, Sorolla decided to switch over to the then highly successful regionalist mode when he was invited to decorate the huge library of the Hispanic Society in New York. Originally he was asked to paint the most important scenes from Spanish history. However, Sorrolla convinced the commissioners that it would be better to represent his native country through its regions. As a consequence he started travelling through the country and dedicated about eight years to painting the various regions of Spain on huge canvasses. In *Castile*, for example, he painted among other events a procession leaving the walled town of Ávila during the so-called 'Fiesta del pan' (The Feast of Bread, plate 9).[2]

Strikingly, in Catalonia, where the regional movement was extremely strong and even started to agitate for political autonomy, regionalist painting was almost non-existent. In the Catalan capital Barcelona there was a flowering art scene that had a strong bond with Paris. Impressionism, Naturalism, Symbolism and Art Nouveau were all rapidly absorbed and the Catalan representatives of these Parisian-born movements were collectively known as *modernistes*. Although regionalist motives and arguments were not absent, most Catalan artists chose to connect their collective identity with international modernity, whereas a conservative minority tightened relations with Catholicism. The most ambitious, such as Pablo Picasso, directly pursued their career in Paris. This does not mean that in Catalonia there was no interest in the traditional folk culture of the countryside, as one of the strongholds of the Catalan movement was formed by the *excursionista* associations.[3]

In the rest of Spain, artistic life was focused on the fairly provincial art scene of Madrid, where the national salon was not organised by the artists themselves, but by government officials.[4] Furthermore, there were only

---

[2] For Zuloaga see: Enrique Lafuente Ferrari, *La vida y el arte de Ignacio Zuloaga* (3rd edn. Barcelona 1990) 83–93. For Sorolla: Pablo Jiménez Burillo ed., *Joaquín Sorolla (1863–1923)* (Madrid 1995) and Priscilla E. Muller and Marcus B. Burke, *Sorolla: The Hispanic Society* (New York 2004).

[3] Francesc Fontbona and Francesc Miralles, *Del modernisme al noucentisme 1888–1917*, Vol. VII, Història de l'art català (Barcelona 1985) and Joan-Lluís Marfany, *La cultura del Catalanisme: El nacionalisme català en els seus inicis* (Barcelona 1995).

[4] Gustav Diercks, 'Die Kunst im heutigen Spanien', *Kunst für Alle* (15 December 1902). See also: Angel Vegue y Goldoni, 'La exposición de Bellas Artes', *La Lectura* (October and November 1910) 181–4 and 287–92.

few art magazines, who generally led a precarious existence. Therefore, outside Catalonia, regionalist painting was seen as a very innovative art movement and was not, as happened elsewhere, rapidly overrun by new, more revolutionary artistic currents.

Spanish regionalist painting should not, however, be considered backward. On the contrary, most painters adopted a somewhat more modern style than most of their French and German counterparts. This was particularly the case with Ignacio Zuloaga, who started his career in Paris, where he kept a studio almost all his life. He only turned to regionalism around 1896, but as he took part in some of the most innovative art circles he produced paintings that differed clearly from those regionalists who still remained under the spell of Impressionism. In Paris he maintained close contact with the impressionist Edgar Degas and with important post-impressionist artists like Eugène Carrière, Paul Gauguin and Henri de Toulouse-Lautrec, and he befriended Emile Bernard and Auguste Rodin as well. In his early years he was influenced by Art Nouveau arabesques and Gauguin and Bernard's *cloisonniste* style; later he did not hesitate to use deformations to stress the expressive strength of his pictures. After he turned to regional themes his work became more stylised, decorative and solid, but somewhat less vivid than that of those who were still captivated by Impressionism such as Simon, Bantzer and Dettmann. He also refused to paint outdoors, or even to make *plein air* sketches as many regionalists still did. A painter, according to Zuloaga, should be guided by his intellect and not only by his eyes, as his task was to interpret reality and not copy it.[5]

Like Gauguin and Bernard, Zuloaga was fascinated by primitivism. In 1895, the same year Gauguin returned to Tahiti and two years after Bernard went to Egypt, Zuloaga did not go to a similar exotic destination, but left Paris for Seville in order to live among beggars, dancers and bullfighters in a 'corral' – a traditional tenement house around a common patio. Here he found the material and inspiration for his paintings. One of the first major results of his new style was *Víspera de la corrida* (The Eve of the Bullfight, 1898, plate 10), in which he painted eight elegantly dressed Andalusian women accompanied by a picador and a greyhound taking a look at the bulls on the eve of the bullfight. In the background we can discern a village, dominated by a church and a castle. Zuloaga was fascinated with the bullfight – he even tried to become a torero himself – but instead of painting the fight itself, he preferred to paint the expectations and the atmosphere on the eve of the event.

[5] See: Lafuente Ferrari, *Ignacio Zuloaga*.

In 1899 Zuloaga discovered the beauty of Segovia and the surrounding countryside. His uncle, Daniel Zuloaga, tried to revive the traditional pottery handicraft in this small Castilian town and Ignacio decided to join him there. Here he would do most of his painting, including *Gregorio en Sepúlveda* (Gregorio in Sepúlveda, 1908) and *El Cristo de la Sangre* (The Christ of Blood, 1911, plate 11), in which he depicted a priest and five members of a brotherhood who are gathered around an enormous macabre crucifix showing a bleeding Christ with real hair and a crown of thorns against the background of the walled town of Ávila (which also figures in Sorolla's *Castille*). These images would cause a stir at the Parisian salon and other international exhibitions. Contrary to the farmers painted by his French and German colleagues, his life-size local types were not generally engaged in any activity, but posed in front of a characteristic village or small town embedded in the landscape, thus harmoniously fusing the environment with remnants from the past.[6]

As with Simon and Cottet, a painting should be a synthesis; it should picture the soul of the specific region. In *Gregorio en Sepúlveda*, for example, the painter had initially placed two taller villagers in the right foreground, next to Gregorio, a somewhat grotesque and deformed wineskin maker positioned on the left. For whatever reason, he decided to cut off part of the foreground and to eliminate these figures in favour of the ancient town and landscape, adding a non-existent crowded bullring in the valley near the river Duratón.[7] Zuloaga thereby stressed the unity between the old town of Sepúlveda, which was draped across the rocky hills of Castile, and its inhabitants, its ancient traditions and surrounding nature. The added bullfight could also be seen as a symbol of the struggle between man and nature, moulded into an elaborate cultural form. Tradition, man and nature were united in this *fiesta nacional*.

Zuloaga was not the only Spanish painter of regional folk life who preferred Castile. Secondary painters like Eduardo Chicharro and Marceliano Santa María were born in this centrally located region and painted it often. Basques, like Zuloaga himself and the Zubiaurre brothers, also had a clear preference for Castilian themes and the same applied to the Valencian Manuel Benedito and the Galician Fernando Álvarez de Sotomayor. They opted for themes similar to those chosen by their French and German colleagues: baptisms, weddings, funerals, religious ceremonies, pilgrimages, local feasts and agricultural work, all in a traditional setting. Unlike Galicia,

---

[6] Ibid.
[7] *Ignacio Zuloaga, 1870–1945* (Bilbao 1990) 174–5.

the Basque country, and Brittany in France, Castile was not a peripheral region, nor especially known for its pre-Roman cultural heritage. On the contrary, it had played a leading role in Spanish national history, colonising the Americas and consequently acquiring enormous economic wealth. The region had been the centre of the Spanish Golden Age in the sixteenth and seventeenth centuries and the nucleus around which Spanish national identity had crystallised. Rapid decline thereafter deprived the region of its prosperity and in the more remote areas life seemed to have stagnated. Thus in many parts of Castile the past seemed to be still alive. Moreover, in earlier times Castile had resisted Roman occupation and led the struggle against the Arab domination in the Peninsula. Thus as it presumably had not suffered under a long occupation or a profound foreign influence it was also often seen as the most authentic and profoundly Spanish part of the country. In this way it performed a similar function as Brittany in France and the coastal areas in Germany. A further resemblance was that Castile, like most German coastal regions and many parts of Brittany, consisted not of lovely green hills or impressive mountains, but of an empty and almost metaphysical plain, under an omnipresent and unrelenting sky, where man was alone, and where, in order to survive, he had to struggle with nature. This type of landscape evidently attracted these painters, who looked for meaning in an apparently senseless world.[8]

The critical reception of this type of painting in Spain was almost completely determined by Zuloaga's international success which dated from the early years of the twentieth century. Whereas in Germany few had commented on the biased image some Worpswede painters gave of their village, in Spain this argument was frequently used against Zuloaga. Many critics even argued that his work was unpatriotic because he perpetuated the myth of Spain as a backward and barbaric country. While in many ways Spain was a modern European country, Zuloaga only showed the decadence of the Spanish countryside and the misery, barbarity and stupidity of its population. His 'ferocious caricatures' made his country

---

[8] Rilke thus explained the preference of his generation for this type of barren landscape: Rilke, Rainer Maria, *Worpswede: Fritz Mackensen, Otto Modersohn, Fritz Overbeck, Hans am Ende, Heinrich Vogeler* (2nd edn., Bielefeld and Leipzig 1905) 15–16. Zuloaga explained that the green hills of his native Basque Country were too lovely and charming for him, therefore as a painter he preferred the barren plains of Castile: Lafuente Ferrari, *Zuloaga* 270. See for a similar interpretation of the landscape Miguel de Unamuno, 'La labor patriótica de Zuloaga', *Hermes*, no. 8 (1917) and for the role of Castile in Spanish nationalism also: Javier Varela, 'El mito de Castilla en la generación del 98', *Claves de la Razón Práctica* (December 1996) 10–18.

look ridiculous in the eyes of the civilised world.[9] He was consequently boycotted by the Spanish art establishment from the very start and his work could only rarely be seen in his native country.

Other authors did not so much criticise Zuloaga's presentation of the Castilian countryside as the heartland of the nation, but its interpretation. Instead of his gloomy, tragic pictures of poor and sometimes even deformed Castilian villagers, they preferred Sorolla's cheerful, brightly coloured images, especially those of the prosperous Valencian coastal region and the huge paintings he did for the Hispanic Society. This discussion of what the two most famous contemporary Spanish painters chose as subject matter did not restrict itself to the specialised magazines but became a national debate.[10]

Zuloaga was chiefly defended by prominent writers from his own generation of whom Ramiro de Maeztu, Azorín and the philosopher Miguel de Unamuno are the best known. All three, at least during part of their career, defended a type of exalted nationalism that had much in common with that of Ganivet and Barrès. Azorín and Maeztu did not always praise Zuloaga's choice of subject, but in general they agreed that the rural Spain represented in his paintings, contrary to the sometimes superficial modernity of the towns, was indeed the real Spain. He depicted the essence of the fatherland. Unamuno even asserted that in few works of art was the Spanish 'soul' better reflected than in Zuloaga's paintings.[11] Unamuno, who like Zuloaga was born in the Basque Country, also contrasted the tragic, austere but profound psychological portraits of Zuloaga to the vigorous, sunny, but somewhat superficial realism of Sorolla. According to him, this opposition was not limited to these two painters but could be applied to the two main tendencies in modern Spanish art: the Basque–Castilian school and the Valencian–Andalusian one. This opposition was echoed by other writers and critics.[12]

In fact, the issue at stake was the same as in France and Germany. A

<hr>

[9]   See for example: José María Salaverría, 'La España pintoresca', *ABC* (19 May 1910) and Vegue y Goldoni, 'La exposición de Bellas Artes' 289–90.

[10]   See: Lafuente Ferrari, *Ignacio Zuloaga* 299–325, Tusell, *Arte, historia y política* 73–155, and Francisco Calvo Serraller, *Paisajes de luz y muert: La pintura española del 98* (Barcelona 1998) 195–233.

[11]   Ramiro de Maeztu, 'Una cuestión de ojos', *Heraldo de Madrid* (20 April 1910), Azorín, 'La realidad española', *ABC* (3 April 1912), and Unamuno, 'La labor patriótica de Zuloaga'.

[12]   Miguel de Unamuno, 'De arte pictorica', *La Nación* (21 July and 8 August 1912) also in: Idem, *Obras completas* (Madrid 1970) VII, 731–42. See also a letter of Maeztu to Zuloaga as cited in: Tusell, *Arte, historia y política* 199, M. Utrillo, 'Los Zubiaurre', *Museum* II (1912) 104–14, especially 104 and José Francés, 'El arte gallego contemporáneo', *El año artístico* (August 1917) 346–63, especially 354–6.

new generation of painters and critics rejected the supposed superficial realism, arbitrary subject choice and bright colours of the impressionists and their followers in favour of a more profound, synthetic and severe style and morally relevant topics. In France these stylistic and aesthetical differences were located in different artistic groups and critics discussed which of these best reflected French national traditions. In Germany, on the contrary, the dissimilarities were projected on two different countries. A superficial French realism was contrasted with a more profound, idealistic German artistic predisposition. In Spain the opposition was embodied in two persons, but at the same time in two parts of the country: the North and Centre versus Andalusia and Valencia. Such a division would be comprehensible in Germany where various rivalling art centres existed. However, as we have seen German painters were very mobile and often visited various art academies and lived in different parts of the country. In Spain the painters were less mobile, at least within the country. It was more common for them to continue their study in Paris or even Rome than at a different Spanish art academy. And most painters established themselves in Madrid, or in their native region. Thus, as was testified by the supposed stylistic division of the country, regional allegiances seemed to be stronger in Spain, whereas the ties that bound artists from the various parts of the country seemed weaker than in France and Germany.

Other painters occasioned less debate than Zuloaga. The critics generally saw their paintings as a striking representation of the local *Volksgeist*. Thus it was said of the Galician painter Sotomayor that he 'reached the Galician race's innermost soul', whereas Chicharro's paintings convincingly characterised Castile's 'tradition and race'. One critic even tried to convince Benedito to stop painting in Brittany and the Dutch fishing village of Volendam and instead find a Spanish region that would correspond with both his own and the general Spanish 'pictorial disposition'.[13]

In contrast to their German colleagues, Spanish critics did not present diligent villagers as an example to the urban working classes. Nevertheless, most painters were praised as exemplary in their seriousness, perseverance and dedication. Zuloaga was even called the 'first among Spanish workers'.[14] Neither did the Spanish critics present the countryside in the first place

[13] Palais, 'Fernando Álvarez de Sotomayor', *Pequeñas Monografías: Revista mensual* (December 1907), Mélida, 'Chicharro', *Museum*, 4 (1914–15) 151–78, especially 168–70, and Aureliano de Beruete y Moret, 'Manuel Benedito', *Museum*, 2 (1912) 353–75, especially 371–5.
[14] Palais, 'Fernando Álvarez de Sotomayor', Rafael Domenech, 'Exposición Benedito', *Pequeñas Monografías: Revista mensual* (May 1907), and Eugenio Noel, 'Ignacio Zuloaga', *El Flamenco: Semanario anti-flamenquista* (19 April 1914) 3.

as an antidote to the alienation suffered by modern man in the big cities. In fact they often had a somewhat ambiguous attitude towards the rural areas of the country, as these both could embody the original and true Spain or symbolise the backwardness of Spain *vis-à-vis* the rest of Europe. Consequently, according to some authors, these painters proved that Spain was not limited to the civilised surface layer of the major cities. After the humiliating defeat in the 1898 war against the United States most Spaniards were very aware of their country's fundamental weaknesses. If Spain were to modernise one could not overlook the disastrous situation of the Spanish countryside as, in fact, many politicians did. Some thus interpreted Zuloaga's paintings as the 'protest of a patriot'. His works, Maeztu remarked, 'offend our vanity [and] strengthen our longing for reform'; another critic called them 'expiatory practices'.[15] In this political interpretation the opposition was not so much between town and countryside, as between Spain and Europe.

Only few critics explicitly saw the countryside as the main source of national regeneration. José Francés, for example, after a visit to an exhibition of Galician art in La Coruña, confirmed that in this region, with its strong Celtic roots, the 'full reintegration of man with nature, which would redeem him from all the civilised artifices and falsities' could still be found. Álvarez de Sotomayor's paintings of isolated hamlets, such as his *Comida de bodas en Bergantiños* (Wedding Breakfast at Bergantiños 1916, plate 12), showed 'the Celtic race in all its purity' particularly well. Another critic asserted that 'the creative fibre of the old national spirit' had almost completely disappeared in Spain's upper classes and that it could only be found in 'anarchical and anachronistic forms' in Spain's 'steppe fields and somnolent towns' where painters like Zuloaga attempted to revive it. After having expressed doubts in earlier years, in 1912 Azorín saw Zuloaga as a painter who tried to capture the most permanent and fundamental characteristics of the Spanish 'spirit'. He even maintained that artists were obliged to discover and express this vigorous and powerful Spanish reality. Implicit in all these remarks was the conviction that a reorientation on the idiosyncratic national characteristics, which were best preserved in the countryside, could help the nation be more faithful to its own spirit and thus regenerate its strength and vigour.[16] More directly than in France and

---

15 Juan de la Encina, 'El exotismo y el arte vasco', *Hermes*, no. 5 (May 1917), Ramiro de Maeztu, 'Los asuntos de Zuloaga', *Heraldo de Madrid* (9 March 1910), Francisco Alcántara, 'Ignacio Zuloaga: Arte y nacionalidad', *El Imparcial* (19 March 1910). See also: Noel, 'Ignacio Zuloaga'.

16 José Francés, 'El arte gallego contemporáneo', *El año artístico* (August 1917), 349 and

Germany, in Spain the debate on the representation of the countryside of one region was intimately connected with the future of the whole nation and the search for concrete political remedies for the supposed ills of the country. One could also interpret this as an implicit plea to more fully recognise the civic rights and economic interests of the rural population, which had been mainly ignored in the past.

Zuloaga himself seemed to have agreed with the interpretation of his paintings by authors such as Maeztu, Azorín and Unamuno. In private letters from around 1912 Zuloaga claimed that he tried to 'synthesise the Castilian soul' and unravel the 'psychology of a race' in his paintings. In 1913, during an unforeseen encounter in Pamplona, he explained to Maeztu that Parisian refinement only meant calculations, numbers and decadence, whereas in the traditional Spanish countryside one could still find strength, passion and vitality. On this occasion Zuloaga was accompanied by the famous composer Maurice Ravel and some other modern French intellectuals, who according to Maeztu were all supporters of Bergson's philosophy and Barrès' writing.[17] In fact, Zuloaga maintained friendly contacts with Barrès, the French propagandist of the new organic nationalism. On the occasion of the publication of his book on El Greco, Zuloaga in 1913 even painted a huge portrait of the French author with El Greco's hometown Toledo in the background. Probably this tells us something about Zuloaga's affinities to this new type of nationalism. Nevertheless, as Zuloaga was neither politically active nor openly expressive of his political opinions until a few decades later, when he became a fervent follower of Franco during and after the Spanish Civil War, we cannot be completely sure that he fully adhered to Barrès' message.

As in France and Germany the relations between the various painters of folkloric themes and the regional movements were surprisingly weak, thus contradicting the accepted view that regionalism was caused by an 'awakening of the regions'. This becomes particularly clear in the Basque Country, where a profoundly catholic and almost reactionary regional movement started to make political claims in the 1890s, especially in the area in and around the fast industrialising town of Bilbao. Adolfo Guiard (1860–1916), the only painter who played an important role in the moderate wing of the Basque Nationalist Party, was not a regionalist,

360, Juan de la Encina, *La trama del arte vasco* (Bilbao 1919) 16–17, and Azorín, 'La realidad española'.

[17] Letters of Zuloaga cited in Lafuente Ferrari, *La vida y el arte de Ignacio Zuloaga* 208, and Jesús María de Arozamena, *Ignacio Zuloaga: El pintor, el hombre* (San Sebastian 1970) 18–19, Ramiro de Maeztu, 'Por la España abrupta', *Heraldo de Madrid* (29 September 1913).

but a propagator of the themes and style of the impressionists. And the leader of the movement, Sabino de Arana, who died at an early age in 1902, seemed to prefer traditional history painting. Only in later years did authors belonging to the Basque movement start to propagate regionalism in painting as well. However, a closer alliance between the movement and various regionalist artists would only come into existence around 1917, when regionalist painting was becoming outdated, with the creation of the Bilbao-based art magazine *Hermes*.[18] Zuloaga, in turn, although he was very proud of his Basque roots, was in the first place a Spanish nationalist. Probably like kindred intellectuals of Basque origin, such as Unamuno and Maeztu who also pursued their career outside the Basque Country, he considered the Basque movement too parochial.

Conclusion

The painters who turned to a new artistic direction during the 1890s adopting regionalist motifs, clearly formed part of a wider regionalism, a broad cultural movement based on a new interest in folklore, typical landscapes, vernacular buildings, dialect, traditional handicrafts, folk songs and other elements of traditional rural popular culture and of which the new organic nationalism and the fast-growing regional movements were also manifestations. However, was regionalist painting really a distinctive and influential artistic current? And how did regionalist painting relate to the new regionalist movement and the new type of exalted nationalism that emerged about the same time?

To answer these questions we must first analyse the characteristics and limitations of this artistic current. It was not a movement with its own manifestos and exhibitions such as Impressionism, Cubism, Futurism or the *blaue Reiter*. Regionalist painters operated within the existing salon system, where formal groupings were not common. Paintings were generally exhibited by genre. Reviewers usually followed this classification, but often linked painters with certain stylistic affinities or those who worked in the same city, village or region. Therefore, at the beginning of their careers, Cottet and Simon were seen as prominent members of the informal *Bande noire*. After this stylistic term became outdated they continued to be discussed together but now as painters of Breton subjects. Furthermore, salon marketing techniques did not include manifestos or separate group

---

[18] Javier González de Durana, *Ideologías artísticas en el País Vasco de 1900: Arte y política en los orígenes de la modernidad* (Bilbao 1992) 50–112.

exhibitions. Painters often tried to impress the general public, the jury and officials by using huge formats, choosing striking subjects, and developing a moderately personal style. Their goal was not artistic innovation for its own sake and they did not direct themselves to a small clientele of connoisseurs as did avant-garde artists later.[19]

Nonetheless, we have seen that this type of painting was clearly distinguished as an important and new current within mainstream art. At least in the initial stages, regionalist painting should be seen as an innovative artistic movement that styled itself in opposition to tendencies such as Realism, Naturalism and particularly Impressionism that had dominated the art scene in the 1880s and early 1890s. It was even seen as one of the main alternatives out of the cul-de-sac to which the triumph of Impressionism had led. It adopted most of the painterly innovations of the earlier movements, and used the regionalist ideology to distance itself from its predecessors and to take art along a new and promising idealistic path, one that stressed the importance of a significant and meaningful subject. In this way, it participated in the subjectivist cultural turn of the fin-de-siècle. Along the way some regionalist painters also incorporated other artistic trends. Thus Zuloaga, Simon and Bantzer produced some very decorative, almost flat pictures in which they omitted drawing in favour of colour, as did Édouard Vuillard and Pierre Bonnard.[20] Zuloaga also adopted Art Nouveau arabesques and Gauguin-like deformations and simplifications, and in this was followed by the brothers Zubiaurre and the Austrian regionalist Albin Egger-Lienz.

After about 1900 regionalist painting was increasingly accepted and successful and slowly became part of the artistic establishment. In Germany this became clear with the appointment of many regionalist painters as professors at the various art academies. Many also began to receive official commissions. The most fortunate in this aspect was Dettmann, who had already won a contest for the decoration of the town hall in Altona in 1898. In the following years he also received commissions for mural paintings in the town hall of Königsberg, the Polytechnic of Dantzig and the University of Kiel. In France, Simon was asked to decorate the Veterinary School in Lyon in 1904 and after the First World War received other commissions, such as the painting of the stairwell of the Senate in Paris. As Zuloaga had a somewhat complicated relationship with Spanish authorities, it was only

[19] See for the avant-garde: Robert Jensen, *Marketing Modernism in Fin-de-Siècle Europe* (Princeton 1994).
[20] See for example Zuloaga's *Toreros de pueblo* (1906), Simon's *Portrait de Charlotte Simon aux tulipes* (1912) and Bantzer's *Waldspaziergang* (1913).

in 1918 that he received a commission to paint a portrait of King Alfonso XIII and, except for some juvenile attempts, he would never produce major decorative paintings. However, in Spain the regionalist painters also rapidly became part of the cultural elite.

Around 1910 regionalist painters and their supporters started to become concerned about the future. At the Parisian *Salon d'Automne* and other international exhibitions, new artists such as the fauves, the cubists, the expressionists and the futurists started to make a furore and their revolutionary works did not please the regionalists at all. Their representations were thought to be incoherent and arbitrary, their style anarchic and their paintings lacking in all positive moral value.[21] Nevertheless, within a few years the avant-garde had almost relegated regionalism to oblivion. Although after the First World War, regionalist painting continued to exist, was present at the various salons and continued to sell well, it was no longer considered very relevant. The international art magazines dedicated only a few pages to the work of some of the regionalists, whereas others almost disappeared from public view, appearing only at local exhibitions and in rare reviews in the regional press.

Nonetheless, regionalist art and discourse were taken seriously by its opponents and it can even be interpreted as an almost completely forgotten negative impetus to twentieth-century avant-garde movements. It seems that avant-garde modernism in the first decades of the twentieth century – at least as later propagandists defined it – constituted a reaction against regionalism, as it embodied almost completely opposite values. Thus, the avant-garde opposed artistic freedom to the contextual determination of cultural expressions, spontaneous creativity to organic growth, form to content and a leading elite to populism. However, the avant-garde artists also adopted part of the regionalist heritage. For example, they radicalised the view that art should be more than a mere copy of reality. Like regionalists, symbolists and other idealist currents, they claimed that truth could only be found beyond visible appearances. Art should therefore give an interpretation and transmit corresponding emotions. Many avant-garde artists also shared the interest in feelings, spirituality, authenticity and expression of the regionalist painters and sometimes even shared their hope that it could be possible to overcome the gap between the artist

[21]   Raymond Bouyer, 'L'Oeuvre de Lucien Simon', *L'Art et les Artistes* 6 (February 1908) 530, Octave Uzanne, 'Fernand Maillaud: A Painter of the Old French Province of Berry', *The Studio* (September 1912) 273–82, Deibel, *Ludwig Dettmann* 1 and 34 and Wilhelm Michel, 'Die Grenzen des Subjektiven in der Kunst', *Kunst für Alle* (1 July 1912) 450–5, especially 454–5.

and the people. However, regionalists and avant-garde artists were in fundamental disagreement on one issue – the representational function of art. The regionalists argued that if outward reality, whatever its nature, did not function as a reference any more, then there would be nothing to interpret. As a result, art, as produced by the avant-garde, was a senseless exercise. According to the regionalists, if the only goal of art was art itself, then painting had lost its fundamental relevance.

With this overview of the rise, flowering and demise of regionalist art we can conclude that it was one of the successors of Impressionism, a highly influential, international artistic trend from about 1890 to 1914 and possibly one of the most important tendencies against which the new avant-garde movements defined themselves. As regionalist art embodied many values that were contrary to avant-garde modernism, it was later generally seen as a reactionary movement, its historical role was forgotten and it gradually slid into oblivion. However, as I hope to have shown, without a proper understanding of regionalist art we get a very incomplete picture of the cultural developments of the first decades of the twentieth century and a very biased image of the rise of the avant-garde and the subsequent triumph of artistic modernism.

Another conclusion is that regionalist art was more intimately related to the new nationalism than it was to the various regional movements. Only a few regionalist painters worked in the region in which they were born. Those who did were generally representatives of a younger generation and only some of them eventually developed connections with the local regional movement. Most painters operated within a national setting. They studied in the major art centres and most of them also lived there, at least for part of the year. They did not work mainly for local or regional art lovers, but directed themselves primarily to the national art market. Even those like Zuloaga who primarily produced for the international market, were seen as typical representatives of their fatherland. Thus, in general, regionalist painters were not so much concerned with the identity of their native region, but with the idiosyncratic characteristics of their nation. They therefore evidenced a clear preference for those areas that were seen as the most typical part of the country. These characteristic regions could be found where foreign influences (especially the unifying influence of the Roman Empire) had been weak and contemporary modern civilisation was almost absent. The soul of the nation could thus be found in an almost pure state in isolated coastal and rural communities in peripheral regions.

Consequently they preferred Brittany in France, the coastal areas in Germany and Castile in Spain. These areas were seen as a kind of heartland of the nation. Backward regions in other countries, such as the Scottish Highlands for Great Britain, Dalarna for Sweden, Karelia for Finland, Kalotaszeg for Hungary and Podhale for the Poles, seemed to perform a similar role.[22] Thus, we may conclude that although these painters certainly played an important role in visually defining the identity of specific regions, they were in fact more concerned with trying to reveal the most profound character of the nation as a whole.

These painters' work, at least as most critics interpreted it, was clearly related to the new, more subjective and populist nationalism. This manifested itself in their stress on regional differences, their quest to discover the true 'soul' of the nation, and their interest in contemporary, popular culture in the countryside. Their interpretation of the nation was also subjective and organic. These painters did not want to depict the outer surface, but sought to penetrate the essence of local folk life and produce a collective psychological portrait by expressing the organic unity of the population with its traditions and natural surroundings. Nevertheless, they emphasised the positive, integrative aspects of this new populist nationalism and clearly omitted the more negative, xenophobic aspects that could be detected with many exalted nationalists.

The regionalist painters also participated in the creation of a truly national culture by consciously choosing national or regional subjects and trying to develop a corresponding national style. In the eyes of the new nationalists, however, their work had a fundamental weakness: painting continued to be a quite elitist art form and was therefore not very well suited to diffusing the new nationalist message. Although illustrated magazines, in which these paintings were reproduced, reached an increasingly large public and some regionalist painters tried to get commissions for wall paintings in public buildings, in general their audience remained mainly limited to parts of the urban upper and middle classes. Other media were better suited to spreading the new nationalist gospel to a broader public and consequently regionalist painting was slightly disregarded by most propagators of the new nationalism.

Regionalist painting was probably least ignored by Spanish nationalists. As organised labour in Spain was still relatively weak and did not constitute a significant menace to the existing political system during the decades

---

22 Anne-Marie Thiesse, *La Creation des identités nationales: Europe XVIII-XXe siècle* (Paris 1999) 23–67 and 113–33 and Jeremy Howard, *Art Nouveau: International and National Styles in Europe* (Manchester 1996) 113 and 128–9.

around 1900, the need to nationalise the masses was less urgent than in France and Germany.[23] Thus the painters' limited audience was not a major disadvantage. As a consequence of the need for reform to combat the relative backwardness of the country, their paintings were generally interpreted as a plea to dedicate more attention to rural areas where the majority of the population lived. Their paintings, and especially some of Zuloaga's best-known works, therefore seemed to give a less idealised picture of an untouched, harmoniously living rural community, and instead also depict more negative aspects such as degeneration, superstition and brutality, which according to some critics could be attributed to the neglectful attitude of the country's politicians.

An argument also heard in Spain and Germany, but most strongly made in France, was that isolated villages such as those painted by the regionalists conserved national traditions that had disappeared elsewhere. To prevent national decadence, France should preserve its character and combine ancient national traditions and customs, found in their purest form in these villages, with international modernity. The strengthening of French culture was first and foremost a middle-class task. Unlike the cosmopolitan upper classes and the uprooted urban working class, middle-class Frenchmen still had a living bond with national tradition as well as knowledge of innovations elsewhere.

More so than in Spain or France, rural villages in Germany – the country where the labour movement was strongest during this period – were presented as harmonious, hard-working communities in which people still lived in close contact with both nature and the past. These organic countryside communities, in which everyone knew their place and performed their duty, were thus presented as an alternative to the internationalist ideologies of the socialists that aimed to overthrow the existing political system and form a classless society in which all the bonds with tradition, the past and the national environment would be broken.

If we compare the discourse on regionalist painting in these three countries, nonetheless, strong similarities among the various interpretations are revealed. The same arguments were used nearly everywhere. While in some countries certain issues received more attention, these differences mostly concerned nuances. Whereas nationalists underlined the differences between countries and regions, in so doing they all used the same rhetoric and arguments. Consequently painters searching for the remains of their

[23] Eric Storm, 'The Problems of the Spanish Nation-Building Process around 1900', *National Identities* VI (2004) 143–57.

original *Volksgeist* went to remote, unspoiled regions to paint hard-working peasants, fishermen and villagers who supposedly still lived in close communion with their surroundings and maintained a living bond with ancestral traditions. By revealing the nation's true soul and developing a corresponding authentic style, they all hoped to bring the nation back on course, identify its 'true' character, stimulate a new sense of belonging and in this way contribute to the regeneration of the fatherland. Their paintings could be seen as, and indeed were considered as, important contributions to, the ever more urgent nation-building efforts of the national elites. Like local folk museums and regional authors, these painters, by converting plain rural themes into high art, transformed local customs, habits, traditions and crafts into an essential part of the country's national culture, thus facilitating the identification of the lower classes with the national heritage and its corresponding identity.

II

Architecture (1900–25)

4

Germany

Introduction

During the nineteenth century, nationalism also had a great impact upon architecture. The greatness of the nation had to become visible in stone. In addition to palaces and cathedrals, which embodied the power of princes and the Church, the nation needed its own impressive buildings – for example, a national museum in which to display its patrimony and artistic treasures, a parliament to provide a worthy forum for its representatives, a national library in which to store the products of its writers, and universities and academies to provide education for the new national elites. At the same time, a new interest in the past resulted in the simultaneous existence of various historical architectural styles. Historicism and eclecticism became the dominant architectural trends, and heated debates were held on such questions as which historical style would best represent the nation or embody national characteristics and which style would best suit the new 'temples' of national culture. Nationalism as a result provided architects with new assignments and profoundly affected stylistic matters.[1]

The process of nation-building accelerated at the end of the nineteenth century. Architects also partook in this new phase by designing monuments and constructing impressive public buildings. The last third of the nineteenth century consequently saw a profound transformation of most western European capitals. In Paris, the inner city was fundamentally transformed by the construction of new boulevards, and the Eiffel tower was erected to commemorate the centennial of the French Revolution. Rome got its huge monument to Victor Emmanuel, Vienna its imposing

---

[1] See, for example: Barry Bergdoll, *European Architecture 1750–1890* (Oxford and New York 2000) 139–205.

Ringstrasse, Berlin its Siegesallee and Madrid acquired an impressive national monument dedicated to Alfonso XII.[2]

But what exactly was the relationship between the new regionalist ideology on the one hand, and architectural thought and practice on the other? This is somewhat more difficult to ascertain due to the fact that, contrary to mainstream nineteenth-century nationalism, its impact could primarily be found not in impressive new buildings in the major urban centres, but in domestic architecture on the fringes of the main cities and in the countryside – which in the 1890s became more accessible because of the introduction of the electric tram and the automobile. Primitive vernacular examples – for instance, traditional farmhouses – functioned as the main source of inspiration for modest constructions such as suburban villas and country houses.

The influence of regionalism on architecture has begun to receive scholarly attention, and in Spain and France the concept of regionalist architecture has already been accepted. Recently, this term has also been applied in the United States and some other European countries. However, in Germany other labels, such as *Heimatarchitektur* (homeland architecture), *Heimatschutzarchitectur* (preservationist architecture), reformist architecture and National Romanticism, are used to define the same trend.[3] Nonetheless, an architecture inspired by vernacular buildings was strongly present in Germany, whereas France and Spain followed more hesitantly. As with painting, regionalist architecture was an innovative trend. It was propagated by the same generation as regionalist painting, born largely in the 1860s and 1870s. Again there was an influential older group that initiated the current and a younger group that adopted an already existing trend.

[2] Eric Hobsbawm, 'Mass-Producing Traditions: Europe, 1870–1914', in: Eric Hobsbawm and Terence Ranger eds., *The Invention of Tradition* (Cambridge 1983) 263–309 and E.J. Hobsbawm, *Nations and Nationalism since 1780: Programme, Myth, Reality* (Cambridge 1990) 101–31.

[3] François Loyer and Bernard Toulier eds., *Le Régionalisme, architecture et identité* (Paris 2001), Vincent B. Canizaro ed., *Architectural Regionalism: Collected Writings on Place, Identity, Modernity, and Tradition* (New York 2007) and Linda van Santvoort, Jan de Maeyer and Tom Verschaffel eds., *Sources of Regionalism in the Nineteenth Century: Art, Architecture and Literature* (Leuven 2008). For Germany: Vittorio Lampugnani and Romana Schneider eds., *Moderne Architektur in Deutschland 1900 bis 1950: Reform und Tradition* (Stuttgart 1992), Sigrid Hofer, *Reformarchitektur 1900–1918. Deutsche Baukünstler auf der Suche nach dem nationalen Stil* (Stuttgart 2005) 34 and Barbara Millar Lane, *National Romanticism and Modern Architecture in Germany and the Scandinavian Countries* (Cambridge 2000) 1–8.

A new domestic architecture not based on existing historical styles but inspired by vernacular precursors first came into existence in England. At least, this was what Hermann Muthesius (1861–1927), the principal propagator of the new English domestic architecture in Germany, maintained in his influential study *Das englische Haus* (The English House). Muthesius, who as a young architect had spent seven years as technical attaché to the German embassy in London, published the three well-illustrated volumes of this book in 1904, one year after his return to Berlin. According to him, England had been the first country to see the rise of a market for commissions for private houses. This was a result of the increasing wealth of the English middle classes. However, neither the mainly unschooled contractors nor the architects, who had been trained to create monumental architecture, were very well equipped to design these new, small buildings. In fact, this was a problem all over Europe, where since the French Revolution the guild system had almost disappeared. In England, however, some architects had found a satisfying way to resolve this impasse, namely by readopting the tradition of the old master masons. From about the 1860s, architects such as Philip Webb (1831–1915), Eden Nesfield (1835–88) and Norman Shaw (1831–1912), influenced by the theories of John Ruskin and William Morris, the founder of the Arts and Crafts Movement, started to build simple, practical houses, while incorporating local materials and construction methods. The buildings that functioned as their source of inspiration were not well-known classical monuments or Italianate villas, but English farmhouses and small-town, middle-class dwellings from the Baroque and, more particularly, the Queen Anne period from the start of the eighteenth century.[4]

Nevertheless, Muthesius did not want to propagate either the Queen Anne or the neo-Gothic style, which was preferred by William Morris. Muthesius especially appreciated the impulse to displace the existing historical styles with a new contemporary style, which could be discerned in the art of both these architects and of the Arts and Crafts movement. Only a second generation of architects – he singled out C. F. A. Voysey (1857–1941), M. H. Baillie Scott (1865–1945) and Charles R. Mackintosh (1868–1928) – would develop a perfect organic unity between the interior (the arrangement of the rooms, the furniture, tapestries and decoration, all designed by themselves or their close collaborators) and the exterior.

---

[4] Hermann Muthesius, *Das englische Haus: Entwicklung, Bedingungen, Anlage, Aufbau, Einrichtung und Innenraum* (1904, 2nd edn., Berlin 1908), I 100–12. See for Muthesius: *Hermann Muthesius, 1861–1927* (Berlin 1977) and John V. Maciuika, *Before the Bauhaus: Architecture, Politics and the German State, 1890–1920* (Cambridge 2005).

Although they found inspiration in the past, they developed their own personal forms, thereby overcoming the historicist dependence on older styles, the traces of which could still be discerned in the buildings of their predecessors. The resulting houses were unpretentious, comfortable and homely.[5]

Although Muthesius recognised that the organic unity of interior and exterior was one of the basic principles of another recent artistic movement – Art Nouveau and its German variant, *Jugendstil* – he did not approve of most of its results. The main representatives of this new continental style jettisoned all historical traditions and, in their search for originality, developed wildly exaggerated and arbitrary forms.[6] A good house, according to the German author, should be practical and simple, and the building materials should be used in a rational and honest way. The architect should take into account the needs and wishes of the commissioner, the peculiarities of the site, the environment, the climate, the local building traditions and techniques, and try to assimilate all these elements into a harmonious unity. Muthesius also preferred the simple, natural beauty of a well-designed cottage to the formal beauty of the perfectly balanced, classical villa in Italian style. Whereas in the latter, windows were placed at regular intervals, and their size and exact location were determined by the geometrical pattern of the façade, even if the opening had no practical function, in the former one looked where in a room a window was needed and adapted the exterior to these inner necessities.[7]

Muthesius explained the lead of English domestic architecture by pointing not only to the effects of the country's early industrialisation – which had caused a rapidly growing awareness of its negative aesthetic effects – but also to the long existing preference of the English nobility and part of the upper-middle class for living in the countryside. He ascribed this ancient tradition to the strong sense of independence, individuality and homeliness of the 'Anglo-Saxon race'. On the Continent, the elites usually lived in the major cities. Thus, whereas most Englishmen had their own houses, generally with small gardens and a living bond with the surrounding nature, people on the Continent increasingly lived in

---

5 Muthesius, *Das englische Haus*, I 161–89. He only criticised Mackintosh's masterpieces as being too refined to live in.

6 Ibid., I 7–9, 158–9 and 183–4. See also his: H. M. [Hermann Muthesius], 'Die Kunst Richard Riemerschmids', *Dekorative Kunst* VII (April 1904) 249–83, especially 249–54, and Hermann Muthesius, *Stilarchitektur und Baukunst: Wandlungen der Architektur und der gewerblichen Künste im 19. Jahrhundert und ihr heutiger Standpunkt* (2nd rev. edn., Mülheim–Ruhr 1903).

7 Ibid., 122–5, 133–40 and 177–82.

cramped, unhealthy apartments in big towns. The newly built country houses consequently reflected the 'nature' of the English people, their sense of family, their moral resolve and gentlemanly restraint. And although the new architects did not imitate historical styles, they did respect the building traditions of the past, particularly those of popular and rural constructions, which were best adapted to both the character of the English people and the peculiarities of the local landscape, soil and climate. Muthesius characterised their architecture as a truly national and modern art form.[8]

Although his study was explicitly meant to present current English domestic architecture as an example to his German contemporaries, Muthesius did not make a plea for slavish imitation. German architects should take into consideration the local circumstances and artistic traditions and the mores and customs of the German people. Fortunately, he wrote, his fatherland still had many rural buildings, which were probably even more imaginative, poetic and sentimental than the vernacular buildings in England.[9] Therefore, nothing could impede a new renaissance of German domestic architecture that in fact, like its English counterpart, could be defined as regionalist.

Thanks partly to Muthesius' voluminous study, the leading role of English architects in the design of this type of 'organic' house, in which interior and exterior were presumably in harmonious unity with the surroundings, would become something of a commonplace in innovative artistic circles in the early decades of the twentieth century, in both Germany and elsewhere on the Continent.[10] Nonetheless, other factors also played an important role in the rise of a new architecture that was inspired by vernacular predecessors. A huge impact was exerted by the various world's fairs. The 1867 International Exhibition in Paris accommodated not only the huge machine hall but also introduced smaller, national pavilions, in which every nation could show its own products, arts and crafts. In order to attract attention, at subsequent fairs these pavilions were increasingly constructed in a striking vernacular style. At the same time, to stress their idiosyncratic identity (which was difficult with new inventions, machines, high art, and historicist buildings, which looked very similar everywhere), countries started to exhibit typical products,

---

[8] Ibid., II–III and 1–10.
[9] Ibid., 10 and 104.
[10] Erich Haenel, 'Fritz Schumacher', *Dekorative Kunst* VI (May 1903) 281–99, especially 293, Otto Bartning, 'Zur Baugeschichte des letzten Jahrzehnts', *Kunstwart* (1 September 1907) 607–11, especially 608–9, Alexander v. Gleichen-Russwurm, 'Das Heim eines Gelehrten', *Dekorative Kunst* XV (October 1911) 1–9, especially 3, and Lang-Danoli, 'Englische Landhäuser', *Deutsche Kunst und Dekoration* XXXI (1912–13) 163.

handicrafts, traditional costumes and other folkloric elements that would clearly distinguish them from their neighbours. It seems that Scandinavia and Eastern Europe took the lead in this aspect. The new stress on popular rural culture was visible at home, too. Regional museums were opened, ancient monuments were protected and restored, and interest in vernacular architecture rapidly grew. Traditional farmhouses, ancient mills and simple rural chapels were even entirely transferred to new open-air museums.[11] Without a doubt, these developments were noticed and often stimulated by architects.

Moreover, already before the publication of Muthesius' book, German architects had started to build in a similar vein as Baillie Scott and Voysey. Particularly *Dekorative Kunst* (Decorative Art), an illustrated monthly that in 1897 had been founded by the influential art critic Julius Meier-Graefe, and which at the start promoted the new international Art Nouveau, was clearly sympathetic to the new trend. In the early years of the new century it published extensive reviews of recent buildings by Richard Riemerschmid (1868–1957), Theodor Fischer (1862–1938), Fritz Schumacher (1869–1947) and others.[12] This interest would only increase in subsequent years and around 1910 the great majority of the many villas and country houses reviewed in this and other journals were executed in a regionalist style.

One aspect of this growing sympathy has been well researched: the applied arts. Partly as a consequence of Muthesius' propaganda, in 1907 the Deutsche Werkbund was founded by, among others, Riemerschmid, Fischer, Schumacher, Peter Behrens (1868–1940) – who later also would be one of the founders of the Bauhaus – the painter, critic and architect Paul Schultze-Naumburg (1869–1949) and the social liberal politician Friedrich Naumann. The Werkbund would unite earlier initiatives to revive the ancient crafts and interior design, such as the United Workshops for Art in Craftworks in Munich, and similar organisations in Vienna, Dresden and

---

[11] Martin Wörner, *Vergnügen und Belehren: Volkskultur auf den Weltausstellungen 1850–1900* (Münster 1999), Bjarne Stoklund, 'How the Peasant House Became a National Symbol: A Chapter in the History of Museums and Nation-Building', *Ethnologia Europaea*, XXIX (1999) 5–18, Catherine Bertho-Lavenir, 'L'Idée régionaliste: naissance et développement' in: François Loyer and Bernard Toulier eds., *Le Régionalisme, architecture et identité* (Paris 2001) 28–48 and Rudy Koshar, *Germany's Transient Pasts: Preservation and National Memory in the Twentieth Century* (Chapel Hill 1998) 17–75.

[12] Hermann Obrist, 'Die Zukunft unserer Architektur', Erich Haenel, 'Theodor Fischer' and Erich Haenel, 'Fritz Schumacher', *Dekorative Kunst*, respectively (June 1901) 329–49, (February 1902) 153–70 and (May 1903) 281–99. See also Maria Rennhofer, *Kunstzeitschriften der Jahrhundertwende in Deutschland und Österreich 1895–1914* (Vienna and Munich 1987) 97–8.

Darmstadt that, contrary to the Arts and Crafts movement, also included industrialists. Under the influence of these artists and organisations, the curriculum of the applied arts schools also underwent a fundamental revision. Instead of a stress on theory and on copying ornaments from earlier styles, teaching was now done mostly in workshops and students had to experiment with various materials and techniques. Consequently, the Werkbund is seen as the main precursor of the artistic innovations that would culminate in Bauhaus after the First World War.[13] However, the regionalist and nationalist outlook of most of these architects has not been given due attention. This can in part be explained by the suspicion with which later modernist architects and historians looked upon nationalist influences on art. Beauty was not and should not be determined by nationality. This belief became particularly pertinent after the Nazis had put art and architecture at the service of their racist ideology.

Villas and country houses

A close analysis of a great number of reviews in the main German architectural and artistic magazines makes it clear that, at the start of the twentieth century, progressive and innovative German architects generally acknowledged their debt to national and regional traditions and presented their work as essentially German. However, architectural critics, many of whom were architects themselves, generally refrained from using an exalted nationalist vocabulary to underline their point of view. In this respect they clearly distinguished themselves from most German art critics who, as we have seen, had no difficulty in using nationalist arguments in their reviews. Possibly this was also related to the fact that, in architecture, England was in the lead and not the arch-enemy France. The architects, who generally worked for a quite mobile upper-class clientele, apparently also did not want to be associated with the provincialism of the majority of the regional movement or with imitations of old vernacular buildings that were constructed by lesser architects or commercial construction companies. In the reviews in the major art magazines of this period, in fact, the term *Heimatarchitektur* or *Heimatkunst* (regionalist architecture or regionalist art) was generally used in a negative way, and *Heimatkünstler* (regionalist artists) were criticised for being too concerned with preservation and conservation, which resulted in the copying of forms from their grandfathers' days

---

[13] Joan Campbell, *The German Werkbund: The Politics of Reform in the Applied Arts* (Princeton 1978), Frederic J. Schwartz, *The Werkbund: Design Theory and Mass Culture before the First World War* (New Haven 1996) and Maciuika, *Before the Bauhaus*.

and other old platitudes, converting architecture into a conventional mask.[14] Only once was an architect, Hugo Eberhardt (1874–1959), called a *Heimatkünstler* in a positive sense, although the author felt obliged to add that Eberhardt was never a slave of his principles and that he applied them in a reasonable and modern way.[15]

As the name *Heimatarchitektur* was rejected, there was no widely accepted label for this new domestic architecture. The term most widely used during the first two decades of the twentieth century was *neue* or *moderne Baukunst* (new or modern architecture) and generally its *künstlerisches* (artistic) character was underlined.[16] Muthesius and his colleagues, moreover, clearly preferred the Germanic term *Baukunst* (architecture or, literally, building art) to *Architektur*, which was disliked because of its Greek, Latin and thus classical and foreign connotations.[17] This stressed both the modern, anti-historicist stance and the artistic pretensions of these architects. They did not produce mere copies taken from European history, but contemporary German artistic creations.

That regionalism was seen as a major up-to-the-minute trend is also illustrated by the fact that many ambitious architects decided to design a country house for themselves in the new style. This was the case with Hans Poelzig (1869–1936) who, after the First World War, would become famous for his expressionist buildings and who in 1905 built himself a villa inspired by vernacular examples in a suburb of Breslau (now Wroclaw in Poland). At around the same time, Paul Korff (1875–1945) constructed a regionalist dwelling just outside Rostock, while Muthesius designed a villa for himself in Nicolassee, Berlin (figure 1). Reformist writers and artists were among the first to order a country house in a neo-vernacular style; for example,

[14] S. Langenberger, 'Landhausbauten: Architekt: Rich. Berndl in München', *Der Baumeister* VI (December 1907) 25–7, Ernst Schur, 'Bruno Paul', *Dekorative Kunst* XIV (November 1910) 57–81, especially 61, Paul Westheim, 'Heimatkunst', *Dekorative Kunst* XIV (January 1911) 187–9, v. A., 'Vom Schwelgen im Dach', *Kunstwart* (1 August 1912) 206–7 and A. Jaumann, 'Ländliche Häuser von Heinrich Straumer', *Deutsche Kunst und Dekoration* XXVII (1910–11) 313–20.

[15] Paul Westheim, 'Haus Ruppel Frankfurt a.Main: Architekt prof. Hugo Eberhardt', *Dekorative Kunst* XVII (January 1914) 153–67, especially 162. See also: H. Werner, 'Die Metzendorf-Häuser an der Hessischen Bergstrasze', *Dekorative Kunst* VIII (December 1904) 113–18.

[16] See, for example: Conrad Buchwald, 'Hans Poelzig als Baukünstler', *Dekorative Kunst* X (March 1907) 225–37, especially 225–8, Georg Jacob Wolf, 'Richard Riemerschmid', *Dekorative Kunst* XV (May 1912) 345–59, especially 345–7, Walter Curt Behrendt, 'Wohnhausbauten von Paul Mebes', *Dekorative Kunst* XVI (March 1913) 249–63, especially 249 and Hermann Muthesius, 'Das Deutsche Haus: Von Paul Ehmig', *Wasmuths Monatshefte für Baukunst* (1918–19) 128–34, especially 134.

[17] Maciuika, *Before the Bauhaus*, 89.

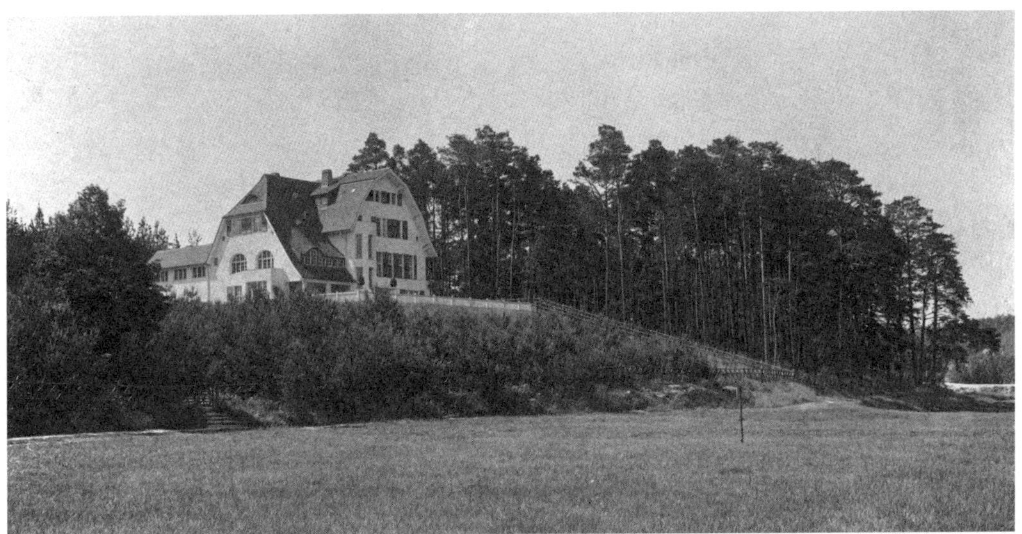

1 Hermann Muthesius, Villa Muthesius, Nicolassee, Berlin, 1906–9.

the famous sociologist Werner Sombart commissioned a country house (figure 2) in Schreiberhau (now Szklarska Porêba in Poland), near Breslau, from Fritz Schumacher, whereas the author and poet Paul Remer even asked the influential Finnish architects Gesellius and Saarinen to design a country house for him somewhere north of Berlin.[18] However, contrary to painters, who had more freedom, architects depended on their clients and generally did not exclusively build in a regionalist style.

The new domestic architecture was seen as an innovative movement. Critics and architects who supported this 'new architecture' consequently distanced themselves – as the regionalist painters had done with history painting and academic conventions – from academic or historicist architecture. The problem, according to them, already started with the architects' academic education, which was detached from reality and practice. Students learned their profession from books and drawings, which led to schematic, imitative and lifeless architecture. Furthermore, academic architecture was conventional and dedicated attention only to the façade, overloading it with ornaments. The resulting pompous mask was not related to the interior and appealed only to the bad taste of parvenus. Particularly the dominant neo-classical style was not suited for Germany,

18 See, respectively: Buchwald, 'Poelzig als Baukünstler' 234, Ernst Schur, 'Rittergut Wendorf und Haus Korff', *Dekorative Kunst* X (June 1907) 353–69, especially 368–9, Maciuika, *Before the Bauhaus* 191–5, Robert Bruck, 'Unsere Bauten: Prof. Fritz Schumacher', *Der Baumeister* (January 1911) 37–42 and Ernst Schur, 'Das Haus Molchow bei Altruppin', *Dekorative Kunst* XI (June 1908) 377–93.

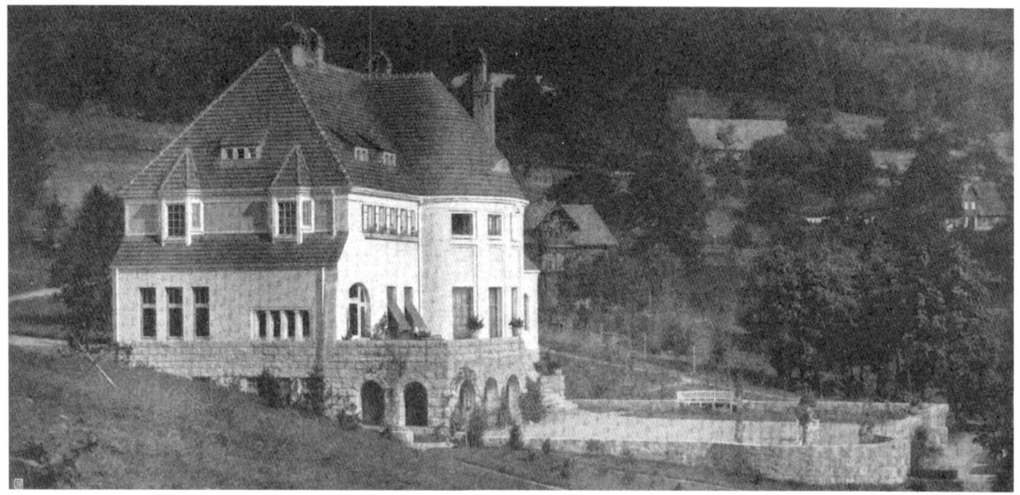

2 Fritz
Schumacher,
Landhaus
Werner
Sombart,
Schreiberhau,
around 1910.

just as it made no sense to plant olive or orange trees in its cold climate. It was therefore not surprising that many of these architects played an important role in the pedagogical reform of the various art academies and schools. According to both critics and architects, other historical styles should also be avoided, as each period and area should have its own architecture; copying buildings from other periods or areas could never have satisfying results.[19] Although Art Nouveau architects did not copy old styles, they were equally dismissed, as their designs were too subjective and arbitrary. This artistic fashion was considered too excessive and frivolous, and was even condemned as an aberration.[20]

The new domestic architects not only rejected past styles, but also tried to build in a modern and rational way. They therefore stressed the importance of hygiene. Good sanitary facilities were indispensable, as was a sufficient supply of light, air and ventilation. Practical considerations should determine the logical plan of a building. Simplicity, clarity, truthfulness and order should be guiding principles in the design process, while honesty was of the utmost importance in the use of materials. The purpose of the

[19] 'Die Pflege heimatlicher Bauweise', *Dekorative Kunst* VII (August 1914) 433–43, Wolf, 'Riemerschmid' 345–7, Bartning, 'Baugeschichte' 607–9, Fritz Stahl, 'Fritz Schumachers Hamburger Bauten', *Wasmuths Monatshefte für Baukunst* (1919–20) 259–60 and Maciuika, *Before the Bauhause* 25–69 and 104–37.
[20] H. M., 'Kunst Riemerschmids' 249–52, Fritz Wichert, 'Curt Stroevings Landhaus am Nuszbaum', *Dekorative Kunst* XII (March 1909) 241–57, especially 241, Bartning, 'Baugeschichte' 608.

different parts of a building and the nature of the materials used should not be concealed.[21]

Part of this 'modernity' was their aversion to the stressful existence in big towns, which according to many contemporary scientists was particularly damaging to the nerves.[22] Thus, living in the countryside, or at least in a park-like suburb, was seen as a hygienic necessity, not only for man's physical well-being but also, and perhaps even more, for his mental health. The town was associated with anarchy, crowdedness, stress and degeneration, and a tranquil home and close contact with nature were seen as good remedies for the overburdened nerves of modern man.[23]

A well-built house should protect its inhabitants from the chaos of modern life, and this could best be done by constructing an organic whole, where man, his house and the surrounding nature formed a harmonious unity. What exactly was meant by 'organic' was explained by the critic Wilhelm Michel in an article on the designer and architect Richard Riemerschmid that was published in *Dekorative Kunst* in 1909. According to Michel, a reaction was taking place all over Europe against the 'cultural anarchy' and the widely felt sense of being 'uprooted', supposedly caused by the artificial, internationalist and academic bourgeois culture that had dominated during the nineteenth century. Art therefore should be 'organic' and avoid both unattached arbitrariness – which was the result of absolute but anarchic freedom and individualism – and a too objective parsimony and poverty, which were generally caused by a lack of true creativity. The author declared that this longing for the organic could be ascribed to the desire of man to reconnect with 'the darker impulses, the unconsciousness, the "Earth" and the "Dionysian"'. Instead of the product of an overcivilised, arbitrary culture, art had to repeat the order of Nature; it should naturally grow out of man's darker impulses and not be 'made'. Art should be a necessity and the artist should 'listen carefully' to the demands posed by

---

[21] Paul Schumann, 'Drei Villen von Fritz Schumacher', *Dekorative Kunst* VIII (June 1905) 345–58, especially 357, Wichert, 'Stroevings Landhaus' 241–2, Max Schmid, 'Wohnhausbauten von Felix Krüger-Köln', *Dekorative Kunst* XVII (March 1914) 249–64, especially 249–52 and 'Bodenständigkeit', *Deutsche Kunst und Dekoration* XXVII (1910–11) 407–8.

[22] See for example: Joachim Radkau, *Das Zeitalter der Nervosität: Deutschland zwischen Bismarck und Hitler* (Darmstadt 1998).

[23] Erich Willrich, 'In partibus infidelium: Zu den Arbeiten Albin Müllers', *Dekorative Kunst* VIII (May 1905) 316–27, especially 320–2, Emil Waldmann, 'Das Landhaus Friese in Bremen', *Dekorative Kunst* XI (February 1908) 185–90, especially 185–6, Wichert, 'Stroevings Landhaus' 244, and Paul Schulze-Naumburg, 'Die Großstadtkrankheit', *Kunstwart* (March 1906) 569–77. See for similar remarks: Muthesius, *Das englische Haus*, I 6 and 219–20.

the aims and materials of a particular project. The architect should therefore depart from the specific requirements of the site, the materials, the official regulations, the budget and the wishes of the client, and 'find' the right form. Only a truly subjective genius like Riemerschmid possessed the sensitivity and insight to create the obvious form that incorporated all the inner necessities of the given assignment.[24]

In this way Michel seemed to imply that German architecture had been denaturalised by following superficial international modes and now had to re-establish an intimate bond with the inner nature of both the country and its inhabitants. Participating in the idealist turn the critic thus thought that architects – and artists in general – had to be intuitive geniuses who better than their less sensitive compatriots could discern the true character of both the nation and its natural habitat.

Michel was not the only critic to equate a well-designed house with an organic whole. Fritz Wichert, in his review of a country house, called its hall the 'heart' and 'lungs' of the building, where the inhaling and exchange of life took place, while the façade was its 'face'. J. Merkl, in his discussion of a regionalist villa, compared the roof with the forehead and the windows with the eyes, while Paul Johannes Rée described a country house by Riemerschmid as being fused with the landscape and a natural cover for its inhabitants, like the shell of a snail. Another metaphor that stressed the harmony of the whole was derived from music. For example, A. Jaumann compared the different parts of a villa designed by Heinrich Straumer (1876–1937) – who in the 1920s would build the functionalist Radio Tower in West Berlin – with the stanzas of a song, and declared that the architecture of a town was like a big orchestra, which ideally should produce a beautiful melody. Another critic, Ernst Schur, compared three country houses by Muthesius with organisms, calling them a 'whole, grown organically out of its purposes'. Like Michel, he underlined the wholesome effects of this type of building. Such buildings were a 'lasting home for people, who wanted to regain their inner nature'.[25] Thus the products of this new type of organic architecture also had a comforting effect on the inhabitants. They could live in a house that was wholly integrated into the

[24] Wilhelm Michel, 'Richard Riemerschmid', *Dekorative Kunst* XII (April 1909) 289–300.

[25] Wichert, 'Stroevings Landhaus' 248–50, J. Merkl, 'Landhäuser von Franz Mayr – Schlederloh', *Dekorative Kunst* XII (May 1909) 353–9, especially 354–5, Paul Johannes Rée, 'Richard Riemerschmid', *Dekorative Kunst* XI (April 1906) 265–300, especially 297, A. Jaumann, 'Heinrich Straumer', *Wasmuths Monatshefte für Baukunst* (1914–15) 493–530, especially 513 and 530 and Ernst Schur, 'Drei Landhäuser von Hermann Muthesius', *Dekorative Kunst* XIII (October 1909) 1–24, especially 22–4.

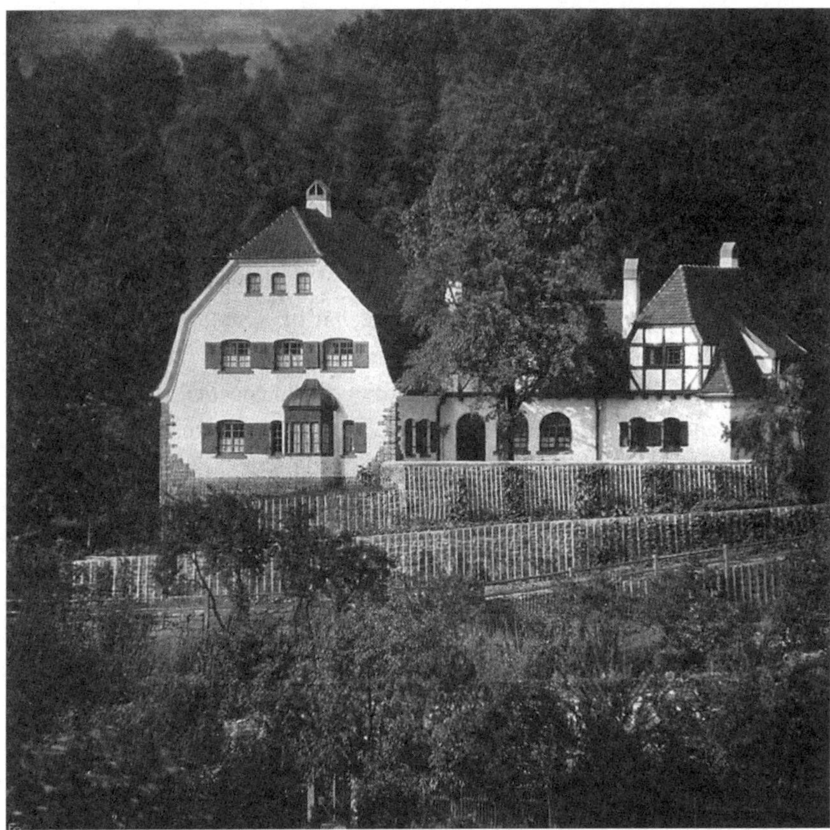

3 Richard Riemerschmid, Villa Frank, Witzenhausen, around 1908. In the middle, on the terrace, is the old pear tree and on its right there is the annex with the kitchen.

environment and thus could reconcile modern man with both his natural surroundings and the historically grown traditions. Here man could truly be himself.

But what practical consequences did this rhetoric have for the architect? Michel mentioned only a few seemingly trivial elements of Riemerschmid's Villa Frank in Witzenhausen (figure 3) that could give us a clue. This country house was designed around an already existing old pear tree. This tree further 'demanded' a terrace. The critic also mentioned the necessity to keep the odour of cooking out of the living rooms, which caused the kitchen and pantry to be placed in an annex at the back of the house. The harmony with the surrounding landscape was underlined by the form of the gables, which repeated in a schematic way the tops of the trees.[26]

Yet more can be deduced from other articles. For example, a few guiding principles should be observed in order to design a truly 'organic'

[26] Michel, 'Riemerschmid' 298–300.

building. Most authors stressed the importance of making a thorough study of the site, the surroundings, the wishes of the client and other practical circumstances. Another guideline can be summed up as 'designing from plan to façade' or 'from the inside to the outside'. Instead of paying most attention to the façade and the impression a building should make on the outside world, an architect should first take into consideration the wishes of the inhabitants and other practical requirements, and then design the plan and the interior. The exterior consequently should be adapted to the inner necessities of the house and reflect the plan. A further factor was the environment. A building should be in harmony with its surroundings, which meant that it should be organically connected with the garden and the landscape, and the rooms should be perfectly oriented. This implied that the architect had to provide natural light, fresh air and a beautiful vista where such were needed, had to protect specific parts of the building from bad weather, from a particular wind direction or from the hot summer sun, and had to connect the rooms with the garden by providing direct access to the garden from some of the main rooms and by constructing balconies, terraces and bow windows, all if possible decorated with plants and flowers.[27] These guidelines also applied to the recent English country houses that had been praised by Muthesius.

However, in order to design an organic whole the architect also had to adapt the house to its geographical and cultural environment, which meant that he also had to take into account the *Volksgeist*. An intimate, organic contact with both natural conditions and ancestral traditions was typical of 'primitive' people. For example, Hermann Obrist – a sculptor who co-founded the United Workshops for Art in Craftworks in Munich in 1897 – asserted that were Aztecs, 'Negroes' or 'Proto-Germanics' given the same material, they would automatically create similar forms, and that this applied to children too. The same materials in the same climate and applied to the same necessities would result in similar 'natural' or 'organic' forms. As time passed and each people added its own ornaments, this could develop into a tradition that completely reflected the particular *Volksgeist*. Foreign influences, however, could confuse this naive 'popular art' and cause it to lose its organic character. A complete return to this naive,

---

[27] See for example: Rée, 'Riemerschmid' 297, Hermann Muthesius, 'Landhäuser', *Dekorative Kunst* XIV (October 1911) 1–20, especially 20, Theodor Heuss, 'Ein Taunuslandhaus von Hugo Eberhardt', *Dekorative Kunst* XVI (December 1912) 105–13, Hermann Muthesius, 'Die Lage des Landhauses zur Sonne und zum Garten', *Der Baumeister* VI (October 1907) 1–6 and Ludw. Bartning, 'Wohnhäuser von Paul Schulze-Naumburg', *Der Baumeister* VIII (June 1910) 97–101, especially 97–9.

organic artistic feeling would be impossible. Nevertheless, Obrist described the architect and designer Bernhard Pankok (1872–1943) as a farmer's son who from the 'depths of his unconscious and almost mystical popular dreams' created the highest splendour in both his country houses and in his interior designs. Although not everybody would agree with his belief in the existence of almost universal 'natural' forms, which did not seem to be determined by local geographical, natural and cultural conditions, many would endorse his view that art and architecture should follow the guidelines provided by the 'spirit of the people', which was best preserved by the traditional peasant population.[28]

Another critic compared Riemerschmid's ornamental forms with figures from 'our folk tales'. His poetic sense could also be found in popular German songs and, according to the same author, in his buildings one could experience the same feelings as in a traditional farmhouse. In another *Dekorative Kunst* article, which dealt with the best new buildings in Austria and the German Empire, it was said that they 'grew self-evidently out of the indigenous soil'. These constructions could not look different and their artistic aspect remained largely unnoticed, as they were not far-fetched and showed no false pomp.[29]

But how exactly should the *Volksgeist* be recognised? In his article in *Der Baukunst*, Friedrich Seesselberg made a clear distinction between old vernacular buildings and new constructions. In former times, farmers and the inhabitants of small towns generally had the same outlook and built as they saw fit. They were not aware that their half-timbered or thatched houses and gables looked as if they were born out of the landscape. This harmony between art and nature had grown as a matter of course from generation to generation. They collectively adapted their constructions, customs and clothing to the surrounding environment, just like a beetle, a fly or a fish did. However, in modern times people had arrived at a higher level of self-consciousness. This was particularly true of the well-educated classes. They knew that other areas and epochs had produced their own art, and that these foreign and ancient styles could now be used in new creations. At the same time, even buildings in the countryside had to be adapted to the new circumstances of the industrialised epoch. Consequently, the ancient, collective 'habitual art' was replaced by 'initiative art'. A truly contemporary architecture that was rooted in the native soil therefore

[28] Hermann Obrist, 'Luxuskunst oder Volkskunst', *Dekorative Kunst* V (December 1901) 81–99, especially 83–90 and 96.

[29] Rée, 'Riemerschmid' 272 and 298, Richard von Schneider, 'Zuerst der Hof und dann das Haus', *Dekorative Kunst* VII (November 1903) 56–76, especially 72.

had to be the conscious creation of a strong artistic personality. In an era with ample knowledge about the past and about other parts of the world, art that both reflected the spirit of the times (*Zeitgeist*) and of the area (*Volksgeist*) had to be the conscious individual creation of a highly gifted and sensitive artist.[30] Thus, new regionalist buildings should not be copies of existing popular types, but well-considered contemporary creations that were inspired by existing vernacular architecture.

The next question was how the *Volksgeist* could be translated into new constructions. First, it should be remarked that, contrary to the situation at the beginning of the nineteenth century, what the authors meant by *Volksgeist* was not so much the 'spirit' of the whole of Germany, but the 'genius' of a specific region or area. Not only was the German Empire clearly divided into a northern and a southern part, each with its own peculiarities, but it could be further divided into many smaller regions each peopled by its own Germanic 'tribe' and with its own specific landscape, soil and climate. Thus, authors spoke of the characteristics of the 'Swabian tribe' or the peculiarities of Brandenburg, Lower Saxony, or North Frisia, or even more specific areas named after river valleys, hills or woods, such as the Hessian Bergstraße (the western slopes of the Odenwald).[31] Consequently, in later decades German ethnologists, geographers and historians, like their colleagues elsewhere, would try to divide the country into clearly delimitated 'cultural regions' based on a classification of all kind of presumably ancient popular traditions. This way they also thoroughly studied the various vernacular building techniques and forms. Although this type of research would be used by the Nazis as a 'scientific' legitimisation of their expansionist policies, arguing that the German cultural space was much larger than the existing German State, the actual results in the end were quite disappointing as the frontiers of the areas of distribution of the various cultural artefacts and popular traditions did not really coincide. So the conclusion in fact was that it was impossible to identify clearly delineated regions, with each a well-defined *Volksgeist*. However, one should be aware that this was not clear at the start of the century.[32]

[30] Friedrich Seesselberg, 'Niedersachsenkunst', *Der Baumeister* VIII (May 1910) 86–96, especially 88–94. See also: Bartning, 'Zur Baugeschichte' 608–10.

[31] J. Baum, 'Arbeiten der Architekten Beutinger und Steiner in Heilbronn', *Dekorative Kunst* XIII (January 1910) 153–7, especially 153, Ernst Schur, 'Bruno Paul', *Dekorative Kunst* XIV (November 1910) 57–81, especially 61, Seesselberg, 'Niedersachsenkunst' 88, K. Mühlke, 'Heimatskunst in Nordfriesland', *Der Baukunst* VIII (February 1910) 49–57 and Werner, 'Metzendorf-Häuser an der Hessischen Bergstrasze' 113.

[32] See, for example: Karl Ditt, 'Der Wandel historischer Raumbegriffe im 20. Jahrhundert

In order to reflect the local *Volksgeist*, according to many critics during the first decades of the twentieth century, architects should restrict themselves to using local building materials and, if possible, local forms and construction techniques. They therefore used, according to the region, timber framing, local stone, brick, or wood. The roofs generally were pitched and covered with tiles, slates or even reed. These materials – compared to the natural stone, marble and exotic wood that were traditionally used in upper-class villas and mansions – were cheap, easily available and generally matched well with the surroundings. If necessary, imported materials should preferably come from the new German colonies.[33] Also the interior should be made of plain, natural materials, which should be used according to their particular characteristics and not be hidden from view. The outside should be cheerful and varied. This should be achieved not by applying unnecessary ornaments and imported pilasters or pillars, but by using the natural colours of the different building materials and by creating a lively ensemble of the various parts. Bow windows, balconies, obviously decorated with indigenous plants,[34] gables and particularly the picturesque silhouette of the various pitched roofs should result in a pleasant view. Nevertheless, if local building traditions and materials were more austere, the new country houses should also adopt a more severe style.

A good example of a country house that was well adapted to the surroundings, the site, the needs of the client and local traditions could be found in an article on a building by Hugo Eberhardt. This was written by the young Theodor Heuss, a publicist and liberal politician who, after the Second World War, would become the first president of the Federal Republic of Germany and who originated from the same town, Heilbronn, as Eberhardt. In 1910 he published a major review of the Adolfshütte (figures 4–5), which the architect had designed for a factory owner in Dillenburg. The site was quite difficult, next to the factory, in an existing park with old trees, between a steep slope and the river Dill. Moreover the terrain was transected by a small industrial canal, which ran parallel to the slope. Eberhardt decided to change the site as little as possible by designing a long house on the small strip under the slope, with

<hr>

und das Beispiel Westfalen', *Geographische Zeitschrift* 93 (2005) 45–61 and Karl Ditt, 'The Idea of German Cultural Regions in the Third Reich: The Work of Franz Petri', *Journal of Historical Geography* 27 (2001) 241–58.

[33] Hans von Poellnitz, 'Schönheit und Ausdruck', *Dekorative Kunst* XL (April 1908) 289–301, especially 289.

[34] Paul Westheim, 'Haus Gluckegönne von Albert Gessner', *Dekorative Kunst* XVI (April 1913) 313–24, especially 316.

some rooms partially over the canal, in this way providing easy access to the broad terrace and the gardens on the other bank. To save a few oak trees the architect pushed the annex somewhat backwards, thus also creating an irregular and lively plan. The different colours of the slates, the stone (both from the region), the plaster and the white window frames blended perfectly in with those of the flowerboxes and the oaks; which together with the gurgling of the fast-flowing water provided a cheerful impression. However, the site, the building materials and the surrounding nature were not the only elements that were skilfully taken into account by the architect, as he also perfectly utilised the orientation. Thus, the main rooms lay on the south to provide natural light, air and views of the valley and garden. The interior was also carefully and logically laid out and decorated by the architect himself. The various pieces all lay

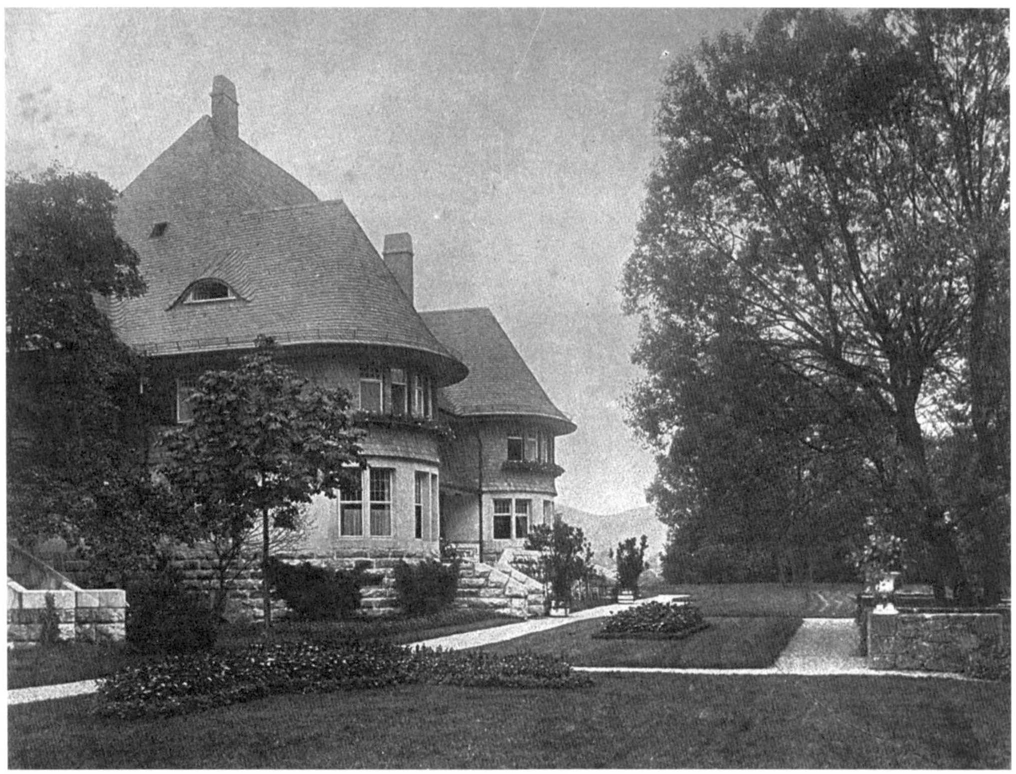

4 (*above*) Hugo Eberhardt, Landhaus Adolfshütte, Dillenburg, 1905–20. On the far left, one of the old oak trees can be seen and the beginnings of a small bridge that crosses the small industrial canal. The façade facing the garden contains the hall and the other main rooms.

5 (*opposite*) Hugo Eberhardt, Landhaus Adolfshütte, Dillenburg, plan.

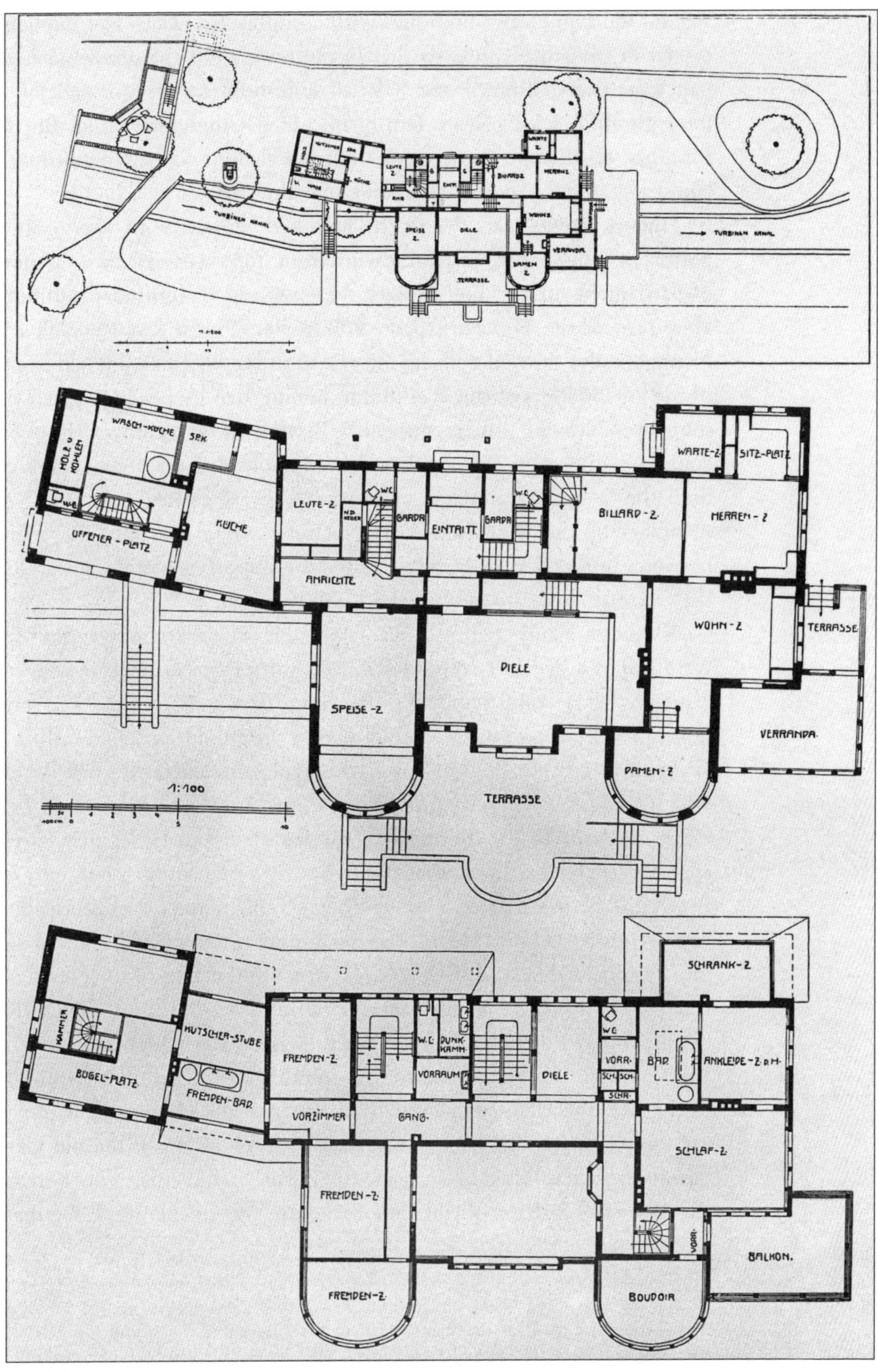
TURBINEN KANAL
TURBINEN KANAL
LEUTE Z.
SPEISE Z.
DIELE
WOHN Z.
VERANDA
DAMEN Z.
TERRASSE
BILLARD Z.
HERREN Z.
WARTE Z.
1:100

HOLZ U KOHLEN
WASCH-KUCHE
SP.K.
WC
OFFENER-PLATZ
KUCHE
LEUTE-Z.
N.D. NEDER
WC
GARDR.
EINTRITT
GARDR.
WC
BILLARD-Z.
MERREN-Z.
WARTE-Z.
SITZ-PLATZ
ANRICHTE
WOHN-Z.
TERRASSE
SPEISE-Z.
DIELE
VERRANDA.
DAMEN-Z.
TERRASSE
1:100

KAMMER
KUTSCHER-STUBE
SCHRANK-Z.
BUGEL-PLATZ
FREMDEN-Z.
W.C.
DUNK-KAMM.
W.C.
VORR.
BAD.
ANKLEIDE-Z. D.H.
FREMDEN-BAD.
VORRAUM
DIELE
VORR.
SCH.SCH.
VORZIMMER
GANG.
SCHR.
SCHLAF-Z.
FREMDEN-Z.
VORR.
BALKON.
FREMDEN-Z.
BOUDOIR

around the two-storey-high hall with a mighty fireplace. The kitchen was placed in the annex, next to the dining room, and the gentlemen's room had a separate entrance and a small anteroom to prevent official visits intermingling with private family life. Heuss therefore called Eberhardt a highly creative designer with a strong feeling for spaces, beauty and landscape; and, he could have added, tradition.[35]

During these years Heuss collaborated closely with the prominent politician Friedrich Naumann, who from 1907 onwards was a member of parliament for the Freisinnigen Vereinigung (Freeminded Union) and after 1910 of the Fortschrittliche Volkspartei (Progressive People's Party). Naumann also showed a strong interest in the applied arts and had been one of the co-founders of the Werkbund, hoping that by producing artistically sound products in a more guild-like setting the position of the workers could be improved. Heuss, like his mentor, was an active member of both the Werkbund and the same social–liberal parties. Like many other members of the Werkbund, of which he would become the manager between 1918 and 1933, he also stressed the importance of designing houses that were in accordance with the local *Volksgeist*.[36]

Although many critics spoke favourably of new country houses that were inspired by old farmhouses, others were more critical. However, the critique that a comfortable country house that was meant for a modern upper-middle-class family should not be disguised as the dwelling of a farmer was only to be heard after this type of architecture had become a widespread fashion practised also by lesser architects and contractors. In 1911 Heuss showed that he did not like the regionalist pastiches that started to appear everywhere. In another positive review of a country house by Hugo Eberhardt he warned of a 'dangerous Romanticism', as historically and socially grown architectural forms were now often applied without taking into consideration the different 'social needs and habits' of the present. This resulted in 'masquerades of Black Forest and Swiss farmhouses as villas for townspeople'. Eberhardt escaped the trap as he was a highly creative artist and found an individual and logical solution to the peculiar requirements of the site, the client, the local traditions and the environment. At about the same time, another critic regretted that adoration of the old German farmhouse had resulted in 'an academic village architecture, which translates the unwieldy dialectal forms into a smooth, presentable High German'.[37]

---

[35] Theodor Heuss, 'Landhaus Adolfshütte', *Dekorative Kunst* XIII (May 1910) 345–57.
[36] See for Heuss and Naumann: Maciuika, *Before the Bauhaus*.
[37] Theodor Heuss, 'Das Landhaus Bubat in Freiburg i. Br.', *Dekorative Kunst* XIV (May 1911) 345–9, especially 345 and Jaumann, 'Ländliche Häuser von Straumer' 314.

A reader's letter in the *Kunstwart* was even more specific. The author criticised the new vogue for high-pitched roofs on farmhouse villas. Nowadays, he wrote:

> the modern small villas prefer to pull the roof down over their ears,
> their shoulders; no, they pull it down below their knees. When one
> walks through a street, in which there are many such nightcap houses,
> one starts to yawn as these well-disguised and safely wrapped up
> goodnight homes look so sleepy, so sealed off.

According to this reader, a house should be designed from a practical point of view. Forms that suit a farmhouse do not necessarily fit a villa for people with urban habits. And instead of adapting itself to the landscape or functioning as a 'decorative piece in a landscape', a house should represent the individuality of the inhabitant.[38]

The inhabitants of the countryside, such as villagers and farmers, generally also seemed to frown upon this type of house. One could deduce, paraphrasing David Lowenthal, that they did not yet see the past nostalgically as a foreign country. When, for example, the architect Paul Korff in his small hometown of Laage in Mecklenburg, tried to convince some well-to-do farmers that he should build a characteristic one-storey house for them, with a pitched roof, a front garden and green shutters, they rejected his proposal since they clearly preferred modern houses, with three symmetrical big windows, as they had seen in the big towns.[39] Neo-vernacular buildings were thus generally built for a modern, urban public.

Most architects and critics saw regionalist architecture as part of a wider reform movement that was to promote a more genuine, truthful existence in harmony with nature and native traditions, and which was directed especially at the middle classes. Although occasionally a regionalist villa was built for someone of noble descent, the clientele consisted almost exclusively of upper-middle-class families. Many critics even stressed the essentially middle-class or bourgeois character of the new 'organic' country houses. Consequently the sources of inspiration could not only be found in the countryside but also in traditional houses built by artisans in provincial towns. Other critics argued that instead of imitating princely and noble

---

[38] 'Vom Schwelgen im Dach' 206–7. However, Avenarius, the editor of this bimonthly, meant that the author exaggerated and that the high-pitched roof perfectly matched the German climate.
[39] David Lowenthal, *The Past is a Foreign Country* (Cambridge 1985) and Schur, 'Rittergut Wendorf' 353.

palaces, this *neu-Deutsch bürgerlichen Baukunst* (new-German bourgeois construction art) should reconnect with the unpretentious, middle-class architecture that had flourished at the end of the eighteenth and the start of the nineteenth century.[40] In this way, a somewhat more generic regionalism also came into existence. Particularly the architects Paul Mebes (1872–1938) and Paul Schultze-Naumburg openly defended the small-town houses and furniture from the years around 1800 and from the Biedermeier period as good examples for the present. Both men were highly influential. In 1908, Mebes published *Um 1800: Architektur und Handwerk im letzten Jahrhundert ihrer traditionellen Entwicklung* (Around 1800: Architecture and Handcrafts in the Last Century of its Traditional Development), while Schulze-Naumburg – the main architectural critic of the *Kunstwart* – wrote nine volumes of *Kulturarbeiten* (Works of Culture), which appeared from 1902 onwards. In them, he juxtaposed what he considered good and bad buildings.[41]

In general, however, most critics agreed that country houses should embody and stimulate both traditional rural and more modern bourgeois values. For example, these family homes should be hospitable and cosy, like a farmhouse. Also the steadiness of the rural population functioned as an example worthy of imitation. Unlike in the towns, where people moved from one rented apartment to another, in the countryside houses were private property and people felt attached to their environment. According to the critic Alfred Eppler, this should also apply to newly built country houses:

> then the house should be a home [*Heimat*] to the family, a place with
> which all members of the family through firm bonds have become one.
> This intimate connection to the ancient family house, that one does not
> change like a jacket, but that belongs to the family, and without which
> it is almost impossible to imagine the family, this intimate connection
> between house and inhabitants is not in the last place, for example,
> what confers its power to the landed gentry.[42]

[40] E. Hänel, 'Das Landhaus Stapf-Möbius in Greiz', *Dekorative Kunst* XIII (June 1910) 436–8.

[41] For Schultze-Naumburg and Mebes see: Norbert Borrmann, *Paul Schultze-Naumburg: 1869–1949, Maler, Publizist, Architekt. Vom Kulturreformer der Jahrhundertwende zum Kulturpolitiker im Dritten Reich: ein Lebens und Zeitdokument* (Essen 1989), Edina Meyer, *Paul Mebes: Miethausbau in Berlin 1906–1938* (Berlin 1972), Wilhelm Bode, 'Paul Schultze-Naumburgs Bauten, *Dekorative Kunst* XI (March 1908) 233–57 and Behrendt, 'Wohnhausbauten Mebes'.

[42] Respectively, Victor Zobel, 'Das Haus Henkel in Wiesbaden', *Dekorative Kunst* XI (October 1907) 1–21, especially 11 and Alfred Eppler, 'Ein modernes Backstein-Haus', *Dekorative Kunst* XII (June 1909) 402–8, especially 402.

Typical middle-class values were also embodied in these houses. In a review of three villas by Fritz Schumacher, the author Paul Schumann maintains that these houses were neither schematic nor too exaggerated: 'On the contrary, everywhere we find complete objectivity and clearness, truthfulness and middle-class thoroughness.' In an article on a villa by Riemerschmid near Munich, Muthesius also praises his 'true-hearted plainness'. Garish colours were excluded as 'everything is tuned down to the unobtrusive bourgeois mentality, but nonetheless one gets solid middle-class fare'. The interior of the villa was also designed by Riemerschmid and reflected the same values. According to Muthesius his furniture 'distinguishes itself for a certain natural simplicity, decency and true-heartedness'. In the rooms he found 'mood, soul and humour, fully governed by reason'. The final result 'is a plain product of sound human reason, which nonetheless strives to employ itself with taste and propriety'.[43]

The architect should provide the inhabitants with the possibility to enjoy a decent family life, often with clearly divided gender roles. What this meant can be deduced from the description of the living room of a 'country seat for a nature-loving bourgeois', which was designed by Riemerschmid, near the Bavarian village of Füssen:

> At the window is a comfortable chair and desk for the father, in the
> bay window extends a small working and chatting corner for the
> mother, along another window stretches a couch around a big table …
> A vast stove with dark coloured tiles heightens the impression of secure
> comfort.

The house had a so-called 'winter room' (figure 6), which 'as a cosy nest is built around a mighty stove … This room is really a family nook, in which one feels oneself a well-protected observer and enjoyer even with storm and heavy weather.'[44] Many critics also stressed the importance of the family's privacy. This should be guaranteed by clearly separating the rooms used by the family members from those parts that were meant for receiving visitors and from the areas – such as the kitchen and pantry – that were the domain of the servants.

Apparently, these architects were not staunch defenders of artistic autonomy, or the cause of art for art's sake. The country houses were constructed for their future inhabitants and had a clear moral goal: they

---

43 Schumann, 'Villen von Schumacher' 357 and H. M., 'Kunst Riemerschmids' 256, 272, 278 and 283.

44 J. Popp, 'Haus Schwalten von Richard Riemerschmid', *Dekorative Kunst* XVII (October 1913) 1–11, especially 8–9.

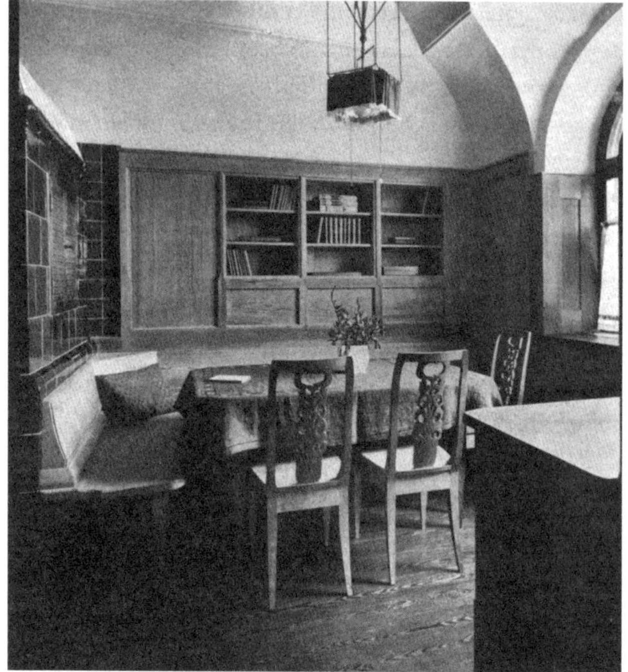

6 Richard Riemerschmid, winter room of Haus Schwalten, Füssen, around 1913. The stove is on the left, with the back of the bench directly attached to it.

were meant to induce their inhabitants to live a decent family life, to behave reasonably – namely in a practical and logical way, to work hard, be thrifty, and to be unpretentious, serious, honest and cheerful. What the architects propagated was not a narrow-minded existence guided by routine and conventions, but a self-conscious, authentic life and a respectful attitude towards nature and traditions. In many ways, the villas and country houses built in a neo-vernacular style and mainly constructed for intellectuals, professors, judges, bankers and industrialists, were thus part of a wider reform movement, which in Germany is known by the term *Lebensreform* (life-reform). The regionalist architects shared a new appreciation of nature, a longing for authenticity, a stress on true creativity and the revaluation of popular traditions with the various *Lebensreform* movements, such as those of the excursionists, vegetarians, educational reformers, nudists and esoterics.[45]

These architects, consequently, also had higher aspirations. Their recipes should not be confined to the country houses and cottages of the upper-middle class but also be applied to other areas. Many architects therefore

---

[45] Kai Buchholz, Rita Latocha, Hilke Peckmann and Klaus Wolbert eds., *Die Lebensreform: Entwürfe zur Neugestaltung von Leben und Kunst um 1900* (Darmstadt 2001) 2 vols.

developed close relations with the various administrations within the German Empire in order to exert influence on their policies; some were even given important jobs. The best example of this is Muthesius, who after returning from his post at the German Embassy in London in 1903 became a high official at the Prussian Commerce Ministry, which because of the lack of a similar national ministry informally functioned for the whole Empire. Here, he designed the fundamental pedagogical reform of the curriculum of the dozens of schools for arts, crafts and trades that depended on the ministry. It was hoped that this would improve the quality of German wares and augment their export. He also collaborated in the organisation of several applied art exhibitions and was one of the most influential leaders of the Werkbund.[46] Others who held important posts were Hans Poelzig, who was appointed director of the Breslau School of Art and Applied Arts in 1903, and Theodor Fischer, who was respectively Munich's city planner, professor at the University of Stuttgart and of Munich's Technical University. Richard Riemerschmid became director of the Applied Arts School in Munich in 1913 and Hugo Eberhardt was nominated building inspector in Frankfurt in 1904 and three years later director of the applied arts school in Offenbach.

Most of these architects also received official commissions, and some of them hoped to apply the new regionalist guidelines as well, as became manifest in an article published in 1902 by Theodor Fischer which dealt with how to build a school. According to him the 'German spirit' in architecture had almost disappeared by the 'deluge of classicism' and other foreign influences; only a few rocks in the 'hills of popular art' were still standing. In order to rediscover its own artistic personality, Germany should try to reconnect with these steady native roots. But how should one proceed when designing a school as, contrary to other building types, there were almost no traditional examples? According to Fischer, this should not be an obstacle as it would be perfectly possible to build simple but artistically sound schools adapting the specific local architectural traditions to the requirements for a modern school building. And this would be as feasible for small village schools as for bigger institutes in the towns. However, Fischer, after his recent conflict with the local city council over a prestigious project at the central Kohleninsel in Munich, was quite pessimistic about the chances for architects to actually build such schools. As long as these issues were decided by 'coincidental majorities' of laymen,

---

[46] Maciuika, *Before the Bauhaus*.

artistic considerations would practically play no role and badly designed, gaudy, characterless structures would continued to be built.[47]

Nevertheless, some years later the new trend also started to get official support. One of the earliest examples of a public building in a neo-vernacular style was the extension of the fifteenth-century town hall of Löwenberg (now Lwówek Slaski, in Poland) designed by Poelzig in 1904.[48] Later others would follow, in both small provincial towns and major cities.

Unquestionably the most influential in this sense was Fritz Schumacher. He was born in Bremen as the son of a diplomat, and gained his first working experience at the office of Gabriel von Seidl in Munich. In 1901 he became a professor of Architecture in Dresden where, in 1906, he would be one of the main organisers of the Third German Applied Art Exhibition. His building activities were fairly limited, although he did design several villas, among which figured the one for Sombart. He felt attracted to the ideas of Naumann and was one of the founders of the Werkbund. His profile therefore was strongly reformist and this apparently was what some influential local politicians were looking for when in 1909 he was appointed Hamburg's main city architect.[49]

Hamburg was an unlikely city to become the main stronghold of regionalist architecture. Although the free city zealously guarded its political autonomy within the German Empire and the special rights of its harbour, Hamburg was a quite cosmopolitan and modern town. At the end of the nineteenth century many parts of the old city had been demolished to make place for a new port and warehouse district. This pragmatic city, in fact, seemed an ideal environment for functionalist architecture. However, when the former city architect retired, Schumacher was appointed as his successor and he almost immediately decreed that all official buildings in the north German town should be designed in a style based on the old Hanseatic tradition and be built mainly in brick. This style glorified the supposedly harmonious artisan traditions of the medieval guilds, whereas at the same time it referred back to the golden age of Hamburg, when commerce prospered and the city was still largely politically independent.

[47]   Theodor Fischer, 'Das Schulgebäude', *Dekorative Kunst* V (February 1902) 170–84, especially 170, 176 and 180.

[48]   Conrad Buchwald, 'Das Löwenburger Rathaus', *Dekorative Kunst* X (October 1906) 11–15.

[49]   See for Schumacher: Hermann Hipp, 'Fritz Schumachers Hamburg: Die reformierte Großstadt', in: Vittorio Lampugnani and Romana Schneider eds., *Moderne Architektur in Deutschland 1900 bis 1950: Reform und Tradition* (Stuttgart 1992) 151–85 and Hartmut Frank ed., *Fritz Schumacher: Reformkultur und Moderne* (Stuttgart 1994).

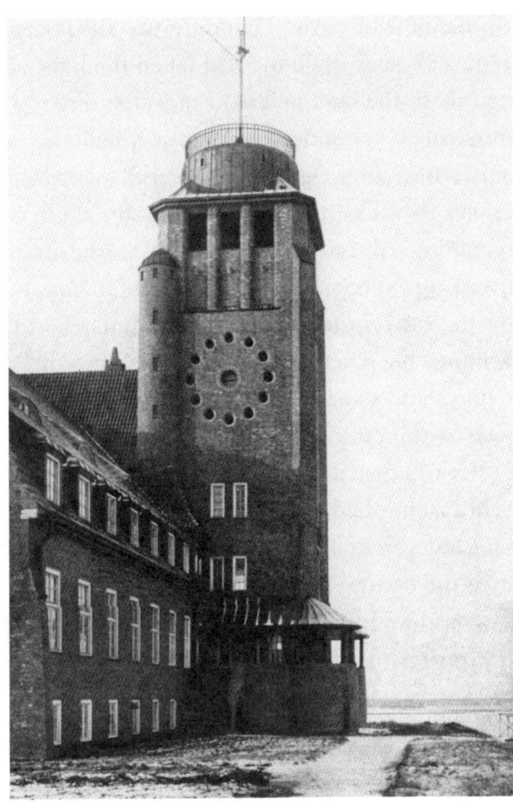

7 Fritz Schumacher, Pilot Station, Hamburg, around 1914.

Although Schumacher was not the first to adopt this style, nor was he very dogmatic in its application, he himself took the lead as he designed several official buildings in brick such as the Tropical Institute and the Pilot Station (figure 7). As he also became active in town planning and social housing, he finally succeeded in almost completely transforming the outlook of the town.[50]

Why precisely did Hamburg, under the guidance of Schumacher, completely convert to regionalist architecture? At least part of the answer can be found in the peculiar political situation of the free city. Whereas since 1890 the socialist party (SPD) occupied all three Hamburg seats in the Reichstag, at the local level the socialists had difficulty in even getting representation in the local assembly. This was due to the high cost of the traditional citizenship fee which severely limited the local suffrage, whereas at the national level general male suffrage had been introduced by

[50] Jennifer Jenkins, *Provincial Modernity: Local Culture and Liberal Politics in Fin-de-Siècle Hamburg* (Ithaca 2003) 150–1, 220–31 and 261–93.

Bismarck. Moreover, Hamburg was the last major European town where in 1892 a cholera epidemic had taken the lives of several thousand inhabitants, mainly in the cramped working-class districts. The strength of the workers' movement, although not an immediate political threat, caused great concern among the city's elites. A reformist section of the city's leading circles therefore tried to convert the workers into responsible citizens. By spreading education and culture to the masses on the one hand, and by inspiring expressions of high culture increasingly on vernacular predecessors on the other, they hoped to integrate the masses into respectable society. Schumacher's activities, including the construction of a *Volkspark*, many schools and social housing in an up-to-date neo-vernacular style, could be seen as the culmination of this broader reformist project.[51]

Critics generally reviewed his work in a positive way. They agreed that Schumacher had built highly sophisticated and purposeful buildings in an updated vernacular style. Also his use of brick was innovative as he fully used the natural potential of the material and in this way revived a tradition that, unlike in Holland and England, had almost disappeared in Germany. Schumacher's activities even compelled German industry to improve its brick production and neutralised the need to import high-quality bricks from the Netherlands. However, he was not the first to return to this north-German tradition, but according to Muthesius in his extensive review of Schumacher's buildings, the somewhat older, but cold and fake Hanoverian neo-Gothic brick architecture had been a mistake.[52] His transformation of Hamburg led him to be presented as one of the country's leading architects who succeeded in not only adapting a building to the local traditions and landscape, but potentially a whole town. According to Fritz Stahl, Schumacher's designs were a sign that the desirable 'decentralisation has started; the proper nature of the German tribes is now being expressed'. Muthesius called Schumacher's north-German building in brick a clear expression of the 'popular' (*völkisch*) longing for artistic unity. Moreover, Schumacher also showed with massive office buildings, schools, the headquarters of the fire brigade and other major assignments

---

[51] This at least is the general thesis of Jenkins, *Provincial Modernity*. Umbach broadly agrees with this interpretation: Maiken Umbach, 'A Tale of Second Cities: Autonomy, Culture, and the Law in Hamburg and Barcelona in the Late Nineteenth Century', *American Historical Review* 110 (2005) 659–92.

[52] Fritz Stahl, 'Lotsenhaus am Hamburger Hafen: Architekt. Stadtbaudirektor Professor Fritz Schumacher', *Wasmuths Monatshefte für Baukunst* (1915–16) 525–30, J. J. Scharvogel, 'Neuer Hamburger Backsteinbau', *Dekorative Kunst* (August 1917) 337–43 and Hermann Muthesius, 'Fritz Schumachers Bauten in Hamburg', *Dekorative Kunst* (January 1919) 93–110, especially 96–7.

that an inspiration in vernacular traditions could also lead to monumental buildings in an urban setting.[53]

Garden cities

Thus, in Germany regionalist and nationalist rhetoric was omnipresent in the debates on a new, innovative architecture which, in turn, was seen as part of a highly influential, wider reform movement with an essentially middle-class background. However, this type of rhetoric not only influenced the architecture of villas, country houses and even monumental buildings, but also profoundly affected the debate on urban planning. Around 1900 many architects and planners began to reject the new broad and straight avenues that should improve both the circulation of traffic and the overall hygiene of the population, and that had come into vogue with Haussmann's restructuring of Paris in the 1850s and 1860s. The new ideas did not originate in Germany but were rapidly absorbed. Highly influential was *Der Städtebau nach seinen künstlerischen Grundsätzen* (City Planning according to Artistic Principles) by the Austrian architect Camilo Sitte (1843–1903), which was first published in 1889. He abhorred the broad, uniform avenues and isolated, symmetrical monumental constructions that had been erected all over Europe, such as Garnier's Opéra in Paris and the main buildings at the Ringstrasse in Vienna. Instead he pleaded for historically grown, irregular squares and streets, where man could feel at home. His ideas would become widely diffused by the magazine *Der Städtebau* (City Planning), which he started together with the German architect Theodor Goecke (1850–1919), and which was published in both Vienna and Berlin. Towns, he wrote in the first issue published in 1904, should again become a 'breeding ground for real patriotism [*Heimatsliebe*]'. A city, according to Sitte, should not be designed on the drawing board by engineers, but by real artists who use their fantasy to develop imaginative, poetic and picturesque spaces.[54]

A more practical influence, however, came from England, where in 1898 Ebenezer Howard (1850–1928) published *To-morrow: A Peaceful Path to Real Reform*. Four years later a second, slightly revised edition appeared

---

[53] Stahl, 'Schumachers Hamburger Bauten' 259 and Muthesius, 'Schumachers Bauten' 94 and passim.

[54] Theodor Goecke and Camilo Sitte, 'An unsere Leser', *Der Städtebau* I (1904) 1–4. See for the influence of Sitte: Eugen Kalkschmidt, 'Der Baumeister und seine Zeit', *Der Baumeister* (March 1908) 66–71 and Richard von Schneider, 'Zuerst der Hof und dann das Haus', *Dekorative Kunst* VII (October 1903) 18–32, especially 26.

under the more resounding title *Garden Cities of Tomorrow*. Howard was a somewhat obscure publicist who had spent several years in the United States and was profoundly influenced by positivist and utopian thinkers such as Herbert Spencer, George Bernard Shaw, Edward Bellamy and the Russian anarchist Piotr Kropotkin. In order to find a solution for both the increasing rural exodus caused by the Great Depression, and the fast-growing slums in the big cities, he proposed the 'garden city' as a solution. By buying up large areas of cheap agricultural land, leasing it out in allotments to the individual inhabitants, connecting it to the railway network and constructing broadly laid-out cities for about 30,000 people, he hoped to combine the advantages of the city with those of the countryside. These new garden cities should provide work, leisure, fresh air and nature. They should not only contain country houses for the upper classes but also provide a decent home for the lower-middle and working classes, thus enabling them to benefit from the wholesome effects of a good house and garden in a healthy and morally elevated setting. His project clearly belonged to the optimistic positivist schemes that were typical of the nineteenth century. Thus, his plan of the city was very schematic, with various circular avenues and straight concentric boulevards. Furthermore, the main part of his book intended to show that his ideas for a garden city, based on the ideal of collective self-help, would be financially feasible. Architecture, on the other hand, did not seem to interest him as he did not specify in what style or way the buildings should be constructed. The Garden City Society he founded in 1899 was a success as it attracted businessmen, politicians from both the Liberal and Conservative Party and artists, and in 1903 the First Garden City Company even started to build the garden city of Letchworth, to the north of London.[55]

The role of Howard rapidly became quite marginal, as he did not have real managerial skills. In contrast, the architects selected to build Letchworth, Raymond Unwin (1863–1940) and Barry Parker (1867–1947), would continue to have a huge impact upon the garden city movement. Unwin and Parker were profoundly influenced by William Morris and the Arts and Crafts movement and showed a similar interest as Howard in social reform through housing. They were attracted by some existing workers' colonies, such as Bournville (1879) outside Birmingham and Port Sunlight (1888) near Liverpool, both of which were constructed by reformist

---

[55] Ebenezer Howard, *Garden Cities of Tomorrow* (London 1902). See also: Peter Hall, *Cities of Tomorrow: An Intellectual History of Urban Planning and Design in the Twentieth Century* (3rd edn., Oxford 2002) 88–104, Standish Meacham, *Regaining Paradise: Englishness and the Early Garden City Movement* (New Haven 1999).

manufacturers and looked like rural villages. Inspired by local vernacular examples, and the informal lay-out of medieval cities and villages, their designs for Letchworth and some other garden cities or suburbs (such as Hampstead Garden Suburb on the outskirts of London, which was started in 1907) completely transformed Howard's rational and almost symmetrical model. With winding streets, irregular squares, cul-de-sacs, and neo-vernacular cottages they hoped to create an organic community, where different classes would live together in harmony. Nonetheless, at the start, in fact, the garden cities attracted especially artistic folk, the middle-class idealists who in Germany formed the core of the *Lebensreform* movement.[56]

The ideas of Howard, dressed up in a neo-vernacular guise by Unwin and Parker, were almost immediately picked up on the Continent. This was particularly true of Germany, where many observers were worried about the high pace of urbanisation and especially about the bad living conditions of the lower classes. Already two years before the publication of Howard's book, the fiercely anti-Semitic author Theodor Fritsch (1852–1933) had come up with a similar plan to build new healthy cities in the countryside. However, Fritsch's goal was to stop the 'decline of the blond race' and create new 'breeding grounds for German life'. Fritsch would remain an outsider and his schematic and racist ideas were ignored by the mainly reformist intellectuals who would embrace the garden city ideal.[57]

Initiatives in the main German towns by manufacturers, workers' co-operatives and limited dividend housing societies had had some positive results already in the 1890s as many projects with affordable and good houses or tenements for the lower classes had been built. Nevertheless, the general situation still was alarming and Howard's plan was welcomed as part of the solution, especially by members of the generation of architects and critics that had been the driving force behind the rise of the regionalist style for villas and cottages. Thus, as early as 1902 the Deutsche Gartenstadtgesellschaft (German Garden City Society) was founded in Berlin by a group of reformist intellectuals with clear socialistic and anarchistic sympathies, many of whom were a member of the literary community in Friedrichshagen, near Berlin. One of these, Bernhard Kampffmeier (1867–1942), would become the most active propagator of the new ideal. After some years the Society, like its English equivalent,

---

[56] Hall, *Cities of Tomorrow* 101–10, and Meacham, *Regaining Paradise.*
[57] Dirk Schubert ed., *Die Gartenstadtidee zwischen reaktionärer Ideologie und pragmatischer Umsetzung: Theodor Fritschs völkische Version der Gartenstadt* (Dortmund 2004) 29 and 38–40.

would become more practical, leaving behind the more utopian aspects, and stimulate the actual building of garden suburbs. It would thus become more influential especially after it succeeded in attracting prominent new members such as Paul Schultze-Naumburg and Ferdinand Avenarius of the *Kunstwart*, Richard Riemerschmid, Hermann Muthesius, Theodor Fischer, Peter Behrens and the social scientist Werner Sombart.[58]

From the beginning of the twentieth century, the English workers' colonies and garden cities received favourable reviews in the German specialised press. In many articles the living conditions of the lower classes in both countries were compared and all authors praised the new English initiatives. However, the comparison also brought to light a few possible difficulties as some authors observed that the English building regulations were less strict than in Germany and that speculation had caused higher land prices than in their own country. Another critic maintained that in Germany the houses would be more expensive as they had to be more solid because of the harsher climate; and letting out land on a long lease, which was at the heart of Howard's financial plan, would not work in Germany, where people were too attached to their own 'soil'.[59]

Starting around 1906 garden cities were built in various parts of the German Empire, although as in England, most were actually suburbs. Almost immediately city councils, state authorities, entrepreneurs such as Krupp, workers' co-operatives and housing societies actively supported the idea. Thus, in 1915 there were already thirty-one garden cities with some 5,600 houses.[60] Some of these were extensively discussed in the various architectural magazines and *Der Städtebau*. As almost all these garden suburbs, like those designed by Unwin and Parker in England, were motivated by vernacular building traditions, the ideas and assumptions expressed in these reviews were very similar to those used when discussing regionalist villas and cottages. Thus, the big cities were depicted as impersonal, destabilising and unhealthy agglomerations. In Berlin, one author asserted, based on a population of some 2 million inhabitants in

---

[58] See: Kristiana Hartmann, *Deutsche Gartenstadtbewegung: Kultur, Politik und Gesellschaftsreform* (Munich 1976) and Axel Schollmeier, *Gartenstädte in Deutschland: Ihre Geschichte, Städtebaulicher Entwicklung und Architektur zu Beginn des 20. Jahrhunderts* (Münster 1990). See for the movement for housing reform and its results: Nicholas Bullock and James Read, *The Movement for Housing Reform in Germany and France 1840–1914* (Cambridge 1985).

[59] Berlepsch-Valendas, 'Englische Arbeiterwohnungen', *Dekorative Kunst* X (May 1907) 313–29, especially 325, Dr Böhmert, 'Englische Arbeiterwohnhaüser in deutscher Beleuchtung', *Der Städtebau* (1909) 15–17, especially 16 and B. Wehl, 'Englische Reiseeindrücke über Gartenstädte und Vororte', *Der Städtebau* (1909) 160–2, especially 161.

[60] Schollmeier, *Gartenstädte in Deutschland* 197 and illustration 9.

1906, the population had increased by about 14 per cent, although actually about 10 per cent had left the city. The most disquieting fact, however, was that almost 1.4 million people moved to another apartment within the city; and as these apartments were generally situated within overcrowded blocks, people had to look for recreation on the streets or in the bar.[61] This was all the more threatening as, according to Hermann Jansen (1869–1945), the editor of the monthly *Der Baumeister* (The Master Builder) and one of the winners of the influential greater Berlin planning contest in 1910, everybody knew that 'the future would belong to the nation with the most healthy and resistant individuals'. Thus architects and city planners had a huge responsibility as they should help to improve the 'human material' of the nation by providing good and healthy houses.[62]

The unhealthy and immoral conditions could be avoided by providing the lower classes with their own house, with enough fresh air and direct light, in new green neighbourhoods where the children would have space to play, where there would no longer be a need to waste time in the bar and where the inhabitants really would feel at home. Garden cities or suburbs could perfectly provide such houses and, consequently, were a 'weapon in the struggle for social peace'.[63] These new quarters therefore should be mixed neighbourhoods where the different classes would live together harmoniously. Their lay-out should be spacious with parks, playgrounds and streets lined with plants and trees. As the terraced houses for the workers should be cheap, a certain uniformity would be unavoidable. However, by varying the colours, roofs and size of the houses, by planting trees and diversifying the lay-out of the streets and public spaces, the whole should provide a pleasant impression. Furthermore these garden cities should possess enterprises, shops, schools and other public buildings, so there would be no need to make frequent visits to the neighbouring town.[64]

All these elements were visible in the first German garden city, Hellerau near Dresden. Hellerau was founded by Karl Schmidt, the owner of the Dresdener Werkstätten für Handwerkskunst (Dresden Workshops for Handcrafted Art) in which he produced simple and *volkstümlich* (popular/

---

61 Erich Haenel, 'Die Gartenstadt Hellerau', *Dekorative Kunst* XIV (April 1911) 297–343, especially 297–9 and 343, and Berlepsch-Valendas, 'Kleine Wohnhäuser', *Dekorative Kunst* XIII (November 1909) 81–7, especially 81. See also: Paul Schultze-Naumburg, 'Kulturarbeiten', *Der Städtebau* (1906) 113–17.
62 Hermann Jansen, 'Wohnhaustypen der Grossstadt', *Der Baumeister* (June 1911) 102–12, especially 102, and 'Einfamilienhäuser', *Der Baumeister* (June 1914) 89–96, especially 89.
63 Quote from: Haenel, 'Hellerau' 343.
64 Karl Henrici, 'Arbeiterkolonien', *Der Städtebau* (1906) 71–6.

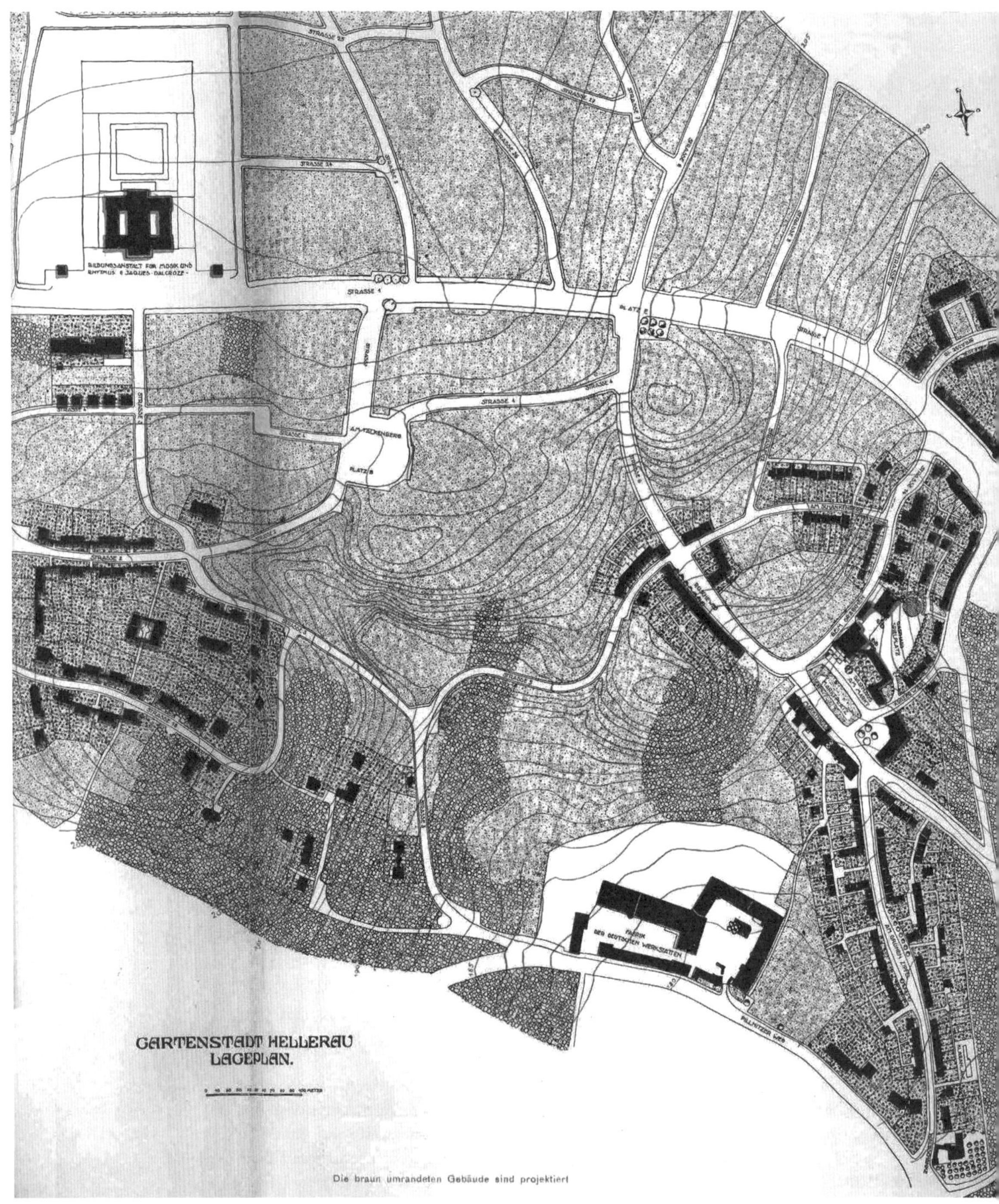

8 Richard Riemerschmid, Plan of Hellerau. The Am grünen Zipfel street of figure 9 is on the lower right corner and next to the huge building of the Workshops for Handcrafted Art, which was constructed around two courtyards. The Institute of Rhythmic Movement and Dance is on the upper left corner.

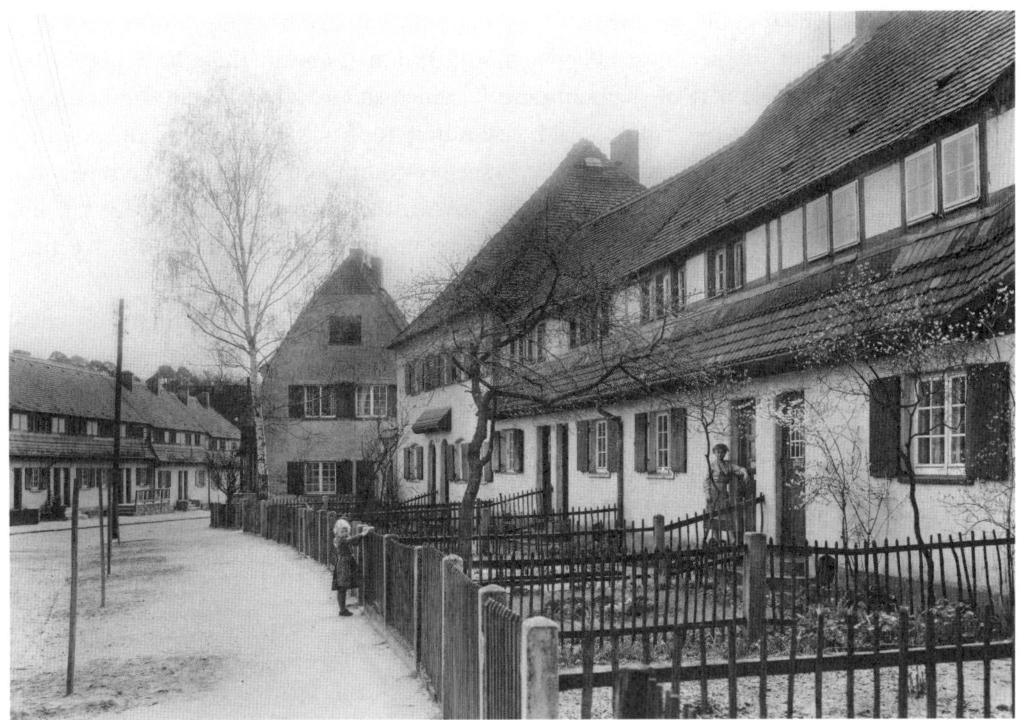

9 Richard Riemerschmid, Hellerau, am grünen Zipfel, 1908–9 (street view of May 1958).

vernacular) furniture designed by renowned artists and architects. In 1906 he decided to move his expanding enterprise to the outskirts of Dresden, where he also planned a new suburb with houses for his workers and the local middle and upper classes. He immediately received support from Naumann, Muthesius and his brother-in-law Riemerschmid, who became the main planner of the project. Schmidt was convinced that it would be easier for his workers to deliver the quality labour needed when provided with a healthy environment, a decent house and a well-designed work place, with sufficient light and fresh air. Riemerschmid came up with a village-like plan, with winding streets, irregular squares and small alleys (figures 8–9). Most of the houses were designed by Riemerschmid and Muthesius, although other architects, among whom were Fischer and Baillie Scott, also designed one or several buildings.[65]

Although the terraced houses were limited to only a few types, with standardised parts for doors, windows and fixtures, Riemerschmid and Muthesius succeeded in giving almost all houses an individual touch,

[65] See for Hellerau: Maciuika, *Before the Bauhaus* 217–48 and Hartmann, *Deutsche Gartenstadtbewegung* 46–102.

which could be enhanced by the personal layout of the flower garden in front of the house. People should feel at home in their own house, but also feel part of the community, which should be visible in the harmonic unity of the whole. And, according to Erich Haenel, in an extensive review of the settlement in *Dekorative Kunst*, by renouncing the superficial outward appearance of the big towns, the inhabitants could together live a healthy and free life in their new environment and thus improve their inner selves.[66]

Slightly different houses were constructed by Heinrich Tessenow (1876–1950), who in the late 1920s would eventually become the teacher of Hitler's favourite architect Albert Speer. As a representative of a younger generation he was less committed to the neo-vernacular reaction against historicist and academic architecture. The groups of houses he designed were much more austere. The white walls were all smooth and although he used gabled roofs that gave the houses a rural appearance, these were simplified to the greatest extent possible. Haenel asserted that because of their 'puritanical character' these houses were less popular with the inhabitants.[67] Open conflict, however, arose over Tessenow's design of the Institute of Rhythmic Movement and Dance, which he built for Émile Jaques-Dalcroze, who had invented eurhythmics, a method of experiencing music through movement. This reformist music pedagogue from Geneva was invited to provide musical and rhythmic education to the youth of the colony. Tessenow designed a monumental building with abstracted classical forms that clashed with the Germanic neo-vernacular style of the rest of the garden suburb. Although a compromise was reached in removing the dance institute from its planned central place, in 1913 Riemerschmid, Muthesius and Fischer resigned from the Hellerau Building Commission. It seems that they did not so much oppose the reformist pedagogy of Jaques-Dalcroze as the austere classicist design of Tessenow.[68] Notwithstanding the difference of opinion over the building, we again see a close alliance between the new type of architecture and the movement for *Lebensreform* embodied in both the organic unity between architecture and environment that was supposed to have a benign influence upon the physical and moral well-being of the inhabitants and in the experimental teachings of Jaques-Dalcroze.

Architects such as Riemerschmid and Muthesius, and critics favourable

---

[66] Haenel, 'Hellerau' 338–43.

[67] Ibid., 327.

[68] Maciuka, *Before the Bauhaus* 242–7 and Hartmann, *Deutsche Gartenstadtbewegung* 90–4.

to the new regionalist trend, showed a remarkable international outlook and generally welcomed and even adopted reformist cultural, educational and architectural trends from abroad. However, with their garden cities they also propagated almost autarkical ideals, which they often combined with a somewhat paternalistic attitude. Thus the garden cities should be almost self-sufficient communities, with their own factories, schools, institutions, shops and entertainment. Some critics explicitly admitted that this was necessary in order to dissuade the workers to go to the town to seek pleasure and therefore be tempted by vice. At the same time, the houses should have both a flower and vegetable garden to educate the aesthetic sense of the workers and provide them with a more independent food supply. With this goal in mind it was even advised that each house should be provided with a small stable in which to house animals.[69] The authors and architects did not advocate this in the same way for the well-to-do inhabitants of the garden cities, as it is difficult to imagine that they would also grow their own food and totally refrain from attending the societies, shops and theatres of the inner city. And whereas these designers were themselves very mobile, having studied in various cities and travelled extensively, they expected the workers to develop roots in one area. Thus Haenel, for example, maintained that the schools in Hellerau and the apprenticeships in Schmidt's workshops would enable the children of the colony to follow in their fathers' footsteps.[70]

Apparently it was important to give these workers a sense of home. Apart from providing a proper house for every family, this could be done by helping the inhabitants to be proud of both their own house and the garden city as a whole. A recognisable, variegated and popular design was therefore important. A pleasant environment, green spaces and nice vistas equally mattered. Also the children should be provided for with small paths, fields and playgrounds. In a review of the garden city of Staaken near Berlin some years later, Fritz Stahl maintained that thanks to such elements, which were naturally present in German provincial towns but were now consciously designed, the children would get 'those lovely memories that a child from the big city never has'.[71]

In Hellerau the careful choice of the location and Riemerschmid's village-like layout served the same purpose. However, another crucial element seemed to be the neo-vernacular design of almost all the buildings,

---

[69]   Henrici, 'Arbeiterkolonien' 72–6.
[70]   Haenel, 'Hellerau' 338.
[71]   Fritz Stahl, 'Die Gartenstadt Staaken', *Wasmuths Monatshefte für Baukunst* (1918–19) 4–5, 137–43, especially 143.

including the factory of Schmidt's Werkstätten. Since the dwellings should also be affordable the design was done in a very sober way and not in the lavish style of the large country houses built by the same architects elsewhere. In general the houses were designed in a style that clearly referred to rural examples and they thus were provided with a steep roof, gables, shutters and pronounced chimneys. However, the reference was quite generic. Haenel thus praised Riemerschmid's houses as he gave them a homely quality by adding 'rural and rustic' elements to 'simple suburban houses'. Only Fischer seemed to try to connect with specific vernacular traditions from the region when he covered the upper storey of his country house in Hellerau with timber in a way that, according to the same critic, was inspired by traditional farm houses in the Thuringian Forest and the Ore Mountains.[72] In other German garden cities similar references to local vernacular examples were made. Thus the settlement of Gebitzendorf in Nuremberg was built in a 'cosy [*anheimelnden*] south-German style' and Staaken was a mixture of a picturesque old German town and a spacious village. Nevertheless, the references were mostly quite general and sometimes they even came from the opposite side of the Empire, when for example Paul Schmitthenner (1884–1972), a student of Riemerschmid who also was responsible for Staaken, applied 'memories of the half-timbered houses' from his native Alsace to a garden suburb of Breslau in Silesia.[73]

But what exactly, apart from mere aesthetic considerations, was the function of the regionalist style? In the case of garden cities, which were generally designed for the middle and lower classes, its purpose most probably was to attach them to a particular region and to Germany as a whole. Therefore the neo-vernacular allusions did not refer to existing states, such as Bavaria or Saxony, but to quite unspecific regions, which could encompass several states (such as Lower Germany) or refer to a very small area. Like folkloric exhibits and regionalist pavilions at world's fairs, they functioned as clearly recognisable signifiers of a common, ethnically based, but diversified *national* identity. The strengthening of a loose regional feeling seemed to be a means to reinforce the national awareness of these groups and especially to stimulate the integration of the working classes in the German Empire. This was all the more urgent as the workers

---

[72] Haenel, 'Hellerau' 326 and 330.
[73] A. Heilmeyer, 'Heimatliches im Städtebau', *Kunstwart* (February 1891) 279–80, Stahl, 'Staaken' 138 and Gustav Wolf, 'Vorstadthäuser bei Breslau, erbaut von Architekt Paul Schmitthenner', *Der Baumeister* XIII (April 1915) 53–60, especially 57.

increasingly voted for the socialist party that clearly opposed the economic system and the existing social and political structure.[74]

Furthermore, it was thought that the agglomeration of the masses in enormous towns could have negative political consequences. Living in the countryside – or at least in a spacious suburb – and adopting its traditions and habits was therefore seen as good medicine against revolutionary agitation. The rural outlook of the garden cities should stimulate this process. Living together with members of the middle and upper classes should also explicitly stimulate the co-operation between the classes, and lead to an organic and harmonious community as presumably existed in the countryside. A happy family life, a proper house with a garden and a healthy environment should convert potential revolutionaries into decent, responsible and law-abiding citizens. A nostalgic and idealised view of a harmonious countryside was therefore consciously propagated as an alternative to the conflict-ridden and cramped working-class districts of the cities.

In the case of neo-vernacular country houses and villas for the upper-middle classes the references to the traditional local architecture seem to be a bit more specific, although most architects were not very dogmatic. They did not seem to be very connected to the various regional movements, nor did they try to reinforce the identity of a particular German state. Even Schumacher, serving the free-state of Hamburg, defined his style as Hanseatic or north-German.

A new era

With the outbreak of the First World War in 1914, the context completely changed. The socialist party, contrary to the ideals of the international solidarity of the workers, sided with the Empire, so national unity seemed complete. Most civil construction projects were halted and around 1917 many architectural journals even suspended publication. Consequently the advance of regionalist architecture and the garden city ideal was postponed until after the war. However, already in August 1914 Russian troops had for a short time invaded and devastated great parts of East Prussia, and plans were needed for their reconstruction. Most architectural journals participated in the debate and they underlined the importance of a co-ordinating role for architects and city planners in both the preparation of

---

[74] Thus the SPD received 27 per cent of the votes in 1898 and almost 35 per cent in 1912.

the reconstruction plans and the actual rebuilding. Most critics also stressed the need to adopt the local building traditions and materials whenever possible. Buildings moreover had to be in harmony with the local landscape and the harsh climate. At the same time the new houses should be up to date and hygienic and preferably should be built in a very efficient and cost-cutting way. Thus standardisation was needed, although this should not lead to monotonous houses and uniform streets.[75]

Muthesius, who actively participated in this debate, even declared that although for the moment it was impossible to continue most building activities, the housing problem was as urgent as ever. As the physical and psychological health of the population was in a great part determined by the way people were housed, providing good houses for the population was a question of 'national self-preservation'. And dwellings in a good setting, with enough green space and fresh air, were of the utmost importance. This, according to Muthesius, had already become obvious before the war when only half the number of young men from the big metropolis, as compared to those of the countryside, were fit enough to serve in the army.[76]

In the circumstances of the war and the resultant shortages it was not very surprising that the authors stressed the need to provide the houses being built with a vegetable garden and a stable. Some even advocated substituting ordinary trees with fruit trees.[77] This tendency was continued in the immediate post-war period. Architectural magazines dedicated more attention than ever to the housing problem and the need to build new spacious suburbs for the lower and middle classes. Unfortunately, it was precisely during these years that the ideals of the architects and critics

[75] See, for example: Gustav Wolf, 'Wohnhausbau in Einheitsformen', *Der Baumeister* (January 1915) 29–31, W. Lindner, 'Ostpreußen', *Der Baumeister* (May 1915) 66–8, W. C. Behrendt, 'Der Wiederaufbau im Osten', *Wasmuths Monatshefte für Baukunst* (December 1914) 65–7, Hans J. Philipp, 'Zu den Abbildungen von Bauten aus dem Wiederaufbau Ostpreussens', *Wasmuths Monatshefte für Baukunst* (1919–20) 321–3, Paul Schultze-Naumburg, 'Der Wiederaufbau Ostpreuszens', *Dekorative Kunst* XVIII (February 1915) 146–50, Walter Curt Behrendt, 'Der Wiederaufbau Ostpreussens', *Dekorative Kunst* XVIII (September 1915) 380–9, C. Gomringer, 'Der Wiederaufbau der zerstörten Teile Ostpreussens', *Der Städtebau* (1915) 5–9. See also: Hartmut Frank, 'Heimatschutz und typologisches Entwerfen: Modernisierung und Tradition beim Wiederaufbau von Ostpreußen 1915–1927' in: Vittorio Lampugnani and Romana Schneider eds., *Moderne Architektur in Deutschland 1900 bis 1950: Reform und Tradition* (Stuttgart 1992) 105–33.
[76] Hermann Muthesius, 'Deutsches Bauschaffen nach dem Kriege', *Wasmuths Monatshefte für Baukunst* (1915–16) 189–93, especially 193.
[77] J. F. Haeuselmann, 'Kriegerheimstätten', *Der Baumeister* (July 1915) 83–4, Behrendt, 'Der Wiederaufbau Ostpreussens' 388, Hermann Muthesius, 'Bebauungsplan für die Kleinsiedlung Tannenwalde bei Königsberg', *Wasmuths Monatshefte für Baukunst* (1919–20) 152–5, Weidenbacher, 'Von der Siedlungstätigkeit in Augsburg: Gartenstadt Augsburg-Spickel', *Der Städtebau* (1921) 100–2.

who before 1914 had defended the new regionalist trend were surpassed by harsh reality. Already during the war many authors had concluded that the shortages and the sharply rising prices made the execution of their plans and ideals very difficult to achieve. After the war these problems continued, and housing shortages and the massive influx of refugees even increased the crisis. Some even concluded that for the moment it would be impossible to continue building single-family dwellings on a grand scale in spacious suburbs. Mass production of small apartments, the use of cheaper materials and standardisation should first mitigate the crisis.[78]

The hyperinflation during the Ruhr crisis of 1923 brought the whole German economy to a halt and in fact destroyed the last hopes of reallocating large layers of the population to neo-vernacular houses in spacious new suburbs. Most architectural journals were again suspended for over a year and when they reappeared they generally paid little attention to regionalist architecture or plans for village-like garden cities with rustic cottages. Instead they increasingly focused on new standardised building techniques and the new modernist architecture, which was actively propagated at the Bauhaus and by architects such as Walter Gropius (1883–1969) and Ludwig Mies van der Rohe (1886–1969). By 1926 most professional journals had been converted to the new gospel, although in practice most buildings were constructed in a simplified traditional style.[79]

However, there were also social and political causes for the decline of the neo-vernacular trend. The upper-middle classes had increasing difficulty in maintaining their economic status, and therefore commissions for new villas were scarce.[80] Furthermore the need to legitimise or claim a leading role in society and politics, and consequently stress the intimate bond with the national community, was far less evident. Democracy had become a fact and the leading position of this group was no longer taken for granted.

This decline in a deferential attitude towards the elite also became clear in the immediate post-war period when inhabitants rejected parts of the regionalist language the architects wanted to impose. Both Bruno

---

[78] See for example: Paul Schmitthenner, 'Die Siedlung Plaue bei Brandenburg a. H.', *Wasmuths Monatshefte für Baukunst* (1919–20) 161–73, H. de Fries, 'Wohnungsnöte und Baustoffsorgen', *Wasmuths Monatshefte für Baukunst* (1920–21) 53–5, 'Die Siedlung Cöpenick', *Wasmuths Monatshefte für Baukunst* (1920–21) 331–2, Paul Wolf, 'Städtische Kleinwohnsiedlungen in Hannover', *Wasmuths Monatshefte für Baukunst* (1921–22) 271–2 and Adolf Rading, 'Neue Kleinmiethaus-Bebauungen', *Der Städtebau* (1920) 105–14.
[79] Barbara Miller Lane, *Architecture and Politics in Germany, 1918–1945* (Cambridge 1968) 27–8, 41–69 and 125–8.
[80] Lane, *Architecture and Politics* 133.

Taut (1880–1938), a student of Fischer and a protégé of Muthesius who shortly afterwards would become an influential expressionist and modernist architect, and Paul Wolf (1879–1957), the city architect of Hanover, were confronted with fierce protests when they used striking bright colours, which according to them were traditionally applied in the region in, respectively, the garden city Falkenberg near Berlin and a new suburb in Hanover. Similarly, during the reconstruction in East Prussia the inhabitants preferred charming south-German houses instead of the local austere types.[81]

Another development which led to the decline of the garden city ideal, at least in its picturesque neo-vernacular guise, was the rise of a new generation of architects that advocated completely different solutions. Architects such as Walter Gropius propagated Le Corbusier's ideal of a metropolis with residential towers in a park-like environment, whereas more practical reformers such as Ernst May (1886–1970), the city architect of Frankfurt, and Martin Wagner (1885–1957), an influential official in the Berlin building administration, planned new green suburbs with highly functionalist apartment buildings. The streets designed by these younger architects generally were straight, the roofs became flat, concrete, steel and glass substituted local materials and references to regional particularities and building traditions were abolished in favour of a new modernist international style.[82] However, as we will see, this did not mean that regionalist architecture completely disappeared.

---

[81] 'Drei Siedlungen: Von Architekt Bruno Taut, Berlin', *Wasmuths Monatshefte für Baukunst* (1919–20) 183–5, 'Die Siedlung Laatzen bei Hannover', *Wasmuths Monatshefte für Baukunst* (1920–21) 299–300 and Fritz Stahl, 'Hans Philipp – Hermann Dernburg', *Wasmuths Monatshefte für Baukunst* (1919–20) 319–20.

[82] Lane, *Architecture and Politics* 87–125.

5

France

The new form of domestic architecture was late to arrive in France, and it seemed to have had somewhat less impact than in the German Empire. There are a variety of reasons for this. In the first place, the market for country houses and suburban cottages was smaller in France. Both industrialisation and urbanisation at the end of the nineteenth and the start of the twentieth century were slower in France than in Germany. However, the lagging demand was caused not so much by the slow urbanisation as by the previous innovations in the major French towns. During the Second Empire, an extremely ambitious programme of expropriation and slum-clearing, led by Napoleon III's prefect Haussmann, had resulted in the complete transformation of the inner city of Paris. The new, broad boulevards provided the upper classes especially with spacious and comfortable apartments. Other French cities had followed the same model, driving most of the poorer inhabitants to the outskirts by expropriating the old, cramped inner-city quarters, while the upper and middle classes moved into the luxurious apartments lining the new central boulevards. In contrast, most German towns, which lacked the possibility of expropriation on a similar scale, followed the tendency that had already become clear in England and the United States, whereby the upper and the middle classes increasingly left the towns to settle in comfortable villas or houses with gardens in the new suburbs or the surrounding countryside.[1]

Another reason for the weakness of neo-vernacular architecture was the dominance of the official École des Beaux-Arts, which attracted the best and most ambitious students of architecture. At the start, the École was controlled by the eight members of the architectural section of the Academy of Beaux-Arts, who also determined the assignments for the

---

[1] See, for example: Donald J. Olsen, *The City as a Work of Art: London, Paris, Vienna* (New Haven and London 1986) and Peter Hall, *Cities of Tomorrow: An Intellectual History of Urban Planning and Design in the Twentieth Century* (3rd edn., Oxford 2002) 48–87.

yearly competition for advanced students and awarded the Prix de Rome to the winners. Although in 1863 the control for this competition passed to the State, this did not lead to any fundamental changes. Commissions for public buildings (which were mainly issued from the central government, even for provincial projects) usually went to previous winners of the Prix de Rome, and the best of them ended up as members of the Academy. At the École des Beaux-Arts, the emphasis was put on the classical tradition and the design of monumental public buildings. During the nineteenth century, a highly eclectic and decorative 'Beaux-Arts style' came into being, which thanks to foreign students and official commissions for French architects was also highly successful abroad. The starting point of the most influential period of the École and its exuberant style was Garnier's opera house in Paris, inaugurated in 1875; its culmination was in the buildings of the 1900 International Exhibition, such as the Petit and the Grand Palais. Although in 1903 new fine arts schools were created in some provincial cities, the Parisian École continued its dominance.[2] Domestic architecture did not receive much attention at the École des Beaux-Arts as it was considered a secondary genre; this attitude did not change at the end of the nineteenth or the beginning of the twentieth century, as it did in some German academies.

Consequently, architects who specialised in the construction of villas and country houses were generally not seen as great architects. It is for this reason that most architects who built in a neo-vernacular style were not very well known, and only a few of the well-known Beaux-Arts architects occasionally built a villa in such a style.[3] The main exceptions were Jean-Louis Pascal (1837–1920) – the winner of the 1866 Prix de Rome and later a *chef d'atelier* at the École des Beaux-Arts – who in 1904 designed the regionalist château du Doux in the Corrèze, and Albert Tournaire (1862–1952) – the winner of the 1888 Prix de Rome and later official architect of the city of Paris – who at about the same time was asked by Edmond Rostand to design a villa in a Basque style (figure 10). Louis Bonnier (1856–1946) and Louis-Marie Cordonnier (1854–1940) were more active promoters of regionalist architecture and also gained fame for their work. Both built various villas and cottages in a neo-vernacular style. Louis Bonnier, who in 1895 had designed Samuel Bing's famous

<hr>

2   A. Drexler ed., *The Architecture of the École des Beaux-Arts* (New York 1977), François Loyer, *Histoire de l'architecture française de la Révolution à nos jours* (Paris 1999) 67–9 and 148–9, and Anthony Sutcliffe, *Paris: An Architectural History* (New Haven and London 1993) 79–81 and 106–10.

3   See Loyer, *Histoire de l'architecture française* 232.

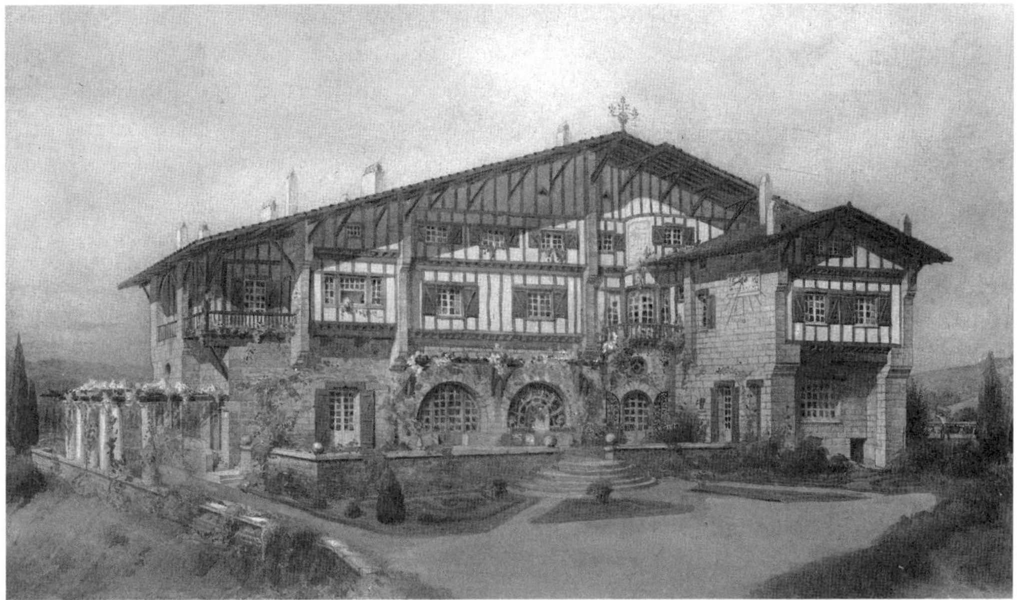

10 Albert Tournaire, Villa d'Arnaga for Edmond Rostand, 1903–6.

Parisian gallery *L'Art Nouveau*, was architect of the city of Paris. In 1902, he was the main author of the revised Paris building regulations, which permitted the break-up of the traditional continuous façades, thus allowing more room for fantasy, variation and picturesque buildings. Cordonnier became the main creator of the neo-Flemish style in France after he returned to Lille having studied at the École de Beaux-Arts. In 1905, he was the highly contested winner of the international competition for the design of the Peace Palace in The Hague, the seat of the International Court of Justice.[4]

Another, related factor was the absence, until quite late, of a proper platform for the new domestic architecture. In both France and Germany, architectural journals mainly restricted themselves to providing practical information on technical developments, new legal regulations, and reports on conferences, books and official commissions. They did not generally publish extensive or outspoken reviews of individual buildings, nor did they comment extensively on stylistic issues. In the German Empire, however, recently created magazines on the applied

---

[4] Ibid., 229–33. His design was especially criticised as being too traditional, at which especially the famous Dutch architect Berlage and his followers protested fiercely. See for Bonnier also: Sutcliffe, *Paris* 120–6 and Bernard Marrey, *Louis Bonnier 1856–1946* (Liège 1988). See for Cordonnier also: Benoît Mihail, *Une Flandre à la française: L'identité régionale à l'épreuve du modèle républicain* (Saintes 2006).

arts – particularly *Dekorative Kunst*, which from 1897 onwards tried to follow the standards set by the widely read English monthly *The Studio* – dedicated considerable attention to architecture and reviewed many new country houses. In France, this was not so often the case, and only *Art et Décoration*, a monthly founded in 1897, published the occasional article on French domestic architecture. Things changed only after the appearance in 1906 of the fortnightly *La Vie à la Campagne* (Life in the Countryside) – which was modelled on the English *Country Life* – as Louis Sézille (1881–1955), the young head of the magazine's architectural service, began a real campaign to stimulate a reform of domestic architecture.[5] This somewhat curious periodical was aimed at affluent inhabitants of the countryside and at those who wanted to live in similar rural circumstances in seaside resorts or new suburbs. It offered information on gardening, plants, animals, agricultural inventions and machinery, as well as on such sports as tennis, field hockey and skiing, and on how to build and decorate a country house and cottage. As it was aimed more at possible clients than at the artistic elite, it probably had less impact on architectural debates than did the journals on decorative arts.

Furthermore, whereas in Britain and Germany the new domestic revival was intimately connected with a thorough innovation of the applied arts, this was lacking in France. There was no structural effort to try to bring together artists and artisans such as the Arts and Crafts movement in England, and the Werkbund in Germany, nor in this period was there a serious reform of the arts and crafts schools, such as had been instigated in Germany. Thus, after the exhibition of decorative artists from Munich at the Parisian *Salon d'Automne* in 1910 had caused a sensation, a German critic commented that whereas France was still in the lead in literature, painting and sculpture, this was not the case in architecture or the applied arts. The artistic revolution in these domains, which in Germany had unseated historicism, remained almost totally ignored and unacknowledged in France. According to this critic, the innovating decorative restraint of contemporary German artists was misunderstood and even valued negatively as a 'direct emanation of the sad German being'.[6]

Although not all French authors endorsed this judgement of France's position, many were aware that the situation of domestic architecture and interior decoration in France was not as favourable as it was in some other

<hr>

[5] Jean-Claude Vigato, *L'Architecture régionaliste: France, 1890–1950* (Paris 1994) 36–51 and Loyer, *Histoire de l'architecture française* 235–6.

[6] Wilhelm Michel, 'Der Deutsche Stil', *Deutsche Kunst und Dekoration* (1910–11) 228–34, especially 234.

countries. For example, in 1912 an anonymous critic declared that the problematic state of the applied arts in France was mainly a result of the abolition of the guilds during the Revolution. National traditions had been broken and instead of a revolution, France now needed a new evolution, in which artists and artisans would try to re-establish the lost bonds with ancient techniques and traditions. Another problem in France was the disdain with which the 'minor arts' were treated. The author suggested that artists and architects should show the way by designing ornaments and furniture, and by guiding the artisans. He also praised the recent initiative to organise a great Exhibition of Decorative Arts, which was to be held in Paris in 1916 and was intended to lead to a revival of the French applied arts.[7] The First World War, however, delayed the exhibition, which would open its doors only in 1925.

Similar remarks appeared in the journal *L'Architecture Moderne*. The critic Pascal Forthuny added that the traditional regional crafts were disappearing in France, thus affecting the smaller, local industries. The German Empire had shown that this problem could be remedied by improving technical education and schools for the applied arts.[8] Even during the First World War, Léandre Vaillat, one of the principle defenders of regionalist art in France, repeated the argument that France should learn from its enemy and particularly from the Werkbund and the intermediary office for applied arts in Munich, which brought producers into contact with appropriate designers.[9]

In general, French critics also signalled the progress that had been made in the design of country houses particularly in England and Germany. Nevertheless, positive comments about English country houses, some of the books published by Hermann Muthesius and the 'movement of architectural renovation' in which he played a prominent role, appeared only quite late from 1907 onwards.[10] In 1911, Sézille even openly

[7] 'Vers un style contemporaine', *La Vie à la Campagne* (15 June 1912) 388.

[8] Marc Croisilles, 'Vers l'art social', *L'Architecture Moderne* I, 1 (1909) 3–5 and Pascal Forthuny, 'À la recherche des beaux métiers régionaux', *L'Architecture Moderne* (June and July 1913) 221–2 and 267–70, especially 222. See for a more extensive analysis: Kenneth E. Silver, *Esprit de Corps: The Art of the Parisian Avant-Garde and the First World War, 1914–1925* (Princeton and London 1989) 171–4 and Nancy J. Troy, *Modernism and the Decorative Arts in France: Art Nouveau to Le Corbusier* (New Haven and London 1991) 52–79.

[9] Léandre Vaillat, *La cité renaissante* (Paris 1918) 19–29 and 93–102.

[10] M.P. Verneuil, 'Maisons de campagne', *Art et Décoration* (1907) I, 91–6, M.P. Verneuil, 'Maisons de campagne anglaises', *Art et Décoration* (1914–19) 21–8, 'Recent English Domestic Architecture, par Mervyn E. Macartney', *L'Architecte* (June 1909) 45–7, 'Landhaus und Garten, par H. Muthesius', *L'Architecte* (July 1907) 59–60 and 'Maisons de campagne de Hermann Muthesius', *L'Architecte* (January 1913) 4–6.

admitted the inferiority of French country house design, especially as compared to England, Belgium and Holland, thus omitting Germany. He complained:

> Whereas France, the country of Art par excellence, sends its architects to foreign countries to execute a great number of their big monuments, state palaces and public buildings that consecrate the success of our academies, she hardly cultivates with any of them the delicate taste of the private home.

According to Sézille, this was mainly due to the gross neglect of domestic architecture at the official establishments of architectural education.[11] In the opening article of the new monthly *L'Architecture Moderne*, which appeared in 1909, Marc Croisilles suggested that the glorious past and rich architectural heritage of France was in fact an obstacle to moving away from historicism. He asserted that the weakness of the French 'movement of regeneration' could mainly be explained by the burden of a very rich past and the 'excessive attachment to the classical styles and the written law', referring both to the dominance of the classically inspired Beaux Arts style and to the abstract and theoretical education that architects received. Croisilles considered it easier to develop a new, free and contemporary style in the Nordic countries, because of their 'heritage of a less glorious and less weighty past'.[12]

The weak position of French regionalist architecture and some of its differences from German domestic architecture also came in for comment in the artistic and architectural press of the period. Because France lacked the strong suburban development that Germany was undergoing, the country houses that were reviewed were generally secondary residences. In general, these houses were affordable only to a rich clientele, and in some ways differed from their foreign counterparts. These differences were noticed by the critics, although generally the comparison was made with Great Britain. In a review of an exhibition of recent English architecture that was held in Paris in May 1914, the author censured the fact that in the new English suburban houses the main living space was no longer the drawing room, meant to receive guests, but the hall, which should be the nucleus of private family life. This was in contrast to French habits, by which he meant those of the upper classes. At about the same time, a similar remark was made in a review of a new French book on English villas and

---

[11]   L. Sézille, 'Quelques maisons de campagne françaises', *La Vie à la Campagne* (15 June 1911) 388–92, especially 388.
[12]   Croisilles, 'Vers l'art social' 4.

cottages. Because most English cottages were small and meant to provide for an intimate family life, most of them were cheap and did not have space for servants. To be without servants, according to the author, was unthinkable in France. Also the elimination of a basement for provisions and especially for wine would be out of the question on the French housing market. The necessity of a basement was probably also connected with the space that was needed for the *calorifère*, the sizeable heating apparatus. The anonymous author also thought that, for the moment, it would be improbable that the French public would accept dissymmetric plans, steep and complicated stairways and matchboarded bedrooms.[13]

The English cottage model was widely accepted in the German Empire, but most of the French country houses that were reviewed were quite large and generally had a basement as well as several rooms for servants. And in contrast to Germany, where the architects generally also supervised or even designed the inner decoration to harmonise with the exterior, in France the rooms were often still done in a neo style. This was the case, for example, in almost all the villas that were discussed in a special issue of *La Vie à la Campagne* that was dedicated to the Norman seaside resort of Deauville, whose famous horse races made it a favourite destination of the Parisian upper classes. From about the turn of the century most new villas were executed in a somewhat exuberant, neo-Norman architecture. However, most interiors were done in the fashionable Louis XV, Louis XVI or Empire style, or at least contained pieces of furniture in one of these neo styles, which would be unthinkable in a villa designed by Riemerschmid or Muthesius.[14]

Villas and country houses

Although weaker, the new domestic architecture did become fashionable in France, and the regionalist discourse could be found in the specialised press and was probably even more outspoken. Contrary to Germany, architects born in the 1860s would only start to propagate regionalism in the 1920s, whereas most of its early advocates, such as Sézille, were born around 1880. Some of the architectural critics were well aware that the

---

13 Charles du Bus, 'Deux aspects de l'art urbain', *La Gazette des Beaux-Arts* XII (August 1916) 368–91, especially 375 and 'Cent cottages et villas anglais, adaptation Française par J.H. Verrey', *L'Architecte* (March 1914) 21–2. See for differences in urban planning: Anthony Sutcliffe, *Towards the Planned City: Germany, Britain, the United States and France 1870–1914* (New York 1981) 134–62 and 189–94.
14 'Les villas et les jardins de Deauville', *La Vie à la Campagne* (15 July 1912) 32–64, especially 48–64.

regionalist movement already existed in other domains and understood that it had now started to influence architecture as well. In 1912, Vaillat, who also belonged to the younger age group, observed in an article in *L'Art et les Artistes* that regionalism had become fashionable: 'These "regionalist" ideas spread in commerce, in industry, rather too little, a little in literature and the arts, and begin to be disseminated in architecture.' Nevertheless, he also remarked that they still were 'not perfectly understood'. Regionalism should not be a mask or a decor, he argued, but could only be fruitfully applied after carefully studying 'the provincial facts'. Until recently, architects 'indiscriminately constructed Provençal houses in Brittany, houses from the Basque Country in Normandy, Breton houses in Provence, and in Savoy, houses from everywhere.'[15] Others critics agreed that building in a neo-vernacular style that did not correspond with the region and mixing elements from various regions in one building was a ridiculous practice. The resulting pretentious and vulgar villas were a blot on the landscape.[16]

Vaillat also suggested a remedy, which was very similar to the regionalist recipes being prescribed in Germany. According to him, architects should know that 'the rural house corresponded to certain permanent laws of climate, temperature, soil, that these physical conditions had not changed substantially, and that by consequence they [the architects] had just to pay attention to the models that were proposed to them by the farmers' architecture.' Therefore, an architect had first to study the relationship between the physical conditions of a certain region or province and its traditional architecture.[17]

How exactly an architect should adopt the existing rural traditions was explained by Louis Sézille in his contributions to *La Vie à la Campagne*. In June 1911, for example, he gave a sort of manual for building a good country house. The first task was to choose an appropriate site that corresponded to the personal taste of the commissioner and assured a good orientation, adequate conditions and a pleasant surrounding. On this site, the architect should find a 'place where, with the best orientation for the living rooms, one discovers the best point of view' undisturbed by possible neighbours. The rooms should be neither too cold nor too hot,

---

15 Léandre Vaillat, 'La Maison en Savoie', *L'Art et les Artistes* VIII (October 1912) 37–41, especially 37–8.
16 L. Sézille, 'La Vraie façade de la maison de campagne', *La Vie à la Campagne* (15 February 1908) 120, Charles Plumet, 'L'Architecture et le paysage', *L'Art et les Artistes* (July–August 1907) 208–12 and 263–7, especially 209 and 263–4.
17 Vaillat, 'La Maison en Savoie' 38.

and depending on the region should be protected from the tropical sun, storms, snow or violent rain showers. The next step was to design the plan, which should not simply be derived from the façade. The layout of the rooms should take into account their future use and they should be related to each other. Instead of a bloodless succession of rectangular rooms all of the same height, it was better to design with more freedom to form an attractive but harmonious ensemble. Communication between the rooms should be logical and easy; there should be enough windows to admit sufficient daylight, while taking into account the future placement of the furniture. Before completing the design of the basement and the attic, one should first continue with the façades.[18]

Having designed a plan that conformed strictly to the practical needs of the client, it was logical, according to Sézille, to create a façade that was adapted to the lines and colouration of the landscape. The architect should try to reconnect with ancient building traditions. But as the plan was modern, assuring up-to-date comfort, an exact copy would be impossible. The silhouette, the materials and the colours should be in harmony with both the natural surroundings and the local traditions. A last element was the garden, which should be modest and connect the house with the landscape, forming a homogeneous whole.[19]

How this recipe would work out in practice was made clear by Maurice Pillard Verneuil, a decorative artist and the main applied art critic of *Art et Décoration*. In 1910, he wrote that he had dreamt of designing a welcoming and comfortable house for himself, but that he had finally decided to ask a professional, Louis Sézille, to design one for him (figures 11–12). He wanted a clear separation between the part dedicated to work – consisting of an atelier-hall, an office, a small drawing-room and a library – and the rooms meant for family life. The vestibule and the staircase isolated the two parts from each other. As Verneuil needed tranquillity for his work, the playroom would be at the opposite end of the house and have easy access to a part of the garden that was especially reserved for the children. The interior was to be connected with the outside by a great variety of openings on all sides. These were intended to let in daylight and fresh air, and to provide a view over the surrounding countryside and the carefully designed garden. The exterior lacked accessory ornamentation and was reduced to the essence: walls and roofs. However, thanks to a well-proportioned distribution of the masses, a picturesque silhouette and a judicious and harmonious use

18 Sézille, 'Quelques maisons de campagne' 388.
19 Ibid., 390–1.

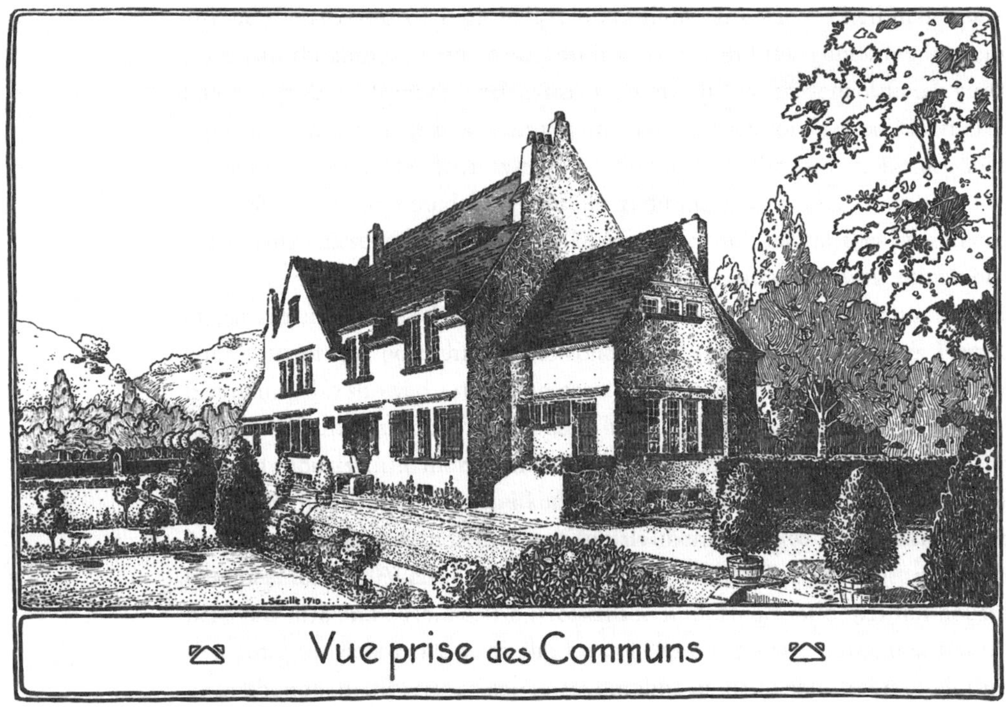

11 Louis Sézille, House of Maurice Pillard Verneuil, Paris, around 1910. The atelier-hall, office, small drawing-room and library are on the left side of the main entrance and on its right are the living rooms. The small door on the right gives access to the children's playroom.

of colour, the house indisputably made an artistic impression. Because of its extreme simplicity and rustic appearance, the house fitted well into its rural surroundings and the author preferred to live, as he expressed it, in a comfortable barn than in a pretentious castle where a pleasant interior was sacrificed to a highly ornamented façade. Finally, the house was built from locally available natural materials, such as whitewashed sandstone and red roof tiles, and the unity between house and garden was stressed by placing flower boxes on the steps and under the windows.[20]

The interconnection between garden and interior was even more necessary in summer residences and other holiday homes. These were generally provided with balconies, loggias, verandas and bow windows to provide views and make it easy to access the exterior and, especially, the garden. Flower boxes, roses and climbers were intended to make the transition from house to garden almost imperceptible, as Sézille made clear in the programme for the construction of a cheap summer cottage just outside Paris, published in *La Vie à la Campagne*. For temporary stays, he argued, the inhabitants did not need the same high level of comfort as they

20 M.P. Verneuil, 'Ma Maison', *Art et Décoration* (1910) II, 65–75.

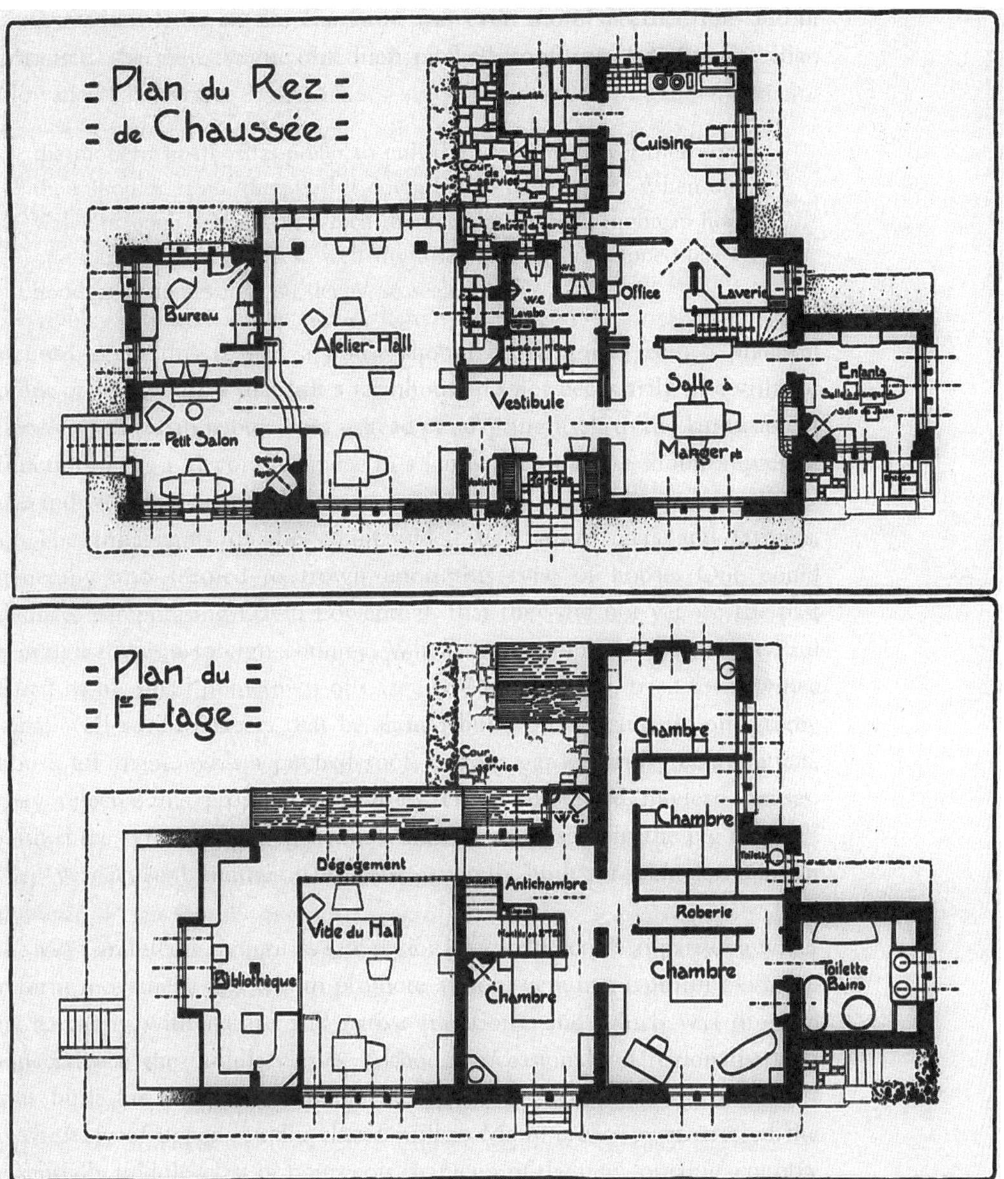

12 Louis Sézille, House of Verneuil, Paris, plan.

did in their modern apartments in town. Thus, instead of a drawing room for ceremonial receptions it was more important to have a covered terrace. Although other critics had warned that this would not be acceptable to French clients, Sézille wrote that the centre of the house could consist of a 'big common room, a kind of Hall, which indiscriminately functioned as dining room, drawing room and office'. This room would be well lit and surrounded by the terrace, which should have a well-protected corner, where a seat, a bench and a table could be installed and where the inhabitants could sit and read or have their meal.[21]

Other authors made similar recommendations for the construction of country houses, to be used either as permanent residences or as holiday homes. Generally, they also stressed, as Muthesius had done in Germany, that the exterior should reflect the interior. The distribution of the various rooms should be easily discernible from the outside 'by the relationship between solids and voids, the movement of the façades without gables, the form of roofs, the location of the openings and the fashion of the dormer windows'.[22] At the same time, the house should provide a pleasant view from both inside and outside. In brief, the rhetoric of these architectural reformers was very similar to that of their German colleagues. The honesty and simplicity of the design and the intimate relationship between interior and exterior were stressed; while the architect should take into account the wishes and particularities of the client, the surrounding landscape and local building traditions.

Nonetheless, the regionalist component in this type of domestic architecture was more pronounced in France than in Germany. Louis Sézille, apart from giving some blueprints for a modern country house, also started a campaign in *La Vie à la Campagne* to promote buildings in a specific regional style. Between December 1907 and January 1910, he gave concrete examples of a country house or cottage for seven different regions of France, publishing articles on Touraine, Normandy, the Côte d'Azur, Alsace, the Basque Country, the Jura and the department du Nord. Each was accompanied by a drawing in perspective and a plan of the ground floor and the first floor, all drawn by the author himself.[23]

In these articles, Sézille made clear that a country house should be adapted to the local geographical and climatic circumstances. His design

---

[21] L. Sézille, 'Un pied-a-terre aux environs de Paris', *La Vie à la Campagne* (1 April 1908) 210–11.

[22] Collin, 'Ce que doit être la maison de campagne', *La Vie à la Campagne* (15 September 1907) 166–7, 'Le Charme des logiques demeures régionales', *La Vie à la Campagne* (15 June 1914) 359–60 and Gabriel Mourey, 'Une maison de campagne: Projet de MM. A. Laverrière et E. Monod', *Art et Décoration* (1903), II 316–21.

[23] 'Une maison de campagne en Touraine', 'Reconstitution d'une gentilhommière normande', 'Une maison blanche sur la Côte d'Azur', 'Une maison forestière en Alsace', 'Une maison en Pays Basque', 'Une maison dans le Jura' and 'Une maison de campagne pour la region du Nord'. All written by Louis Sézille and published in *La Vie à la Campagne*, respectively (1 December 1907) 335; (15 June 1908) 343–4; (1 January 1909) 29–30; (1 March 1909) 149–50; (1 September 1909) 153–4; (1 November 1909) 283–4; (15 January 1910) 59–60.

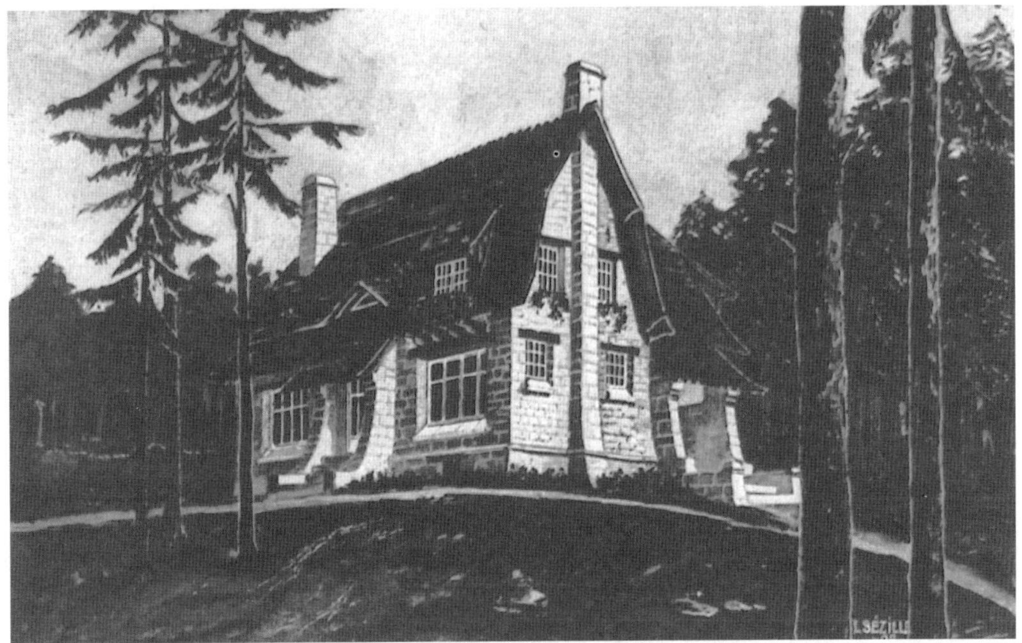

13 Louis Sézille, A house in the forest, Alsace, 1909.

for a house to be built on a slope in a spruce forest near Hohneck, Alsace (figure 13) was a monolithic but homogeneous cottage with walls of locally available granite, wood and tiles. He said that the roof was very plain in order to avoid hollows where the wind could amass snow, pushing it under the tiles and thus causing serious damage. It was pitched to encourage the snow to slide off it. The lower part was less inclined in order to slow the snow down before it slid off the roof, and to cast it further from the walls when it did slide off. The porch was entirely sheltered by a roof, and side walls protected it from gusts of wind. The snow could therefore not accumulate in front of the door. The drawing-room or hall and the dining-room occupied the side that faced the valley. With an eye to the interminable winter evenings, both side walls were provided with a fireplace, which had a soft bench on both sides. Thus, in all its aspects the house gave an impression of fitting perfectly in its natural surroundings, while at the same time protecting the inhabitants from the elements.[24]

This conscious adaptation to local circumstances was not a theoretical exercise carried out by an eccentric critic, but something that was put into practice by architects. Probably one of the first to apply these principles

[24] Louis Sézille, 'Une maison forestière en Alsace', *La Vie à la Campagne* (1 March 1909) 149–50.

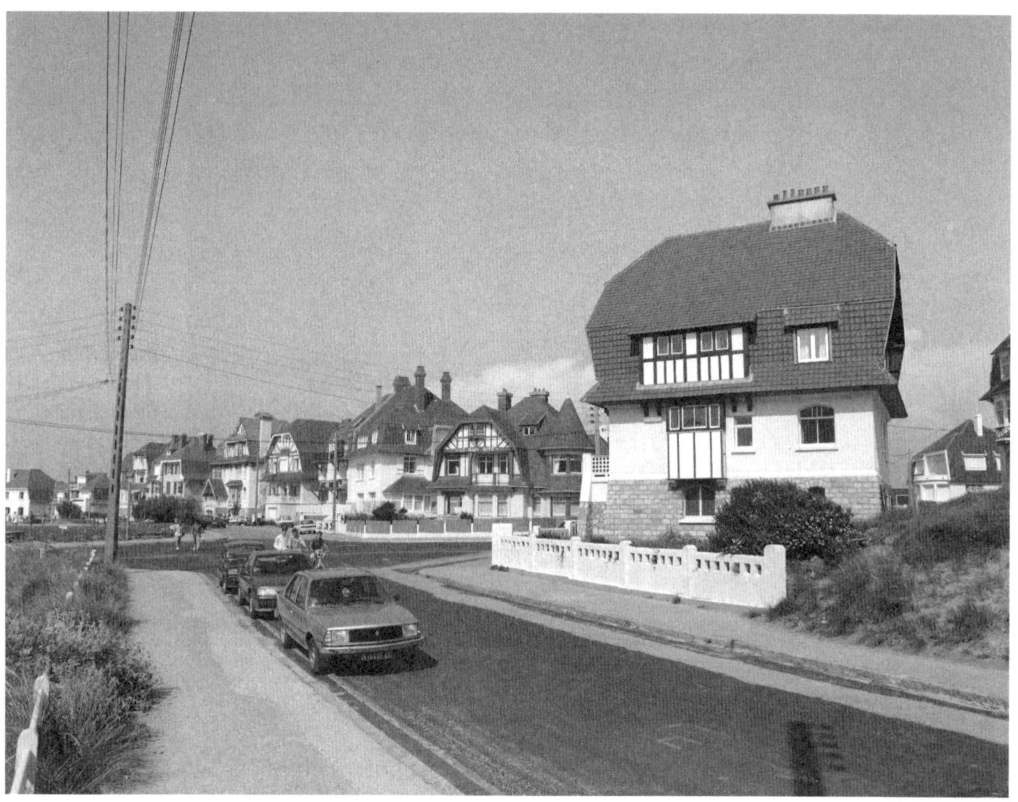

14 Louis-Marie Cordonnier, Villa Wilhelmine, built for himself around 1908, Hardelot. Most of the other villas, facing the tennis-court on the left (not visible on this photo from the 1980s), were also constructed by him.

was the Parisian architect Louis Bonnier, who in 1891 built four cottages for members of his family at Ambleteuse, on the Channel coast just north of Boulogne-sur-Mer.[25] These 'small familiar cottages' in an unpretentious style were constructed in the dunes, next to the sea. Their orientation was therefore of the utmost importance, as remarked by the critic who reviewed these holiday homes more than a decade later. The inhabitants were to gain maximum profit from the spectacular view of the sea and the interior was to receive sufficient direct sunlight. On the other hand, the projecting pitched roof was designed to protect the house from rain showers and strong winds. Not only did Bonnier fulfil these requirements, but by using local materials and a fortunate choice of colours, and by perpetuating the 'character of the local architecture', he also integrated these highly picturesque buildings into their privileged natural decor.[26]

[25] Loyer maintains that they were inspired by the American shingle style: Loyer, *Histoire de l'architecture française* 229–31.

[26] Charles Saunier, 'Deux cottages de Louis Bonnier', *Art et Décoration* (1907), I 187–92. See also: Plumet, 'L'Architecture et le paysage' 210–1.

Less than 20 km to the south, Louis-Marie Cordonnier followed the example of Bonnier by building a whole range of villas (one of which was meant for himself) around a tennis court in the new seaside resort of Hardelot. The villas reflected the barren dune landscape: they were built in local materials, and were solid and rude (figure 14). According to the author of an extensive review in *La Vie à la Campagne*, they were either completely or partially inspired by traditional buildings in the neighbouring areas.[27] The protruding roofs seemed to protect the houses from strong winds, whereas the balconies, bow windows and terraces provided a view of the sea and facilitated the taking of a sun or an air bath during almost every part of the day or year.

In Brittany the way houses were traditionally constructed was also determined by harsh circumstances. Generally, according to Vaillat in *L'Art et les Artistes*, the houses were oriented with their backs towards the dominant wind direction. Only the opposite side had a few small openings, giving the houses a hermetic and mysterious air. The walls of local granite and the thatched roofs accentuated their sturdy character. Horizontal lines dominated these constructions and the landscape, and their silhouettes were simple. The interior and the furniture had the same austerity. Although the overall impression was one of reserve and resignation, this harmony with the surrounding nature, the author felt, should be preserved when designing new buildings.[28]

However, houses should not only provide shelter against snow, rain and wind, but also – particularly in the south of France – protect the inhabitants from heat and the sun. Louis Bonnier, for example, also built a villa with local materials in Cagnes, near Nice (figure 15). Its thick walls were meant to protect the inhabitants not from the cold coming off the Channel, but from the intense heat of a Provençal summer. A covered terrace, with a view of the Mediterranean, made it possible to be outside in reasonable comfort throughout almost the entire year.[29]

Why ancient building traditions should be respected was clearly explained by Sézille in his article on a house in the Basque Country. In their construction techniques, the Basque artists and artisans of the past had perfected their own characteristic way of building, thus creating a style that was perfectly suited to the local geographical and climatic conditions. They

27 C. Boutibonne, 'Cottages modernes d'une robuste structure', *La Vie à la Campagne* (15 June 1913) 381–406.
28 Léandre Vaillat, 'La Maison en Bretagne', *L'Art et les Artistes* (March 1913) 281–4.
29 Plumet, 'L'Architecture et le paysage' 209–10 and Sézille, 'Quelques maisons de campagne' 392.

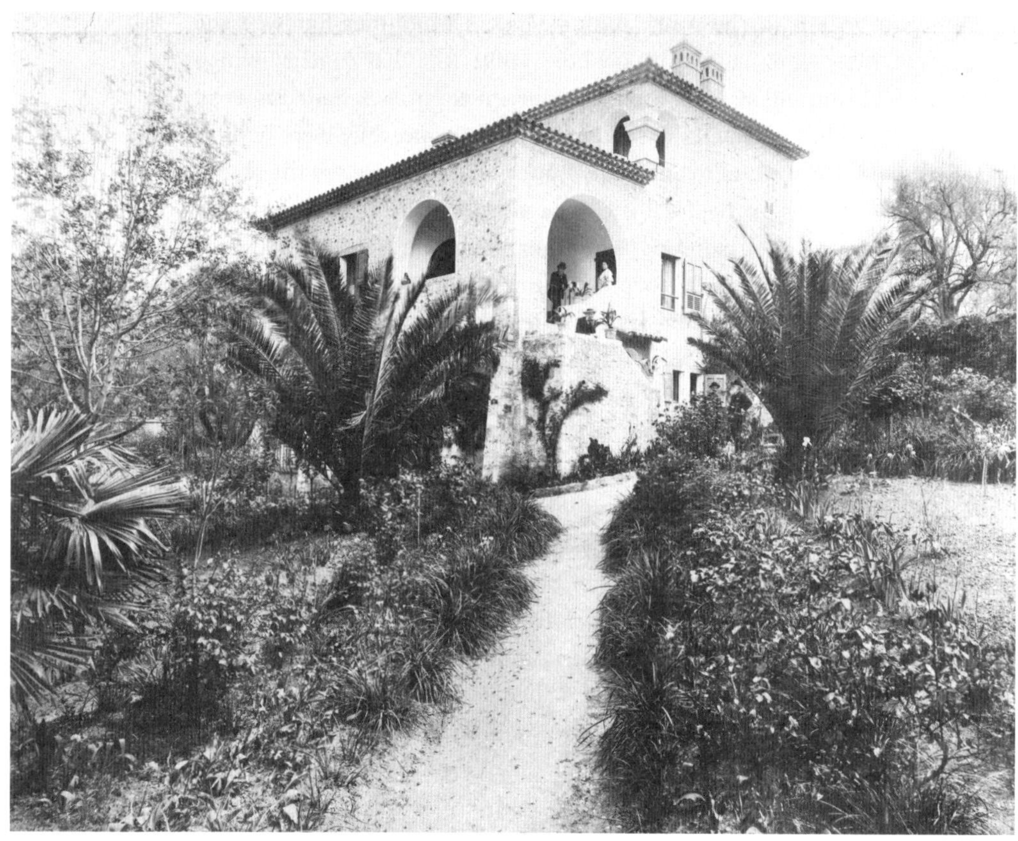

15 Louis Bonnier, Villa La Bégude, Cagnes, 1900–22.

had succeeded in doing this by assimilating only a few useful inventions and innovations from elsewhere, never copying them or completely adopting foreign styles. According to the critic:

> they had remained themselves, by only putting their acquired science in contact with foreigners in order to perfect their way of working. But never would this manner, this very special genre, disappear and give way to these sole foreign methods. And this way the artists, perfecting ceaselessly their local methods, have arrived at the mastery that surprises us: this is a precious lesson, and to equal them we thus have to imitate them in their way of working and of studying.

Consequently, it would be logical for contemporary architects who were building in the Basque Country to follow these traditions.[30]

[30] Louis Sézille, 'Une maison en Pays Basque', *La Vie à la Campagne* (1 September 1909) 153–4.

Sézille admitted that adopting ancient traditions could in some cases lead to a less logical solution. In his article on Normandy, he lamented the poor condition of the forests in France, which had led to a rise in the price of timber. A modern Norman gentry-house with a timber framework would therefore cost about one-third more than a current construction. Nonetheless, he maintained that 'if you wish to realise an interesting artistic effect you could not do better than adopt this eminently French genre of constructing in the old Norman style'. There were alternative and cheaper ways to create the same effect, but these were severely condemned by the author. Timber framing was not 'a vulgar ornament that one could create by adding strips of wood to a wall' or produce by 'an invented combination executed in plaster'. Nevertheless, feigning timber framing had become quite a common practice, as made clear by the review of villas in Deauville where only one out of eight villas in Norman style had a real timber framework.[31]

The need to faithfully follow ancient rural examples did not necessitate architects copying old buildings. All critics admitted to the need to adapt the new country houses to present needs and to equip them with modern comforts. Vaillat made this perfectly clear when he described the traditional farmhouses in Brittany. New constructions could never be exact copies, as nobody would put a 'dunghill in front of his door, nor all sleep in the same room, live on tamped soil, never use forks, only eat porridge, allow chickens in to the kitchen, and have bunk beds'. Nevertheless, according to Vaillat, it was always possible to let oneself be inspired by these 'ancient rural houses, which by instinct submit themselves to the physical necessities' that have not changed since prehistoric times.[32]

Surprisingly, not all the country houses proposed by Sézille were inspired by these almost instinctive and naive vernacular traditions. In the south of France, he argued, a house should have thick walls and few windows to protect it from the heat of the sun and it should be located in a well-aired place, preferably with some shadow. The best adaptation to this type of climate, he argued, had been the Roman villa. In his design for a white villa on the Côte d'Azur, he therefore adopted the plan of a

---

[31] Louis Sézille, 'Reconstitution d'une gentilhommière normande', *La Vie à la Campagne* (15 June 1908) 343–4 and 'Les villas de Deauville' 48–64. According to François Loyer, the rise in the price of traditional building materials and construction techniques is one of the main explanations for the decline of 'pure' regionalism: Loyer, *Histoire de l'architecture française*, 236–8 and Bernard Toulier, 'L'Assimilation du régionalisme dans l'architecture balnéaire', in: François Loyer and Bernard Toulier eds., *Le Régionalisme, architecture et identité* (Paris 2001) 96–110, especially 103.
[32] Vaillat, 'La Maison en Bretagne' 284.

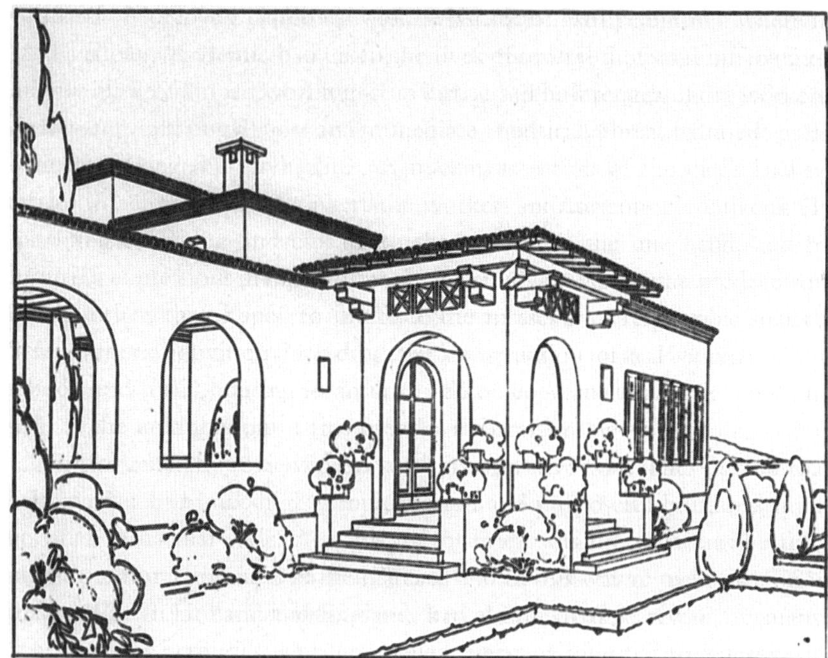

16 Adolphe Thiers, A villa in the Roussillon, around 1920.

Roman villa: 'an interior courtyard preceded by a peristyle and flanked by different reception rooms and terraces.' He even maintained that in the northern parts of France, 'the absence of such a brilliant civilisation as the Latin epoch' had forced the architects to develop new forms that were inspired by the primitive vernacular models. In the south it was not necessary to do new research, as the simple, antique forms could be adopted almost completely. They would need some modification only in the decoration of the details.[33]

A few years after the First World War, another critic made similar comments in his review of a villa in the Roussillon (figure 16), presenting rural architecture from antiquity as an inspiring native tradition for the south of France. The architect, Adolphe Thiers (1878–1938), had been inspired by medieval and Roman traditions to adapt the villa to the climate and to use materials and methods of construction that were still familiar to the local workers. In this way, he had produced a building like those that 'were erected in Gallia until the invasions of the Barbarians'.[34]

[33] Louis Sézille, 'Une maison blanche sur la Côte d'Azur', *La Vie à la Campagne* (1 January 1909) 29–30.
[34] Lionel Landry, 'Une villa dans le Roussillon', *Art et Décoration* (1922), II 27–32, especially 32.

Such a positive remark about classical antiquity, although referring to rural architecture, was very hard to find in reviews of a German country house and, as we have seen, Tessenow's classicist design for Hellerau was fiercely criticised by Riemerschmid, Muthesius and Fischer. Thus, whereas the Mediterranean heritage of classical antiquity was cherished as proper and native in parts of France, in Germany references were generally made to vernacular architecture of a presumably pure German or Germanic origin. This difference might also explain why in France more stress was put on the specific regional character of the new constructions. By also appropriating the Roman heritage, the variety in vernacular constructions seems to be greater than in the German Empire or England. Whereas vernacular constructions in the north, east and west – such as the typical mountain constructions in the Alpine regions, the buildings made of brick in the north and of granite in Brittany, and the half-timbered buildings in different styles in such dispersed regions as Alsace, Normandy and the Basque Country – should mainly protect the inhabitants from the wind, rain, cold and snow, in the south, the Mediterranean building traditions (which could refer both to medieval precedents and to classical antiquity) were primarily aimed at providing shelter from the heat and blazing sun. This probably caused a greater awareness of fundamental regional differences, whereas in Germany critics often restricted themselves to making a general reference to the need to adapt a building to the climate, natural surroundings and building traditions, without specifying the particular characteristics of a certain region or its vernacular traditions.

Another reason for the more pronounced regional awareness in France was the growing aversion to the country's strongly centralised administration. Official buildings, including those in the provinces, were closely controlled by a council of the central government, and until 1903 a thorough architectural education was available only in Paris.[35] The situation was quite different in the German Empire. Although Germany had been unified in 1871, the former states and their administrations remained in place. In artistic and educational matters, rivalry between the various princes and administrations continued to exist and the central government had no formal power in these domains. Local differences and traditions thus continued to exist. Therefore, in Germany there was no need to protect regional traditions from an encroaching, centralising state.[36]

---

[35] Daniel Le Couédic, *Les Architectes et l'idée bretonne 1904–1945: D'un renouveau des arts à la renaissance d'une identité* (Saint-Brieuc 1995) 34–49 and Vigato, *L'Architecture régionaliste*, 16–17.

[36] Nonetheless, regions that had been absorbed into another state (e.g. the Palatinate,

The French critics who defended the new domestic architecture attacked not so much historicist and eclectic architecture (both of which they disliked), as their like-minded German colleagues did, as the strong centralisation that existed in France and was embodied by the dominance of the École des Beaux-Arts. The main problem was that the official architectural education did not take regional differences into account. Or as Pascal Forthuny formulated it in 1913: 'There is unity of doctrine that began in Paris, was promulgated in Paris, is centrally taught in Paris, and that imposes upon all the young people who want to become an architect, the same discipline and the same path to the consecrating diploma.' He spoke of 'the inflexible bible where the law of lines and volumes is continued according to the glorious consecrated examples'. This only resulted in 'cliché' buildings.[37] More than ten years earlier, in a review of the country house that the poet and art critic Gabriel Mourey (1865–1943) had designed for himself, the decorative artist, architect and critic Charles Plumet (1861–1928) had condemned the 'immobilised catechism' of the École des Beaux-Arts in similar terms, ridiculing the 'sacrosanct principles that constituted the spirit and the letter of the official education'. In 1910, Sézille criticised the École des Beaux-Arts, where instead of teaching how to build a modern, logical and sincere house, they still focused on the principal façade, preached symmetry and upheld superfluous ornamentation.[38]

In 1903, Mourey – the director of *L'Art décoratif* who defended the regionalist art of Simon and Cottet – criticised the architects who remained 'slaves of the traditions', who drew their inspiration only from the 'examples of the past, from the graveyard of the dead truths'. They were probably excellent 'copyists', but they were not 'creators, because they never create something from nature or from life'. Architects therefore had to free themselves of the dead weight of their academic education and the examples of 'great' architecture which, as Forthuny stated, had in any case been imported from abroad. Instead, he continued, artists and architects should try to reconnect with vernacular traditions. After all, the work of the ancient artisans was spontaneous, instinctive and free.[39]

which had been absorbed into Bavaria) occasionally opposed centralising tendencies, thus not of the Empire but of the smaller states. See: Celia Applegate, *A Nation of Provincials: The German Idea of Heimat* (Berkeley 1990).

[37] Forthuny, 'Des beaux métiers régionaux' 268–9.

[38] Charles Plumet, 'Une maison de campagne', *Art et Décoration* (1902), II 198–200 and L. Sézille, 'Trois cottages aux environs de Paris', *Art et Décoration* (1910) 25–31, especially 26 and 30. See also: Plumet, 'L'Architecture et le paysage' 211–12.

[39] Mourey, 'Une maison de campagne' 316 and Forthuny, 'Des beaux métiers régionaux' 268.

Compared with academic practice, the architecture these critics proposed was free and the result of a creative process. According to them, however, artistic freedom should not be totally unbounded, as the buildings should be adapted to local climatic and natural circumstances as well as to existing traditions. Consequently, Art Nouveau architecture, for which the English term 'modern style' was mostly used, was condemned as being too eccentric and exaggerated. It was the outcome not of a long process but of a radical break with all traditions.[40]

In general, as in Germany, the new domestic architecture was seen by its practitioners and propagandists as a modern and highly innovative artistic movement. Innovative architects and artists therefore did not hesitate to build or to commission a house in a neo-vernacular style. For example, Bonnier, Mourey, Cordonnier and the artist Charles Coppier (1867–1948) built houses for themselves. Bonnier further constructed a regionalist villa for the Belgian musician George Flé and the famous writer André Gide, while Tournaire designed the country house of Rostand. The sculptor Pierre Roche, the decorative artist Verneuil, the painter Albert Besnard and the editor Arthème Fayard also commissioned regionalist villas. Most of these houses were built quite early, that is, during the first decade of the twentieth century.[41]

The most generally used labels for this type of innovative architecture, especially in the beginning, were 'new', 'modern' and 'contemporary'. The adaptation to the environment and local traditions was generally called 'logical' and 'rational'.[42] The new style could also be named after the region where it found its inspiration. The neo-Norman style in particular was quite popular and often mentioned. Nonetheless, when reviewing a neo-Norman villa built by Sézille for the widow of one of the Renault brothers at the Norman seaside resort of Cabourg, Sézille and the director of *La Vie à la Campagne*, Albert Maumené, explicitly called these various

---

[40] However, most of the negative remarks were made after 1907, by which time Art Nouveau was already out of fashion. Many critics and architects, such as Plumet, Verneuil and Bonnier, had been active in the French Art Nouveau movement. See for the critical remarks: Sézille, 'Reconstitution d'une gentilhommière normande' 343, Sézille, 'Quelques maisons de campagne' 390, Maurice Guillemot, 'Habitations d'employés', *Art et Décoration* (1911), II 209–16, especially 209–10 and Vaillat, *La Cité renaissante* 10.

[41] See for the houses of Coppier and Besnard: Vaillat, 'La Maison en Savoie' 41; for those of Bonnier and Tournaire: Loyer, *Histoire de l'architecture Française* 231–3; and of Fayard: Marc Croisilles, 'Une villa à Pinterville (Eure)', *L'Architecture Moderne* (February 1912) 31–4.

[42] See for example: Plumet, 'Une maison de campagne' 200; Plumet, 'L'Architecture et le paysage' 266–7, L. Sézille, 'Une maison moderne très simple', *La Vie à la Campagne* (1 June 1909) 337–8, Sézille, 'Trois cottages' 30; Verneuil, 'Maisons de campagne anglaises' 28.

new regional styles a truly or eminently 'French style'.[43] Hesitantly, the term 'regionalism' also came into use, generally as 'regional architecture' (which could also refer to vernacular architecture from a particular region) or as 'regionalism in architecture'. Surprisingly, the clearest use of the term could be found in a review of a new book on country houses by Muthesius. The movement of architectural renovation of which he formed part, according to the author, moved in the direction of 'rationalism and regionalism'.[44] It seems that the exposition of regional architecture, which was held in Paris in 1917 to provide examples for the reconstruction of the devastated regions of northern France, and the ensuing debates, helped to establish 'regional architecture' as a generally accepted term, although it was not completely clear whether this referred to vernacular buildings or to new creations. Only later would 'regionalist architecture' become a more widely used label in France for this neo-vernacular trend.[45]

Although the French market for regionalist architecture was smaller and more oriented towards secondary residences, it has become clear that the reformist architectural ideals were almost identical to those in Germany. The regionalist character was even more marked than in the German Empire, as several regions with building traditions that were adapted to the local circumstances were clearly identified. However, it should be remarked that these presumed regional traditions generally were the traditions of a very specific part – such as the Labourd area of the Basque Country – or of a very specific type of building,[46] such as the ancient half-timbered manor houses of Normandy that provided the 'vernacular' examples for neo-Norman villas. Other elements of the reformist ideology were less pronounced in the French specialised press. As most French inner cities had been thoroughly reformed, anti-urban remarks, which in Germany could be frequently found in architectural reviews of this period, were almost completely absent from French periodicals. And when an occasional author

43 Sézille, 'Reconstitution d'une gentilhommière normande' 344, Sézille, 'Quelques maisons de campagne' 390, Albert Maumené, 'Sweet home, villa du littoral normand: À Mme Fernand Renault, Cabourg (Calvados)', *La Vie à la Campagne* (1 January 1913) 11–17, especially 12 and 17.
44 Sézille,'Les Villas de Deauville' 56 and Vaillat, 'La Maison en Savoie' 37, 'Maisons de campagne de Hermann Muthesius 4.
45 See Vigato, *L'Architecture régionaliste* 93–118. Vigato's pioneering study surprisingly interprets the decades after the First World War as the heyday of regionalist architecture. Loyer, in various publications, asserts that this should be located in the pre-1914 period, which is in agreement with my own findings.
46 Claude Lasserre, 'Le Néo-basque: une autre face de la modernité (1920–1940)', *Monuments Historiques* (October–November 1986) 65–73, especially 69. See also: Louis Colas, *L'Habitation basque: De l'art regional en France* (Paris 1926) 5–7.

complained about the big city he called the new apartments impersonal like 'cabins on a packet boat' and did not speak of the physical and psychological dangers that threatened modern man in the big agglomerations, as was often done in Germany.[47] The same applies to the open defence by various German critics of the new country house architecture as essentially bourgeois, meant for hard-working, unpretentious and honest middle-class families.

Probably because of the considerable proportion of aristocratic clients (although most seem to have been recently ennobled), French critics did not openly stress the middle-class nature of the new country houses. However, like their German colleagues, they underlined the importance of family life. The greatest emphasis was put on intimacy and on privacy *vis-à-vis* visitors, neighbours and personnel. Dining rooms should be cosy to stimulate the intimacy of the family. Reception rooms and offices therefore should be clearly separated from the living areas. The same was true for possible guest rooms, and even more so for the areas used by servants. Louis Sézille, in particular, put considerable stress on this aspect. In his articles he often dedicated a few lines to the personnel, criticising for example the habit of lodging the maids and servants in garrets under the roof. This was not only uncomfortable for them, as these small rooms were hot in the summer and cold in the winter, but also inconvenient for the owners of the house as they were often disturbed or even woken up by the noises above their head. Moreover, if there was not a specified staircase for the servants one might meet them in every part of the house. Consequently, in his own designs he always tried to find a logical and somewhat isolated place in the house for them, be it in the basement, on the ground floor or in a separate wing of the first floor.[48]

Other practical measures promoted the neatness and decency of the house. For example, some of the bigger villas were provided with a separate tradesmen's entrance that provided direct access to the kitchen or basement. Major country houses at the beach, such as the ones constructed by Sézille in Cabourg and La Baule, often had a small entrance that gave access to the basement, where a well-equipped bathroom allowed the inhabitants to take

[47]   Camille Mauclair, 'L'Âme de la maison française', *Revue bleue* V (24 February 1906) 242–6, especially 243.
[48]   L. Sézille, 'Un cottage sur une plage de l'océan', *La Vie à la Campagne*' (15 July 1908) 48–9, Sézille, 'Une maison moderne' 338, Sézille, 'Trois cottages' 29. And for houses constructed by Sézille: M.P. Verneuil, 'Type d'un spacieux et confortable cottage', *La Vie à la Campagne* (15 June 1909) 371–2, Maumené, 'Sweet home' 12–13 and L.P. Sézille, 'Conception d'une grande villa à Cabourg: Les plans de "Sweet Home", maison normande', *La Vie à la Campagne* (1 February 1913) 87–90.

a bath and carry out their toilette before entering the principal rooms of the house, thus 'removing from the rooms all the causes of dirtiness originating from the sand brought along with the wet clothes'. In these villas, Sézille even made provisions for disposing of dirty laundry via a tube that led directly to a basket in the basement.[49] This aspect was equally important in smaller cottages. In his article on an Alsatian house, Sézille designed a well-protected porch where one could shake off one's clothes and shoes, thus removing snow and mud before entering the house. He added that 'this way the interior of the house will gain in cleanliness'.[50]

Nonetheless, as in Germany, French critics also saw the countryside as a regenerative force. The pure beauty and tranquillity of nature and a simple and harmonious existence in the countryside would protect the inhabitants of the country houses from the feverish and noisy non-stop activity of the big city, the bad taste of the parvenus and the lure of night life.[51] Verneuil compared the rural country house that Sézille had designed for him with a pretentious villa with a highly decorated façade. These were like a 'beautiful countryside girl, at ease with her casque and rustic dress, and the other who was rigged out with a pathetic hat and a frock of bad taste'. His own house fitted in organically with its surroundings like a country girl 'running freely over the paths'. In another article he established a similar parallel:

> The one, the house in an old local style, is the good song of the area, which goes straight to the heart, the farmer's song always fresh and young, that speaks the soul of the country; the other, the pretentious villa of bad taste, is the song of the honky-tonk, dumb and perverse, that one brings along from the town and that is pitifully out of tune among the healthy nature and before the calm horizons.[52]

Thus, although less outspoken, regionalist architecture in France was also intimately connected with a longing for a more natural and authentic life, one free from the stress, routine and rigid conventions that characterised existence in the big urban centres. This could be achieved by living in a rural and organic setting in harmony with nature and historically grown traditions. Sézille remarked, in his description of a house in the Jura, that

---

49   See, respectively 'Les Villas de Deauville' 62, Sézille, 'Grande villa a Cabourg' 88 and 90, and Verneuil, 'Type de cottage' 371–2.
50   Sézille, 'Une maison en Alsace' 149.
51   Plumet, 'L'Architecture et le paysage' 208–9, Sézille, 'Trois cottages' 28–9, and Guillemot, 'Habitations d'employés' 215.
52   Verneuil, 'Ma Maison' 73 and Verneuil, 'Maisons de campagne anglaises' 24.

after some years the house would acquire the patina of time and 'would take its place in the great village family to contribute to the general harmony of the work of humankind with the surrounding nature'.[53] And according to these critics, building a neo-vernacular house in the countryside was a logical and rational solution. However, by 'logic' they did not mean a cold, rational, mathematical or capitalist logic, but the logic according to the ideology of *Volksgeist* in its new regionalist guise. Every region had its own 'spirit' or 'genius', which was the cultural product of the age-long struggle of mankind to cope with the local natural and geographic circumstances. Thus when constructing in the countryside, according to Verneuil, it would be very illogical not to follow the local styles that were the product of a 'profound and prolonged knowledge of local materials and of the climate of the area'.[54]

But was this regionalist architecture also stimulated from the regions themselves? This is particularly interesting as in France the rise of regionalism and the growing aversion to the dominance of Paris resulted in 1900 in the creation of the Fédération Régionaliste Française, led by the energetic Jean Charles-Brun, who pleaded for political decentralisation.[55] Furthermore there were regions, with Brittany in first place, with a strong regional movement that began to formulate claims for autonomy. Thus in Brittany in 1898 the Union Régionaliste Bretonne was founded and in 1911 even a Parti Nationaliste Breton saw the light. Nevertheless, regionalist architecture, like regionalist painting, arrived – shortly after the turn of the century – at the hands of architects from outside the region in the form of new cottages and villas, almost exclusively for Parisians who wanted to spend the summer at the Breton coast. Some installed themselves permanently in Brittany, such as the Parisian architect Georges Lefort (1875–1954), who in 1906 decided to remain in Guincamp. Later on, local architects, some of whom studied at the newly created regional school of architecture in Rennes, also began to build in a neo-Breton style. It seems that in other regions the situation was very similar.[56]

53   L. Sézille, 'Une maison dans le Jura', *La Vie à la Campagne* (1 November 1909) 283–4, especially 284.
54   Verneuil, 'Maisons de campagne anglaises' 23–4.
55   Anne-Marie Thiesse, *Écrire la France: Le mouvement littéraire régionaliste de langue française entre la Belle Epoque et la Libération* (Paris 1991) and Julian Wright, *The Regionalist Movement in France 1890–1914: Jean Charles-Brun and French Political Thought* (Oxford 2003).
56   Le Couédic, *Les Architectes et l'idée bretonne* 102–61 and 308–24, Hélène Guéné and François Loyer, *L'Église, l'état et les architectes: Rennes 1870–1940* (Paris 1995) 243–66. See also the detailed study of the interaction between Paris and French Flanders: Mihail, *Une Flandre à la française.*

Moreover, most members of the Breton movement frowned upon the new regionalist cottages that appeared at the various seaside resorts – some even called it 'bretonnerie' for tourists. Later on some artists and architects who sympathised with the Breton movement nonetheless also adopted the regionalist rhetoric and style. Surprisingly, however, architects of a younger generation who in the interwar period would become heavily involved in the regional or even national movement openly dismissed regionalist architecture. Thus, James Bouillé (1894–1945), a conservative Catholic who strove for political autonomy for Brittany, rejected the idea that art was mainly determined by the environment. According to him, the Celts, to whom the Bretons belonged, had maintained their personality intact even if they were 'exiled' in different territories. Thus, like many Nazi ideologues afterwards, he found racial factors more important than environmental influences. Bouillé therefore tried to revive the Celtic art of his ancestors. Instead of returning to the vernacular buildings from medieval times, he preferred the prehistoric Celtic period.[57] The more secular Breton nationalist architects Maurice Marchal (1900–63) – who in 1925 would design the Breton flag – and Olivier Mordrelle (1901–85) on the contrary condemned regionalism as backward and false, preferring the international style of Le Corbusier (1887–1965). Regionalist architecture gave an exotic image of Brittany and thus, according to them, was in fact a French style, because a true Breton would never view himself as exotic. They hoped Breton architects would develop a personal but highly modern architectural style, helping Brittany fully to participate in the international architectural developments of the day instead of remaining a picturesque but backward region of France.[58]

Garden cities

The new neo-vernacular trend also became visible outside the domain of country houses and suburban villas. However, in contrast to the situation in Germany the reformist critics and architects who had advocated the regionalist architecture at the start did not become actively involved in the French garden city movement, which would almost completely be dominated by young architects and intellectuals. Nonetheless, the garden city trend came into being at almost the same time as in Germany. The most influential propagator of the garden city ideal in France would

---

[57] Le Couédic, *Les Architectes et l'idée bretonne* 266–8, 317–22, 403–4 and 447–52.
[58] Ibid., 338–45, 377–89 and 530–3.

be the young lawyer Georges Benoît-Lévy (1880–1970). In 1903 he was asked to make a trip to England, to study the new garden city ideal, by the Musée Social, an association of intellectuals and politicians founded in 1894 to study and propose measures that would improve the living conditions of the poor. He thus visited Bournville and Port Sunlight and extensively studied Howard's ideas. Back in France he started a true publicity campaign that began in 1904 with the creation of the Association des cités-jardins de France (The Association of Garden Cities of France) and the publication of *La cité-jardin*. This book contained a foreword by the influential reformist economist Charles Gide who, like Werner Sombart in Germany, was a proponent of the historical approach of economics and became an influential propagator of the co-operative movement and the main theoretician of *Solidarisme*, the French version of social liberalism.[59] However, whereas the English and German counterparts of his Association succeeded in translating their ideals into the practical foundation of a garden city, this did not take place in France.

This was somewhat surprising as the living conditions of the urban poor in France were probably worse than in Germany and England. Although the urbanisation process was much slower in France than in Germany, little was done to improve the living conditions of the poor. After the inner cities had been reformed, providing new apartments for the upper classes, nothing comparable had been done for the lower classes. Private housing associations and worker-led co-operatives did build some low-cost housing, but compared to Germany and other West European countries the numbers were very disappointing. Although the government from 1894 onwards passed some laws that sought to improve the situation by lowering taxes and providing loans at favourable terms, until 1914 this did not really result in massive housing schemes. Consequently the majority of the poor continued to live in slums on the outskirts of the big towns, generally having only one room per family.[60]

Benoît-Lévy thus had every reason to continue publishing articles and books on garden cities both on a more theoretical level, and in the form of descriptions of projects that were actually built elsewhere in Europe

---

59 Christian Topalov, 'Les "Réformateurs" et leurs reseaux: Enjeux d'un objet de recherche' in: Idem ed., *Laboratoires du nouveau siècle: La nébuleuse réformatrice et ses réseaux en France, 1880–1914* (Paris 1999) 11–61, especially 21–9 and Jean-Pierre Gaudin, 'The French Garden City' in: Stephan V. Ward ed., *The Garden City: Past, Present and Future* (London 1992) 52–69. See for the Musée Social: Janet R. Horne, *A Social Laboratory for Modern France: The Musée Social and the Rise of the Welfare State* (Durham and London 2002).
60 Anne Power, *Hovels to High Rise: State Housing in Europe since 1850* (London and New York 1993).

and in the United States. Initially, however, he remained a rather lonely voice in the specialised press as only Louis Sézille published two articles in *La Vie à la Campagne* in which he presented his own design for a small garden city, which had been exhibited at the *Salon d'Automne* of 1910. In fact, it consisted of six regionalist villas for an imaginary Parisian suburb. Benoît-Lévy, however, emphasised that a garden city was intended to be a community of different social classes and not as a villa quarter or a workers' settlement. He further stressed that in the English garden cities especially a traditional design and lay-out of the cottages was combined with modern facilities, giving every family an independent 'home' and providing both poor and rich with a minimum of 'comfort, beauty and hygiene'. The English model should be adapted to French needs and peculiarities and this could best be done by designing modern cottages inspired on 'our old regional styles that represent a bit the soul of the country'.[61]

In contrast to England and Germany, the upper and upper-middle classes showed no interest in buying a house in a garden city. Thus, in the early years no garden city was actually constructed around Paris, where it was most needed, and when garden cities were eventually started they were all workers' settlements, and generally quite modest in scale. The first garden cities in France were the initiative of entrepreneurs. From about 1906 various manufacturers in the Franche-Comté and Lorraine regions, such as Peugeot, constructed quarters for their workers along the lines of Howard's ideas; all made use of the services of the young local architect Jean Walter (1883–1957). In 1912 Walter had already designed nineteen small workers' settlements in the east of France. Only when the first plans for a garden city were well under way in Paris were his activities reviewed in *Art et Décoration*. The settlements designed by Walter, according to the author, greatly improved the health and well-being of the workers and their families. Instead of living in dark houses in narrow streets where tuberculosis and other diseases were rampant, they could now live in a comfortable cottage, with enough air and light, a proper garden and space where the children could play. This would also have a positive effect on the 'morality of the masses', as the inhabitants would almost automatically avoid bars, bad company and vicious habits. Although the houses were clearly inspired by vernacular examples, this was only hinted at by the author, as he wrote that the houses were well protected in the 'bad season' by using

---

[61] L. Sézille, 'Une cité-jardin aux environs de Paris', *La Vie à la Campagne* (15 January 1911) 51–2 and L. Sézille, 'Deux cottages voisins de la cité-jardin', *La Vie à la Campagne* (1 March 1911) 136 and Georges Benoît-Lévy, 'La Cité-jardin', *La Gazette des Beaux-Arts* (February 1910), III 157–69, especially 158–60 and 167–8.

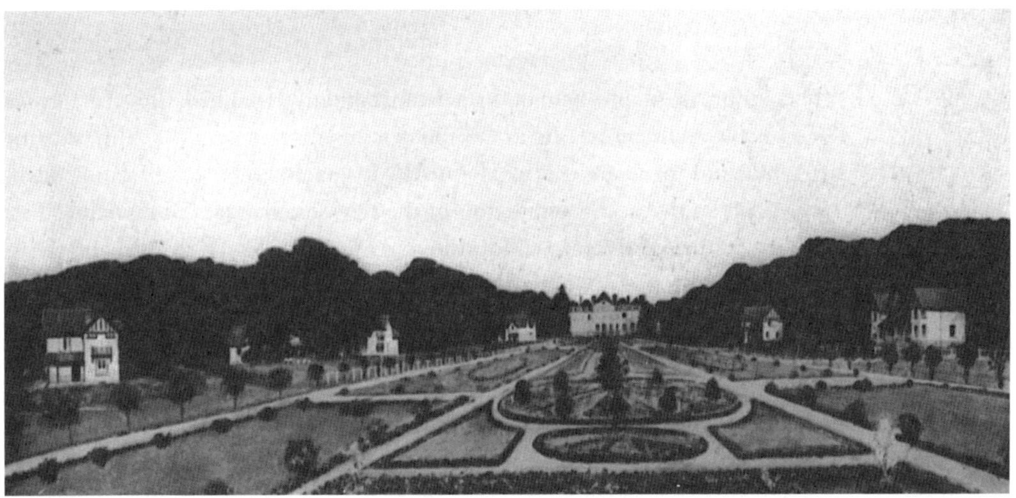

17 Jean Walter, Garden city at Draveil, Paris, around 1913. At the end of the main axis of the park is the country seat and on the sides there are a few of the newly built cottages and semi-detached houses.

eaves and porches, whereas the half-timbered upper storeys gave a discrete decorative effect.[62]

The first garden city near Paris was also a workers' settlement and was realised by a co-operative of 300 labourers, which in 1911 bought the seventeenth-century country seat of Draveil, just south of Paris. The park of the estate, which had been designed by Louis XIV's gardener Le Nôtre, was converted into a garden city for the workers and their families, whereas the mansion functioned as the community centre. Jean Walter drew up the overall plan in which he respected the existing park as far as possible, and he also designed the low-cost cottages in harmony with the surroundings and according to the needs and wishes of the families (figure 17). According to the critic of *Art et Décoration* some resembled villas from Normandy, whereas others shared the beauty of English cottages. Nevertheless, they all formed an organic unity. Walter himself did not refer to the regionalist style of the cottages in his own article on 'the first garden city of France' in *L'Architecture*. He only wanted to highlight the 'efforts which we have made to realise a social dream, to create at the entrance of Paris a joyful city full of flowers with sunny and healthy houses, small kingdoms of health and happiness'.[63]

[62] Maurice Guillemot, 'Logis d'ouvriers', *Art et Décoration* (1912), II 79–88, especially 79–81 and 83.
[63] Maurice Guillemot, 'Un cité-jardin à Draveil', *Art et Décoration* (1914), I 49–54 and Jean Walter, 'La Première cité-jardin de France: Cité cooperative de Draveil', *L'Architecture* (11 July 1914) 237–41, especially 241.

A new era

The outbreak of the war in 1914 fundamentally changed the situation of regionalist architecture. As in Germany, construction activities almost came to a halt and many architectural journals suspended their publications. Plans were made for the reconstruction of the devastated areas. But whereas East Prussia had been reconquered almost immediately and the debate on its reconstruction already began in 1914, this was not the case in France. The devastated areas were much greater and during the war were mostly too close to the battlefront or even occupied by German troops to effectively allow rebuilding. Already in 1915 some members of the recently created Société Française des Architectes Urbanistes (French Society of Town Planning Architects), which was domiciled at the office of the Musée Social, published a book on 'how to rebuild our destroyed cities'. They naturally pleaded that every town should be obliged to first draw up a development plan before starting to rebuild. They also advocated the use of local materials and building traditions in both public and private buildings and the creation of garden cities for workers.[64] However, their book received little interest.

More debate was provoked when in May 1916 an exhibition on 'La Cité reconstituée' (The Reconstituted City), organised by the General Association of Hygienists and Municipal Technicians, which also had its offices at the Musée Social,[65] opened its doors in the gardens of the Tuileries, in the heart of Paris. This exhibition provided models for the reconstruction of the infrastructure and also displayed barracks and cheap building materials that could be used to house the refugees on a temporary basis. This provoked a reaction from the ranks of the architects who were disappointed by the proposed solutions. Thus, Léandre Vaillat, one of the main propagators of regionalist architecture, began a series of articles, polemically called 'La Cité renaissante' (The Reviving City), in the major evening paper *Le Temps*, which in 1918 was also published as a book. In these articles he wrote that plans were needed for a more definite reconstruction and that these should not be wholly determined by arguments of efficiency. According to him it was necessary to adapt the buildings to the local landscape and climate and take into account the existing local and regional construction traditions.[66]

---

64 Alfred Agache, Marcel Auburtin and Edouard Redont, *Comment reconstruire nos cités détruites: Notions d'urbanisme s'appliquant aux villes, bourgs et villages* (Paris 1915) 3–7, 20–1 and 106–8.

65 Loyer, *Histoire de l'architecture française* 218.

66 Vigato, *L'Architecture régionaliste* 76–93 and Vaillat, *La Cité renaissante* 10–12, 43–4 and 51–2.

Consequently, before starting work on the reconstruction a thorough knowledge of existing building traditions in the destroyed areas was required. This was also realised by one of the major associations of architects, the Société des Architectes Diplômés par le Gouvernement (Society of Architects with a State Diploma), and the French State, represented by Paul Léon, the highest official for Architecture, who together organised an exposition on the traditional architecture of the devastated areas. The exhibition, which was inaugurated in January 1917 in the Galeries Goupil, showed almost 600 photographs, paintings, engravings, drawings, etc. of vernacular buildings classified per region. The introduction of the catalogue was written by Vaillat, whereas Paul Léon wrote a highly positive review of the exhibition in *Les Arts*, which was edited by Goupil. In this article he wrote that it was a patriotic duty to use French materials, stimulate the national economy and follow local building traditions. In fact, the exhibition implicitly maintained that regionalism should be the guiding principle in the rebuilding process and, consequently, that the reconstruction could not be left solely to engineers, but that a prominent role should be given to architects. In these difficult times, the architects thus claimed a new domain for themselves, the field of small rural constructions, which until then had generally been built without the services of a trained architect.[67]

The exhibition seemed to be a success as some months later the undersecretary of Fine Arts, together with the interministerial Council for the Reconstruction of the Invaded and Destroyed Regions, which was presided over by Léon Bourgeois, Minister of State and the main propagator of the *Solidariste* current within the Radical Party, announced a contest for the creation of types that should function 'as models for the reconstruction of rural houses in the devastated regions'. The buildings should be up to date and respect the 'regional styles'. In order to facilitate the participation of architects who had been mobilised by the army the first round consisted only of a small sketch. A jury, with prominent regionalists such as Léon and Cordonnier, made a selection which was shown in July 1917. Six months later the winning designs of the second round were exhibited in the Museum for Decorative Arts. Most of the awarded projects, however, were the work of Parisian architects, among whom was Louis Sézille.[68]

---

[67] Vigato, *L'Architecture régionaliste* 93–100 and Paul Léon, 'L'Architecture régionale dans les provinces envahies', *Les Arts* (January 1917), no. 157 12–19.

[68] Ibid., 102–18. See for some positive reviews: F. Honoré, 'Les Maisons de demain dans les régions libérées', *L'Illustration* (26 January 1918) 86–93 and Paul de Rutte,

Thus, regionalist architecture, at least on paper, had become a mainstream movement during the war and now received a strong backing by the government. Nevertheless, the practice of the reconstruction turned out to be quite disappointing. The post-war economic crisis and shortages made the reconstruction very difficult and slow. The need for standardisation, the use of cheap materials and concrete and the lack of time and interest by many local authorities and building societies in the end did not favour the cause of regionalism.[69]

However, there were a few exceptions. Thus in Reims the local low-cost housing society, led by the active social-catholic entrepreneur Georges Charbonneaux, constructed various garden cities.[70] More impressive was the effort of the Compagnie des Chemins de Fer du Nord (the Railway Company of the North), which constructed twenty-six garden suburbs with about 11,000 houses in a striking regionalist style for its workers in the destroyed zones of the North of France (figure 18). This was due to the company's own initiative, and was executed by its efficient head engineer Raoul Dautry (1880–1951) almost without any financial support from the government. As the railway company was often threatened with strikes by their highly unionised personnel one of the explicit goals of the garden cities was to maintain social peace. Thus, the workers could rent a cottage with a garden in a pleasant green and picturesque environment, but those who participated in a strike were expelled. The garden cities were constructed close to the railway hubs or depots and far from the inner cities. They had their own schools, post office, shops, cinema and community centre.[71] So there was no need to leave the area and visit the bars of the town, as the critic of *Art et Décoration* remarked. Both the suburbs and the buildings were methodically designed and rapidly constructed. Nonetheless, by dissymmetrical plans and varying the types and disposition of the houses, too great a uniformity was avoided. Most

'Maisons des champs et villages', *La Vie à la Campagne* (1 July 1919) 109–52, especially 110–11.

[69] Ibid., 118–28. See also: Hugh Clout, *After the Ruins: Restoring the Countryside of Northern France after the Great War* (Exeter 1996) and Hugh Clout, 'The Great Reconstruction of Towns and Cities in France 1918–1935', *Planning Perspectives* (2005) 1–34.

[70] Delphine Henry, *Chemin vert: L'oeuvre d'éducation populaire dans une cité jardin emblématique, Reims 1919–1939* (Reims 2002) and Clout, 'The Great Reconstruction' 21–3.

[71] Chantal Petillon and Didier Terrier, 'Une corporation cheminote: Le travail et les hommes à la Compagnie de chemins de fer du Nord (1832–1937)' published on: www.commission-historique59.com/bulletins/avril2005.html consulted on 30 July 2007. In 1939–40 Dautry would be minister of Armament in the last government of the Third Republic, and De Gaulle also named him minister of Reconstruction and City Planning in the first post-war cabinet of 1944.

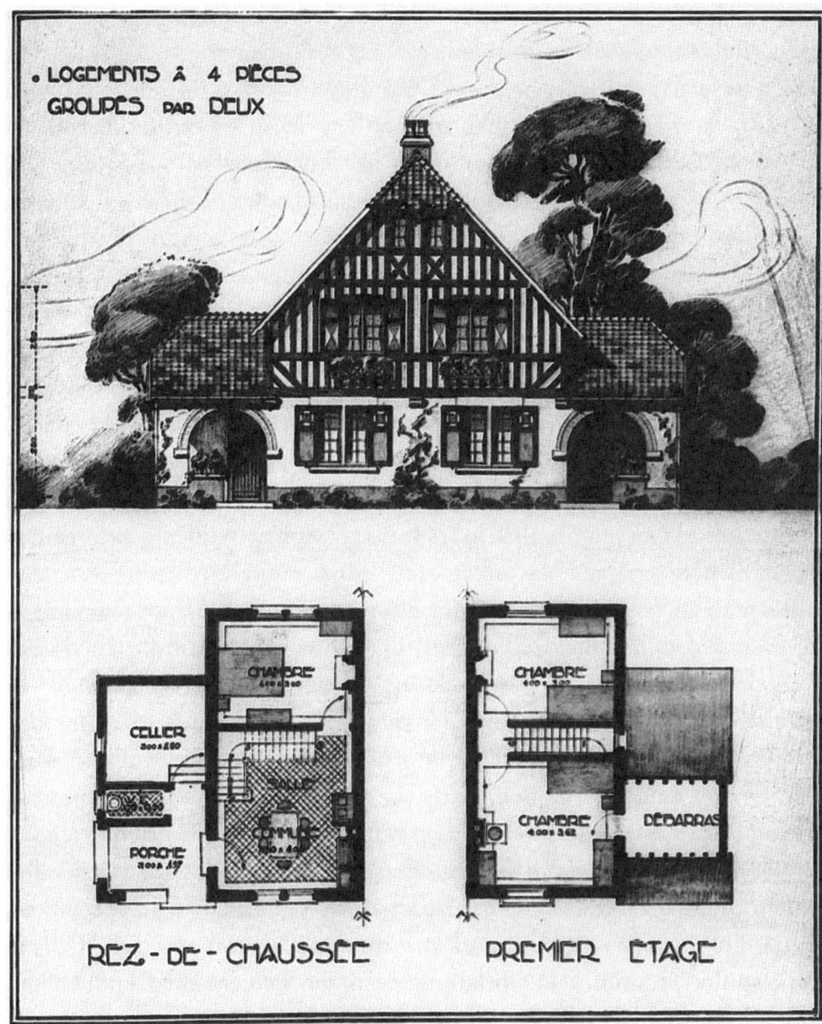

18 Gustave Umbdenstock, two semi-detached houses with four rooms, Garden city of the Compagnie des Chemins de Fer du Nord, 1922.

houses had a porch, 'like the old French farm houses', where the children could play in bad weather, where the laundry could dry and where the family could eat in the summer. The colours were lively; the steep roofs protected the houses without obstructing light and air and, according to the same critic, they thus were very similar to the 'rustic houses of Picardy and Flanders'. His only criticism was about the use of false half-timber gables, which moreover were not common in the region.[72]

72 René Chavance, 'Les Cités-jardins de la Compagnie du Nord', *Art et Décoration* (1922) 2, 111–28.

On another front regionalism also gained ground as an ambitious programme of constructing garden cities for the urban poor was initiated in the greater Paris area. Just before the war a new law was introduced, which for the first time allowed public involvement in social housing, destined exclusively for families with more than three children. Municipalities and departments could now create and subsidise autonomous *Sociétés d'habitations à bon marché* (Low-cost housing societies), which should actively stimulate the building of cheap rented apartments and houses for the poor. The war, however, prevented any progress in this field and a further measure would hamper the growth of housing construction during almost the whole of the interwar period. To prevent protests among the population the government namely continued the very strict rent control that had been introduced during the war, thus making private investments in housing projects highly uneconomic. Nevertheless, the *Société d'habitations à bon marché* of the Seine department led by Henri Sellier (1883–1943) would, with the help of co-operative housing societies and special loans, eventually create nineteen garden cities around Paris.[73] Contrary to most propagandists of regionalism Sellier was a man of humble origins, his father being an ordinary worker from Bourges. Already at a very young age he became a socialist and in 1919 he was elected mayor – first for the communist party, which in 1924 he left for the French socialist party – of the industrial town of Suresnes, slightly west of Paris. Consequently, he was familiar with the miserable living conditions of the working classes.[74]

Sellier also undertook the task of making the projected garden cities known to a specialised audience. He therefore published two large articles in *La Vie Urbaine*. The goal of the new settlements was to give the workers the possibility to withdraw from the overcrowded city and to lead a fortified and healthy life in a comfortable and pleasant house at the countryside. Therefore Sellier wanted to copy the garden city as it had developed in Great Britain – he particularly liked the designs of Unwin – and Germany, although adapting the model to the French customs and traditions. Thus he proposed a combination of straight French lanes and winding English streets, using trees that were accustomed to the French climate, to create lively ensembles of terraced houses as in the English and

---

[73]   Power, *Hovels to High Rise* 36–9 and Le Couédic, *Les Architectes et l'idée bretonne* 284–6. These problems were also noticed by foreign observers: Albert Heymann, 'Wohnungsbau in Paris', *Die Baupolitik* (1929) 23–4.

[74]   See for Henri Sellier: Roger-Henri Guerrand and Christine Moissinac, *Henri Sellier, urbaniste et réformateur social* (Paris 2005). In 1936 Sellier would even become minister of Public Health in the Popular Front government of Léon Blum.

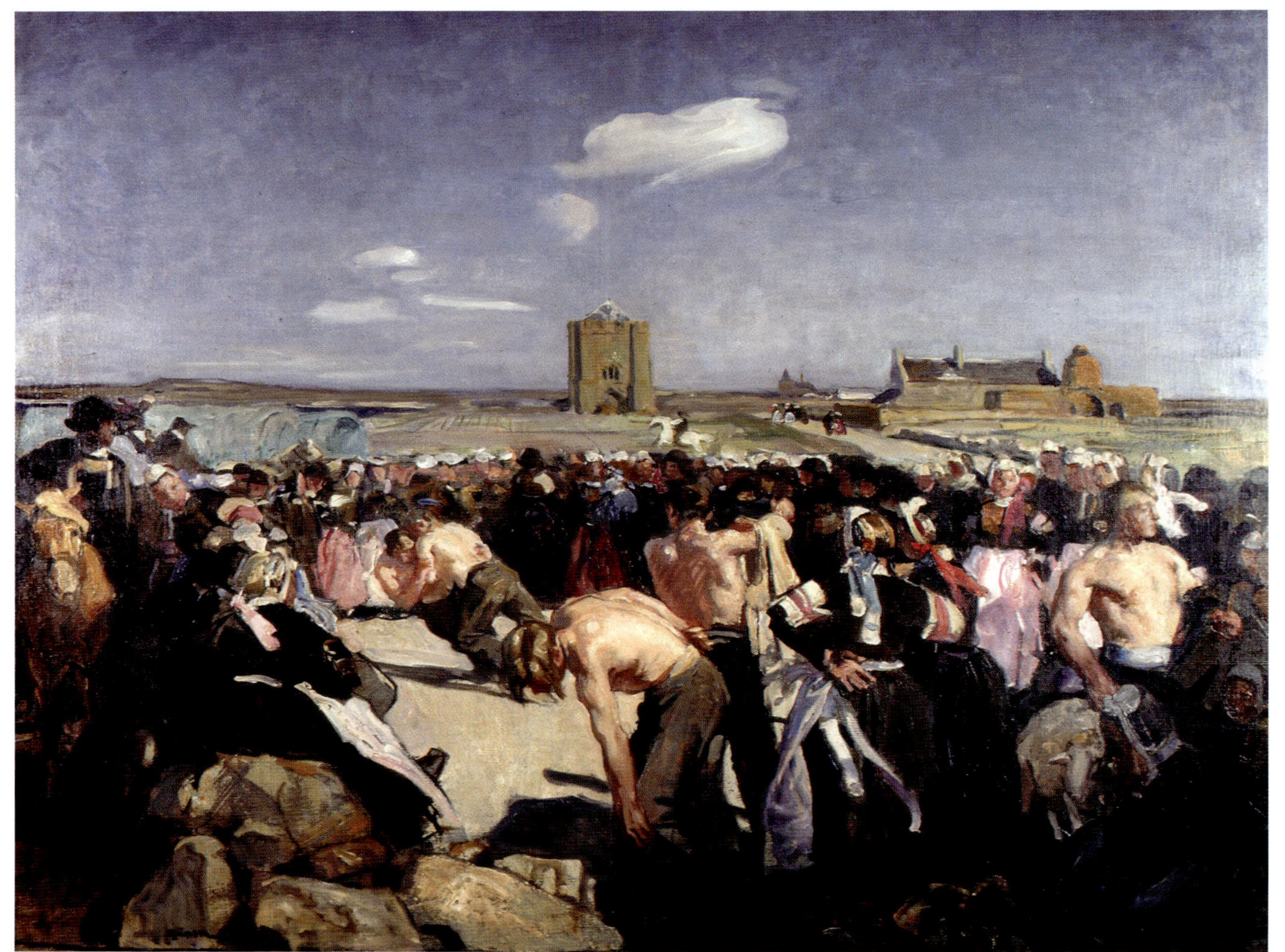

1 Lucien Simon, *Les lutteurs, Penmarc'h* (The Wrestling Match, Penmarc'h), 1898; 111 × 146 cm.

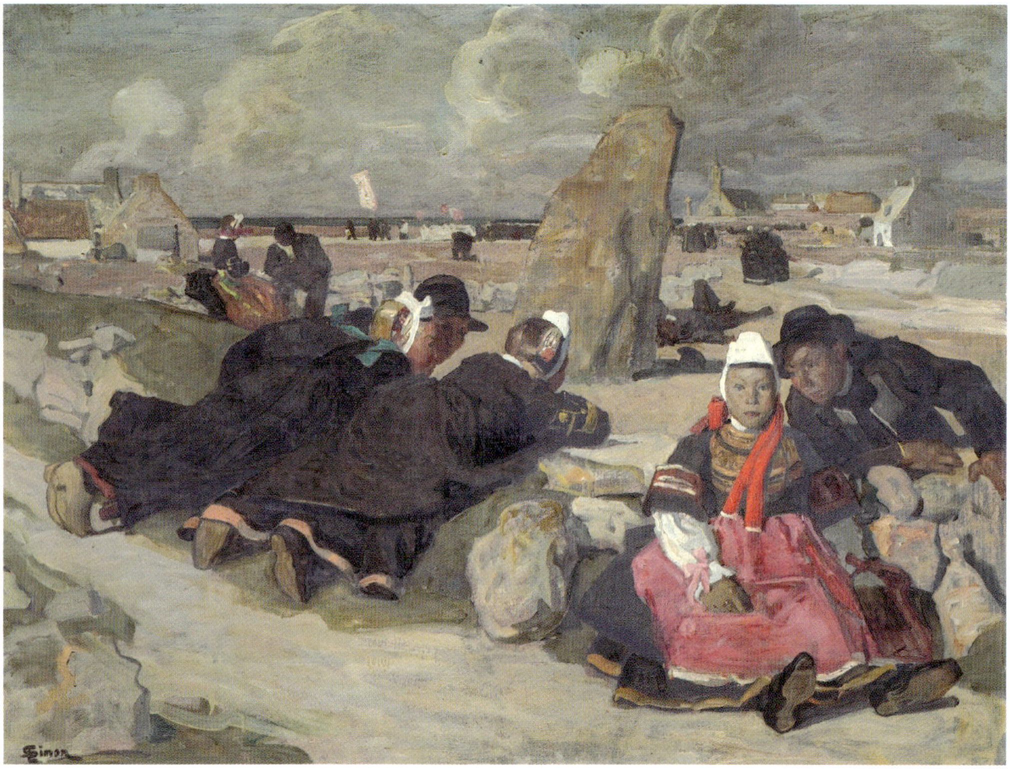

2 Lucien Simon, *Le menhir* (The Menhir), 1900; 98 × 131 cm.

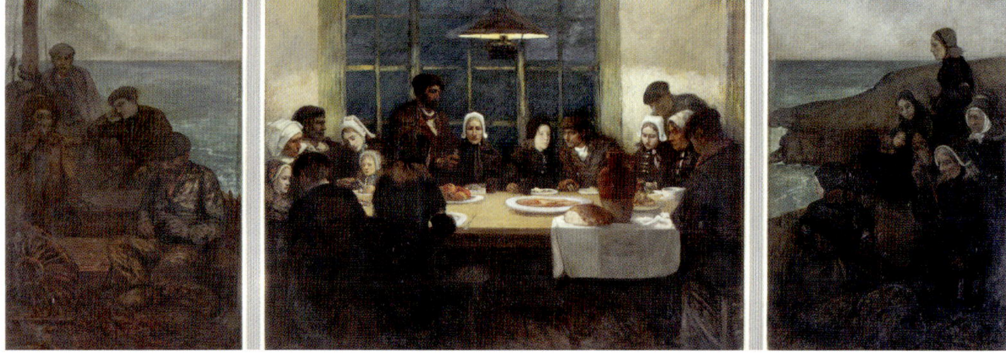

3 Charles Cottet, *Repas d'adieu* (Farewell Dinner), 1898; 176 × 475 cm.

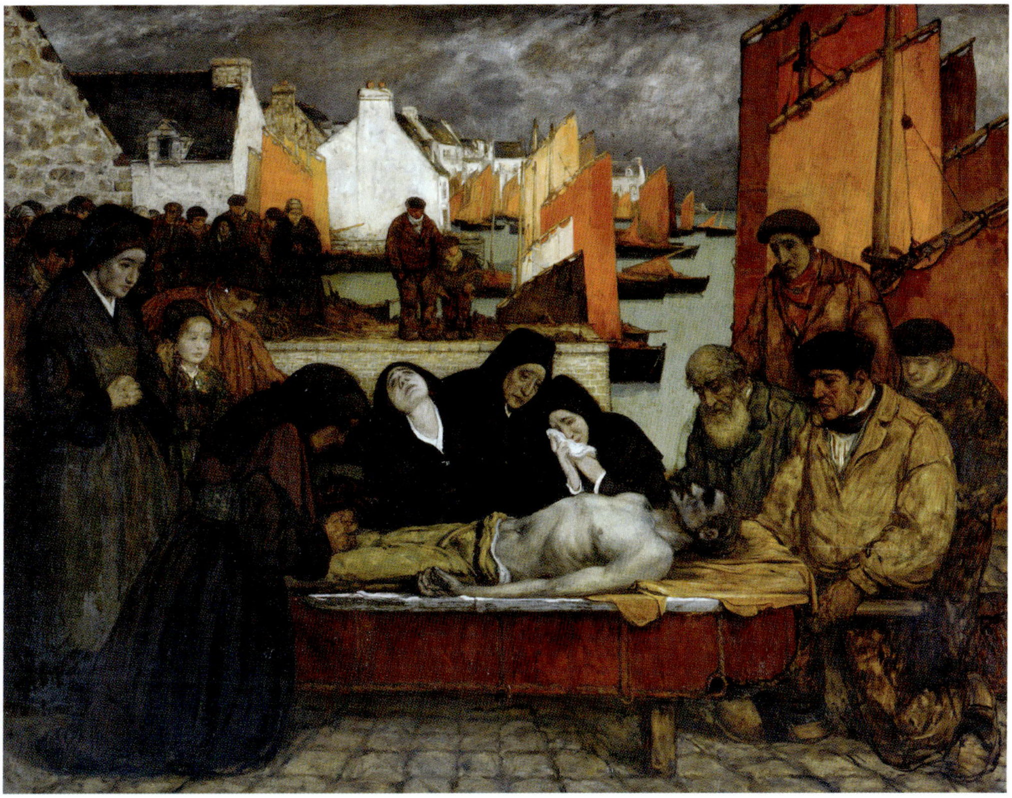

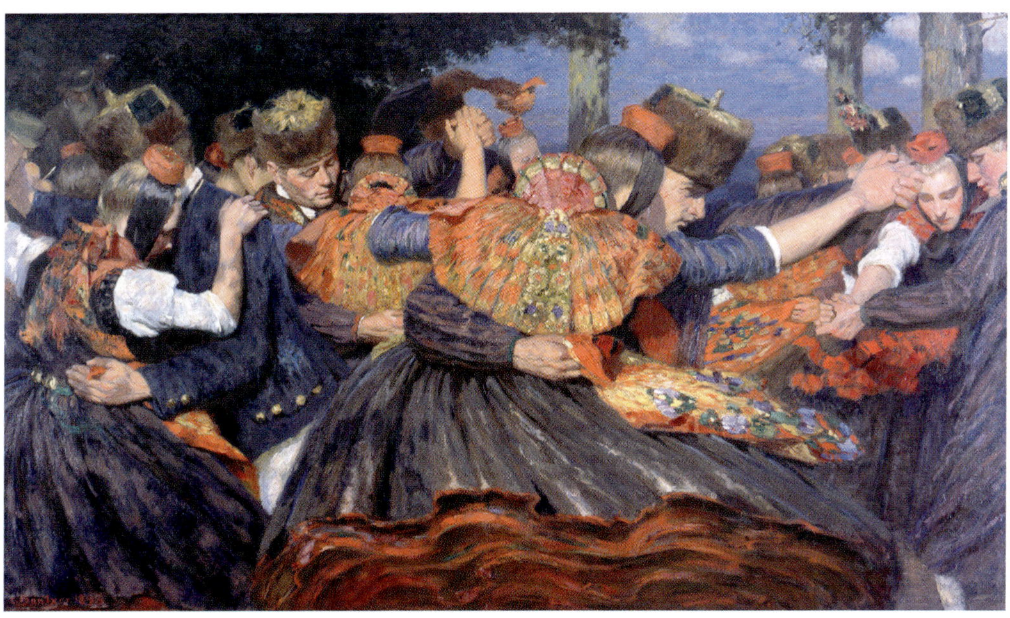

4 Charles Cottet, *Douleur au pays de la mer* (Sorrow at the Land by the Sea), 1908; 264 × 345 cm.

5 Carl Bantzer, *Schwälmer Tanz* (Dance from the Schwalm), 1898; 97 × 167 cm.

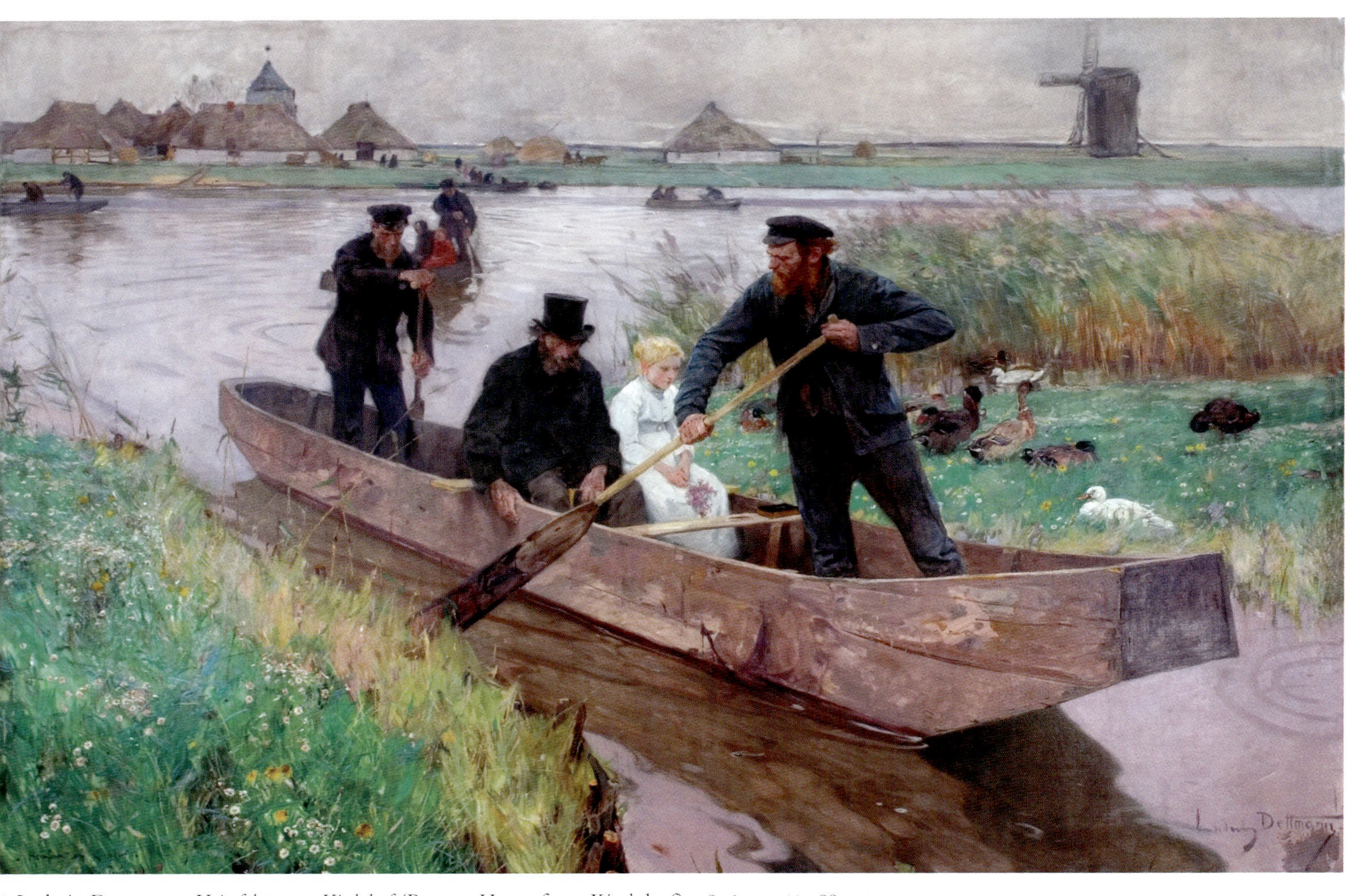

6 Ludwig Dettmann, *Heimfahrt vom Kirchdorf* (Return Home from Kirchdorf), 1896, 191 × 288 cm.

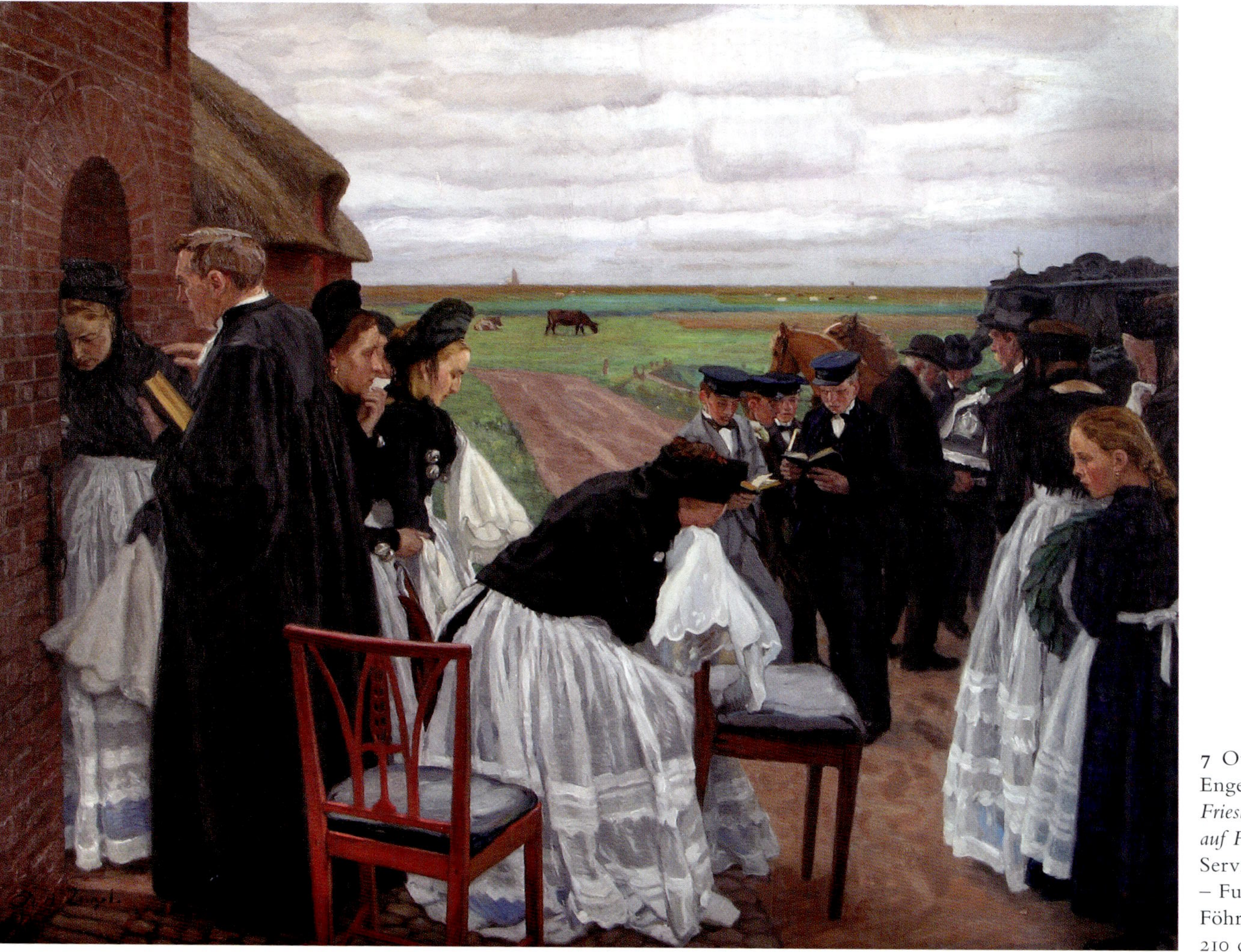

7 Otto Heinrich Engel, *Trauerfeier in Friesland – Begräbnis auf Föhr* (Memorial Service in Frisia – Funeral on Föhr), 1904; 174 × 210 cm.

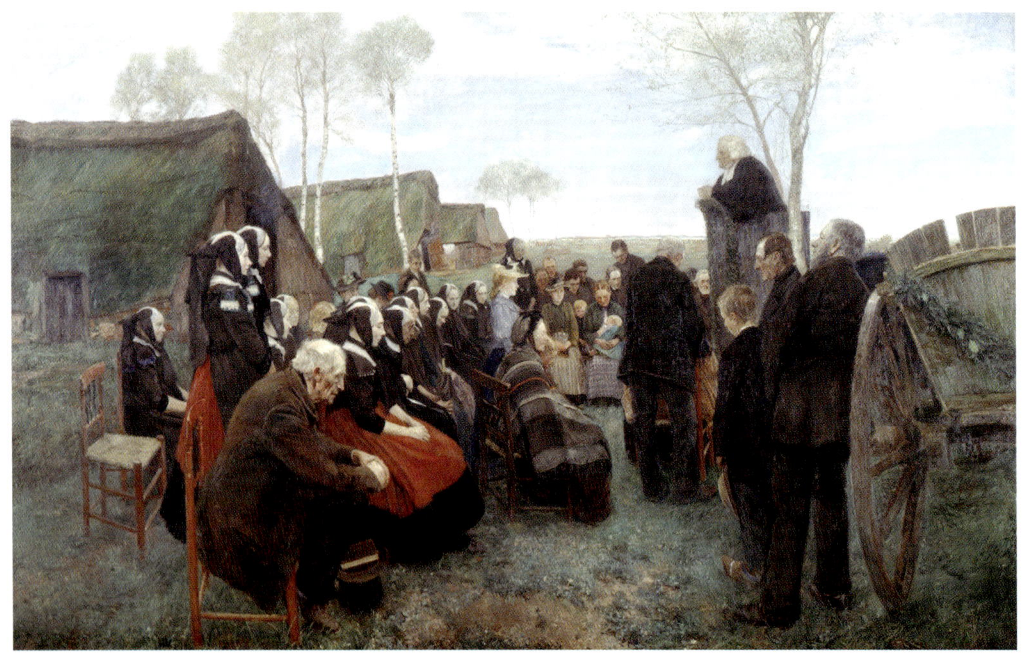

8 Fritz Mackensen, *Gottesdienst im Freien* (Open Air Service), 1895; 235 × 376 cm.

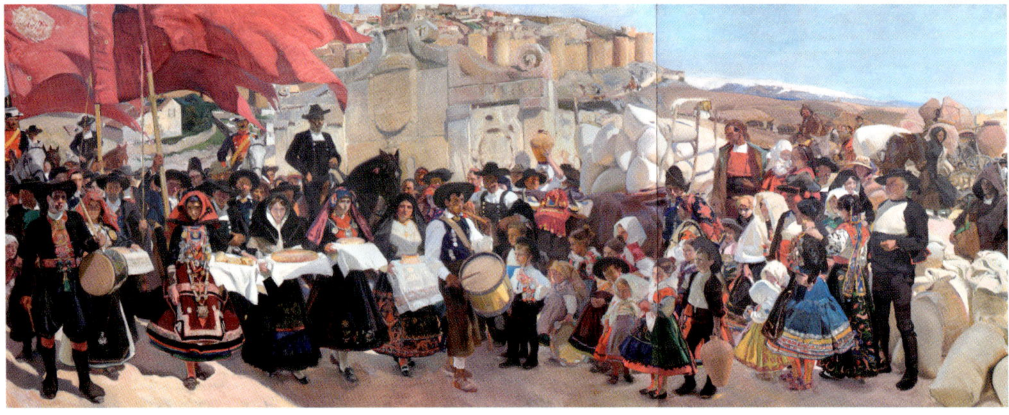

9 Joaquín Sorolla, *Las regiones de España: Castilla – La fiesta del pan* (The Regions of Spain: Castile – The Feast of Bread [which is only the left half of the painting on Castile]), 1913; 351 × 1392 cm.

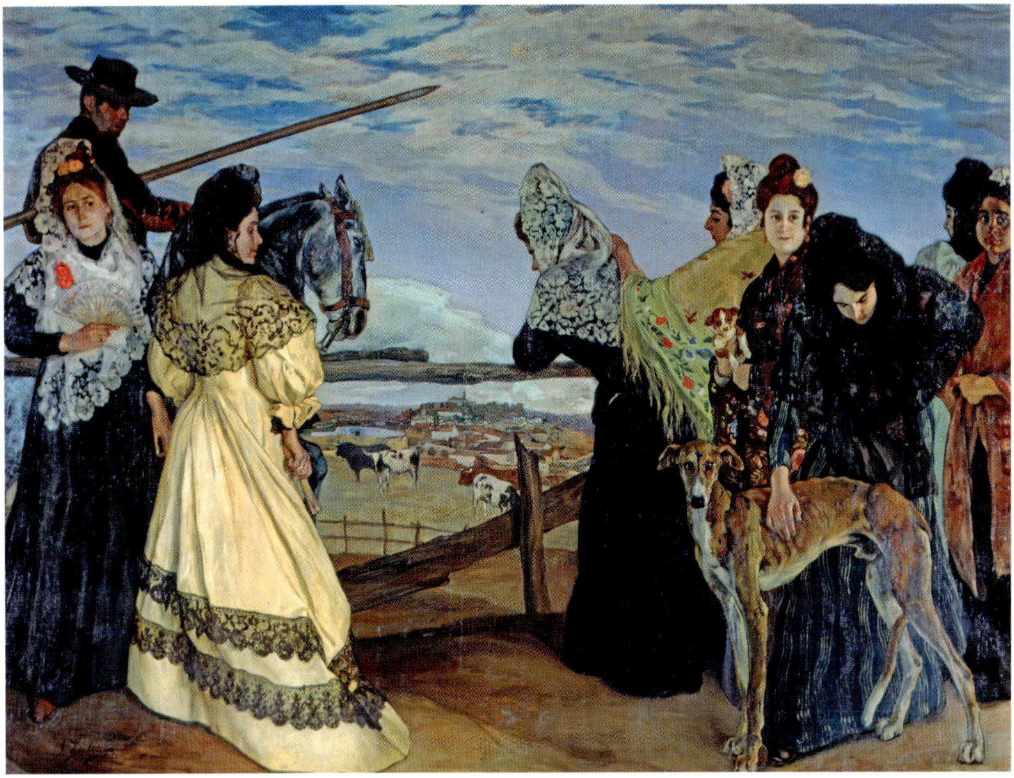

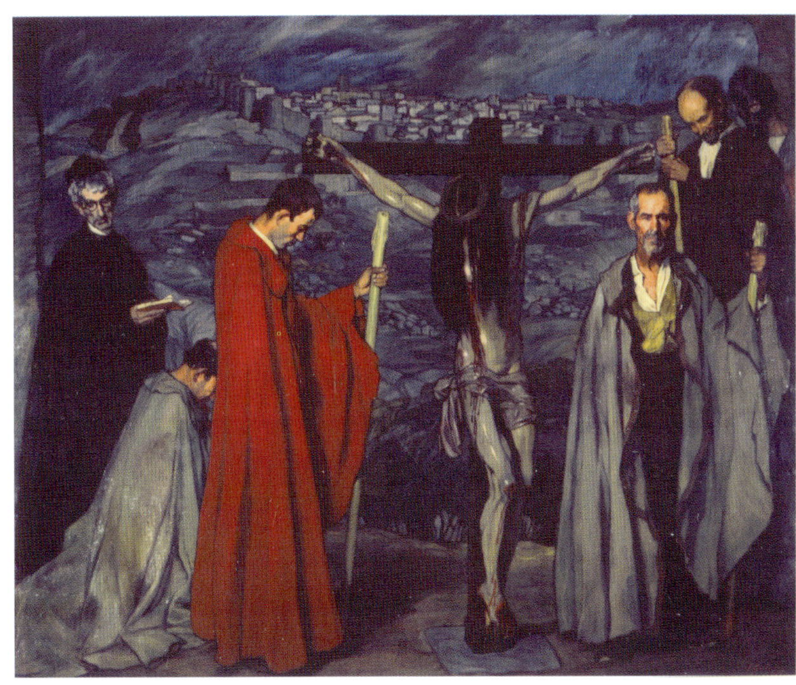

10 Ignacio Zuloaga, *Víspera de la corrida* (The Eve of the Bullfight), 1898; 222 × 302 cm.

11 Ignacio Zuloaga, *El Cristo de la Sangre* (The Christ of Blood), 1911; 248 × 302 cm.

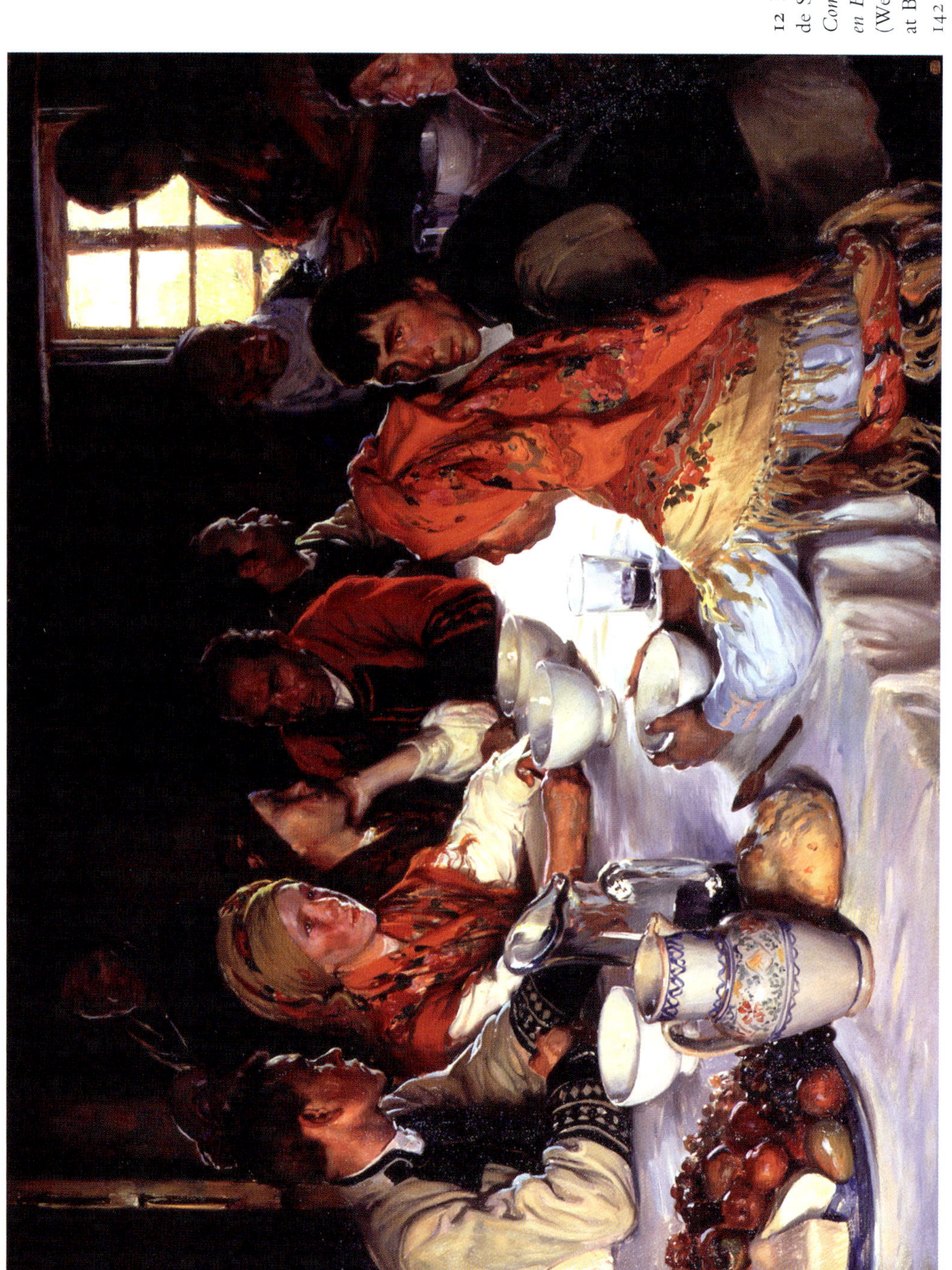

12 Fernando Álvarez de Sotomayor, *Comida de bodas en Bergantiños* (Wedding Breakfast at Bergantiños), 1916; 142 × 180 cm.

German garden cities.[75] In the end, most of the garden cities were quite small and were in no way the self-sufficient towns Howard had intended. In contrast to Germany, where big towns often possessed or acquired great plots of land for future expansion, in France, where municipalities did not have this possibility, the land had to be bought in a complicated process from various owners. In total, the garden cities therefore contained only about 15,000 houses, and being the main social housing scheme in fact meant a drop in the ocean of the Parisian banlieu.[76]

As in France garden cities were in fact intended for the blue collar workers, there was no mention of a new reformed middle-class lifestyle as was advocated by most English and German garden city propagandists. However, the healthy aspects of living in the countryside were emphasised, as were the possible positive moral aspects of such a lifestyle. A healthy family life in a proper house, where sons, daughters and parents would sleep in a separate room, in a green environment was to be preferred to the unhygienic living conditions in the slums or in the one- or two-room apartments, where the constant lure of night life, bars and alcohol had disastrous effects. Gardening, playing with the children or going to the cinema or community centre of the garden city should replace bad habits. As a consequence, in most garden cities bars and often even the sale of alcohol were explicitly forbidden.[77] The critic Paul Wallon even claimed that by combating alcoholism one could also fight socialism, as the socialists used the bistros to 'preach their class hatred'.[78]

According to the critics the new garden cities could also help solve another urgent problem in France, the threat of depopulation, which after the lagging birth rates during the nineteenth century and the enormous massacre of the First World War became a national preoccupation. Sellier and others meant that the new workers' settlements would lower the infant mortality rate and, by offering a pleasant environment for small children, increase the birth rate.[79] The regulations of a garden city in the recovered

[75]   H. S. [Henri Sellier], 'Cités-jardins et groupes d'habitations de Paris et du departement de la Seine', *La Vie Urbaine* (15 August and 15 October 1923) 21–2, 326–81, especially 361–2 and Henri Sellier, 'L'Extension de Paris au Sud: La cité-jardin du Grand Paris', *La Vie Urbaine* (1920) 5, 63–76, especially 63–4, 69–70 and 72.
[76]   Power, *Hovels to High Rise* 38, Loyer, *Histoire de l'architecture française* 222 and Bullock and Read, *The Movement for Housing Reform* 532–4.
[77]   Guillemot, 'Logis d'ouvriers' 79 and 83, Chavance, 'Les Cités-jardins de la Compagnie du Nord' 128, and H. S., 'Cités-jardins' 359 and 379.
[78]   Paul Wallon, 'Les Habitations à bon marché', *L'Architecture* (13 April 1912) 125–8, especially 126.
[79]   Sellier, 'L'Extension de Paris Sud' 63–4. See also: de Rutte, 'Maisons des champs et villages' 116.

town of Strasbourg, built by the food company Ungemach as a deed of charity and strongly supported by the socialist mayor Jacques Peirotes, stipulated that young worker families with children who displayed good behaviour should have priority in the allocation of the new cottages in the 'style of the region'. Preferably the mother should stay at home to take care of the children and families that did not have enough offspring could in theory lose their right to rent a house.[80] Social housing thus was explicitly used to discipline the working classes by rewarding those who observed their (patriotic) duties with a spacious cottage in a pleasant environment.

As in Germany and England, during the 1920s standardisation and the use of modern construction techniques led to increasingly simplified designs for the houses and cottages in the French garden cities. Planning was professionalised and large-scale building operations in the name of efficiency were increasingly preferred. Consequently the neo-vernacular architecture was slowly replaced by more functionalist models. At the end of the decade even Sellier was converted to the new modernist ideals as in Drancy he developed a 'cité-jardin verticale' as propagated by Le Corbusier with large apartment blocks and five fifteen-storey-high skyscrapers in a park-like landscape.[81] However, as only relatively few garden cities were built, social housing did not play the innovative role as, for example, in Frankfurt, Berlin, Vienna, Belgium and the Netherlands.[82]

[80] Jean Porcher, 'Les "Jardins Ungemach" à Strasbourg', *L'Architecte* (May 1927) 33–7. See also: Stéphane Jonas, 'Les Jardins d'Ungemach à Strasbourg: Une cité-jardin d'origine nataliste (1923–1950)' in: Paulette Girard and Bruno Fayolle Lusac eds., *Cités, cités-jardins: Une histoire européene. Actes du colloque de Toulouse des 18 et 19 novembre 1993* (Toulouse 1996) 65–87.
[81] Rémi Baudouï, 'La Cité-jardin française entre mythes et réalités' in: Paulette Girard and Bruno Fayolle Lusac eds., *Cités, cités-jardins: Une histoire européene. Actes du colloque de Toulouse des 18 et 19 novembre 1993* (Toulouse 1996) 88–100, especially 97, Jean-Claude Vigato, 'La Cité-jardin et l'architecture régionaliste' in: Paulette Girard and Bruno Fayolle Lusac eds., *Cités, cités-jardins: Une histoire européene. Actes du colloque de Toulouse des 18 et 19 novembre 1993* (Toulouse 1996) 115–26, especially 121, and Stanley Buder, *Visionaries and Planners: The Garden City Movement and the Modern Community* (Oxford and New York 1990) 142–56. See also: Anthony Sutcliffe, 'Le Contexte urbanistique de l'oeuvre d'Henri Sellier: La transcription du modèle anglais de la cité-jardin' in: Katherine Burlen ed., *La Banlieue oasis: Henri Sellier et les cités-jardins, 1900–1940* (Saint-Denis 1987) 67–80, especially 78–9 and Susanna Magri and Christian Topalov, 'De la cité-jardin à la ville rationalisée: Un tournant du projet réformateur, 1905–1925. Etude comparative France, Grande-Bretagne, Italie, Etats-Unis', *Revue française de sociologie* (1987) 417–51.
[82] Already during the First World War the enormous effort of the Federal War Housing project in the United States, constructing more than 200 workers' settlements by using

Thus, contrary to the outcome of the debates during the war, regionalist architecture played only a minor role in the reconstruction of the devastated areas of Northern France; the few major social housing projects that were realised did not really provide an influential alternative. Nonetheless, regionalism was accepted by both the authorities and mainstream architects as a viable alternative, particularly for constructions in suburban or rural areas. This became especially clear on paper. Thus, between 1923 and 1926 Charles Letrosne (1868–1939), the head architect of the state agency for Civil Buildings and National Palaces, published a three-volume treatise on regionalist architecture called *Murs et toits pour le pays de chez nous* (Walls and Roofs for Our Homeland). In this book, which was prefaced by Léandre Vaillat, he proposed up-to-date neo-vernacular models for all types of public and private buildings arranged by region. The Parisian publisher Massin from about 1924 issued a 'collection of regional art in France', containing twelve volumes dedicated to regionalist furniture and nine to the domestic architecture of a specific region, among whom one was surprisingly on the Tunisian house. And a prominent architect such as Gustave Umbdenstock (1866–1940), who had designed several houses for the garden cities of the Railway Company of the North, dedicated some 200 pages of his published architectural course at the Polytechnic to French regionalist architecture.[83]

Whereas villa suburbs were still rare in France, the main areas where regionalist architecture continued to flourish were tourist areas. Nonetheless, in general these villas did not exhibit any innovative features and became a mere fashionable envelope. Many architects in the seaside resorts gave their clients a choice; they could have a villa with a specified lay-out built either in a regionalist or modern style. Sometimes even a choice could be made between various neo-vernacular models such as Breton or Anglo-Normand.[84] Local authorities also started to apply regionalist recipes, thus in Deauville in the interwar period the railway station, the market and the houses for the customs officials were built in a neo-Normand style. Private

standardised materials and serial construction was reviewed positively in France: J.L., 'Cités-jardins et villes ouvrières aux États-Unis', *Art et Décoration* (1914–19) 59–64. See for the innovative role of social housing elsewhere: Heymann, 'Wohnungsbau in Paris' and Bullock and Read, *Movement for Housing Reform* 532–4.
[83] Vigato, *L'Architecture régionaliste* 139–78, Deborah Dawson Hurtt, 'Rivalry and Representation: Regionalist Architecture and the Road to the 1937 Paris Exposition' (PhD dissertation, University of Virginia, 2005) 49–59 and Jean-Étienne Grislain, 'Simplicité et distinction', *Monuments historiques* 144 (April–May 1986) 57–63.
[84] Le Couédic, *Les Architectes et l'idée bretonne* 414 and Toulier, 'Régionalisme dans l'architecture balnéaire' 101–2.

companies also participated in the venture as shops, hotels and even a petrol station were constructed in the same style.[85]

Compared to Germany, however, the strength and implications of regionalist architecture were quite different. It received support from the same reform-minded upper-class circles as in Germany, such as the Musée Social and individual politicians and entrepreneurs. Most were social-liberals, others reformist conservatives or social-Catholics. After the war social-democrats also began to play an important role. All were very preoccupied with the social question in general and the living conditions of the working classes in particular and wanted to break with the still dominant laissez-faire attitude. However, most of them were quite isolated and their support had less effect than in Germany. The garden city recipe with its neo-vernacular cottages or terraced houses was only applied to workers' colonies, but resulted in far too few new dwellings to seriously help solve the housing question. The upper and middle classes apparently felt no need to show their solidarity by moving into a mixed garden suburb. Probably, this could be explained as in France there was less need to fear a socialist revolution since the labour movement was weaker than in Germany and at least until the 1930s constituted no immediate threat to the political system of the Third Republic.[86] Consequently, compared to Germany, the French social welfare provisions were rather precarious and, as also became manifest in the garden cities, were mainly limited to the 'worthy poor' and directed to raising the birth rate. Thus neglect and repression were preferred to an ambitious and well-co-ordinated programme of social reform.[87]

Notwithstanding the weakness of regionalist architecture in France, the regionalist character was more pronounced than in Germany. Every region had its own neo-vernacular style. However, the regions that were identified, such as Normandy, Brittany and Provence did not correspond with the existing administrative units of the departments. Instead they mostly coincided with the historical provinces that had been abolished during the French Revolution and that referred to supposedly well-defined underlying ethnic identities. Regionalist architecture as a consequence implicitly criticised the strong centralism of the French State and the

---

[85]   Marie-Noël Tournoux, *Deauville: Les styles normands: Itinéraires du patrimoine* (Deauville 1999).

[86]   The French Socialist and the Communist Party together had no more than 23 per cent of the seats in the National Assembly in 1924; only in 1936 would they reach 38 per cent.

[87]   Timothy B. Smith, 'The Plight of the Able-Bodied Poor and Unemployed in Urban France, 1880–1914', *European History Quarterly* (2000) 147–84.

artificial division of the country in equal-sized departments which stifled the organic growth of the nation's vital forces. Thus, as in the French regionalist movement and the Fédération Régionaliste Française (with which many architects and critics sympathised or even had close contacts), identification with the nation through ethnically and historically defined regions was combined with a plea for decentralisation, which in this case was mostly left implicit.

6

Spain

Probably the most striking aspect of neo-vernacular architecture in Spain was its rare appearance in Catalonia, the region with the strongest self-awareness. The Catalan movement had gained influence during the second half of the nineteenth century, although initially it was mainly focused on the cultural domain. At the beginning of the 1890s, however, it also formulated a political programme and already by 1913 the region received some political autonomy with the creation of the *Mancomunitat*, a common authority for the four Catalan provinces. After the creation in 1871 of a new Provincial School for Architecture in Barcelona, architects also tried to distinguish themselves from the rest of the country. Thus, during the last few decades of the nineteenth century, the historicist architecture in Catalonia was strongly inspired by the Gothic tradition, which was widely present in the region but quite rare in most other parts of Spain. Like the painters, Catalan architects and commissioners were also eager to adopt new international trends. Thus, at the end of the nineteenth century, a new generation of artists and architects adopted highly modern styles, such as Art Nouveau and Symbolism, which in Catalonia became known collectively as Modernismo, or *Modernisme* in the now more widely used Catalan language. Although the local variant of Art Nouveau received a particular flavour and some Catalan accents, vernacular elements played only a subordinate and decorative role. This is all the more surprising in light of the fact that the best-known *modernista* architects were prominent propagandists of the Catalan movement. Lluis Domènech i Montaner (1850–1923) was one of its early leaders, and Josep Puig i Cadafalch (1867–1956) would in 1917 become the second president of the *Mancomunidad*, whereas Antoni Gaudí (1852–1926) combined his strong Catholicism with an equally fervent Catalanism. After about 1906, an aesthetic reaction set in under the leadership of the writer Eugenio d'Ors, also an influential Catalanist. Against the disorder, individuality and aestheticism of *Modernisme*, he defended a new *Noucentisme* (an 'ism' derived from the Catalan word for 'twentieth century'), a new social art, based on an ordered, Mediterranean classicism, which again left little space for vernacular influences.[1]

Although in general the cultural, political and economic elites of Barcelona preferred to connect the Catalan identity with international, urban modernity, regionalist architecture was not completely absent in Catalonia. Thus, as in the south of France, rural construction traditions from Roman antiquity were also considered native and could inspire regionalist country houses. Some architects even used medieval rural architecture for their villas and cottages, and in this way the traditional farmhouse – the *masia* – became a model for at least some new villas and small public buildings.[2] Nonetheless, neo-vernacular architecture was much stronger in other parts of Spain. As in France, where the regionalist architecture was strongly present on the Atlantic coast and along the Channel, in Spain it particularly flourished in the main, fashionable seaside resorts of the period, which were situated on the Bay of Biscay. Other strongholds could be found in the Basque town of Bilbao and in Seville.

Villas and country houses

Regionalist architecture arrived late in Spain compared to Germany and France, and most of its prominent advocates were born only in the 1870s. As the country was somewhat smaller and considerably poorer, the market for new villas and country houses was weaker than it was in Germany and France. There was almost no exodus of the middle and upper classes from the inner cities to new suburbs or the countryside, although there had been no thorough reform of the inner cities, such as had occurred in France. The generally quite modest towns were extended with new, luxurious quarters just outside the old city, of which the most ambitious was without a doubt the Eixample in Barcelona, after the highly original plan of Ildefons Cerdà. Initially, these were meant to be quite spacious, but most ended up as rather densely developed urban quarters. In these new neighbourhoods only the very rich could afford a free-standing villa,

[1] Javier Hernando, *Arquitectura en España, 1770–1900* (Madrid 1989) 199–204, Ángel Urrutia, *Arquitectura española del siglo XX* (Madrid 1997) 47–84 and 185–91.

[2] L.F.T., 'La arquitectura suburbana en Barcelona', *La Construcción Moderna* XI, 8 (30 April 1913) 113–24 and 'Arquitectura catalana', *La Construcción Moderna* XI, 20 (30 October 1913) 305–18. See also: Esteban Castañer, 'Catalogne: À la recherche d'une architecture nationaliste' in: François Loyer and Bernard Toulier eds., *Le Régionalisme, architecture et identité* (Paris 2001) 208–20.

whereas the middle classes generally had to content themselves with an apartment, as was the case in France.[3]

Spain, particularly after the disastrous war against the United States in 1898, in which it lost the last remnants of its once glorious empire, was generally seen as a backward and peripheral European power. Nor was it at the forefront in cultural matters. However, the Spanish elites were aware of developments abroad and generally kept themselves well informed about all kinds of new cultural and artistic trends by reading foreign and especially French periodicals. This was also the case with architecture. As in France and Germany, the architectural journals in Spain mainly contained short factual reports on technical and legal issues, reviews of conferences and books, and the occasional essay or lecture. In contrast to France and Germany, there were no magazines devoted to the decorative arts and the few more general art periodicals paid no attention to architecture. Nonetheless, from about 1912 a substantial number of the more general articles in the professional journals were dedicated to regionalist architecture.

Also the content of these articles and essays was quite different from what was to be found in the French and German specialised press. In Germany, most articles were reviews of individual country houses or suburban cottages. The writings of Muthesius and others were very concrete and their arguments were strictly professional; they revealed their ideals in the detailed analysis of specific buildings. In France, articles generally were more theoretical: they did not discuss houses that had actually been built, but showed how a good country house should be built. This was particularly clear in Sézille's writings, in which he usually proposed a model for a house in a very specific location. In Spain, reviews of individual constructions were almost non-existent. Nor was there a self-appointed propagandist who produced models for various regions and sites. On the contrary, most essays in the architectural journals dealt with more abstract issues without giving actual examples. One of the most widely debated issues, however, was whether the neo-vernacular should be the national architectural style.

This debate was in fact part of a wider discussion on the Spanish national identity and especially on the role of art in the regeneration of the country. Architects and critics referred to well-known writers and intellectuals, and some of them also intervened in the architectural

---

[3] Fernando de Terán, *Historia del urbanismo en España III Siglos XIX y XX* (Madrid 1999).

debates, generally favouring a new orientation towards local vernacular constructions. For example, in 1909 the novelist Azorín, who also defended Zuloaga, criticised the proposition of the Fifth National Conference of Architects in Valencia that architects should extend their activities to small villages as he feared that they would introduce the bombastic historicist style into the countryside. In his almost daily column in the conservative newspaper *ABC*, Azorín maintained that, judging from recent monumental buildings in Madrid, architecture had slipped into complete decadence and architects were producing only 'pretentious and eye-catching houses' that imitated the sumptuous buildings in the big cities. 'No, let the local genius of the constructors and masons develop freely and according to tradition. The modern architects operate in the abstract; they do not take into account the climate, the temperature, the major or minor transparency of the air, the surrounding constructions, the landscape, etc., etc.' This was not such a problem in a town, but according to the author in the small villages 'the landscape dominates construction and the climate is more in control than man'. Azorín argued that it was necessary to first study the natural conditions and traditions, maintaining that the 'profound instinct of life and harmony' of the traditional artisans led them automatically to produce houses that were perfectly adapted to the local circumstances.[4] Thus instead of pushing aside local craftsmen, architects should learn from them.

Other authors referred positively to Ángel Ganivet who, although he committed suicide in 1898, could be seen as the main Spanish ideologue of a new organic nationalism and who already in 1896 in his *Granada la Bella* (Granada the Beautiful) had come up with a plea similar to Azorín's in favour of a more organic architecture that reflected local circumstances and traditions and drew its inspiration from existing rural constructions. According to Ganivet, art and architecture should reflect the environment, and this was best done in simple and spontaneous popular creations. Following vernacular examples was both logical and economical, according to the author: 'The typical is the primitive, and is the first thing men create when they take possession of the environment in which they live; and the first has to be and is what requires less consumption of forces.'[5] A

---

[4] Azorín, 'La arquitectura', *ABC* (9 July 1909) 6. Azorín in turn was criticised by an architect for having oversimplified ideas: Pedro Cerdan, 'Carta abierta: La arquitectura', *La Construcción Moderna* (1909) 331–2.

[5] Ángel Ganivet, *Granada la Bella* (1896) in: Idem, *Obras completas* (Madrid 1962), I 59–147, especially 123–5. See for the references to Ganivet: Leonardo Rucabado, 'La tradición en arquitectura', *Arquitectura y Construcción* (1917) 27–42, especially 38 and Eduardo Gallego, 'La educación estética del pueblo: El arte público en Madrid', *La Construcción Moderna* (1920) 178–80, especially 178.

truly national regeneration could only be produced by a reorientation to the specific circumstances at a regional level. Regionalism and nationalism for Ganivet thus were two sides of the same coin.

The professor at the School for Architecture in Madrid, Manuel Aníbal Álvarez (1850–1930), was one of the first architects to adopt the point of view that in designing a building one should take into account regional differences. In his inaugural lecture in 1910 at the Royal Academy of Fine Arts, he maintained that every country, because of its different climate and traditions, had its own customs. It would therefore be wrong to import foreign architectural modes. However, in the past Spanish architecture had been dominated by foreign styles, sometimes as a result of a foreign occupation, sometimes because of kings who brought in architects from abroad. He thus doubted the existence of a truly Spanish style in the past. Nonetheless, he expressed the hope that a new, up-to-date national style would be created in which interior decoration and exterior were in harmony with 'the light, the sky, the atmosphere and the vegetation of every locality'.[6]

A somewhat more positive interpretation of the Spanish architectural past was given by Vicente Lampérez y Romea (1861–1923), a professor of architectural history at the School for Architecture in Madrid, who had been responsible for the restoration of medieval monuments, such as the Cathedral of Burgos. At the opening of the First Salon for Architecture in Madrid in 1911 Lampérez defended the need to follow those national architectural traditions that had been made truly Spanish and could still be adopted: 'The architectural forms that are a part of certain historical styles are the decantation, over centuries and generations, of principles and laws, so variable in one factor (the habits), perennial in others (the spirit of the races, the conditions of the country).' He especially referred to the styles that were in use during the most brilliant period in Spanish history, namely from the end of the Middle Ages until the seventeenth century. On the other hand, he also distinguished 'exotic' styles, which were imitations 'of foreign styles and dispositions, contrary in the majority of cases to the needs, the uses, the materials and the climate of the country: only for the supreme reason that is *fashion*' (italics in the original). He agreed with Álvarez that it was necessary to develop a new national style that was adapted to 'our actual life, and our spirit'.[7]

---

[6] Manuel Aníbal Álvarez, 'Lo que pudiera ser la arquitectura española contemporánea: Discurso leído por el autor en el acto de su recepción en la Real Academia de Bellas Artes de San Fernando', *Arquitectura y Construcción* (1910) 139–50.

[7] Vicente Lampérez y Romea, 'La arquitectura española contemporánea: Tradicionalismos

Reviewing what he saw at the Salon, he distinguished two groups: the Catalan and the Castilian, which in fact amounted to the respective spheres of influence of the schools for architecture in Barcelona and Madrid. According to Lampérez, in the Catalan sphere most architects followed the traditions of the country, which in the Catalan case meant the Gothic style, which was the only style that had undergone a powerful development and had local characteristics. The problem in the rest of the country was caused not so much by the architects – who generally wanted to build in an updated national style – as by the clients, who requested imitations of foreign trends. The new national style propagated by Lampérez, like that promoted by Álvarez, should take into account regional differences. Thus, in Andalusia it was logical to construct houses with a patio and an awning as in Roman times, whereas in the region around Santander houses should be solid and closed like the Celtic dwellings.[8]

Over the subsequent few years, Lampérez continued his preaching in favour of a new national architecture in a substantial number of lectures and articles. He even emphasised the need to look for inspiration in vernacular architecture. In a lecture he gave at the Royal Geographical Society in Madrid he maintained that the vernacular architecture of former times was in particular subjected to the 'tyranny' of geographical factors, declaring that 'exotic constructions' – most of which had been built for the aristocracy, who rebelled against these factors – soon decayed or had to be renovated. On another occasion he reviewed some of the main regional building traditions. He concluded that by studying this type of vernacular building:

> one perceives the embryo of the Spanish regional architecture, adapted
> in its entirety to the particular soil, climate, needs and materials
> of every region, whose characteristics confer a great archaeological
> interest to these modest types of constructions, and which indicates
> to the modern architects the course we have to steer to Hispanicise
> our architecture, putting aside the exoticisms, based on fashion,
> which could never be real Art, which always has to be inspired in
> Nature, the master of all human creations; and just like the painter
> and sculptor have to study her, the architect should not disdain with

y exotismos. Conferencia dada en el "Salon de Arquitectura" el 19 de junio 1911', *Arquitectura y Construcción* (1911) 194–9, especially 195–6. Lampérez particularly saw the Gothic, *mudéjar* and Renaissance styles as still apt to be adopted, whereas elements from Muslim architecture and the Baroque *churrigueresco* style could also be used.

[8] Lampérez, 'La arquitectura española' 195–8. See also: 'La arquitectura civil: Conferencias dadas en el curso de estudios superiores del Ateneo de Madrid, por D. Vicente Lampérez y Romea', *Arquitectura y Construcción* (1913) 50–8.

absurd constructions the elements that the same Nature provides him to distinguish his works.[9]

At the Salon for Architecture, Manuel Vega y March (1871–1931), the director and owner of *Arquitectura y Construcción*, the main platform for architectural debate in the country, and the critic and architect Luis María Cabello y Lapiedra (1861–1936), who regularly published in the same monthly, also advocated a new national style. Although the journal was edited in Barcelona, Vega was highly critical of both the Catalan movement and the *Modernista* architecture. Nevertheless, he strongly supported the renovation of the decorative arts that was taking place at about the same time, a process in which the *modernistas* had a prominent role. Like Lampérez, in his article on the Salon, Vega pleaded for a new, modern Spanish style, based on national, regional and popular traditions. Cabello y Lapiedra also defended the need to find inspiration in national traditions. In 1917, he even dedicated a complete book, called *The Spanish House*, to the issue.[10]

Similar opinions were published in the other important architectural journal of the period, *La Construcción Moderna*, although this fortnightly journal put more stress on technical and engineering questions than did *Arquitectura y Construcción*. Some of the lectures given by Lampérez were summarised in its pages. In a short article, José María Donosty maintained that 'the Spanish house' varied from region to region as this reflected the regional diversity of the nation. This had not only geographical and climatic causes, but also 'racial' ones. The diversity in Spain, according to him, 'arises from life itself, from its topographical contrasts, the relief of its soil, the latitudinal influences, the differences of its invading races and even the modified autochthonous sediment.'[11]

The most polemical contribution to the debate was a joint lecture by Leonardo Rucabado (1875–1918) and Aníbal González Álvarez (1876–1929) at the sixth National Conference of Architects, which was held in San Sebastián in 1915. Over the subsequent few years, Rucabado and González

<hr>

[9] Luis S[áinz]. de los Terreros, 'Conferencia del Sr. Lampérez', *La Construcción Moderna* (1917) 22 and A. Alcaide, 'Arquitectura regional (Conferencia en el Ateneo de Madrid)', *La Construcción Moderna* (1916) 325–6.

[10] Manuel Vega y March, 'Divagaciones sobre el tema Salón de Arquitectura', *Arquitecture y Construcción* (1911) 209–13 and Luis María Cabello Lapiedra, 'El Salón de Arquitectura', *Arquitectura y Construcción* (1911) 199–208. His book was called *La casa española: Consideracones acerca de una arquitectura nacional*. See also: Ángel Isac, *Eclecticismo y pensamiento arquitectónico en España: Discursos, revistas, congresos 1846–1919* (Granada 1987) 224–50 and 343–6.

[11] José María Donosty, 'La casa española', *La Construcción Moderna* (1914) 85–6.

Álvarez became the most prominent exponents of the new style. The former was born in the province of Santander but also worked in the Basque Country, whereas the latter was active in Seville. They had decided to defend their point of view in a lecture entitled 'Orientations for the Resurgence of a National Architecture'. Again, one can detect the same mixture of regionalist and nationalist elements. A national regeneration according to both speakers could only come about by respecting regional differences and identities.

At this occasion Rucabado and González Álvarez maintained that a devotion to tradition was one of the characteristics of the Spanish 'race'. However, a too pronounced orientation towards foreign and thus 'exotic' examples had led to the loss of the bond with the national architectural tradition. The best way to repair this bond was to start imitating the ancient traditions and styles. Just like the Greek temple and the Gothic cathedral – which they considered the most sublime examples of a perfect harmony of spiritual and mechanical principles – had been the product of infinite repetitions of only a few elements, the Spanish architects should also start to repeat ancient forms. After a period of study and initiation, they could begin to permit themselves some more liberty, and with the passing of time and by perfecting what they already had, a new and modern national style could come into existence.[12]

According to the speakers, complete freedom did not exist in art or architecture. As the French historian Taine had shown, every work of an artist was intimately connected with his entire oeuvre, which in turn was intimately connected with the school or family of artists of the same country and the same period to which he belonged. In its turn, this group depended on the state of the customs and the 'universal spirit' of the period. Thus, the advice to all artists should be: 'Investigate your origins and you will know your aptitudes, and you will be able to walk over the true path of your destinies.' Consequently, progress was possible only by following tradition. This meant that in every Spanish region the architects had to adapt themselves to the local topography, climate and temperament. This reorientation towards historical and ethnographical traditions had already taken place to some extent in Catalonia and the Basque Country. The two architects now hoped that the other regions would follow and thus fill the 'wide national river-bed', fusing themselves in the unity of the fatherland. They finished their presentation with an appeal to both their colleagues

---

[12] Leonardo Rucabado and Aníbal González, 'Orientaciones para el resurgimiento de una arquitectura nacional', *Arte Español* (1915) 379–86 and 437–53, especially 383–4, 437–40 and 451–3.

and the national and local authorities to stimulate awareness of the national architectural traditions and to propagate a new architecture that was rooted in national and regional traditions.[13]

Shortly after his presentation, Rucabado published an extensive article in *Arquitectura y Construcción* in which he further explained his understanding of the term 'tradition'. Referring to his lecture in San Sebastián, he wrote that he had not wanted to prescribe how architects should work. However, he remained convinced that progress in architecture could only be achieved by the evolutionary repetition of mechanical and ornamental forms. But which old styles should serve as an example for contemporary architects? According to Rucabado, nations are like individuals in that they have their own character and predilections for certain forms, manners and ways of expression. These are determined by the collective psychology, the historical contingencies, as well as by 'the material conditions of the locality, its topography, its climate and even the qualities of the disposable materials'. The architect thus had to look for inspiration in the tradition that best reflected the local collective personality.[14]

A more moderate point of view – and an implicit criticism of the position of Rucabado and González Álvarez – was expressed by Leopoldo Torres Balbás (1888–1960), the main editor of *Arquitectura*, the official organ of the Central Society of Architects. In June 1918, in one of the first issues of this new monthly, he criticised the use of the recently fashionable term 'Spanish style'. A false nationalism, according to him, would only result in pastiches, that is, the application of ancient exterior forms to modern constructions. Those who advocated an imitation of past styles did not understand that the great architects of the past never imitated their predecessors. Instead he argued for another, more 'truly' nationalistic attitude, whereby one would be open to foreign influences *and* study the buildings of the national past. More than monumental buildings one should look for inspiration in the 'ordinary, popular and anonymous architecture, in whose forms one sees the perpetuation of a secular tradition and in which we can better discern the constructive spirit of our race'. Instead of imitating the decoration and mouldings one should assimilate the essence, that is, 'the proportions, the relationship between masses and volumes, the distribution of the decoration, etcetera'. A good architect consequently should 'translate the traditional spirit of Spanish architecture into modern forms'. An architect thus should try to discover

---

[13] Rucabado and González, 'Orientaciones' 382, 385, 440, 446–7 and 453.
[14] Leonardo Rucabado, 'La tradición en la arquitectura', *Arquitectura y Construcción* (1917) 27–42, especially 35, 38–9.

the intimate, profound and peculiar collective personality of a certain region or nation and its genuine tradition.[15]

Although the nuances were different, all these critics defended the need for architects to reconnect with the Spanish *Volksgeist* and its regional variants and adapt old architectural styles and traditions in order to create a new national style. This is even more surprising if one bears in mind that the political affinities of these critics and architects differed widely and covered almost the entire spectrum, although none of them seemed to embrace the now widely criticised laissez-faire liberalism that had dominated the past decades. For example, Cabello y Lapiedra supported the ultramontanist Carlist cause, which hoped to replace the Bourbons with a reactionary, dissident branch of the royal family. Judging by his citations, Rucabado seemed to adhere to the conservative Catholic ideology of the great historian Marcelino Menéndez Pelayo, who also originated from the province of Santander. And his main Maecenas was Tomás Allende, a rich entrepreneur who was a senator for the Conservative Party. After a brief flirtation with anarchism, Azorín also had become a member of parliament for the Conservative Party, although his ideas could be better defined as neo-conservative and were similar to those of Maurice Barrès in France. Torres Balbás, on the other hand, had progressive liberal or even republican sympathies and welcomed the Bolshevist revolution in Russia, while Manuel Vega y March became town councillor in Barcelona for the Radical Republican Party of the populist Alejandro Lerroux.[16]

However, not everybody adhered to the new nationalist slogans. At the National Conference of Architects in San Sebastián, the main opponent of Rucabado and González was the Valencian architect Demetrio Ribes (1875–1921), who argued that a new national architecture, based on tradition, would only amount to copying details of ancient buildings. Instead of imitating others, he preferred artistic freedom. He did not want to reject all traditions but, according to him, it was more important to study new forms and techniques that corresponded to the present needs.[17]

---

15 Leopoldo Torres Balbás, 'Mientras labran los sillares', *Arquitectura* (1918) 31–4, especially 33–4. The central argument and terminology of Torres Balbás strongly reflected the ideas, rhetoric and nationalism of Unamuno, and particularly of his influential book on Spanish identity *En torno al casticismo* (1895).

16 See for Cabello y Lapiedra, Rucabado, Torres Balbás and Vega y March: Isac, *Eclecticismo y pensamiento arquitectónico*, respectively 344, 347–8, 351–3 and 232 and for Azorín: Eric Storm, *La perspectiva del progreso: Pensamiento político en la España del cambio de siglo (1890–1914)* (Madrid 2001) 265–89.

17 Demetrio Ribes, 'La tradición en arquitectura', *Arquitectura y Construcción* (1918) 21–8. See also: Isac, *Eclecticismo y pensamiento arquitectónico* 349–51.

Another striking issue, especially when compared with Germany, was that those who called for a national architecture proposed examples from both high architecture and vernacular traditions. This is understandable, as the debate was held in general terms, often in the form of lectures for a more general public. Moreover, this new Spanish style should also be applied to monumental buildings. But how did this work out in domestic architecture?

Until the early 1920s, the architectural press paid almost exclusive attention to the new domestic architecture in the Basque Country and Cantabria (of which Santander is the capital). The strong regionalist nucleus around Aníbal González in Seville would be reviewed only in later years. The interest in Cantabria was focused almost exclusively on the architect Rucabado. After his study in Barcelona, where Domènech had been his preferred teacher, Rucabado had started working in the rapidly industrialising town of Bilbao. In the new quarters of the city he built luxurious villas for the enriched bourgeoisie and some aristocrats in a great variety of styles, ranging from French Beaux-Arts style, to English neo-Gothic, French and Belgian Art Nouveau, the Viennese *Sezession* and the English cottage style. However, around 1909 he decided to change his orientation. Instead of importing new foreign modes, he now wanted to derive his inspiration from the traditions of his native region, the Montaña (the area around Santander). For the following few years he spent considerable time travelling the whole province to make sketches, notes and pictures of typical buildings and construction traditions.[18]

Rucabado's new orientation became visible in 1911, when he won one of the prizes in the architectural contest at the first Salon for Architecture, with his palace for a noble in the Montaña (figure 19). Although one of the themes of the contest was the design of a small country house, Rucabado had consciously chosen to participate in the 'private palace or public building' section, probably because he had more experience in working for a rich clientele. He included in his project elements from various palaces and houses in his native region from about the fifteenth until the eighteenth

---

[18] Leonardo Rucabado, 'Arquitectura española contemporánea: Casa de Don Escauriaza. Bilbao. Arquitecto: Don Leonardo Rucabado', *Arquitectura y Construcción* (1916) 1–9, especially 2 and 8. See also Vicente Lampérez y Romea, 'Leonardo Rucabado', *Arquitectura* (1918) 217–24, especially 217, 'Casa hotel en Castro-Urdiales (Santander). Arquitecto: D. Leonardo Rucabado', *Pequeñas monografías de arte* I, 4 (August 1907) and Nieves Basurto, *Leonardo Rucabado y la arquitectura montañes* (Madrid 1986).

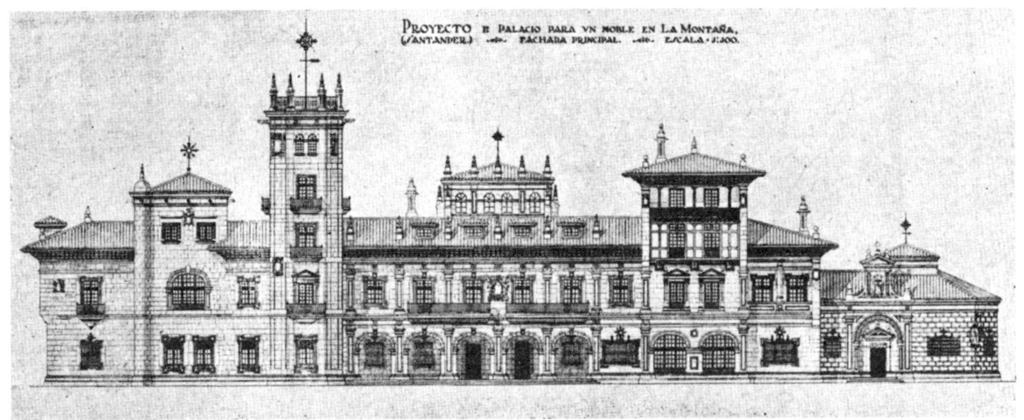

19 Leonardo Rucabado, Project: palace for a noble in the Montaña, 1911.

century. Thus, his interests included not only the vernacular traditions, but also more monumental buildings in historical styles that supposedly fitted well into the region.[19]

Lampérez asserted in a long obituary of Rucabado, who in 1918 had been one of the many victims of the Spanish flu, that his friend was not a slavish imitator but shrewdly adapted old elements and especially the 'intimate spirit' of ancient traditions to create new modern constructions. His many buildings in a Montañés or Basque style showed that he knew better than anyone else how to replace the English hall, the bow window, the loggia and the silhouette of an English cottage or a French *hôtel* with native equivalents.[20]

One of Rucabado's last commissions, for an apartment building (figure 20) in the centre of Madrid, received a lot of attention in the specialised press. Lampérez tells us that Rucabado wanted to construct on the narrow site an elegant, modern and ultra-European building with a Spanish façade, combining elements from various epochs and regions. The final result was judged by Torres Balbás in the pages of *Arquitectura*. According to Torres Balbás, the building perfectly embodied both the qualities and the faults of Rucabado's architecture. He particularly praised the meticulous attention the architect had paid to the details of the building and to the interior. Rucabado had also shown his mastery in giving the whole a certain unity, although the building consisted of a lot of different elements. This was the main problem, as many of Rucabado's designs were not natural and logical, but profuse and affected. According to Torres Balbás, he had combined too

---

[19] See Isac, *Eclecticismo y pensamiento arquitectónico* 337–8 and Basurto, *Leonardo Rucabado* 46–7.

[20] Lampérez, 'Rucabado', 220.

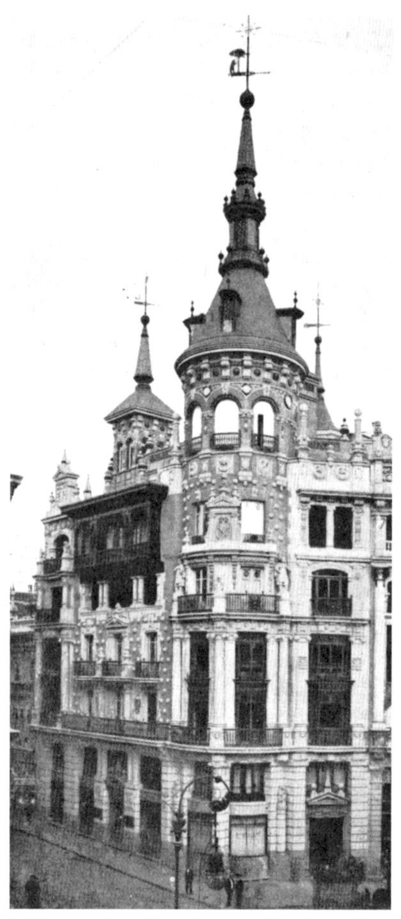

20 Leonardo
Rucabado,
Apartment
building, Plaza
de Canalejas,
Madrid, 1920.

many different architectural elements, for example fragments of the classical architecture of Toledo, a gallery from Cantabria, decorative shells from palaces in Salamanca, Andalusian brick towers and spires from Madrid.[21]

According to the same critic, artistic nationalism and regionalism had become an international trend. He complained that in the area around Santander, many rich people – especially those who had profited from Spain's neutrality during the First World War and those who had been ennobled in the previous decades – wished to follow this new fashion. They:

> wanted to live in mansions, chalets and palaces, constructed in the
> so-called Montañés style; and to furnish them they bought old chests,

---

[21] Ibid., 224 and Leopoldo Torres Balbás, 'La última obra de Rucabado', *Arquitectura* (1920) 132–9, especially 132 and 135–6.

heavy walnut cupboards, solid chestnut seats, benches with turned
balusters, even coats of arms ripped off ancient palaces, and entrance
gates that were reconstructed afterwards on their estates. Surrounding
themselves with an ancient and noble atmosphere, they possibly
pretended to age their recent blazon, which they acquired more by
their fortune than by proper merits, which they lacked.

The problem, however, was not only the bad taste of this parvenu clientele,
but also the lack among architects of knowledge of the region's traditional
architecture. Rucabado had made a profound study of the typical buildings
in the province of Santander, but he was an exception. According to the
critic the *estilo montañés* that he had inaugurated had thus degenerated into
a superficial pseudo-style that was applied to the tramway lamps, public
dustbins and even blast-furnaces.[22]

A more fundamental critique appeared four years later in the same
journal. Unlike Torres Balbás, who in 1918 had approved of a moderate
and open nationalistic attitude in architecture, the author of this article,
Elías Ortíz de la Torre, asserted that an architect had to be a man of his
own times and should not use an antiquated language to express modern
ideas. A neo-vernacular villa in an urban surrounding seemed to him like
a man 'who dressed up like a villager and walks through the streets of
the town with a rake on his shoulders and letting his clogs sound on the
asphalt'. He admitted that Rucabado had succeeded in creating a modern
type of Montaña house, in which 'the typical traditional elements have
their representation or rather, their more or less transformed recollection'.
Rucabado did not continue or revive an ancient tradition, but simply used
traditional elements taken from a wide variety of buildings and epochs
in a very different setting. Rucabado thus transformed the aristocratic
tower, which originally had a defensive purpose, into a graceful and
transparent watchtower. The gallery, which had a rustic origin, was not
placed on one side but repeated on almost all façades. And the typical
portico was sometimes placed under the tower, thus dispossessing the latter
of its majestic and robust character. According to the critic, the modern
principles of a lively plan and an uneven silhouette, which were usually
applied by Rucabado, were at least as important for the final picturesque
result as these recollections of ancient architecture. Younger architects
showed even less respect for the historical function of the various elements,
and they did not have much knowledge of the difference between the

---

22 Torres Balbás, 'La última obra de Rucabado' 132–5.

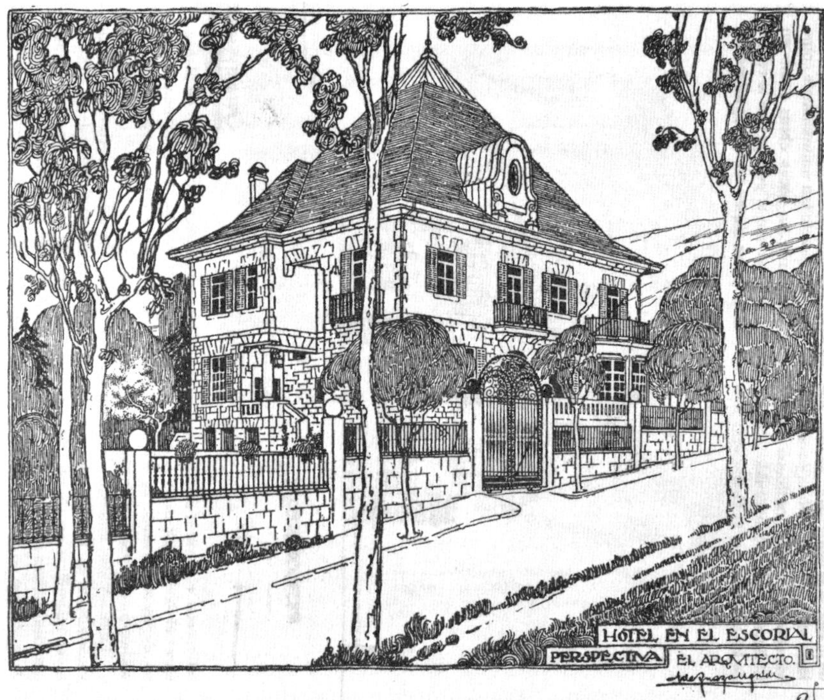

21 Secundino Zuazo Ugalde, Villa in the Sierra de Guadarrama, 1920.

various epochs. As a consequence, they produced even worse villas than those of Rucabado.[23]

The surprising mixture of vernacular and historicist elements in Rucabado's buildings could also be found in the work of other architects and in other regions. In a review of a villa (figure 21) by the Basque architect Secundino Zuazo Ugalde (1887–1970) in the mountains near Madrid, Torres Balbás made clear that he sincerely liked this plain and original piece of 'healthy regionalism'. He explained that most recently constructed chalets and country houses were too pretentious, used materials that were not traditionally applied in the area and revealed the bad taste of their inhabitants. On the contrary, the traditional popular dwellings were perfectly adapted to the barren, granite soil and the hard, bleak climate. Nonetheless, by using the same granite the great monumental buildings of the past looked as if they had organically grown out of the soil. Particularly El Escorial – the palace-monastery that had been built for Philip II – harmonised with the countryside around it and, according to the author, its lines and masses could help us to interpret

23   Elías Ortiz de la Torre, 'El estilo montañés', *Arquitectura* (1926) 450–61.

the 'spirit' of the surrounding nature.[24] Thus, Torres Balbás presented both vernacular dwellings and some consciously designed monumental constructions as being perfectly adapted to the local geographical and climatic circumstances. Consequently, both could function as a source of inspiration for modern architects.

The articles dedicated to the Basque Country also presented both vernacular dwellings and more monumental constructions as possible sources of inspiration. However, here more than elsewhere the authors preferred the rustic constructions. The engineer Joaquín de Yrizar, for example, opined that the isolated farmstead was as characteristic of the Basque 'race' as its language and its music. According to him, the villagers who had constructed these farmsteads were not preoccupied with a specific historical style, nor did they have the preconceived intention to achieve an artistic effect; they were inspired only by their own well-being. '[T]he constructive systems are those imposed by the climate and the materials' and the distribution of the floors 'is principally the result of the agricultural needs'.[25]

The Basque architect Pedro Guimón expressed a similar opinion. Just as the face is the mirror of the soul, the artistic manifestations of a people reflect that people's soul. Thus, the simple art of the ordinary people was 'the archive, the depot of documents where all artists who pretend to make regional art have to search'. The regional 'soul' could best be studied in its primitive pureness in the intimate family life of those who were bound to the earth in the countryside. And the building that best responded to the characteristics of both the people and the natural conditions was without a doubt the typical isolated Basque farmstead. The inhabitants of the countryside had intuitively made this 'Basque house, with a Basque soul and a Basque appearance'. Like the German critic Seesselberg, Guimón recognised that for a modern, educated architect it would be very difficult to do the same. He, for example, was not satisfied with the villa he had constructed at Zumaya beach for Ignacio Zuloaga (figure 22). Because of the sometimes conflicting wishes of the owner it had become a Basque–Parisian–Segovian house, and consequently it was a picturesque but soulless construction.[26]

---

[24] Leopoldo Torres Balbás, 'La arquitectura moderna en la Sierra de Guadarrama: Una obra de Zuazo en El Escorial', *Arquitectura* (1920) 78–84.

[25] Joaquín de Yrizar, 'Arquitectura vasca: Ensayo sobre el problema arquitectónico vasco', *La Construcción Moderna* (1926) 37–42, especially 38 and 42.

[26] Pedro Guimón, 'El alma vasca en su arquitectura', *Arquitectura* (1924) 166–73, especially 169–72.

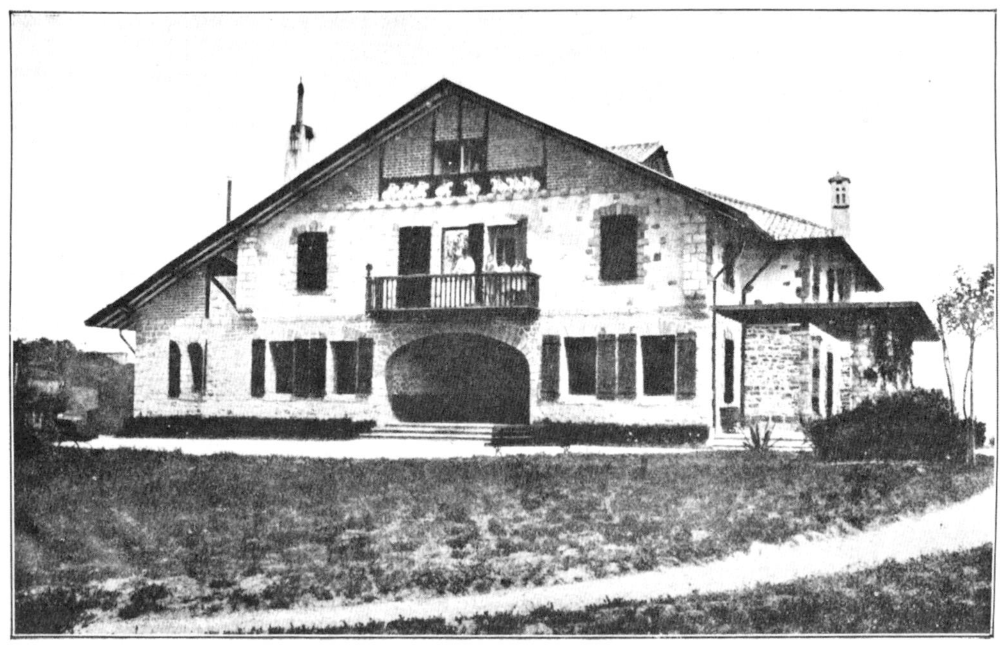

22 Pedro Guimón, House for Ignacio Zuloaga, Zumaya, around 1914.

This difficulty was also signalled by other authors. Yrizar wrote that the main problem for architects was how to combine the traditional forms with the modern construction techniques without just copying a few superficial elements. He strongly rejected the habit of imitating the timber framing of traditional houses by using 'cement strips besmirched in green or blue' as if they were made of wood. Eduardo Gallego was much less severe. He explained that the exposed wooden parts suffered from the weather and that it was quite logical to replace them with reinforced concrete. Gallego, an engineer and one of the two directors of *La Construcción Moderna*, published an illustrated report on the new buildings he had seen during his trip along the Basque beaches, in both Spain and France. According to him, nowhere had 'regional architecture' become more popular than in the Basque region. Apart from technical innovations, the new houses were adapted to the inhabitants. The saddle roof, the portico and the exposed framework of the Basque farmstead were adopted in the Basque chalet or villa. However, these were not built for farmers but for wealthy people, mostly the bourgeois who did not have to work the land. The portico thus was not needed to watch the cattle, and the architects provided more galleries and terraces so that the inhabitants could enjoy the fresh air. These modifications did not disturb the author, and he even welcomed hotels and apartment blocks in a Basque style.[27]

During the first two decades of the twentieth century, regionalism became a major architectural trend in Spain. Regionalism was widely adopted in the tourist sector, and already in 1915 the national post and telegraph company decided that the new central post offices should include in their facades 'the national historical styles and, above all, those typical of the locality in which the new building was to be constructed'. At around the same time, the railway and the national telephone company opted to apply regionalist elements in their newly built stations and offices throughout the country, even though the latter company was a daughter of the American multinational ITT.[28]

Regionalism even became the dominant architectural style in the Andalusian town of Seville. In 1910, in fact, it became the semi-official building style of the town. This was only one year after Hamburg had taken a similar step. And in many ways the almost complete dominance of the 'estilo sevillano' in subsequent decades was very similar to what was achieved in Hamburg by Schumacher. However, in Seville the fast rise of regionalism was not caused by a city architect who imposed a new regionalist style on all public buildings, but by a resolution of the conservative municipal councillor Francisco Javier de Lepe that fell on fertile ground. Lepe proposed to reward new house façades that adapted themselves to the peculiar local styles with prizes and an exemption from certain imposts. In this way the town could improve its image in the wake of the Spanish–American Exhibition, which had been recently assigned to Seville and was scheduled for 1914. In 1912 this would result in an official municipal contest. Both local architects and proprietors responded enthusiastically to Lepe's initiative, whereas the local ceramics artisans, who with the support of the local school for applied arts had improved their designs and techniques, were prepared to collaborate.[29]

The main exponent of this new architectural trend was Aníbal González Álvarez. Like Rucabado he was not very dogmatic and combined historicist

[27]   Yrizar, 'Arquitectura vasca' 41–2 and Eduardo Gallego, 'La casa vasca' *La Construcción Moderna* (1914) 273–5, 289–91, 305–8 and 321–3, especially 273–4 and 289–91.
[28]   Pedro Navascués Palacio, 'Regionalismo y arquitectura en España (1900–1930)', *Arquitectura & Vivienda* 3 (1985) 28–36.
[29]   See the exemplary and detailed study: Alberto Villar Movellán, *Arquitectura del regionalismo en Sevilla: 1900–1935* (Seville 1979) 167–87.

and vernacular elements alike. His main sources were the major buildings in the local Mudéjar (a late medieval architectural style of Moorish craftsmen who worked in Christian territories) and Renaissance style, which both referred to the most glorious period of the Sevilian past. However, he did not copy these buildings, but by selecting typical local elements, such as eaves, the aristocratic corner turret, balconies, barred windows, Arabic tiles and ceramic adornments, he gave his constructions a clear Sevilian character, and so did many of his fellow architects. The regionalist aspect, however, was most clearly visible in the creative use of brick, ceramics, traditional tiles, ironwork and other local materials and crafts. Thus, as in Hamburg a variant of regionalism had arrived, mainly based on brick and a free interpretation of traditional urban models, that could easily be applied to more monumental buildings as well, such as those of the exhibition (see chapter 7). However, whereas in Hamburg this new type of architecture was generally called 'Hanseatic' or 'north German', in Spain this style was named after the town. Nevertheless, the 'estilo sevillano' would also become popular in adjacent parts of Andalusia and Extremadura.[30]

The rising demand and higher prices caused by the First World War brought prosperity to the great Andalusian landowners. As a consequence regionalism was also exported to the countryside. This was mainly done by two younger architects. Vicente Traver (1888–1966), an architect from Castellón who only came to Seville in 1913, started to look for inspiration in the traditional buildings from the countryside, which he combined with an interest in traditional buildings in the, until then generally despised, Baroque style. The same combination of Baroque and rural influences could be detected in the work of Juan Talavera (1880–1960). On this basis he even developed a new 'white architecture', which by its success elsewhere in the region could also be called a more truly Andalusian regionalism. One of the early highlights of this new style, although situated in the urban setting of Seville's traditional Barrio de Santa Cruz, would be his house for Jerónimo Armario (figure 23), built around 1922. However, as in Normandy, the sources of inspiration could hardly be called vernacular, as the eighteenth-century farm houses (*cortijos* and *haciendas*) that functioned as models for this

---

[30] Villar Movellán, *Arquitectura del regionalismo en Sevilla* 204–5, 221, 238–70 and 348–54. Whereas Maiken Umbach compared the role of architecture in the self-definition of the 'second cities' of Hamburg and Barcelona at the end of the nineteenth century and the beginning of the twentieth, a comparison between Hamburg and Seville – also a port city and, like Hamburg, better integrated into the nation – would probably have been more interesting and fruitful. Maiken Umbach, 'A Tale of Second Cities: Autonomy, Culture, and the Law in Hamburg and Barcelona in the Late Nineteenth Century', *American Historical Review* 110 (2005) 659–92.

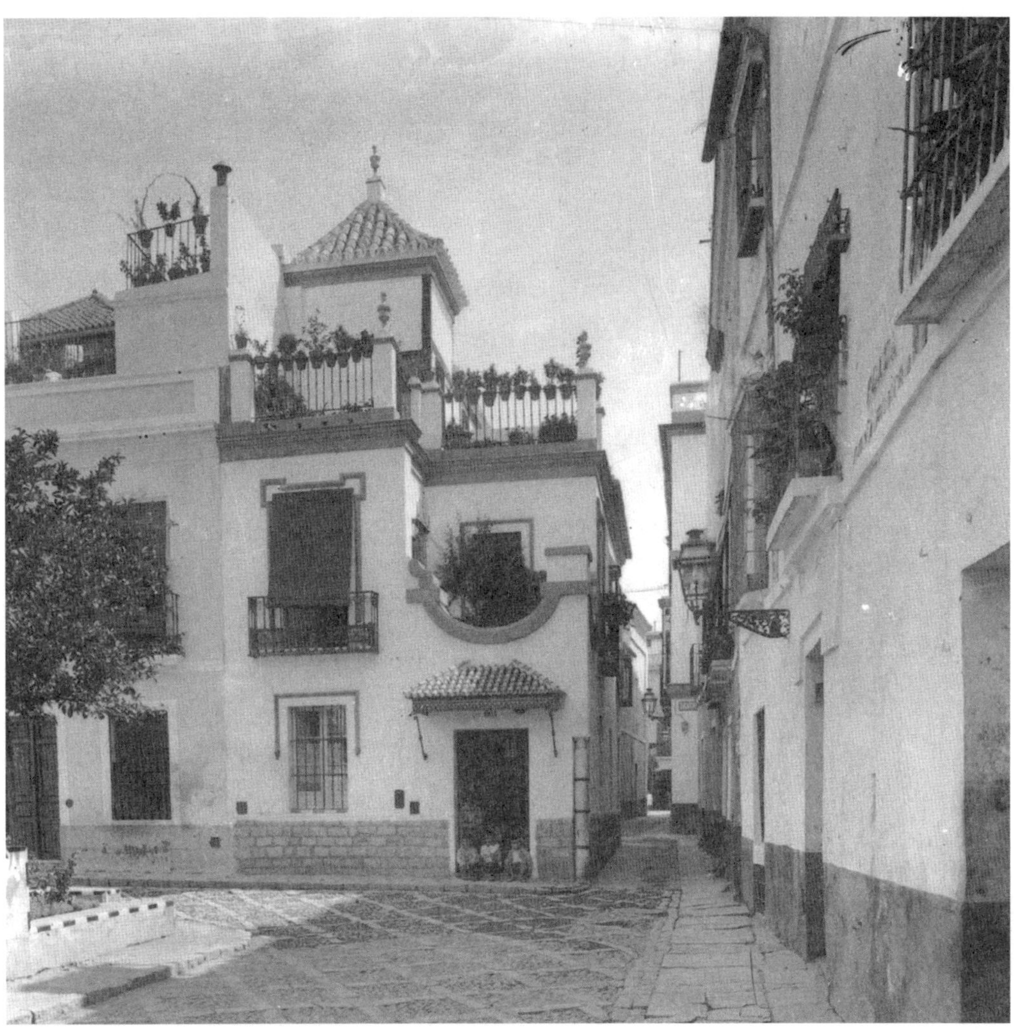

23 Juan Talavera, House for Jerónimo Armario, Plaza de Doña Elvira, Seville, around 1922.

'white architecture' generally were the residence of the landed aristocracy who owned almost all the arable land in this part of Spain.[31]

Another interesting issue, which maybe was more obvious in Seville than elsewhere, was that regionalist architects in fact had to fundamentally change the tradition they claimed to be continuing as they adapted vernacular models to different types of buildings. The traditional houses of the upper classes in Seville, based on both Roman and Arabic predecessors, generally had a richly decorated patio and a very sober façade. As at the start of the twentieth century most assignments concerned apartment

[31]   Ibid., 204–5, 313–27 and 355–65.

buildings or free-standing villas and chalets, the façades now moved to centre stage. Both building types were oriented towards the exterior instead of towards a private interior patio. Thus, as the traditional exteriors offered no attractive examples, most regionalist architects in Seville adopted the decorative elements and materials of the traditional patios for the façades of their new constructions. In this way the new streets lined with picturesque new houses completely differed from the winding alleys with almost plain walls in the old town. Consequently, Aníbal González preferred straight and wide streets to make it possible to admire the new buildings.[32]

In contrast to what had happened in Germany and France, the new type of domestic architecture in Spain was not generally presented as a reform movement, propagating a new, and more natural and authentic lifestyle away from the cramped urban centres. Only a few authors advised their readers to move to the more uplifting and healthy countryside or criticised the vulgar taste of parvenus, thus implicitly longing for a more genuine existence in a harmonious and carefully designed environment.[33] However, the reformist aspect in German and French architectural critiques came to the fore particularly in the discussion about the plan of the house and the decoration of the interior. As we have seen, in Spain, where no magazines on decorative arts were published, almost no individual houses were discussed and the distribution of the various pieces and its consequences for the inhabitants did not receive attention. Consequently, these new country houses were not explicitly presented as part of a new reformist middle-class culture, as had happened in Germany.

Nonetheless, other factors also played a role. In most Spanish towns, the effects of urbanisation and industrialisation were not comparable with the effects they had in Germany, and consequently the need to flee the big cities and find a different, more natural lifestyle in the countryside was not felt very strongly. Another factor seems to have been the lack of a substantial, progressive cultural elite – consisting of writers, artists, intellectuals and professors – that had sufficient means to buy a carefully designed villa and could have taken the lead in the introduction of this new domestic architecture, as had happened especially in Germany. Consequently, Spanish architects had to deal with a well-to-do bourgeois

---

32 Ibid., 217–20.
33 Álvarez, 'Lo que pudiera ser la arquitectura española' 146–8, L.F.T., 'La arquitectura suburbana en Barcelona' 113–16, Donosty, 'La casa española' 86 and Torres Balbás, 'Una obra de Zuazo en El Escorial' 78.

and aristocratic public that probably had a more conventional taste. In Seville, for example, by far the largest group of commissioners of regionalist buildings were rich landowners, often aristocrats, living in the town, whereas intellectuals and artists only constituted about 1 per cent of the clients.[34] In this aspect, perhaps Barcelona was an exception, but as we have seen, in Catalonia architects and clients opted primarily for the Art Nouveau of the *Modernistas* and the new Mediterranean classicism of the *Noucentistas*.

The terminology used to designate the new domestic architecture also differed in Spain. Although some critics stressed that the new style had to be contemporary, the adjectives 'new' and 'modern' were not frequently attached to this type of building, contrary to the situation in France and Germany. Prominent proponents of the new trend, such as Leonardo Rucabado and Aníbal González, even stressed its traditional character. Nonetheless, the most widely used qualification, especially at the start, was 'national' or 'Spanish'. This was probably due to the less strictly professional and therefore more general issues that dominated the Spanish architectural debate. Instead of reviewing particular designs, or proposing a new type of country house, many relevant articles (which often had already been presented as a lecture) in the architectural press dealt with a 'new national style', 'the Spanish house', or other broad topics. However, this did not mean that a new uniform, historicist style was proposed for the whole country, as had often been done during the nineteenth century. Everywhere in Spain, according to the advocates of the new style, architects should study both the local climatic and geographical circumstances and the existing construction techniques and traditions in order to create a new national style that would embody the Spanish *Volksgeist* in all its regional variety.

At the same time, the new style was known for its regional variants, most clearly as Montañés, Basque, or Sevilian. And, as in neighbouring France, the rather vague term 'regional architecture' came into use during the First World War, while in recent scholarly studies 'regionalist architecture' is preferred, a designation that has become widely accepted. In this respect Spain followed the same pattern as France. In Spain, differences between regions and their respective vernacular traditions were clearly distinguished. Natural and climatic circumstances differed widely, as did the historical traditions, in which pre-Roman, Celtic, Roman, Germanic, or Arab traces were discernible, depending on the region. This

---

34 Alberto Villar Movellán, 'Tres aspectos del historicismo regionalista: Ética, libertad y clientela' in: José Joaquín Yarza Luaces and Francesca Español Bertrán eds., *Ve Congrés espanyol d'història de l'art* (Barcelona 1987) 199–204.

interchange between regional and national as qualifications for the same neo-vernacular architecture (which could also be found in French articles, although less frequently), also shows that a strong, ethnically defined, regional identity was not regarded as being opposed to national sentiments. On the contrary, they appear to be mutually enhancing. At the same time, internal differences within regions apparently did not matter. Whether vernacular examples originated from the mountains, the plains, the coast, the town, or the countryside seemed unimportant. This was also the case in Seville, where inspiration was derived from the city and its immediate surroundings. Nonetheless, the Sevilian style became emblematic for almost the whole South-West of Spain.[35]

Spanish regionalist architecture and its defenders were generally less orthodox than their French and German counterparts. In France and Germany most critics and architects who favoured the neo-vernacular trend abhorred the historicist and eclectic styles that still dominated the architectural scene around the turn of the century, and fiercely opposed the international Beaux-Arts style and the too theoretical education at the academies. This type of criticism, however, was almost completely absent from the Spanish architectural discourse. Moreover, many proponents of regionalism did not make a clear distinction between high architecture and historical styles, on the one hand, and vernacular examples, on the other. Both could be sources of inspiration, the only criterion being that a building was in harmony with its environment and the local traditions. Consequently, regionalism is characterised by many Spanish architectural historians as a 'last revival', or as the last phase of historicism.[36]

Nonetheless, this less than purist attitude can perhaps also be explained by the absence from many parts of Spain of a prosperous class of independent farmers who lived on their land. The dwellings of small farmers and agricultural workers, mostly assembled in villages or small towns, were generally extremely simple and poor and often lacked a garden. On the other hand, in most areas the houses of the aristocracy and landed gentry – who mostly resided in towns – as well as the churches and chapels, were built of local materials and showed a great regional variety. They could thus function, like the houses of the better-off farmers did in other countries or in the Basque Country, as specific regional sources of inspiration. As a consequence, in Spain it was probably easier to apply

---

[35] Villar Movellán, *Arquitectura del regionalismo en Sevilla* 204–7.
[36] See, for example: Ramón Rodríguez Llera, 'Rucabado en Santander', *Arquitectos*, 57 (June 1982) 32–50, especially 32, Navascués Palacio, 'Regionalismo y arquitectura' 30 and Isac, *Eclecticismo y pensamiento arquitectónico* 347.

the new style to more monumental buildings, as was aptly shown in the designs of Aníbal González for the main pavilions of the Ibero-American Exhibition in Seville.

Another striking issue is that regionalist architecture arrived late in Spain, although regionalist sentiments were already quite pronounced. As in France and Germany, the relationship between the new architectural trend and the various regional movements was not very close, at least at the start. This became particularly clear in the Basque case. Here, the new regionalist villas were mainly built for the aristocracy and the new bourgeois elite, who were generally well integrated into the national political system and the dominant Conservative and Liberal Party who alternated in power. The only exception was the industrialist Ramón Sota y Llano, who became one of the leaders of the Basque movement. Surprisingly the buildings he commissioned from the regionalist architect Manuel María Smith Ibarra (1879–1956) were not in a neo-Basque style.[37]

Likewise in painting there seems to have been no clear link between regionalist architecture and the Basque movement, which already in 1895 had founded the Basque Nationalist Party and had its roots in the ultramontane Carlist movement. Basque regionalism found its supporters mainly among independent farmers and the lower-middle classes, who obviously could not afford a splendid villa, and when – like Sota – they could afford such a luxury, they apparently did not favour the new neo-Basque trend. As a reaction to the rapid influx of poor immigrants from other parts of Spain, the party was anti-capitalist and openly hostile to non-Basques, although it later adopted a more moderate tone. Thus, the regional movement was a clear opponent of the modern liberal bourgeoisie, and the occasional aristocrat, who were involved in the modern capitalist sectors of the rapidly expanding local economy and who decided to build their new country houses and suburban villas in a Basque style. [38]

In the booming industrial town of Bilbao, which at the same time was the centre of the neo-Basque architecture, the main bastion of the regional movement, and the first stronghold of an increasingly self-confident labour movement, the choice to build a villa in a neo-Basque style must have been a conscious one. Already during the first decades of the twentieth century the political dominance of the local industrial elite was challenged

---

[37] D. Fullaonda, *Manuel María Smith Ibarra, arquitecto 1879–1956* (Madrid 1980) and Maite Paliza Monduate, *Manuel María de Smith Ibarra; Arquitecto* (Bilbao 1990).
[38] José Luis de la Granja, *El siglo de Euskadi: El nacionalismo vasco en la España del siglo XX* (Madrid 2003).

by the Basque Nationalist Party and the Spanish Socialist Party, which mainly recruited its voters from migrant workers from other parts of Spain. It seems that the decision to build in a regionalist style was at least partially prompted by fear of their political opponents. This step by the local upper classes was probably meant to stimulate a more pronounced sense of belonging among the working classes, while at the same time, by presenting themselves as true Basques, they tried to cut the electoral ground from under the feet of the regional movement. It seems very unlikely that in this politically polarised environment they would have based their choice merely on aesthetic considerations.

In Seville, regionalist architecture was also supported by the local upper classes, probably, like their Basque colleagues, in order to find support among the increasingly self-conscious middle classes, who had started to feel attracted to the Andalusian regional movement, and among the working classes that increasingly came under the spell of anarcho-syndicalists. As in the Basque Country, the political and economic elite was strongly opposed to the calls for regional autonomy that were formulated by the more radical leaders of the regional movement which, given its weakness in a profoundly agricultural region, were not taken very seriously. In fact the political situation in Seville had more in common with Hamburg, where the lower classes were excluded from the suffrage. In Seville, as in the rest of Spain all adult males could vote, but in practice the elections were 'organised' by the national and local political leaders in such a way that the regular alternation between Liberals and Conservatives, which was decided in Madrid, was assured. This way, the local elite had no difficulty in severely limiting the political influence of both the workers' parties and the regional movement.[39] Thus, regionalist architecture in none of these regions was a direct consequence of an 'awakening of the regions', nor maintained intimate connections with any form of political regionalism.

Garden cities

Regionalist architecture was also applied to social housing and garden cities, although as in France this did not happen very fast. Nevertheless, the ideas of Ebenezer Howard entered Spain quite early, almost separately in Madrid, Bilbao and Barcelona. The first to explain the garden city ideal to a Spanish public was Arturo Soria y Mata (1844–1920), an idealist who

---

[39] Villar Movellán, *Arquitectura del regionalismo en Sevilla* 75–92. In Barcelona and Bilbao, this political system, based on a demobilised electorate and manipulated elections, did not function any longer after about 1900.

in some ways resembled Howard. After a short political career during the progressive Sexenio (1868–74), Soria began a business career in Madrid, while at the same time publishing his various curious technical inventions and more or less philosophical ideas. In 1882 he launched the idea of the Ciudad Lineal (Linear City), which over the next ten years he would further develop. A linear city would be a new spacious and green town constructed along a broad central avenue with various train and tramway lines in the middle. On both sides of the avenue houses with a flower and a vegetable garden for both rich and poor should be built, with schools, shops, recreation facilities and public buildings. In his imagination these new linear towns should connect the old urban centres and he even dreamed of a linear town along the whole Mediterranean coast of Spain, which in the future could even be extended to Saint Petersburg.[40]

However, he was also a very practical man. In 1892, as the director of a tramway company he acquired the concession for a new circular tramway line that had to connect the different villages just outside Madrid. Two years later he started the construction of the first 5 km of his linear city along a tramway line North-East of Madrid. To hawk his enterprise and to explain his ideas he began to publish the first magazine on urban planning, called *La Ciudad Lineal*. Nevertheless, the project never went beyond this first stretch. This did not impede Soria from continuing to play an influential role in Spanish debates, and his ideas were even picked up abroad. Already in 1899 he had reviewed the ideas of Howard in the pages of his magazine. In subsequent years the journal would continue to give attention to the English garden city movement, but Soria and others generally emphasised the superiority of its Spanish alternative.[41]

The garden city ideal also arrived quite early in Bilbao, the booming town that maintained close commercial relations with Great Britain. Shortly after the turn of the century the new villa suburbs of Las Arenas and Neguri, between the coast and Bilbao, were laid out according to the new ideas. Similar suburbs were also constructed near Barcelona. However, it would be more than a decade before a garden city society was founded, as in Madrid the idea of a linear city prevailed and in Bilbao no one took the initiative to further diffuse the new garden city ideal. Only in 1912 did a group of mainly Catalan intellectuals and businessmen found the Civic Society 'La Ciudad Jardín', which had its base in the Museo Social in

---

[40] Terán, *Historia del urbanismo* 105–11.

[41] See respectively, Terán, *Historia del urbanismo* 110–11 and 160–2, and María Castrillo Romón, *Reformismo, vivienda y ciudad: Orígenes y desarrollo del debate en España 1850–1920* (Valladolid 2001) 106–7.

Barcelona.[42] It seemed that people like Cipriano de Montoliú (1873–1923), the great instigator of the society, had become aware that something had to be done to improve the situation of the working classes as Spanish authors primarily saw garden cities as a means to tone down class conflict. This was particularly urgent in Barcelona, where during the Tragic Week of July 1909 a rebellion had broken out after the Government had called up reserve troops to reinforce the military positions in Spanish Morocco and which turned into an orgy of violence and bloodshed.

Like Georges Benoît-Lévy in France, Montoliú organised lectures and published various books and articles to promote the garden city ideal, although like its French counterpart his society did not succeed in founding its own garden city. In their writings he and others gave much attention to garden cities abroad, publishing several articles on developments in England, Germany, France and even the United States. Apart from a factual description of the lay-out and organisation of the various garden cities, these reviews generally were rather explicit on their social and moral implications. Thus, according to Montoliú, the combination of the advantages of the countryside with those of the town in a garden city would combat speculation and stimulate the co-operation between the inhabitants. And a hygienic, beautiful and cheap home in a pleasant environment would contribute to the physical and moral progress of the 'race'.[43] A quite descriptive review of Hellerau, by another Catalan critic, concluded that by having their own house in this beautiful garden city the workers lived 'happy and satisfied'. He underlined that the architecture and lay-out of the plant and colony also had an ethical component as it invited people 'to work, but not the hard and obligatory work, but the free and cheerful work'.[44]

An official pamphlet of Montoliú's society was even more straightforward in its explanation of why garden cities were necessary. Although in Spain the urbanisation process had not progressed as much as in other European countries, the bad living conditions of the working classes had engendered 'immorality, alcoholism, tuberculosis, high morbidity and death rates, physical degeneration, etc.'. The text continued by arguing that 'the ugliness and vulgarity of the environment would in the end have fatal consequences for the soul' and that 'the bitter contrast between the extreme

---

[42] Castrillo Romón, *Reformismo, vivienda y ciudad* 106–9.
[43] C. Montoliú, 'La ciudad jardín', *Museum* IV (1914–15) 75–99, especially 77–82 and 92–8.
[44] A. Badrinas y Escudé, 'Hellerau', *Museum* IV (1914–15) 100–6, respectively 105 and 102.

luxury and the extreme misery ... would add fuel to the fire of class hatred'. In Spain, this problem was aggravated by the low cultural level of the population. The alarming 'physical degeneration' of the Spanish people was in a great part caused by the absorption of 'all the vital reserves of the rural population' by the cities. The new 'organic and social concept' of the city, embodied in the garden city, however, could remedy this situation by combining the advantages of the city with those of the countryside. This way town life would become more ordered, sane and beautiful.[45]

Authors from Madrid also expressed themselves in similar ways. Thus Cabello y Lapiedra in 1905 maintained that cheap housing, which could also be provided in the form of garden cities, would be the 'big dyke that could check the overflowing of the social mass, disrupted continually by economic disequilibrium, tuberculosis, alcoholism and emigration'.[46] The main propagator of the ideas of Arturo Soria, the writer and diplomat Hilarión González del Castillo, also meant that the garden city, but even more the linear city that already existed in Madrid, would be able to at least partially solve 'the great social plagues: of emigration, alcoholism, criminality, lack of civilisation, prostitution, tuberculosis, social conflict and misery'.[47] Another author, the prominent architect Enrique María Repullés y Vargas (1845–1922), also underscored the uplifting effects of a garden city. Well-lit and ventilated plants and healthy and comfortable houses combined with sport facilities, libraries, conferences, concerts and the possibility to work in a proper garden would provide the worker with 'the peace and tranquillity of a life in the countryside', without having to give up the advantages of the city.[48]

Whereas the moral component in the propaganda for garden cities was much more explicit in Spain, almost no attention was given to the design of their houses. This is all the more surprising in a country where heated debates were held on the question if regionalist traditionalism constituted a new national style. Compared to technical issues and the need to improve the housing conditions of the urban poor, this aspect apparently seemed of marginal importance. Moreover, no one even bothered to underline the need of a design that took into account the regional traditions and geographical conditions. This can probably be explained by the fact that

<hr>

[45] 'La "Ciudad Jardín"', *Arquitectura y Construcción* (April 1913) 82–6, especially 83–4.
[46] Luis María Cabello y Lapiedra, 'Habitaciones económicas', *La Construcción Moderna* (30 March 1905) 101–7, especially 105.
[47] H. G. del Castillo, 'Ciudades jardines y ciudades lineales (Conclusión)', *La Construcción Moderna* (1914) 36–45, especially 41 and 44.
[48] E.M. Repullés, 'La ciudad jardín', *La Construcción Moderna* (1920) 38–41.

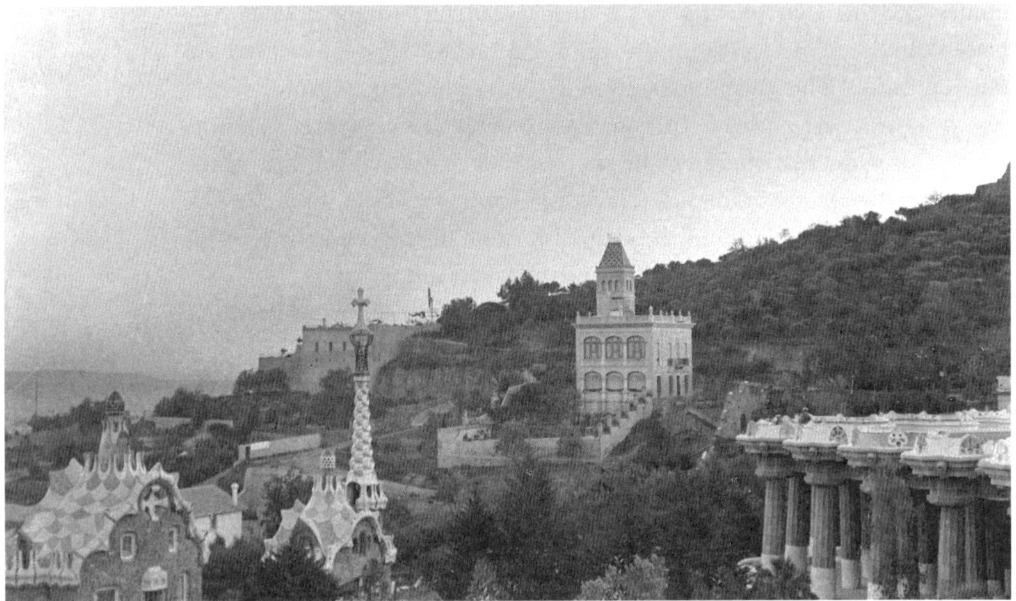

24 Antoní Gaudí, Park Güell, Barcelona, 1899–1914 (photo between 1915 and 1920). On the left there are the two small fairytale pavilions which flank the main entrance; on the right is the central hall supported by Doric columns, which was meant to held markets. The roof consists of a large terrace, where Gaudí constructed his famous tiled serpentine bench. The house in the background is located just outside the park.

most authors looked at garden cities from the point of view of an engineer or a city-planner; and because only a few reviews of actually built garden cities were published, starting only in 1920.[49]

This does not mean that almost no garden cities were constructed in Spain. However, most of them were commercial projects and not all of them prospered. Probably the best-known example of this is Park Güell in Barcelona (figure 24). Eusebi Güell was a rich manufacturer with close connections to England and he would become a member of Monoliú's garden city society. Already around 1900 he had asked Gaudí to design a residential park with villas on the slope of a hill overlooking Barcelona.[50] But whereas the park was built, only two of the sixty intended villas were actually constructed.

Only in the decades after about 1915 were a substantial number of garden cities built. Most of them were either commercial projects on a very

---

49   X., 'Burgos y la ciudad jardín', *La Construcción Moderna* (1920) 14–15 and Anasagasti, 'Ciudad-jardín en Irún', *La Construcción Moderna* (1925) 145–8.
50   Castrillo Romón, *Reformismo, vivienda y ciudad* 108.

modest scale or the initiative of co-operatives, generally of middle-class professionals. Some tried to profit from the subsidies that became available after the social-liberal government of José Canalejas passed the first law on cheap housing in 1912. In fact most houses with a garden in these new suburbs were destined for the middle or lower middle classes. Thus, contrary to what Montoliú and others had hoped, not much was done to solve the social question.[51] The situation in Spain also differed from that in Germany, where mixed garden cities, namely those containing all classes of people, seemed to have been preferred and France, where almost only workers' colonies came into being. Nonetheless, although it has not been mentioned by the critics, many of the Spanish garden suburbs, like their counterparts elsewhere, were constructed in a regionalist style.[52]

Conclusion

Although in general it is understood that nationalism and *völkisch* inclinations were very strong in pre-war Germany, in architectural discourse the nationalist and regionalist rhetoric was less prominent in Germany than in France and Spain. This was most probably due to the higher level of professionalism that was to be found in the German specialised press, at least when concerned with architectural topics. Most articles were reviews of individual buildings and the authors limited themselves to architectural and artistic issues, while in France fewer articles were published on individual projects. However, *La Vie à la Campagne* – a magazine aimed more at potential clients than at professional architects – published many more abstract essays, proposing a model country house for a specific region. In Spain, on the contrary, many articles on regionalist architecture were originally written as a lecture for a more general, well-educated public. The authors thus embedded their architectural views in a discussion of more general cultural issues, and some of them particularly stressed the nationalist content of the architecture they proposed.

Another striking point is that in Germany the new domestic architecture was intimately connected with a revival of the decorative arts and with the longing for a new, more authentic, reformist lifestyle. Most German

[51] Urrutia, *Arquitectura española* 197–205, Terán, *Historia del urbanismo* 156–60 and María Castrillo Romón, 'Les lois des habitations à bon marché et la construction des colonies résidentielle en Espagne' in: Paulette Girard and Bruno Fayolle Lussac eds., *Cités, cités-jardins: Une histoire européenne* (Talence 1996) 161–9.

[52] Urrutia, *Arquitectura española*, 199–204. See for Madrid also: Enrique Fidel, 'La Ciudad jardín madrileña: colonias del Ensanche' in: http://urbancidades.wordpress.com/2007/09/29/la-ciudad-jardin-madrilena consulted on 31 October 2007.

architects also designed, or at least supervised, the interior and the furnishing of their country houses and villas, and some played a major role in the craft revival that was taking place in the country. This was somewhat less the case in France and Spain, where some houses even received a conventional historicist or eclectic interior. The German country houses and suburban cottages were also consciously presented as the ideal, natural environment for a new, more harmonious and modest lifestyle, far away from the unhealthy conditions of the big industrialised cities and from the false pomp and conventions of a pretentious parvenu milieu. In France, on the other hand, the new boulevards provided a beautiful and luxurious living space for the upper-middle classes, and thus the need to flee the towns was not as strong as elsewhere. The drift to the countryside was equally weak in Spain, although this was due to the slower urbanisation process. As a consequence of these differences, the arguments in favour of a new, more genuine lifestyle that was close to nature were heard less frequently in France and were almost totally absent in Spain. Additionally, fewer country houses and suburban villas were built in France and Spain, and those that were built, often as secondary residences, were generally destined for a more upscale and probably less reform-minded clientele.

A similar difference could be seen with regard to the garden cities. Whereas in Germany, garden cities were considered as part of a new reformed lifestyle, combining the advantages of the countryside with those of the town in new, interclass communities, in France and Spain these were merely seen as a new way to improve the living conditions – and indirectly also the moral standards – of the urban working classes. It seems that in Germany the social question, probably because of the greater threat of a socialist take-over, was taken more seriously by the middle and upper classes, and many concluded that the best way to uplift the workers was to provide them with respectable examples to emulate in their own environment. Some were even prepared to share a new green suburb with lower-class families. Many of the best-known reformist architects did their bit by participating in the German garden city movement and by designing plans and neo-vernacular buildings for one or various garden cities or suburbs. Howard's ideas were also received with enthusiasm in France and Spain; however, this did not result in the creation of garden cities where different social groups mingled. Apparently the need to uplift the working classes was not that urgent and both the propagation and design of garden cities was left to writers and architects who had just started their career. As a consequence, only workers' settlements were created in France, whereas in Spain only modest, socially homogeneous suburbs were built, either for the upper classes, middle-class professionals or labourers. Some of these garden cities were even explicitly presented as a way to discipline and edify the working classes.

Notwithstanding these differences, the basic regionalist argument was equally present in all three countries under review. Architects and critics argued that a country house or suburban cottage should be designed in accordance with the local climatic, geographic and natural circumstances, and should be integrated into the surrounding landscape by using locally available materials and traditional construction techniques. As the farmers and local artisans had lived in these natural conditions for centuries, they had adapted themselves to these circumstances, developing vernacular building traditions that perfectly matched their situation. They had assimilated only those foreign innovations that were useful to them, taking care that their native traditions were not overwhelmed by influences that contrasted with their collective personality. This argumentation in terms of a *Volksgeist*, according to which every region had its own identity that should be respected or even rediscovered and propagated, unmistakably formed the ideological background in the discourse on the new regionalist architecture in Germany, France and Spain. In Spain, however, some advocates of the new style were less orthodox and implicitly maintained that the local collective 'spirit' could also be detected in high architecture, such as palaces and churches, although these had to be recognisable as belonging to a specific region. In practice, however, in all three countries most clients, and consequently also the architects, were less dogmatic and applied picturesque vernacular elements and models from other regions as well. Thus, in many cases a more dogmatic regionalism was soon diluted to a more generic identification with the countryside and its vernacular traditions. This process gained momentum in the first post-war years, when the difficult economic situation and the urgency of the housing shortage forced architects to abandon any possible orthodox neo-vernacular ambitions they may have had for the reconstruction of the devastated areas and major social housing projects.

A more general identification with the vernacular architecture of the countryside also prevailed in the case of most garden cities. Apparently, it was taken for granted that the architecture should reflect the rural values that were part of the garden city ideology at large and that the buildings should fit in well with the natural environment and if possible adopt local construction traditions and materials. Following the designs of Unwin, until the 1920s most garden cities and suburbs in Germany, France and Spain were executed in a somewhat simplified regionalist style. As most cottages and terraced houses should be cheap and consequently required little intervention from the architects, their work received relatively little attention from the specialised press, although Germany was somewhat of an exception. Nonetheless, it seemed that for these semi-rural settings nobody needed to be told that the architecture should follow vernacular models.

A striking difference between the three countries, however, is that in Germany the regional *Volksgeist* was only loosely defined. Many authors stressed the need to integrate a newly built country house into the local environment, but their references could be to broad areas such as the north of Germany, to more specific regions such as Lower Saxony or North Frisia, or to smaller areas, such as a particular river valley, chain of hills, or town. Often they were even less specific, simply asserting that the building perfectly merged with the surrounding countryside. Authors apparently did not want to define a particular style linked to a specific region, many of which were still actually existing States within the German Empire, each with its prince, government and bureaucracy. And where such a State actively stimulated regionalist architecture, as was the case with the Free City of Hamburg, it was defined in a broad way as Hanseatic or north-German. Particularism, seemingly, should be avoided.

In France and Spain, on the other hand, critics almost always referred to particular regional styles. Each historical region possessed its own unique style, and ethnic identity, hence implicitly effacing local differences within the region which, as was the case with Flanders and the Basque Country, could even transgress national borders. However, as in Germany, the areas to which architects and critics referred were not actually existing political entities, like the French departments or the Spanish provinces. These had been outlined on the drawing board and therefore, contrary to the historically grown ancient provinces, were seen as artificial units. The stress on specific regions can probably be explained as a reaction to the strong centralist and abstract political system, which was increasingly considered a disadvantage by various sectors of the middle classes. An injection of local and regional autonomy could infuse the country with new life, it was thought. As the nation was an organic unity its health depended not only on the capital or the centre, but on the vitality of its various parts. In Germany – where the memory of national unification was still fresh and the existing local and regional autonomy was not seriously threatened by the national administration – it was apparently less urgent to support existing regional identities that could supplement or even replace the existing national identity. The popular but vague term *Heimat*, which referred to both the local or regional homeland and the greater fatherland,

and which thus connected the familiar local level to the nation, seemed perfectly adequate. Similarly, in all three countries, a generic reference to the vernacular architecture of the countryside seemed to suffice in many of the garden cities.

Nevertheless, the relationship between regionalist architecture and the various regional movements, which were becoming particularly demanding in some parts of Spain and France, was not very strong, at least during the first two decades of the twentieth century. Most architects of the new regionalist trend operated at a national level. Thus in Germany, many architects were quite mobile, and often built country houses and villas in various parts of the country, and most of their clients seemed to share this national or even international outlook. In France, most domestic architects studied and worked in Paris. Although many assignments were actually carried out in the provinces, a large proportion of the commissioners also lived in the French capital. It appears that in Spain architects were more attached to their native region, nonetheless, they participated in national debates and contests and worked for both a local upper-class clientele and for members of the national elite. The notable exception was Catalonia, with Barcelona as its indisputable centre, where proper, more cosmopolitan and modern trends were cherished by both the architects and their prosperous clients. Thus, paradoxically, in the only region where architects actually became prominent leaders of the regional movement, vernacular sources played only a secondary role in the creation of an idiosyncratic collective identity and of an architecture that was intended to be its concretisation. In Brittany and the Basque Country the regional movement also was suspicious of regionalist architecture, which was even seen as an importation from elsewhere. And the case of Seville made clear that those who sponsored regionalist architecture were generally rather distrustful of the Andalusian movement that pleaded for political autonomy.

Thus, as we have seen, regionalist architecture in all three countries was more connected with the centre than with the periphery. We therefore can conclude that regionalist architecture did not come about primarily by an awakening of the provinces, in which every region tried to strengthen its own peculiar identity, as has been suggested more or less explicitly by various scholars. On the other hand, a close analysis of regionalist architecture confirms the findings of recent studies on regionalism at large that it should be understood in the first place as a new stage in the nation-building process. In order to find new allies in a period of universal suffrage and the breakdown of traditional political loyalties, the regionalists consciously broadened the national identity that the lower and middle strata should adopt, by including local folk culture and regional traditions in their artistic productions. In the past, monuments were erected to kings, generals, scientists, writers and artists or other members of the political and cultural elite as national heroes with whom the population should identify, but now they provided a new, more inclusive national identity, one that was based on a heterogeneous, but recognisable, rural low culture. And regionalist architects clearly participated in this venture. By proclaiming farmsteads and barns to be part of the national heritage and examples worthy of imitation, architects and critics tried to induce wider sections of the population to identify with the nation and thus become 'responsible' citizens. This became most clearly visible in the garden cities, which at least in part were destined for members of the 'uprooted' working classes. Giving them a comfortable home with a garden in a pleasant environment, dressed in a semi-rural and neo-vernacular guise, should again tie them to the soil and the nation. Thus by stimulating the identification with a recognisable and concrete region and the values of the countryside, it was thought that the lower classes would also increasingly feel attached to the much more abstract and distant nation and the existing political system. Surprisingly, in those countries where less was done to improve the living conditions of the workers, such as France and Spain, the authors generally were more explicit on the importance of the garden cities as a means of pacifying the labouring classes by integrating them into the nation.

But what about the clients? We can only speculate about their motives, although it seems probable that they shared the concerns of the regionalist architects. Most of the commissioners of regionalist cottages and country houses did not need to stress their adherence to the nation-state. Instead their choice seemed more a statement placed before the lower classes and meant to underline their adherence to the region and its rural values. By moulding their houses on vernacular models, the owners stated that they formed an integral part of the national community that was best embodied by the ordinary population of the countryside and had its roots in primordial times. In this way they probably claimed that they were not part of a cosmopolitan plutocrat elite that had no eye for the interests of the nation and the ordinary people, but formed an integral part of local society. By knowing well its particular circumstances, traditions and customs, they more or less assured the population that they would faithfully serve the common good. It seems plausible that in this manner they hoped to legitimise and even to reinforce their leading position in society that seemed particularly threatened by the rise of the workers' movement. Surprisingly, the farmers and inhabitants of the countryside themselves seemed to be the only people immune to the new architectural trend and to prefer urban models.

Remarkably, apart from some Spanish architects who cited Ganivet, the ideologue of an organic Spanish nationalism, there were almost no direct references to a more exalted, *völkisch* nationalism that was clearly on the rise in the years around the turn of the century. However, the populism, the rhetoric in terms of *Volksgeist*, and the emphasis on a presumed harmonious community, unmistakeably connected the propagators of the neo-vernacular trend to this type of organic nationalism. Nonetheless, there is also a clear difference as they did not stress the threats and dangers that outsiders or foreign powers constituted, but solely emphasised the unity of a regionally variegated but fundamentally harmonious national community. What was needed was a reorientation on the true spirit of the people that was best embodied by the inhabitants of the countryside who still had a living bond with tradition and the surrounding nature. It seems that by adopting part of the *völkisch* rhetoric they in some way wanted to neutralise the influence of more exalted nationalists. Thus, anti-Semites, such as Theodor Fritsch in Germany, had no practical influence on the debates on regionalist architecture. In France no mention was made of the anti-Semitism of some of the anti-Dreyfusards, nor of the fierce anti-clericalism of many Dreyfusards. This was a conflict that permeated political debates of the period, but was invisible in architectural discourse. Traces from the similarly heated debates in Spain that arose as a result of the fierce opposition of the liberals and republicans to the neo-conservative and corporatist reform policy of Antonio Maura's cabinet (1907–9), were also completely absent from architectural debates of the period. Consequently, it seemed that regionalism – probably like imperialism – was a kind of neutral, depoliticised common ground on which all reformist groups could agree.

This rapprochement with the countryside, disguised as a neutral new interest in vernacular culture, thus, had a double political message. The main enemy of those who propagated the new regionalist trend was the revolutionary labour movement, which was seen as the major threat to society and the existing political constellation, and was condemned as uprooted, internationalist, urban, degenerate and, consequently, unpatriotic. At the same time, however, most critics and architects saw the social question as very urgent, and some even sympathised with many of the objectives of the labour movement. As a consequence their other target was the, already somewhat out-of-date, laissez-faire ideology, the cosmopolitan outlook of the old political and cultural elite, and the accompanying optimistic and elitist nineteenth-century high culture. The social question and other related problems were so urgent that the State, guided by the reformist cycles of which these architects and intellectuals formed part, should intervene. Charity or abstract new laws and policies had not bridged the growing gap between rich and poor. Specific measures that took into account the regional and national peculiarities and a more interventionist attitude of the State – for example, actively supporting the creation of new garden cities or improving the education of the artisans, and the propagation of a more inclusive and diversified national identity – should help convert the masses into responsible citizens.

As has become clear, regionalist architecture could not be classified as politically reactionary. Regionalism appealed to various ideological groups within the existing political spectrum, which in general could be classified as reformist.[53] Most prominent among the defenders of this new architectural trend in all three countries, although not everybody openly expressed their political allegiances, seemed to have been social liberals; but also social-Catholics, social-minded conservatives and, after the First World War, social-democrats played a role in the advance of its cause. All in fact wanted to avoid revolution by promoting a more gradual and organic evolution. At the same time, they hoped to cut the ground from under the feet of the nationalists of the extreme right who seemed to address the same audience with a more exalted and alarming rhetoric. In this they increasingly received support. It seems that apart from laissez-faire liberals and conservatives who were against a more active social policy or preferred outright oppression and accordingly were at best lukewarm towards the reformist implications of regionalist architecture, only revolutionaries, such as socialists and anarchists, and some political regionalists, such as members of the Catalan, Basque, or Breton movement, did not support the cause of regionalist architecture. The strength of this opposition differed from country to country. In Germany regionalist architecture found a fertile ground, as a reformist social policy – which was implemented by the State – did not encounter much opposition, political regionalism was almost completely absent and the labour movement was strong but mainly moderate and reformist. In France and Spain this was much less the case as support for social reform was much weaker and a great part of the leading classes thus were openly indifferent to the reformist aspects of regionalist architecture. Moreover, the weaker labour movements in these countries

[53] In this way the proponents of regionalist architecture resembled the adherents of the Fédération Régionaliste Française, and German reformist societies, such as the *Deutsche Gartenstadtgesellschaft*, the *Werkbund* and the *Heimatschutz*.

were more radical and thus less inclined to support reformist policies and political regionalism made headway in various parts of the country. This was especially of importance in Spain, where around the turn of the century the elite of Catalonia, the country's most prosperous region, massively converted to political regionalism.

Thus, architectural regionalism had a critical but often neglected political role, which cannot be dismissed as being merely reactionary. The same applies to the cultural domain as, together with Art Nouveau it can be understood as the principal hinge between the various neo-styles and the eclecticism of the nineteenth century and the functionalist and modernist avant-garde that became prominent in the 1920s. This was even more obvious than in the case of regionalist painting. The new domestic architecture that broke with historicism to find inspiration in vernacular traditions was a clearly recognisable, new architectural trend, although those behind it did not produce provocative manifestos or sensational exhibitions. Their reformist attitude even seemed to disqualify them for the avant-garde. The stress on modesty, reform and tradition was not compatible with a revolutionary, high-profiled avant-garde attitude. However, the trend was propagated by many critics and architects, and did have well-known advocates such as Muthesius, Sézille and Rucabado. Consequently, at the start of the twentieth century regionalism was a widely influential reform movement and was prominent in the architectural debates. In its stress on creativity, constructive honesty, hygienic measures, restrained designs and the importance of air and light, its plea for an up-to-date contemporary style, and its criticism of superfluous decoration, imitations of historical elements and styles, it was a clear precursor of twentieth-century functionalism and modernism. At the same time, it became the main target of the new modernist prophets such as Le Corbusier, Behrens and Mies van der Rohe. After the First World War, the values of the architectural modernism were increasingly profiled in contrast to those of regionalism. Thus, modernity was opposed to tradition, internationalism to regionalism, functionalism to the picturesque, individual genius to vernacular inspiration, form to plan, town to countryside, machine to artisan and progress to evolution.

We can now also reject alternative labels for regionalist architecture. 'National Romanticism' has been proposed, but does not seem very apt. Although Romantic elements can be discerned, the political and cultural constellation at the start of the twentieth century was completely different from that of the early nineteenth century. Furthermore, the adjective 'national' does not reflect the references to the rural popular or vernacular culture that were the main source of inspiration for the new movement. And although nationalist inspiration was important, 'national' has a very vague meaning, especially if we take into account that regionalist architecture did not respect national borders, as evidenced by the neo-Basque style. The term *Heimatarchitektur*, which is sometimes used in Germany, although generally in a condescending way, perfectly captures the different connotations of the neo-vernacular trend, as *Heimat* signifies home, birthplace, homeland, native region and fatherland at the same time. However, in this way it seems a unique German phenomenon, which clearly was not the case. In my view, the more specific term 'regionalist architecture' is a better option, as it is already applied in southern European countries such as France and Spain, and as it makes clear that this movement was connected to a new and rapidly growing interest in local vernacular culture. And although we have seen that there are some important differences, it also seems perfectly applicable to the German case.

III

International Exhibitions (1910–39)

7

Barcelona and Seville

Introduction

Painters had more freedom to adopt regionalism than architects, who often had to follow the aesthetic preferences of their clients. However, from the early years of the twentieth century private commissioners began to show an interest in having their houses built in a regionalist style. A few corporations and enterprises soon followed, especially when garden cities were concerned. However, more than a decade passed before local, regional and national authorities began to select regionalist models for some of their commissions. In this period this architectural trend had already lost its main innovative drive. Surprisingly, in the late 1920s and 1930s, at the instigation of some municipal and national governments, regionalist architecture received a pivotal place at major exhibitions in Barcelona, Seville, Paris, Munich and Düsseldorf. Although these immense shows were partially meant to revive regionalism, in the end they would only confirm its inevitable decline. It became obvious that regionalism had increasing difficulty in living up to its own principles of honesty, authenticity and rationality and – at least in its existing form – would have an afterlife in only two domains: in an exuberant version it continued to be useful for commercial purposes especially in the tourist sector, whereas in a simplified form it still was an attractive option for suburban developments.

Elements of vernacular culture already had a place in the many grandiose international exhibitions that were organised every few years, although this was not the case at the early World's Fairs, such as the first Great Exhibition of 1851. In Joseph Paxton's enormous Crystal Palace in London's Hyde Park one could admire machines, technical inventions, new products and high art. Within this enormous space every participating nation had its own section. At the Paris Universal Exposition of 1867, the participating countries were for the first time encouraged to present their exhibits not only in the great central exhibition palace, but also in a proper pavilion. Each of these temporary structures should be erected in a style that was considered typical of the country represented. The organisers also anticipated that archaeological findings and historical objects would document each country's past. This way the exhibition was no longer restricted to a competition in modernity but also became a contest between national cultures. At the next World's Fair in Vienna in 1873, the planned international village was not a great success as only nine farmhouses were constructed. However, at subsequent exhibitions copies or pastiches of typical old buildings, from both towns and the countryside, started to appear in growing numbers, be it in the form of a *Rue des nations*, an old Antwerp, Paris, or Vienna or a Russian, German, or Swiss village. Ethnographic and colonial shows also became an indispensible part of these expositions and greatly contributed to their commercial success by attracting large numbers of visitors.[1]

It seems that most countries increasingly preferred to construct their national pavilions in a typical style to distinguish themselves from the neighbouring buildings. Past architectural styles, such as Gothic or Renaissance, had clear geographical variations, but these were not always easy to distinguish for the untrained visitor. Particularly the Scandinavian and East European countries, which probably had problems competing with monumental examples from their own architectural past, started to dress their pavilions in a vernacular guise. By choosing the most peculiar and striking vernacular style they succeeded in standing out among the mass of historicist buildings of other countries. This meant that generally very peripheral and often rather primitive areas were now presented as quintessentially national. Thus copies of rural buildings form Dalarna represented Sweden, constructions from Telemarken symbolised Norway, and the Pusztas stood for Hungary. As a result, from the end of the nineteenth century, vernacular architecture, traditional costumes and popular arts and handicrafts were no longer shown as a picturesque complement to cover up modernity, but rather as the essence of the nation. In Paris, at the World's Fair of 1900, some national pavilions could even be labelled regionalist, as vernacular inspiration was used to create highly picturesque modern buildings. The best-known example of this new trend was the Finnish

---

[1] See, for example, Winfried Kretschmer, *Geschichte der Weltausstellungen* (Frankfurt and New York 1999) and Martin Wörner, *Vergnügen und Belehren: Volkskultur auf den Weltausstellungen 1850–1900* (Münster 1999).

pavilion, designed by Eliel Saarinen and loosely moulded on vernacular buildings from the peripheral Karelia region.[2]

This advance of vernacular elements also had to do with the transformation of the universal expositions during this period, which would be in full swing after the First World War. As more and more specialised trade fairs and international congresses were organised, the world's fairs slowly lost their function as a central meeting ground for professionals from all kind of areas and started to direct themselves to a more general public. Industrial products and technical inventions in consequence lost ground to consumer products and entertainment.[3] Regionalist architecture increasingly played a role in this new type of spectacular mass event as it offered a highly picturesque and recognisable background for folkloric shows and an attractive visual display to stimulate tourism. This also happened in the three countries under review, where from the 1920s onwards regionalist architecture became more prominent and was even used to represent the host nation. Surprisingly, latecomer Spain took the lead. The question remains why the organisers decided to apply regionalist recipes, and if this also meant that the authorities subscribed to the implicit political agenda of regionalism?

The 1929 International Exhibition of Barcelona

Whereas in France all international exhibitions were organised by the government and consequently took place in the capital, in Spain the initiative was taken by the economic and political elite of major provincial towns, such as Barcelona and Seville. Consequently the more modest exhibitions took place on an irregular basis and local authorities were in charge of their organisation. Barcelona organised its first World's Fair in 1888 and vernacular elements played only a very subordinate role. Although the organisers, after the Parisian *Rue des nations* of 1878 had been a success, planned a *Calle de España*, where all Spanish regions would have their own pavilion, eventually only two regional pavilions were constructed in a typical historicist style. Thus Seville was represented by a neo-Arab

<hr>

[2] Bjarne Stoklund, 'How the Peasant House Became a National Symbol', *Ethnologia Europaea* XXIX (1995) 5–18, Bjarne Stoklund, 'The Role of International Exhibitions in the Construction of National Cultures in the 19th Century', *Ethnologia Europaea* XXIV (1994) 35–45 and Jeremy Howard, *Art Nouveau: International and National Styles in Europe* (Manchester 1996) 170–4.
[3] Pieter van Wesemael, *Architecture of Instruction and Delight: A Socio-Historical Analysis of World Exhibitions as a Didactic Phenomenon (1798–1851–1970)* (Rotterdam 2001).

building.[4] More impact, understandably, had the comprehensive *Pueblo Español* (Spanish Village) that could be found at Barcelona's next universal exposition in 1929.

Although the 1888 exhibition had ended with large debts, some politicians, particularly those of the Catalanist movement, dreamt of repeating the experience. Thus, in 1905, the architect Josep Puig i Cadafalch came up with the idea to organise another international exhibition. Puig i Cadafalch was also a prominent member of the Lliga Regionalista, a conservative Catalanist political party that had won the 1901 municipal elections in Barcelona, thus definitively breaking the dominance of the two national parties on a local level. Two years later the Lliga had been defeated by the populist Radical Republicans, who with a highly Spanish nationalist programme had mobilised the working classes that in great part had emigrated from other Spanish regions. Immediately before the municipal elections of November 1905 Puig i Cadafalch published an appeal in the Catalanist daily *La Veu de Catalunya* (The Voice of Catalonia), in which he shrewdly linked a new universal exposition with an electoral victory of his party. The leader of the main local employers' association decided to back the initiative and subsequently lobbied to get the support of the various authorities. However, only in 1913 was a mixed commission formed, consisting of representatives of the employers' association and all major political forces of Barcelona, among whom were Puig i Cadafalch and the undisputed leader of the Lliga Regionalista Francesc Cambó.[5]

The initial idea was to celebrate an International Exhibition of Electric Industries in 1917 at the east end of the town, near the Plaza de las Glorias Catalanas. However, paradoxically, the committee finally decided to locate it next to the Plaza de España, in the west of the town on the slopes of the Montjuïc hill, which proved to be a daring and visually attractive setting for the exhibition, thanks in great part to Puig i Cadafalch, who made the first overall design. A monumental entrance gave access to a broad avenue flanked with pavilions that led to a kind of baroque stairway to the eye-catching central, domed National Palace at the top of the hill. The whole was designed in a mixture of the international Beaux-Arts style, which could be found at most preceding exhibitions, and the new classicist *Noucentisme* trend. Most minor pavilions, in a variety of styles, were scattered over the rest of the hill. Puig i Cadafalch, who in 1917 became the

<hr>

[4] Eduardo Rodríguez Bernal, *Historia de la Exposición Ibero-Americana de Sevilla de 1929* (Seville 1994) 35.

[5] Ignasi de Solà-Morales, *La Exposición Internacional de Barcelona 1914–1929: Arquitectura y Ciudad* (Barcelona 1985) 9–19 and 53–5.

second president of the *Mancomunitat*, also planned a picturesque transversal axe with reproductions of vernacular buildings from the whole of Spain called *Tipos de la vida española* (Types from Spanish Life).[6]

This part was explicitly endorsed by the Catalanists within the organising committee. Thus, already in the spring of 1914 Cambó explained in the town council of Barcelona that the exhibition should not merely show one branch of industry. As Barcelona would not be able to surpass San Francisco, organising a very ambitious and costly World's Fair for 1915, it should try to impress in areas in which it had a clear advantage. Compared to the United States Barcelona could not offer a more modern industry, but it surely could compete with its history and traditions. Therefore, he concluded, the exhibition should also show the great national past, by which he meant the Spanish national past, by displaying artistic highlights and archaeological and historical artefacts from all over the country. Traditional handicrafts could be shown in 'an exhibition of Spanish towns', which three years later would find its way into the design of his political associate Puig i Cadafalch.[7]

However, because of the First World War the exhibition had to be postponed until 1923. But even this date proved to be too early, as the construction advanced only slowly because of the post-war crisis and a lack of funds. In 1923 the coup of general Miguel Primo de Rivera, an admirer of Mussolini who with the implicit approval of the king installed a military dictatorship, caused further delay. As captain general of Catalonia Primo de Rivera had received support for his coup from leading Catalanist politicians and from the Barcelonese business elite. They were dismayed by the recurring violence and terrorist attacks by the anarchists, which after 1918 degenerated into open class war. They hoped that Primo de Rivera would restore order, support their autonomist aspirations and take into account their economic interests. However, the dictator revealed himself to be a staunch Spanish nationalist – prohibiting the public use of Catalan and Basque – and he soon clashed with the political ambitions of the Catalanists.[8] As a consequence, Puig i Cadafalch resigned as president of the Catalan *Mancomunitat* which shortly afterwards was dissolved by the dictator. Other Catalanists now decided to step down from the board of

[6] Solà-Morales, *La Exposición de Barcelona* 54–61 and Jordana Mendelson, *Documenting Spain: Artists, Exhibition Culture, and the Modern Nation, 1929–1939* (University Park 2005) 6–11.

[7] The speech was delivered on 30 April 1914 and is cited in: Jesús Pabón, *Cambó 1876–1918* (Barcelona 1952) 423–4.

[8] See for the dictatorship of Primo de Rivera: Shlomo Ben-Ami, *Fascism from Above: The Dictatorship of Primo de Rivera in Spain 1923–1930* (Oxford 1983).

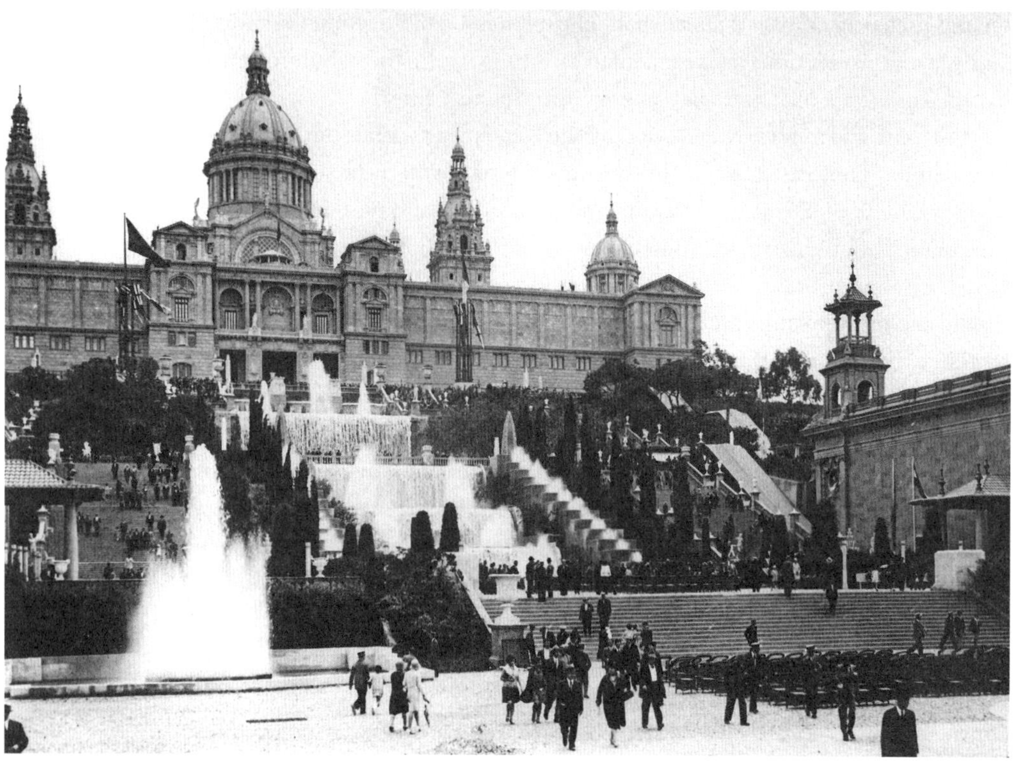

25 The National Palace, with the baroque stairways on top of the Montjuïc, at the International Exhibition, Barcelona, 1929. On the right is the Pavilion of Queen Victoria Eugenia, designed by Puig i Cadafalch, and behind it one could find the Pueblo Español in figure 26.

the Exhibition. For the moment these political changes did not favour the progress of the exposition.

Only in 1925, after the dictator decided to transform his military dictatorship into a civil regime and change some of his policies to get more support from the population, were construction activities resumed with new vigour, now strictly supervised by a new royal commissioner, the marquis of Foronda, a retired cavalry officer. The Spanish government also decided to fix the date of 1929 for the exposition, which would now focus on industry, art and sports. Nonetheless, it still would be the first World's Fair after the First World War. The dictatorship was now clearly in charge, as it controlled both the national government and the municipal authorities of Barcelona that supplied most of the budget. The lay-out of the exhibition was not drastically changed; only new architects were selected for the National Palace, which was destined for the masterpieces of Spanish art and the treasures of the national past and which was finally constructed in a Spanish Renaissance style (figure 25). The most visible change occurred one year before the opening, when it was decided to pull down the four columns on the central avenue – which had been constructed by Puig i Cadafalch – as it was feared that this reference to the four bars of the Catalan flag would anger the dictator.[9]

Regionalism did not play an important role in the exhibition. It is now mostly remembered because of the path-breaking modernist German pavilion designed by Mies van der Rohe, which in the 1980s was reconstructed on the same spot, in front of the Pavilion of Queen Victoria Eugenia. Only Norway, Denmark and Romania built a pavilion in a regionalist style. Nonetheless, the Pueblo Español could be seen as a kind of a vernacular complement to the high art in the National Palace. Although the plan to build a street with typical buildings from the different Spanish regions had disappeared after the first plan, the idea seemed to have stayed in the air, as from the start a part of the exhibition was dedicated to Spanish crafts. Moreover, earlier ethnographic villages, such as the Village Suisse at the Parisian World's Fair of 1900, had been a huge commercial success. And Brussels and Ghent, where in 1910 and 1913 the last World's Fairs before the war had been held, had showed the way with an Old Brussels and an Old Flanders quarter. Thus in 1925, the poet Joaquín Montaner, the newly nominated secretary of the organising committee, included a Spanish village in the revised plans, and the next year, the architect Francesc Folguera (1891–1960) was designated to direct the construction of a 'typical Spanish village', which compared to its predecessors at former exhibitions was a rather ambitious small town.[10]

Apart from Folguera the village was the work of the architect Ramón Reventós (1892–1976) and the artists Miguel Utrillo (1862–1934) and Xavier Nogués (1873–1940), all of them Catalans. The role of inspirer and main organiser seemed to have been played by Utrillo, a secondary artist but a leading figure in Barcelona's cultural life, who around the turn of the century had helped to introduce modern artistic trends such as Symbolism and Art Nouveau to Catalonia. He was one of the founders of the café *Els Quatre Gats*, the famous hang-out for Picasso and other ambitious young artists. According to Utrillo, when interviewed by a journalist from the Catalan weekly *Mirador*, he had come up with a plan for a Spanish village, when asked by Fernando Álvarez de la Campa, who in 1923 had been

---

9   Solà-Morales, *La Exposición de Barcelona* 62–74.

10   Ibid., 110–20 and 133–41. 'La paternitat del Poble Espanyol: La primitiva idea es deu a don Ignasi Girona?', *Mirador* 31 (29 August 1929) 3 and Salvador Sellés, 'La Exposición de Barcelona "El Pueblo Español"', *Revista del Cuerpo de Arquitectos Municipales de España* I, 5 (August 1929) 75–9, especially 76. Grandas somewhat malevolently maintains that the only precedent for the Spanish village had been the colonial exhibit of the African village of 1889: M. Carmen Grandas, *L'Exposició Internacional de Barcelona de 1929* (Barcelona 1988) 27.

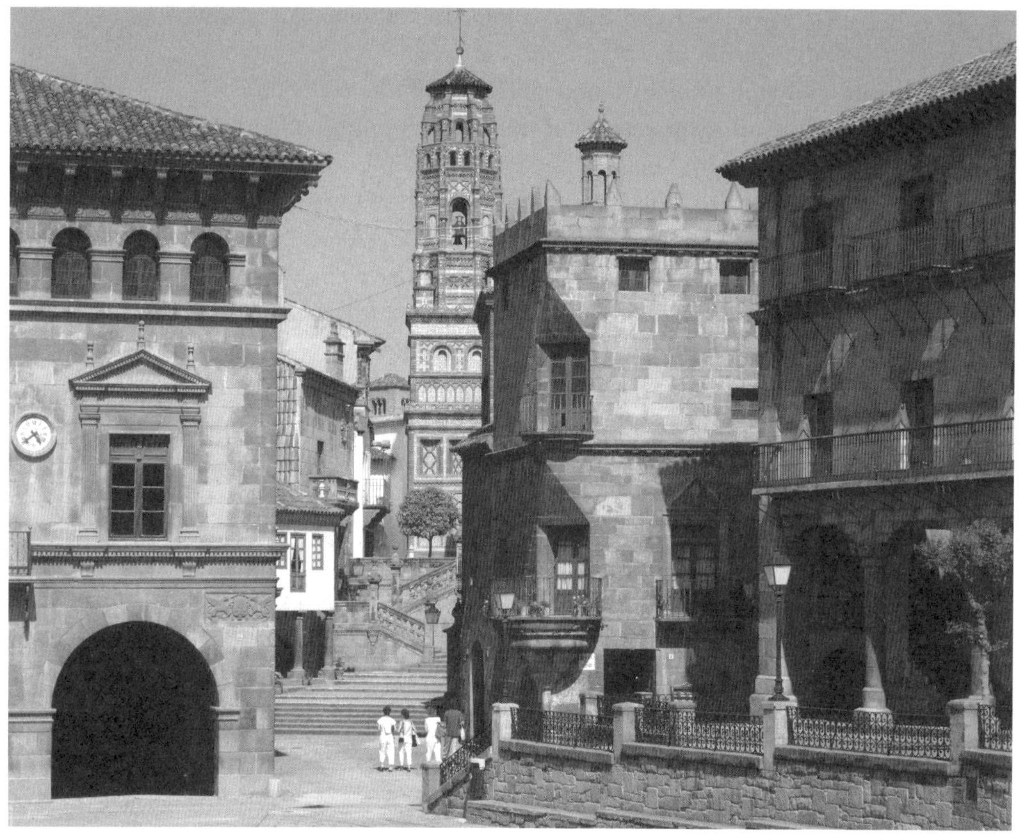

26 Pueblo Español, International Exhibition, Barcelona, 1929. View from the Main Square. On the left is the townhouse of Valderrobres (Teruel), then some houses from Galicia and the stairways of Santiago de Compostela, and in the background, the tower of Utebo (Aragón).

nominated mayor of Barcelona by Primo de Rivera. However, at this stage the project, like the rest of the exhibition, did not advance.[11]

After being appointed the four men decided to take examples from both high architecture and vernacular models and try to combine them in a harmonic ensemble. The hundred or so buildings, built on the slopes of the Montjuïc, would form a small walled town with some twenty streets, eight squares, churches, monasteries, a town hall, two gates, a bridge and various bars and restaurants (figure 26). As the regional division of the country was respected the village constituted a miniature Spain. The buildings were fake copies of armoured concrete and plaster; however to give the village an authentic air, especially when seen from the hill, the tiles were real and partially were even taken from old houses. Dioramas, presentations of local products and crafts, and typical dishes should present

[11] 'La paternitat del Poble Espanyol' and Mendelson, *Documenting Spain* 17–20. See for Utrillo, Marilyn McCully, *Els Quatre Gats: Art in Barcelona around 1900* (Princeton 1978).

the regional variety of the country, whereas concerts, local fiestas, dances, cavalcades and rustic sports should enliven the whole.[12] As the Pueblo Español was a huge success, instead of demolishing it after the exhibition as was planned, it was decided to keep it open and it still is one of the major tourist attractions of Barcelona.

Although in 1929 Primo de Rivera's regime rapidly lost support, the Pueblo Español was received favourably by the artistic and architectural press. It has to be remarked that because of the censorship – which was rather mild – it was impossible to openly criticise concrete measures by the authorities, but more general negative remarks were not prohibited.[13] However, in the reviews only praise for the makers of the village could be found, although its interpretation varied. In general, journals from Madrid were delighted that a village showing the beauty and organic unity of the country had been constructed in Barcelona by Catalan artists. The authors, still slightly worried by the Catalan pleas for autonomy from the recent past, expressed their satisfaction that even Barcelona now understood the importance of national unity. This was most obvious in those magazines that interpreted the Spanish Village in a highly nationalistic vein. Thus, the illustrated cultural magazine *La Esfera* exclaimed that 'the totality of the Spanish village gives an idea of an indissolubly united Spain, of a single Spain with different aspects'. The anonymous author even somewhat optimistically concluded that this culmination of the Exhibition showed that Barcelona 'wanted to have Spain in its heart'.[14]

Already one year before the opening, *Construcción Moderna*, which was also published in Madrid, gave a somewhat more neutral description of the various exhibition pavilions, while also discussing the Pueblo Español. The anonymous author asserted that this 'typical Spanish village' shows 'the humble, quiet and laborious life of our small rural small towns' and added that it constituted 'one of the most appealing attractions' of the exhibition.[15] In January 1930, two weeks after the closure of the exhibition, the magazine repeated this judgement. The anonymous author also declared that the designers had carried out their task perfectly:

[12] Solà-Morales, *La Exposición de Barcelona* 134–40 and Sellés, 'El Pueblo Español'.

[13] See for the censorship: María Cruz Seoane and María Dolores Sáiz, *Historia del periodismo en España 3: El siglo XX. 1898–1936* (Madrid 1996) 322–6.

[14] 'De la Exposición de Barcelona: El maravilloso Pueblo Español', *La Esfera* (1 June 1929) 6.

[15] 'La Exposición Internacional de Barcelona (continuación)', *La Construcción Moderna* (1 August 1928) 209–15, especially 212–14.

> Every street, every house, every corner, every stone of the Spanish
> Village has the taste of the soil it represents. And being like this,
> everything is grouped with such a sense of harmony that the village is a
> perfect unity; which brings about the miracle of making of the souls of
> the Spanish peoples [*pueblos*], which it represents, a single soul, a single
> spirit. Let's add that this lesson of unity is given in Barcelona and that it
> is realised by Catalan artists.[16]

The critic of the *Revista del Cuerpo de Arquitectos Municipales de España*,
which was edited in Barcelona, was more outspoken in his judgement,
but implicitly claimed the success of the exhibition for Catalonia and
hoped that it would contribute indirectly to the regeneration of the whole
of Spain. In his review of the National Palace, which he presented as a
masterpiece, he maintained that 'our' exhibition, realised exclusively by
local architects, is 'the best of all until the present'. This also applied to
the Pueblo Español, as nowhere:

> not even in the North-American nation of gigantic enterprises, have
> they constructed in one year a whole village and made it alive ...
> a village in which people pray, work, teach and amuse themselves,
> a village which is not a necropolis of dispersed and incomplete
> remainders of others that were, but the life itself of other periods,
> revived and purified by a miracle of art and science.

He hoped that the village would be an incentive to visitors to appreciate
and protect the artistic riches they possessed in their own villages or
towns. He particularly praised the villagers of Utebo, who had gone to the
provincial capital of Zaragoza to demand money to repair the bell tower
of their church, arguing that the replica in the Pueblo Español was in a
better state and more beautiful than the original. At the same time the
Spanish village, according to the critic, could stimulate 'artistic tourism'
within Spain, especially by foreigners.[17]

Thus, although small differences could be found, in fact both the main
protagonists and the reviewers agreed that apart from industrial progress
some aspects of the great Spanish past should also be shown. Leading
conservative Catalanists such as Cambó and Puig i Cadafalch even took
the initiative to include buildings or pavilions from the different Spanish

---

16 'De la Exposición de Barcelona: El Pueblo Español', *La Construcción Moderna* (30
January 1930) 17–20, especially 18.
17 Salvador Sellés, 'La Exposición de Barcelona: El Palacio Nacional', *Revista del Cuerpo
de Arquitectos Municipales de España* (July 1929) 62–7, especially 62 and Sellés, 'El Pueblo
Español' 76–7.

regions in the plans for the exhibition. The dictatorship of Primo de Rivera wholeheartedly endorsed this part of the program, although concrete steps to realise a Spanish village were taken only in 1925 and 1926. All critics seemed to agree that the creators of the village had perfectly succeeded in conveying the image of unity through variety. Despite clear ideological differences, all seemed to agree that the main lesson of the village was, and should be, that differences did not impede unity; on the contrary, by supplementing each other the various regions of Spain formed an organic national whole. Nevertheless, regionalism was confined to the picturesque Spanish part of the exhibition, the rest was mainly constructed in a monumental, neo-classical style, with which the organisers apparently preferred to associate their town.

The 1929 Ibero-American Exhibition of Seville

The Ibero-American Exhibition of Seville, which was also inaugurated in May 1929, was the first international exposition in which regionalism was the main architectural style. Like its Catalan counterpart, the exposition in Seville had been mainly a local affair, although on this occasion the initiative had been taken by some members of the business community. Luis Rodríguez de Caso, a retired artillery officer and the proprietor of a glass manufacturing enterprise, had the idea to organise an international exhibition in Seville. In this way he hoped to contribute to the regeneration of the country which, especially after the loss of the last main colonies after the disastrous Spanish–American War of 1898, seemed more urgent than ever. In 1905 he had been rewarded for his Art Nouveau display at a small exhibition of Sevillan products and he also had been the main driving force behind the fiesta 'Spain in Seville', which was held in the spring of 1908 to commemorate the centennial of the uprising of the Spanish people against Napoleon. During this feast folkloric groups from all Spanish regions were invited to Seville to glorify national unity. During the central event the flags of all the Spanish regions and the Spanish American states were gathered around the national ensign. At the same time, residents originating from the different parts of Spain were invited to construct their own stand at the local April Fair in a typical regional architectural style. As both the industrial exhibition and the fiesta had been a success, Rodríguez de Caso in June 1909 suggested that the town should host a major international exhibition. The local press immediately supported the idea but only in 1910, after the king had given his explicit support to Seville and the Liberals had replaced the Conservative Party in both the

Town Hall and in the national government, would the plans receive official recognition and the first subsidy from Madrid.[18]

A local organisation committee was formed that consisted of representatives of the main political parties and members of the economic and social elite. The date for the opening was fixed for 1914. However, as in Barcelona the project did not advance very quickly, and the First World War caused further delay. But even after the war progress was slow and only after Primo de Rivera decided to step up efforts in 1925 did the construction activities advance more rapidly. The government also decided to celebrate the Ibero-American Exhibition in 1928, although it later had to be postponed for one more year, thus finally coinciding with the International Exhibition in Barcelona. It also took away the reins from the local organisation committee by nominating José Cruz Conde, a former officer who had no bonds with Seville, as new Royal Commissioner. To assure the success of the enterprise and guarantee that the fruits were reaped by the dictatorship, Cruz Conde was also appointed civil governor of the province of Seville and head of the local branch of the Unión Patriótica, the political movement created to mobilise support for the regime.[19] Thus, the transition from a military to a civil regime, which was decided upon by the dictator in 1925, had major consequences for both Seville and Barcelona. The dictator now decided to use both exhibitions as a way of increasing support for his regime and of improving his image abroad. Although the exhibitions would finally open as planned, the dictatorship would fail in its objectives as the number of visitors to both events was disappointing.[20] Moreover the growing economic and political difficulties at home forced him to step down on 28 January 1930, even before the Ibero-American Exhibition had closed its doors.

But what reasons had seduced the somewhat sleepy town of Seville into embarking upon such a great adventure? Clearly the main motives were economic. The business community wanted to give a burst to the local economy, whereas the town council hoped to attract subsidies from the

[18]   Eduardo Rodríguez Bernal, *La Exposición Ibero-Americana de Sevilla de 1929 a través de la prensa local: Su génesis y primeras manifestaciones (1905–1914)* (Seville 1981) 37–152 and Alberto Villar Movellán, *Arquitectura del regionalismo en Sevilla. 1900–1935* (Seville 1979) 182–6. It seems that king Alfonso XIII took a special interest in the exhibition and intervened various times in behalf of Seville. See: Alfonso Braojos Garrido, *Alfonso XIII y la Exposición Iberoamericana de Sevilla de 1929* (Seville 1992).

[19]   Rodríguez Bernal, *Historia de la Exposición Ibero-Americana* 57–81 and Braojos Garrido, *Alfonso XIII y la Exposición Iberoamericana* 72–7.

[20]   For both exhibitions there are no clear data although the exhibition in Seville probably received less than two million visitors, whereas Barcelona possibly welcomed somewhat more people.

national government to pay at least a part of the town extension and urban reforms that were badly needed. The exhibition should also enhance or re-establish the commercial bonds between the former American colonies and Seville, and convert the town into a major tourist destination.[21]

At the same time, feelings of local pride and nationalistic motives were equally paramount. Seville's elite hoped that the exhibition would make a contribution to the national regeneration. However, in a world dominated by huge colonial empires this would not suffice to regain a prominent place on the international stage. Tightening the bonds with kindred nations in order to form a kind of loose commonwealth could to some extent make up for the loss of the once glorious Spanish empire. Instead of subjecting new areas, many Spaniards now hoped to unite the former American colonies in a new kind of commonwealth with the motherland, and the exhibition could be a good starting point. Thus, initially the exhibition was meant to be Hispano-American, but as Portugal, Brazil and the United States also showed an interest in participating, it was decided in 1922 to change the name to Ibero-American. The participation of Portugal, which would be one of the main exhibitors, could also function as a stimulus for more co-operation on the Iberian Peninsula, which eventually could also increase the weight of Spain in the international arena. Somewhat later it was decided to also include pavilions for the remaining Spanish colonial possessions in Africa.[22]

The decision to also invite the Spanish regions had already been taken in 1911 and would never be recalled. The assembly of all regions would show that love for the regional homeland was fully compatible with national unity. Rodríguez Caso, in a renewed proposal of 1923, openly argued that in a period when Catalan regionalism had 'degenerated into separatism', this demonstration of unity was even more urgent than before.[23] Thus, cultural regionalism in fact was used to counter the political regionalism

---

[21] Rodríguez Bernal, *Historia de la Exposición Ibero-Americana* 42 and 274–5 and Manuel Trillo de Leyva, *La Exposición Iberoamericana: La transformación urbana de Sevilla* (Seville 1980) 34–50.

[22] See for Hispanismo and Iberismo: Frederick B. Pike, *Hispanismo, 1898–1936: Spanish Conservatives and Liberals and their Relations with Spanish-America* (Notre Dame 1971) and Juan Antonio Rocamora, 'Un nacionalismo fracasado: El Iberismo', *Espacio, Tiempo y Forma*, V *Historia Contemporánea* (1989) 2, 29–56. Luis Ángel Sánchez Gómez, 'África en Sevilla: La Exhibición colonial de la Exposición Iberoamericana de 1929', *Hispania* (2006) 1,045–82.

[23] Rodríguez Caso as cited in: Rodríguez Bernal, *Historia de la Exposición Ibero-Americana* 115–16. He also opposed the inclusion of a section for machines and industrial products as he feared that the somewhat backward Spanish industry could not withstand the comparison with foreign companies. See: Ibid., 86–90.

that was on the rise in Catalonia and that was increasingly perceived as a threat to the integrity of the fatherland.

The first details of the programme for the exhibition were revealed in April 1911 when the organisation committee announced the terms for the architectural contest. The exhibition should take place in three different areas surrounding the María Luisa Park that connected the old town with the new port under construction. The redesigning of the park had already been assigned to the foremost French garden architect Jean Claude Nicolas Forestier, who had promised to adapt his designs to the Islamic Andalusian garden traditions of Seville. Initially the organisers thought of admitting only local architects who should not 'copy other Expositions celebrated abroad, but should give to the design foreseen in Seville a typical character, in harmony with the climate, customs, sky and soil of this area and with the style and manner of its renowned monuments'. In the end, however, the contest was open to all Spanish architects and no stylistic limitations were imposed.[24]

Most local architects deemed the budget and space too limited and thus refrained from participating. In the final event, only three projects were submitted of which the regionalist proposal of Aníbal González Álvarez was by far the most convincing. The young Sevilian, who would become one of the most important regionalist architects of Spain, had already started to adopt regionalist elements in some of his houses. Nevertheless in an interview, which was published three months after the announcement of the contest, he maintained that the exhibition was something 'exotic' and consequently could not be conceived entirely in a local style. However, that same summer he seemed to have changed his mind. Probably he was influenced by the local politicians who encouraged the use of regionalism, as in the preceding year the town council had accepted the proposal of Javier de Lepe to reward new private constructions in a peculiar Sevilian style. Nevertheless, it seems that a theoretical contribution had a more direct impact on the architect. Thus, in the report that accompanied his design for the exhibition Aníbal González cited the conference by Vicente Lampérez from the July issue of *Arquitectura y Construcción*, in which he pleaded for a new national style inspired by the architectural traditions of the most glorious periods of Spanish history. This was exactly what González tried to do in his project, although he added that the style of the major buildings was 'a regional traditionalism, since all the elements and

---

24 Conde de Urbina as cited in: Trillo de Leyva, *La Exposición Iberoamericana* 58–9. See also: Villar Movellán, *Arquitectura del regionalismo* 119–21, 230–2 and 234 and Rodríguez Bernal, *Historia de la Exposición Ibero-Americano* 159.

materials are typical, and most of them genuinely local'. The regionalist character of the buildings and decoration, according to him, would also distinguish the exhibition from earlier ones.[25]

The main buildings of the exhibition were hence designed in styles that referred to the golden age of Seville in the late medieval and early modern period. By using local materials and construction techniques, the architect hoped to reinforce the Sevilian character of the buildings and stimulate the local economy. The Royal Academy of Fine Arts of Seville subscribed to the former goal as it recommended acceptance of the project by Aníbal González because it formed a 'purely Spanish and eminently regional composition', and by executing this project 'Seville could show itself very Sevilian'.[26] As a result, he was awarded the first prize and shortly afterwards was nominated chief architect of the exhibition.

González Álvarez now began to concretise his projects, starting with the central open space that he had baptised Triumph Square, but which the organising committee shortly afterwards renamed Plaza de América. Around the square he planned three permanent buildings, each in a different historical style. Thus, the monumental Pavilion of Fine Arts was built in the Spanish Renaissance style, the Pavilion for Industry and Decorative Arts in the local neo-Mudéjar style (figure 27), whereas the smaller Royal Pavilion showed the neo-Gothic style characteristic of the reign of the Catholic Monarchs, who in the late fifteenth century had united the various Spanish kingdoms and had supported Columbus' discovery of America. By using local brick and glazed ceramic he gave this last building a strong local touch. The fourth side was to be crowned by a monument to the Spanish language symbolised by the greatest writer of the Golden Age, Miguel de Cervantes. But as the ambitious monument designed by the sculptor Lorenzo Coullaut was far too expensive, it was substituted by a small roundabout dedicated to the author of *Don Quixote* designed by the architect himself.[27]

González Álvarez' design for the Plaza de América could be seen as an illustration to the lecture he gave in 1915 with Leonardo Rucabado at the sixth National Conference for Architects. In this lecture, which as we have seen became the manifesto of Spanish regionalist architecture, they argued

---

[25] Aníbal González cited in: Villar Movellán, *Arquitectura del regionalismo* 234. See also 170–9 and 186–7.

[26] Dictamen de la Real Academia de Bellas Artes de Sevilla del 25 de septiembre de 1911 as cited in: Ibid., 237–8.

[27] Ibid., 232–4 and 274–83. The magnificent monument by Coullaut would later on arise at the Plaza de España in Madrid: Rodríguez Bernal, *Historia de la Exposición Ibero-Americana* 158.

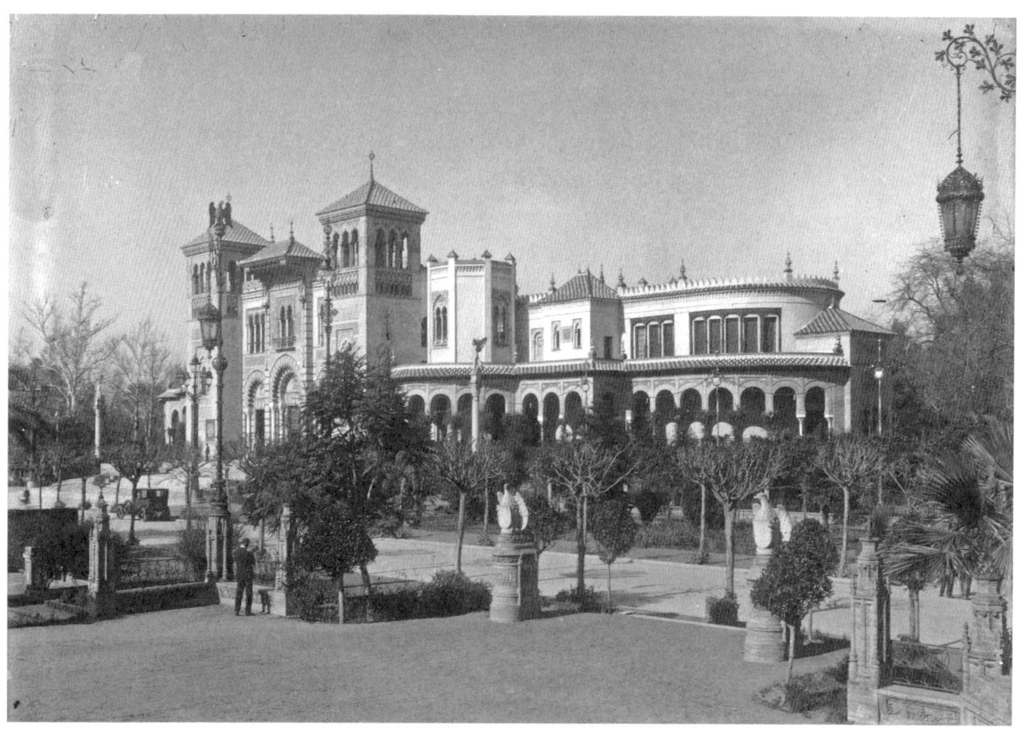

27 Aníbal González Álvarez, Pavilion for Industry and Decorative Arts, Plaza de América, Seville, 1929.

that in order to develop a new, modern but truly national architectural style architects should start repeating traditional historical forms while taking into account the specific local climatic and geographical circumstances.[28] The Sevilian architect applied these principles by using the styles, materials and ornaments he deemed most typical, and consequently most in accordance with the spirit of both Spain and Seville. His regionalism, nevertheless, was not completely orthodox. Thus, contrary to Rucabado, González Álvarez almost entirely ignored rural influences, whereas both men coincided in making no serious distinction between regionalism and nationalism, or between historicist and vernacular sources of inspiration.

Like Rucabado had done with his well-known apartment building in the centre of Madrid, González Álvarez also tried to synthesise Spanish architecture in one magnificent building. Whereas Rucabado's picturesque assemblage of decorative elements from many different regions in a great variety of materials constituted an interesting, but very eclectic whole, González Álvarez' Plaza de España would become a real masterpiece

[28]   Leonardo Rucabado and Aníbal González, 'Orientaciones para el resurgimiento de una arquitectura nacional', *Arte Español* (1915) 379–86 and 437–53.

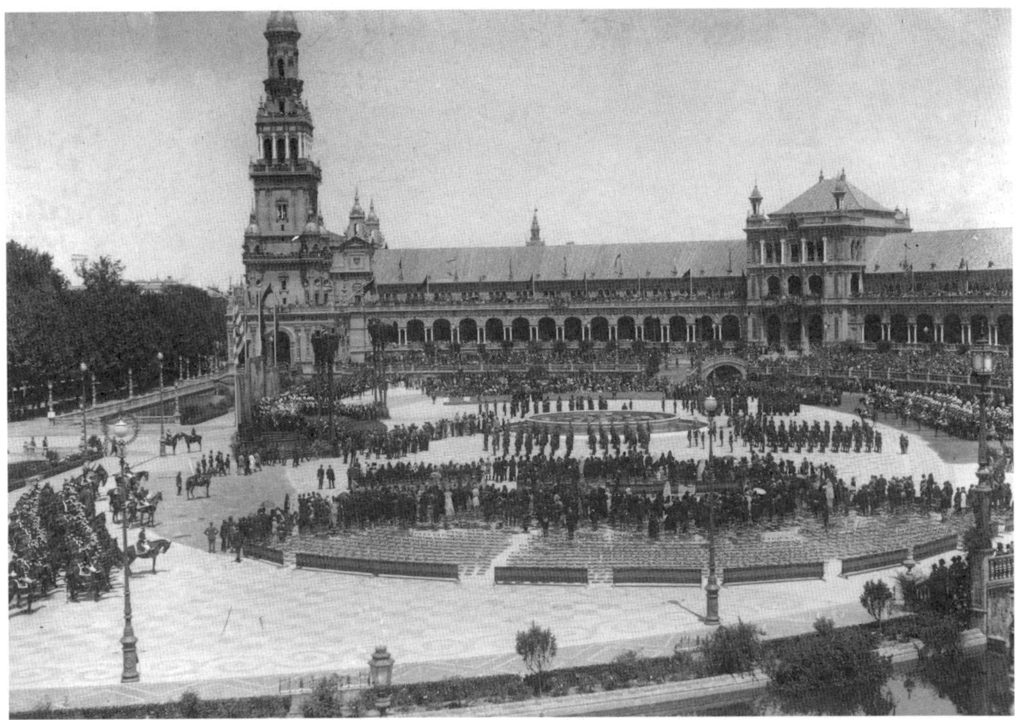

(figure 28). Although he also assembled elements and forms from all over Spain, González Álvarez succeeded in giving the huge complex a uniform aspect. He used a symmetrical layout and a unified formal language taken from the Renaissance and the Baroque; nonetheless he particularly created a harmonious outlook by applying almost exclusively typical Sevilian materials, such as brick, tiles and glazed ceramics, which completely covered the structure of the building that was built in concrete.

The Plaza de España, however, would take more time to build than the Plaza de América. The first revised plan of 1912 envisaged a stadium close to the entrance of the exhibition area. Somewhat later the organising committee decided to locate the stadium – currently used by Betis Sevilla – on newly added terrain at the far end of the fair ground and to name the remaining square Plaza de España. In July 1914 González Álvarez' more detailed plan was approved. In fact, the architect had retained the function of the stadium as he designed a huge symmetrical and semi-elliptical space surrounded by three temporary pavilions which were connected by a colonnade with a terrace on the first floor. A small canal separated the central circus – which measured about 170 by 100 m – from a broad promenade and the buildings that together could house thousands of spectators. The trees of the María

28 Official inauguration of the Ibero-American Exhibition, 9 May 1929, Plaza de España, Seville.

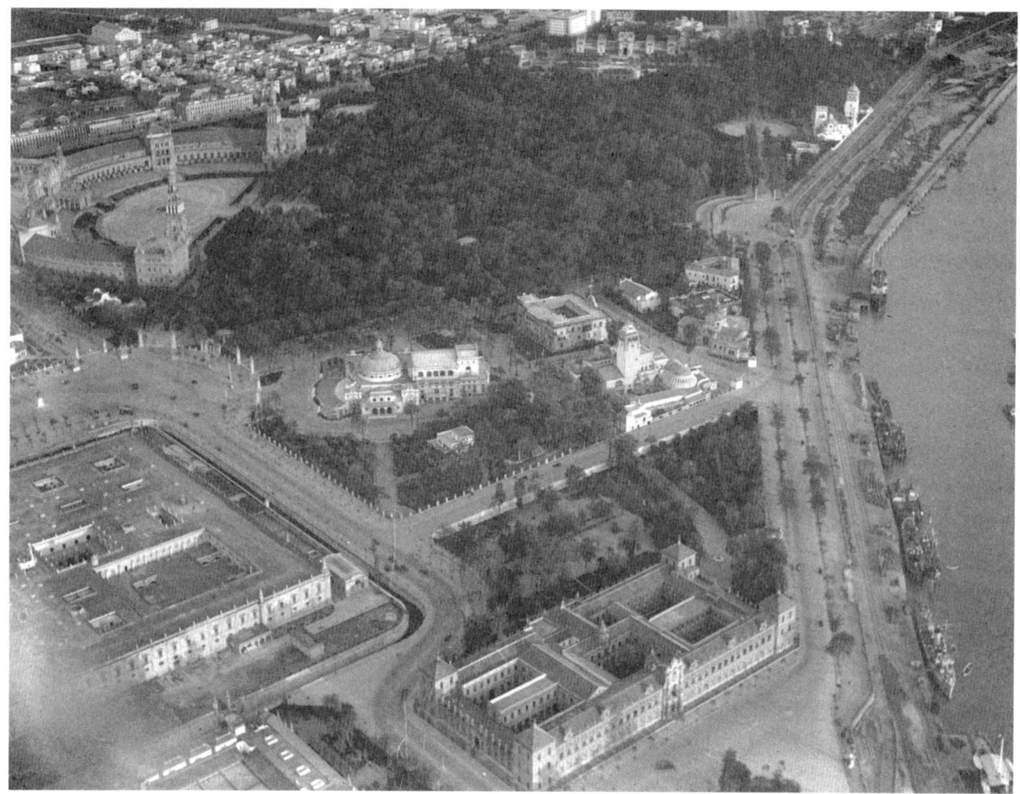

29 Aerial view of the Ibero-American Exhibition, Seville, 1929. On the left is the Plaza de España. At the right of the entrance are the pavilions of Seville, Peru, Chile, and then, next to the river Uruguay, the United States and, a bit further on, Argentina. On the upper part one can discern the rectangular Plaza de América. The Avenida de la Raza, which was the main axis of the rest of the exhibition ground, began right above the pavilion of Argentina, and is just outside the picture.

Luisa Park functioned as a kind of background for this central stage. During the war it was decided that the buildings should be permanent and González Álvarez consequently revised his plan, transforming the three pavilions and the colonnades into one huge building.[29]

Although the canal evoked memories of Venice and the plan was reminiscent of the sixteenth-century Italian architect Palladio, Aníbal González explicitly inspired his designs in the ornaments of several Renaissance and Baroque monuments from various parts of Spain, which was particularly clear in the two towers that flanked the building.

[29] Rodríguez Bernal, *Historia de la Exposición Ibero-Americana* 161–2, Trillo de Leyva, *La Exposición Iberoamericana* 77–90 and Villar Movellán, *Arquitectura del regionalismo* 283–5 and 421–7.

Eventually, the whole sense of the building and the experience of space were botched by Vicente Traver, who succeeded González in 1926, when the latter resigned in protest at the change of orientation and the diminishing of his personal influence following the arrival of Cruz Conde. Traver decided to introduce an illuminated fountain in the middle of the plaza, thus replacing the human activities or spectacle that should have occupied centre stage. The fountain now induced the people to stroll around it, admiring the picturesque building, whereas this was primarily intended to be an interesting backdrop to the assembled masses.[30]

The nationalist and regionalist character of the exposition did not only become manifest in the architecture, but was also made clear from the names of the main squares and streets (figure 29). Apart from the Plaza de América and the Plaza de España, there was an Avenida de la Raza (Avenue of the Race), where the pavilions of most American participants were planned, and which referred to the common descent of the peoples from Spain and Spanish America.[31] The Plaza de España further had four bridges that were named after the main kingdoms of medieval Spain: Castile, Leon, Navarre, and Aragon. Aníbal González also constructed, as a transition from the semi-elliptical promenade to the main building, forty-eight benches with ceramics that represented the provinces of Spain (figure 30). The Plaza de España, where all the provinces and ancient kingdoms were thus assembled, was placed at the end of the avenue that crossed the park and began at the river; thus it symbolically spread its arms to welcome the visitors from America.[32]

But to whom should the regionalist and nationalist message be conveyed? As the lowest entrance fee – 50 cents on Thursdays and Sundays – was still considered quite expensive, the exhibition clearly catered to a well-to-do public.[33] However, both the organising committee and its chief architect tried to direct themselves to a more lower-class audience as well. Thus when the plans for the Plaza de España were revised the now permanent building was destined to become a workers' university. Later on this changed to a Spanish–American college and a school for applied arts. It was Aníbal González Álvarez who constantly tried to emphasise the didactic aspect of the exhibition and thus also bring the poor into contact with the

---

[30] Trillo de Leyva, *La Exposición Iberoamericana* 86–90 and Villar Movellán, *Arquitectura del regionalismo* 283–5 and 421–7.
[31] In 1918 the Discovery of America on 12 October was proclaimed a national holiday in Spain as the 'Fiesta de la Raza'.
[32] Rodríguez Bernal, *Historia de la Exposición Ibero-Americano* 161–2.
[33] Ibid., 348–56.

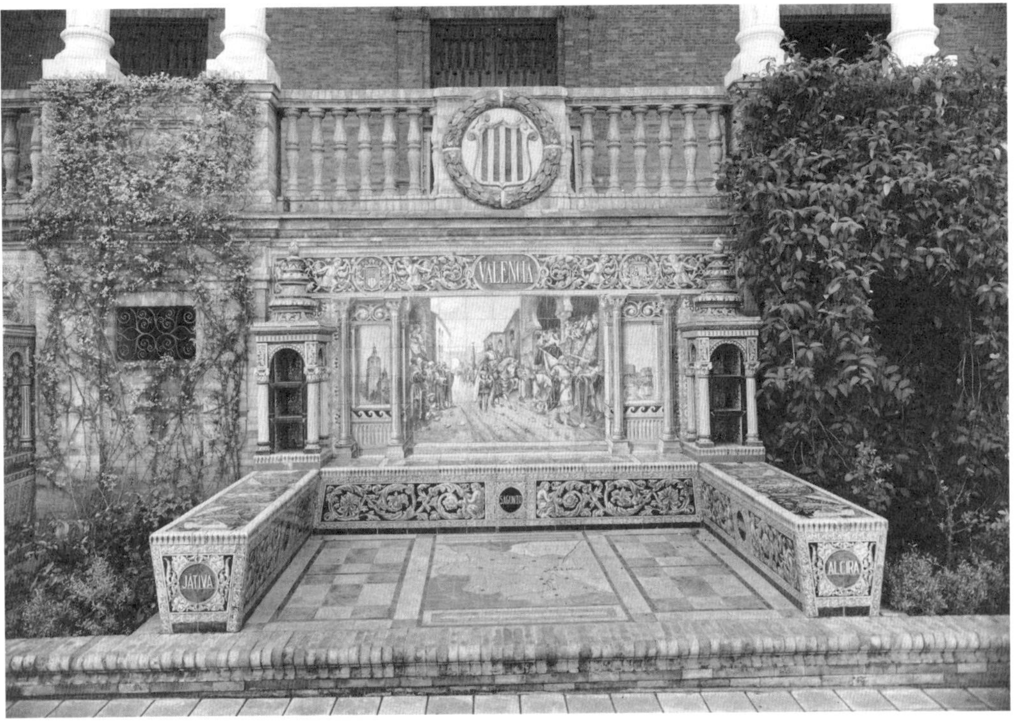

30 Aníbal
González
Álvarez, Bench
dedicated to
the province
of Valencia
at the Plaza
de España,
1915–29, Seville.
Photo from
1929.

national and local cultural heritage, although his ideas were also approved by the organising committee. Already in 1912 he proposed the erection of a kiosk in the María Luisa Park, next to the recently constructed monument for Gustavo Adolfo Bécquer, where the books of this great Sevilian poet could be read, thus giving access to his writings to those who could not afford to purchase a book. This should be the first step of his plan to convert the Park to a museum of regional literature and an open-air public library. During the next few years five more monuments were erected to commemorate local authors and all were provided with their works. Obviously also González Álvarez' roundabout dedicated to Cervantes was equipped with books and benches.[34]

One of the main goals of González Álvarez' designs was to provide work for the local artisans and indirectly to improve the artistic quality of their products. In this, like German architects such as Riemerschmid, Muthesius and Schumacher, he clearly subscribed to the ideals of the Arts and Crafts movement. He particularly favoured the traditional ceramics workshops, because their painted tiles could also easily be used for pedagogic purposes.

[34]   Trillo de Leyva, *La Exposición Iberoamericana* 45–8 and 74.

The architect made profuse use of these tiles to bring home the nationalist message. Thus, the tableau of each of the forty-eight benches of the Plaza de España showed a characteristic historical event of the depicted province and some representative buildings and coats of arms. The floor in front of the U-shaped benches, which formed small, almost separate spaces on a human scale, was decorated with a map of the province. Finally the benches were flanked with small ceramic shelves where the public could find maps, guides, leaflets, magazines and journals from each province.[35] However, the Spanish nation as represented in the Plaza de España should not only encompass all provinces, but also all layers of society. By designing a regionalist building, visibly founded on the humble but dignified work of masons, ceramists and other artisans, González Álvarez seemed to imply that the heroic deeds depicted on the tableaux – which generally showed kings, nobles, bishops, explorers and politicians – could only be performed while they were based on the anonymous efforts of millions of ordinary Spaniards.

Furthermore, to the architect, the protagonist of the Plaza de España was not the building, but the visitor. He (or she) had the central role, he had to become active and experience the space on his own by watching the tableaux, sitting on one of the benches, reading the leaflets or books, and thus becoming familiar with the diverse geography and history of the fatherland, or by hiring one of the rowing boats on the canal. The plaza therefore – which still is the most popular part of the María Luisa Park – was a democratic monument to the Spanish people, which could be enjoyed while at the same time honouring the past, the regional diversity and living present of the nation. It seemed that even the architect's political adversaries recognised his zeal in an effort to give the ordinary worker a dignified place within the nation as during the 1920 terrorist campaign some local anarchists tried to assassinate him.[36] For González Álvarez, who survived the attempt, regionalism thus was part of a broader reform programme that aimed at incorporating the working classes into the national community.

It seemed that Primo de Rivera could subscribe to this programme. Although in 1925 the government took the reins from the local organising committee, this merely caused a speeding up of the existing project. The various Spanish regions and all Andalusian provinces were more effectively pushed to participate in this national venture. Nevertheless, they did so

---

[35] Ibid., 79–88 and Rodríguez Bernal, *Historia de la Exposición Ibero-Americana* 150–1 and 162.

[36] Villar Movellán, *Arquitectura del regionalismo* 303–4.

hesitantly as most of the pavilions, which could be seen in a somewhat remote part of the fairground, were only finished several months after the inauguration. They mostly chose a style inspired by typical vernacular constructions from the countryside, although others preferred a more historicist approach and some even reproduced a well-known historical building. As had been the intention from the start, most other buildings were also constructed in a regionalist style. The Agricultural Pavilion by Juan Talavera, for example, made quite an impact as one of the first examples of a new Andalusian 'white architecture', inspired by eighteenth-century farm houses of the Sevilian countryside. At the same time the government actively urged the American countries to build a proper pavilion. Most American participants also selected a neo-vernacular design for their representations. Thus the Mexican architect Manuel Amábilis Domínguez constructed a neo-Maya pavilion, Juan Martínez Gutiérrez a 'nationalist' Chilean building, and William Templeton Johnson chose an appropriate 'Californian' or Spanish Revival style to represent the United States.[37]

Contrary to its counterpart in Barcelona, the Ibero-American Exhibition was almost completely ignored by the architectural press, which apparently considered the architectural concept somewhat outdated. Cultural magazines from Madrid, however, exalted the work done by the organisers and architects. Critics of *La Esfera* even boasted that 'nothing similar was ever made in the world' and that the new regionalist hotel Alfonso XII was the 'most complete and rich top class hotel of the world'. In an editorial the magazine sustained that thanks to the 'new Cid', with which it referred to Primo de Rivera, a new, renovated Spain had arisen.[38] The 'splendid buildings' of the exhibition showed 'the soul and effort of the represented nations and of our own nation, province by province. For one time, the Hispanic world comes together on the fecund soil of the procreating mother, and creates, cordially, one sole people, exemplary, free and sovereign, that during one whole year will dictate laws of love and peace.' In its review of the opening *La Esfera* called the Plaza de España the culmination of the exhibition, and in an obituary of González Álvarez, who died a month later, it even maintained that his pavilions 'would have no rival in the world'.[39]

37 Ibid., 429–65 and Rodríguez Bernal, *Historia de la Exposición Ibero-Americana* 201–13 and 367–80.

38 O. de P., 'Crónica de Sevilla: Preparando la Exposición Iberoamericana', *La Esfera* (19 January 1929) 12–13, José Andrés Vazquez, 'Crónica de Sevilla: Los hospedajes durante la Exposición', *La Esfera* (24 November 1929) 2–3 and 'La Esfera', 'Significación nacional de las exposiciones', *La Esfera* (4 May 1929) 4.

39 José Andrés Vazquez, 'Crónica de Sevilla: Homenjes a las Repúblicas durante la

Similarly the Madrid-based weekly *Blanco y Negro*, although less exaggerated, called Aníbal González Álvarez a 'genius' and praised the 'magnificent' Plaza de América. The anonymous author particularly liked the Plaza de España and the benches that each depicted a Spanish province, which were like a 'facet of the great Spanish diamond, like a stanza of the triumphal, sovereign and unanimous song'. The author thus especially eulogised the architect for stressing the fundamental unity of the fatherland in his masterpiece.[40]

The architectural magazines, on the contrary, did not feel the need to deal extensively with the exhibition in Seville. *Arquitectura* waited until 1930 to publish a very factual description of the exposition, whereas *Construcción Moderna* only republished a short review from the royalist newspaper *ABC* and an obituary of González Álvarez. The anonymous journalist from *ABC* merely described the road González Álvarez had covered to arrive at his 'original decorative architecture in which mudéjar bricks and ceramics triumph with the brilliant lights of their enamel'. According to him the exhibition had been a success and thanks to the architect was a 'symphony of ceramics and cast iron'.[41] Thus insofar as the specialised press dedicated attention to the exhibition it was in a positive way; all, like the dictator himself, seemed to subscribe to the original regionalist concept of the organisers and the main architect. However, the silence of the architectural magazines probably should also be seen as a sign that this type of architecture was now considered to be something from the past, which did not have to be explained extensively to its public.

Both exhibitions, in brief, continued the local architectural trends that were already visible before 1914. Thus, the exhibition board in Barcelona in fact did not regard regionalism as a serious architectural option and preferred an international orientation for the main buildings. Regionalism, in the form of fake copies, was only considered apt for the Spanish village, where vernacular buildings and handicrafts were shown. Nonetheless, this was not an imposition from Madrid; the choice even seemed to have originated with leading Catalanists. In Seville, on the other hand, it was decided to dress even the monumental main buildings in the rather eclectic regionalist

Exposición', *La Esfera* (1 December 1928) 8–9, 'Sus Majestades inauguran solemnemente la magnífica Exposición sevillana', *La Esfera* (11 May 1929) 5–7 and J. Cascales Muñoz, 'Aníbal González Álvarez-Ossorio', *La Esfera* (8 June 1929) 39.

40 'Plaza de España', *Blanco y Negro* (5 May 1929).

41 'Inauguración de la Exposición Iberoamericana de Sevilla', *La Construcción Moderna* (15 May 1929) 129–30. The other articles were 'Aníbal González', *La Construcción Moderna* (15 June 1929) 161–4 and 'Sobre la actividad arquitectónica en España', *Arquitectura* (April 1930) 99–110, especially 101–3.

attire that was the hallmark of González Álvarez, who mixed national and local elements from both high architecture and vernacular examples. By paying most attention to the picturesque façade of his festive buildings, he continued to turn the traditional patio-centred buildings inside out. Moreover, he now also used concrete for the structure of his buildings, which was completely hidden from view. This meant that it had become almost impossible to convincingly assert that his constructions were an honest and logical continuation of an authentic tradition. Nonetheless, both the main buildings of González Álvarez and the Spanish village perfectly fulfilled their main objective: attract and entertain visitors.

The political implications of these regionalist structures were most clearly visible in the Plaza de España and the other highly didactic projects of González Álvarez. They showed that he directed himself to a broad public and especially to the poorer classes. Stimulating local pride, and reinforcing local identity, also implied the strengthening of national feelings. This message seemed to have the support of the oligarchic elite of Seville, the more democratically elected authorities of Barcelona and the military dictatorship. Thus in Barcelona even fierce champions of regional autonomy proposed combining a clear emphasis on Catalan elements with a central place for the Spanish heritage. One could probably argue that by connecting Catalonia with modernity and Spain with the past, they implicitly claimed more of a leading political role for their own region. Primo de Rivera possibly put more emphasis on national greatness, but in general he did not oppose cultural regionalism. Expressions of political regionalism were not tolerated, but this was the case with all open opposition and, in fact, the strong central control of the exhibitions by his regime was resented in both Barcelona and Seville.

8

Paris

At the 1937 International Exhibition in Paris, regionalism also played a major, although almost forgotten role. The exposition is mostly remembered for an impressive painting that came to symbolise the drama of the Spanish Civil War and two buildings that perfectly visualised the current ideological clash between fascism and communism. Thus, the monumental pavilions of Nazi Germany and the Soviet Union aggressively opposed each other at the Place du Trocadéro, whereas Picasso's *Guernica*, the cry of outrage against the bombardment of the emblematic Basque town of Guernica by German air planes, could be seen in the pavilion of the Spanish Republic. These powerful images completely overshadowed the picturesque *Centre régional* (Regional Centre) that was the principal representation of the host country and which has, until recently, sunk into oblivion. In a monograph on the exhibition, James D. Herbert maintains that nobody could take the various regional pavilions as a serious representation of France. Consequently, he completely ignored them in the rest of his book.[1] Nonetheless, the Regional Centre received the support of representatives from a broad political spectrum and regionalists of the first generation held many of the leading positions in the exhibition's organising committee.

In France universal expositions were the prerogative of Paris and strictly supervised by the national government. The Parisian World's Fairs, which between 1867 and 1900 took place with an interval of eleven years, had been among the most influential and visited of all expositions, and only some exhibitions in the United States, such as the one in Chicago in 1893 or in Saint Louis in 1904, could equal those of France. Since the turn of the century Paris had housed two more specialised, successful expositions, the International Exhibition of Modern Decorative and Industrial Arts in 1925 and the International Colonial Exhibition of 1931. Regionalist

---

[1] James D. Herbert, *Paris 1937: Worlds on Exhibition* (Ithaca 1998) 19.

architecture – apart from most colonial pavilions which, like those from American countries in the Sevilian exhibition, drew on the same genius loci sources as regionalism – did not play a major role at these exhibitions. In 1900 the idea to add a *Rue des Provinces* to the *Rue des Nations* had been discarded in favour of a *Rue de Paris*. And in 1925 the international Art Deco triumphed in most pavilions, whereas the improvised French village was deceptively small. Only seven provincial cities and seven regions took the initiative to participate as they had to fund their own representation. As a result, their pavilions lacked stylistic unity. A few consisted of copies of old buildings; some were modern constructions, whereas others were more orthodox regionalist examples.[2]

The 1937 International Exhibition of Paris

Things would be different in 1937. The initiative was taken three weeks after the Wall Street Crash of October 1929, when Julien Durand, a Radical deputy, proposed to celebrate another international exhibition in 1935, dedicated again to the decorative arts. His proposal was accepted by the right-wing government led by André Tardieu and by both chambers of the French parliament. However, since the opening of the expositions in Barcelona and Seville the international political and economic climate had drastically changed. The Golden Twenties, with various years of steady economic growth and international détente, ended with the crash. Although the Great Depression did not hit France as hard as other countries, economic recovery was slower than elsewhere and seriously affected domestic politics as well. Cabinets were more short-lived and suffered increasing pressure from both the extreme left and right. Riots, demonstrations and fierce protests were the order of the day. With the rise to power of Adolf Hitler in Germany in 1933, the international situation became ever more tense as well. Both the more difficult economic situation and the growing political instability would have a considerable impact on the exhibition, which finally was scheduled for 1937.

At the start of 1932, when little had been done to realise the exposition of decorative arts, the Republican Socialist senator Isidore Tournan proposed

---

2 Isabelle Collet, 'Le Monde rural aux expositions universelles de 1900 et 1937' in: *Muséologie et ethnologie* (Paris 1987) 100–40, especially 110–16, Léandre Vaillat, 'Le village français à l'exposition', *L'Illustration* (8 August 1925) 131–5, Léandre Vaillat, 'À l'exposition des Arts Décoratifs: La tendance régionale', *L'Illustration* (22 August 1925) 187–90 and Daniel Le Couédic, *Les Architectes et l'idée bretonne 1904–1945: D'un renouveau des arts à la renaissance d'une identité* (Saint-Brieuc 1995) 348–72.

to celebrate an International Exposition of Civilisation also, dedicated to science, literature and fine arts, with the aim of promoting international intellectual co-operation. His proposal was accepted unanimously by the Senate. In June 1932, after new elections had brought a victory for the *Cartel des Gauches* (a left-wing coalition of Radicals and Socialists), a Socialist deputy, Eugène Fiancette, came up with the idea of adding another exposition to the already accepted plans, dedicated to 'the life of workers and peasants'. Durand, who had become minister of Commerce in the new progressive cabinet of Edouard Herriot, combined the three proposals in one project that he submitted in October 1932 to the recently created *Bureau Internationale des Expositions*, which had its offices in Paris. Shortly afterwards, Aimé Berthod, another Radical who had been minister of Pensions with Herriot, was nominated general commissioner of the exhibition.[3]

In the meantime, all kind of associations and individuals came up with ideas for the exhibition. Thus, already in July 1932, probably responding to the proposal of Fiancette, the *Association Provinciale des Architectes Français* proposed to dedicate a section of the exhibition to the French provinces, where every province could construct both a traditional building and a modern one. The former most likely should attract visitors and tourists, whereas the latter should provide commissions to members of the provincial association of architects and show their capabilities of adopting modern techniques without losing sight of the idiosyncracies of their region. Others proposed to take advantage of the occasion to construct a permanent open-air museum.[4]

Several architects now submitted plans for the exhibition. The prominent regionalist Charles Letrosne, the author of the three-volume 'bible of regionalism' in the 1920s, located the main part of the exhibition in the centre of Paris, but also envisaged a second site south of Paris for a cluster of villages where Fiancette's worker and peasant life could be shown. In April 1933, however, it was decided to reduce the size of the exhibition, limiting it to the area around the Eiffel Tower and the Place du Trocadéro. At the same time Letrosne was nominated head architect of the exhibition.

[3] Edmond Labbé, *Exposition Internationale des Arts et Techniques: Paris 1937: Rapport Générale* (Paris 1938), I 33–43, Madeleine Rebérioux, 'L'Exposition de 1937 et le contexte politique des années trente' in: Bertrand Lemoine ed., *Cinquantenaire de l'Exposition Internationale des Arts et des Techniques dans la Vie Moderne* (Paris 1987) 26–30 and Shanny Peer, *France on Display: Peasants, Provincials, and Folklore in the 1937 Paris World's Fair* (New York 1998) 22–4.

[4] Le Couédic, *Les Architectes et l'idée bretonne* 660–2 and Collet, 'Le Monde rural aux expositions' 116–17.

He was assisted by the considerably younger Jacques Greber (1882–1969), who specialised in city-planning and garden architecture and had worked for several years in the United States where he designed the monumental Fairmount Parkway in Philadelphia. They immediately produced a new master plan in which the workers and peasants would have their place along the Seine in a Regional Centre and a Centre for the Applied Arts and Artistic Crafts, flanking the Eiffel Tower from both sides.[5]

During the spring, Anatole de Monzie, the Republican-Socialist minister of Education in a new left-wing cabinet led by Edouard Daladier, tried to wrest the responsibility for the exhibition from the ministry of Commerce. Apparently he also had different ideas about the exhibition as he asked Auguste Perret (1874–1954), the most important French modernist architect of the first generation, to design an alternative plan. Perret proposed to create a new monumental axis, a kind of second Champs Elysées from the Trocadéro to the École Militaire, which should be extended on both sides to the outskirts of the town. In this plan, which in August was published in *L'Illustration*, he also anticipated a French village, called *Vieille France*, and a model working-class neighbourhood for the peasants' and workers' exhibition, both next to the Eiffel Tower. If this highly symmetrical plan had been accepted the German and Soviet pavilion would have been merely two of a whole range of imposing French constructions. At the same time, there would be no space for regionalist architecture as the Old France quarter should obviously consist of picturesque copies of old buildings. Probably instigated by Monzie or Perret, a few weeks later the journalist Raymond Ritter published an elaborate plan for a French equivalent of the Pueblo Español in *L'Illustration* that after 1937 could function as a kind of open-air museum of all French regions.[6]

However, everything soon came to a halt. At the end of January 1934 the somewhat more moderate government of Camille Chautemps which was increasingly under fire because of political and financial scandals, decided to cancel the whole project shortly before resigning. This was most probably due to budgetary difficulties and continuing disagreement over

[5] Deborah Dawson Hurtt, 'Rivalry and Representation: Regionalist Architecture and the Road to the 1937 Paris Exposition' (PhD dissertation, University of Virginia 2005) 178–9 and Danilo Udovicki, 'Projets et concours', in: Bertrand Lemoine ed., *Cinquantenaire de l'Exposition Internationale des Arts et des Techniques dans la Vie Moderne* (Paris 1987) 44–66, especially 44–51.

[6] Hurtt, 'Rivalry and Representation' 179–82, Udovicki, 'Projets et concours' 51–2, Joseph Abram, 'Perret et l'exposition' in: Bertrand Lemoine ed., *Cinquantenaire de l'Exposition Internationale des Arts et des Techniques dans la Vie Moderne* (Paris 1987) 66–72, and Le Couédic, *Les Architectes et l'idée bretonne* 662.

all sorts of questions between the city of Paris, the general commissioner and various ministries. The decision did not meet with much approval; particularly Parisian business and commercial circles protested, as did artists and artisans. All had hoped that the exhibition would improve the depressed economic situation and provide work, commissions and revenues. The Parisian town council, which also participated in the organisation of the exhibition, supported their cause.[7]

The fall of the government, however, did not solve the political crisis. On 6 February anti-parliamentarian and fascist leagues assembled for a huge demonstration, which ended in a full-scale attack on the National Assembly. The police finally held out against the rioters, several of whom were armed, but sixteen people were killed and 2,000 injured. Former president Gaston Doumergue, a conservative Radical, now formed a government of national union to save the Third Republic and re-establish public order. Conservative and progressive politicians decided to work together to avoid a fascist take-over. One way to rally support for the republic was to reverse the decision on the exposition. Pressed by the conservative town council of Paris, which was prepared to augment its financial contribution, the government finally decided to submit a new request for a limited and specialist fair to the Bureau International des Expositions. This also fitted well into its economic recovery programme that particularly aimed at diminishing the unemployment in the Parisian region and improving the situation of the 'art industries'.[8]

A few days later, in July 1934, Edmond Labbé, a retired high civil servant and a friend of Doumergue, was appointed as the new general commissioner. He had been the head engineer of the reconstruction in the department du Nord and later became general director of technical education in the Ministry of Education. He thus was a specialist in applied and industrial arts and consequently decided to rename the enterprise the *Exhibition internationale des Arts et Techniques dans la vie moderne* (International Exhibition of Arts and Techniques in Modern Life). In this way he also took into consideration the expressive wish of the *Union corporative de l'Art français* (UCAF: Corporative Union of French Art), a kind of umbrella organisation for unions and associations of both artists and artisans, which had been created in 1932, partly to exert influence upon the plans for the exhibition. In contrast to the German Werkbund and its French equivalent

[7] Hurtt, 'Rivalry and Representation' 175–6 and Labbé, *Exposition Internationale*, I 44–5.
[8] Labbé, *Exposition Internationale*, I 45 and Rebérioux, 'L'Exposition de 1937 et le contexte politique' 28.

the *Union des artistes modernes* (UAM: Union of Modern Artists) created in 1929, which were free associations of artists, architects and entrepreneurs with an innovative artistic program, this corporatist organisation had to defend the interest of all of its some one million members. Already at the end of 1932 it had published a manifesto in which it expressed the hope that the new exposition would be less elitist and less focused on luxury products than the one in 1925. It therefore argued in favour of the removal of the distinction between fine, applied, industrial and popular art and against retrospective overviews. The exposition should merely show the whole range of products made by contemporary French artists and artisans.[9]

Shortly after taking office, general commissioner Labbé decided to reject the division of the exposition into three sections, and to concentrate on arts and crafts. He wanted the exhibition to have a 'regionalist character' and be more democratic than its 1925 predecessor. He hoped to achieve this by involving a great number of organisations and associations to make it an exposition of the whole of France. These decisions were in accordance with the original idea of 1929, the demands of the UCAF and the intentions of the Doumergue government. Contrary to most former Parisian World's Fairs, this time there would be no central building. The site was laid out according to the plan of Letrosne – who again was appointed as head architect – as a kind of garden city with a great number of smaller and larger buildings. Apart from the many thematic pavilions, the country was principally represented by the *Centre régional*, which had already appeared on Letrosne's earlier map. How could the artisanal industries of France be shown better than by the whole variety of national trades and crafts in an assembly of regional pavilions? According to Labbé the Regional Centre, shaped like a 'lively tableau of our French provinces', should be one of the punchlines of the exhibition and the French reply to the foreign sections.[10] But should this be fashioned in a nostalgic-looking village, such as the Pueblo Español, or in a more modern way?

Edmond Labbé, like Letrosne, was a clear adherent of regionalism and the underlying *Volksgeist* ideology. Although in his general report – which was published in eleven volumes after the exposition – he defended the need for international co-operation, he clearly stated that '[e]very nation should, without a doubt, conserve its particular physiognomy, becoming

---

[9] Jean-François Pinchon, 'La Conception et l'organisation de l'exposition' in: Bertrand Lemoine ed., *Cinquantenaire de l'Exposition Internationale des Arts et des Techniques dans la Vie Moderne* (Paris 1987) 36–43 and Hurtt, 'Rivalry and Representation' 172–7.

[10] Labbé, *Exposition Internationale*, I 58 and 219, Peer, *France on Display* 66 and Hurtt, 'Rivalry and Representation' 167–72.

aware of all its possibilities, and contribute to the extent of its capacities to the enrichment of humanity'. He therefore did not believe in 'cosmopolitan art'. Modern art, he already claimed in September 1934 in his address to the newly constituted Superior Council of the exhibition, was too abstract, whereas modern architecture had produced great monotony by constructing the same buildings everywhere. A house should not be merely a 'machine à habiter' (machine for living), as Le Corbusier championed, but should also be a home. As regionalist art could introduce 'flexibility, variety, warmth and its inimitable nuances that could not be expected from pure reasoning', the exhibition should reflect the regional diversity of France. This would not be difficult, as according to Labbé every province could offer artists a 'hundred opportunities to show their originality, an originality adapted to the climate, customs, and local traditions or, more precisely, an originality born by the very effort, made by the creators to adapt themselves to all its particular conditions'.[11]

In order to show the diversity of France in the Regional Centre the various parts of the country should be grouped into regions, each with its own pavilion. Early in 1935, Greber consequently charted a map of seventeen regions, based on existing 'centres of regional architecture'. Later on, by subdividing several of them, this would be extended to twenty-seven. Labbé and his collaborators thus consciously rejected the idea of adopting the existing administrative borders by giving each of the ninety departments proper representation. Nor did they think of showing an assembly of all the ancient provinces. Later on the general commissioner explained that the map had been drawn by taking into account natural ('soils, reliefs and climates') and cultural differences, whereas culture referred as much to economic and intellectual relations as to the folklore of 'adages and songs'.[12] This did not contradict the explanation given by Greber, as regional architecture from their point of view always reflected the natural and cultural peculiarities of a specific area.

According to the organisers, each pavilion should be a 'microcosm of a French region'. Paintings, murals, photographs and dioramas should show the most picturesque aspects of the region, whereas traditional artisanal products and objects should evoke its activities. This way the exposition would contribute to the 'recovery of business and the renaissance of tourism', also outside of Paris. To prevent the Regional Centre from becoming a 'necropolis', every week one region would get the possibility to stage its

11   See, respectively: Labbé, *Exposition Internationale*, I 220–1 and VIII, *Annexes* 91.
12   Ibid., VIII, xviii and Hurtt, 'Rivalry and Representation' 183–4.

feasts, dances, songs and music. Lectures, plays and performances should provide further opportunities to present the region's treasures, whereas restaurants could present the highlights of the local cuisine. The Centre would therefore also be 'a gastronomic map' of a country where culinary habits were an indispensable part of the 'national character'.[13]

In line with Jean Charles-Brun, the highly esteemed leader of the Fédération Régionaliste Française, Labbé maintained that regionalism was not a movement that looked back to the past. On the contrary, it only took from the past what was still alive: 'salutary traditions' instead of routine. Regionalism consequently would not lead to 'pastiche and reproduction'. This should also be reflected in the style of the pavilions in the *Centre régionale*. The architects, thus, should borrow the particular 'permanent elements' of the represented region, whereas the constructions should correlate with its 'environment and landscape'. At the same time the pavilions should be modern by broadmindedly interpreting tradition, while using new construction techniques and complying with all present-day requirements.[14]

Two to three decades before, this would have sounded logical to all proponents of regionalist architecture, be it in France or elsewhere. They had, after all, defined regionalism as an innovative movement that consciously broke with the false and pompous Academic and historicist architecture that had lost any connection to both tradition and nature. However, during the late 1920s and 1930s their position had come under attack from a younger generation of architects and critics. Thus, Labbé's remarks should be understood in the light of the architectural debates of the interwar period.

In Spain, the rise of modernism would happen quite late – the first modernist association was only founded in 1929 by young architects in Barcelona – and did not seriously influence the debates over the exhibitions in Barcelona and Seville. In Germany and France, however, the critique, especially by Ludwig Mies van der Rohe, Walter Gropius and Le Corbusier, would be very harsh and in the end extremely influential. In France, nevertheless, the debates would only really begin in the early 1930s. In February 1933, for example, the young and polemical architect Raymond Fischer (1898–1988) maintained in a public debate that the railroads and new materials such as iron and concrete had made it illogical to limit oneself to local materials. The introduction of central heating had

---

13 Ibid., VIII, xii–xiii and xix–xxii.
14 Ibid., VIII, xix and Hurtt, 'Rivalry and Representation' 181–92.

even freed the architect from the need to take the influence of climate into consideration. The machine had made regionalism obsolete.[15] Others, like Le Corbusier and Robert Mallet-Stevens (1886–1945), both members of the UAM, argued that the artistic aspect in new modernist buildings did not express itself in a beautiful and harmoniously decorated envelope, but in freely designing a hygienic, pure and well-lit space with balanced forms, materials and volumes. Consequently, they criticised regionalism for making copies and pastiches and for being irrational and backward. They in fact denied that regionalist architecture was modern or could be creative.[16]

Fiercely nationalist authors, particularly from the *Association des Architectes Anciens Combatants* (Association of Veteran Architects), among whom was its honorary president Gustave Umbdenstock, counter-attacked. They criticised the modernists for being cold rationalists, internationalists, for importing 'German' models and therefore for being anti-French, and for producing inhuman, exchangeable, 'nudist' constructions. By not using artisans they moreover increased the unemployment figures. To defend themselves, modernist architects asserted that by sticking to outdated technologies their opponents, in fact, were complicating the economic recovery of France. More surprisingly however, they also adopted part of the *Volksgeist* ideology – which thus became almost all-pervasive – by denying that they were anti-French; they even portrayed themselves as those who truly updated the glorious French architectural traditions. Most of them further admitted that their buildings should also be adapted to the local natural circumstances and preferably made of French materials.[17]

Thus by demanding the regional pavilions be constructed in a modern regionalist style, Labbé clearly took a stance in the debate between traditionalists and modernists. He clearly rejected both Le Corbusier's internationalist 'machines for living' and the backward-looking attitude of the staunch nationalists. A renewed regionalism should in his view overcome the false antagonism between tradition and modernity. Although obviously not everybody greeted it with enthusiasm, Labbé's decision was widely supported, particularly by the main architectural associations and the UCAF. This also made clear that the great majority of critics and

---

15 Raymond Fischer in *Construction Moderne* (19 March 1933) as cited in: Hurtt, 'Rivalry and Representation' 128–31.
16 Hurtt, 'Rivalry and Representation' 87–165.
17 Ibid.. See also Jean-Claude Vigato, *L'Architecture régionaliste: France, 1890–1950* (Paris 1994) 179–88 and 229–63 and Romy Golan, *Modernity and Nostalgia: Art and Politics in France between the Wars* (New Haven and London 1995) 89–97.

architects tried to keep a middle position between the two opposing camps and Labbé would recruit most of his staff members from this group.

Labbé surrounded himself with experienced collaborators, many of whom were foremost regionalists. Thus his adjunct was Paul Léon, the former highest civil servant for Fine Arts and Architecture, who had been responsible for the architectural contest for the reconstructed areas during the First World War and the deputy general commissioner for the international exhibition of 1925. Louis Bonnier, who had also been active at the exhibition of 1925, was one of the representatives of the UCAF in the exhibition's Superior Council, whereas Letrosne was head architect. The same applied to the Regionalism Commission that was established in 1934 to organise the *Centre régional* and that was presided over by the conservative politician Maurice Petsche. The commission included the famous folklorist Georges-Henri Rivière, three representatives of the Fédération Régionaliste Française, among whom were Charles-Brun and Edmond Chaix from the Touring-Club de France, and for the UCAF one of the foremost advocates of regionalist architecture, Léandre Vaillat.[18]

Supported by the UCAF, the Regionalism Commission now proceeded to form regional committees that should organise the participation on a local level, thus fulfilling one of the promises of the organisers that the exhibition should be more democratic and less centralised than previous expositions. As little progress was made, it was decided to organise a conference in Paris in April 1935 to debate all kinds of issues concerning regional art in general, and more specifically the plans for the *Centre régional*. Organisers, experts and over 300 regional delegates discussed the programme, goal and content of the Regional Centre, while at the same time it was hoped that the meeting would generate publicity and enthusiasm for the project among the regions.[19]

In their speeches some members of the Regionalism Commission showed their preoccupation with the actual situation of crisis. Petsche, for example, spoke of 'an epoch during which we observe throughout the world profound transformations that put the old structures of the nineteenth century in the shade'. Accordingly he pleaded for the need to replace 'our old individualism', which only engendered division and conflicting interests, with a more corporate organisation of society. The members of the UCAF had shown the way by creating an 'organism of collective life in which, by maintaining the personal initiative of all of

18   Ibid., 176 and 183 and Peer, *France on Display* 66.
19   Ibid., 184–5 and 192–5.

you, you succeed in co-ordinating the energies and make effective your common responsibilities'. He consequently hoped that they would also help to form a 'bundle of all people of good will to realise this work of beauty and French grandeur': the Regional Centre. For 'bundle' he used the word *faisceau*, which was the French equivalent of the Italian *fasces*, the symbol of Mussolini's fascism and the name of a short-lived French fascist movement. This probably also indicated where his sympathies lay. The architect Joseph Hiriart, a member of both the UCAF and the Regionalism Commission, came to a similar conclusion as he also presented the UCAF as a good solution to the current 'universal disorder' and economic crisis. He further asserted that this 'modest work of reconstruction' converted the artists and art manufacturers in the 'avant-garde of the social reconstruction of tomorrow' one more time.[20]

Nonetheless, most lectures and debates concerned more practical issues. Thus, chief architect Letrosne, who later that year would resign because of ill health (Greber would be his logical successor), made clear that 'international architecture', with which he meant modernistic buildings, would be excluded from the Regional Centre. According to him, architects had the task to 'understand and express a reflection of the soul' of the different peoples by using local materials and taking into consideration the 'climate and the character of the inhabitants', whereas at the same time they had to reckon with 'our current needs'.[21]

The architectural programme was outlined in more detail by Louis Hautecoeur, the chief curator of the Musée du Luxembourg in Paris and artistic director of the exposition. He made clear that the goal of the Regional Centre was not merely to combat modernist architecture, but to overcome it. The process of modernisation and increasing communications between different parts of the world had inevitably led to a growing uniformity. This was particularly visible in architecture, where the 'international style' had resulted in similar buildings everywhere, as new materials such as iron and reinforced concrete were necessarily treated the same way in China, Germany, Russia and France. In France this 'standardised architecture' could already be seen in 'all our provinces'. This uniformity could also be found in furniture, on passenger boats, in hotels, restaurants and even meals. However, according to him, every excess will be followed by a reaction and the exhibition of 1937 will be a perfect occasion for an examination of conscience in this respect. One cannot

---

20 'Discours de M. Petsche' and 'Exposé de M. Hiriart' in: Labbé, *Exposition Internationale*, VIII, *Annexes*, respectively 94–5 and 96–7.
21 'Discours de M. Letrosne' in: Labbé, *Exposition Internationale*, VIII, *Annexes* 105–7.

deny, he argued, that in architecture the climate determines some specific forms, whereas the available materials and the customs of the inhabitants also impose certain requirements, and these should be taken into account. Nonetheless, the introduction of new materials, electricity and central heating also has had important effects. Consequently the time has come to reconcile the necessary traditions with the forms and techniques of today. The Regional Centre, accordingly, should be a great laboratory where every region would show how one could logically adapt the 'new procedures to the local needs, conditions and habits'.[22]

Other speakers also stressed the need to combine regional traditions with modern inventions, materials and methods, although they did not use exactly the same arguments. Paul Léon, for example, presented a more deterministic and atavistic point of view. According to him the best representatives of regionalist art transformed their products 'without being afraid of modernism, nor did they repudiate the tradition that should not be seen as a voluntary acceptance of the past, but that one carries in one's blood and in which one is not more free to avert the effects than one is in evading the laws of heredity'.[23]

In the preceding year Labbé had already decided that the *Centre régional* should reconcile modernity and tradition. In his closing remarks he expressed the hope that the renovation of regional traditions would also strengthen national unity. By increasing the knowledge of each other, Paris, the provinces and even the colonies would form a more powerful 'unity in diversity'. He also expected that the exhibition would give work to the 'greatest possible number of workers', stimulate French production, 'breathe new life into the endangered crafts', defend French quality, promote tourism and be a great feast that would show that 'our old nation is not a tired nation'.[24]

Greber's map that divided the country into seventeen regions was also presented at the conference. Léandre Vaillat somewhat optimistically presented the map as in conformity with the data provided by the science of human geography which in France had been developed by Paul Vidal de la Blache and Jean Brunhes. Thus instead of choosing the provinces of

[22] 'Exposé de M. Hautecoeur' in: Labbé, *Exposition Internationale*, VIII, *Annexes* 97–102, especially 98–100.
[23] 'Discours de M. Paul Léon', in: Labbé, *Exposition Internationale*, VIII, *Annexes* 93–4. See for a similar view also: 'Discours de M. François Carnot', in Ibid., 102–4.
[24] 'Discours prononcé à la séance de clôture du congrès de l'art regional par M. Edmond Labbé' and 'Discours prononcé par M. Edmond Labbé au banquet de clôture du congrès de l'art régional' in: Labbé, *Exposition Internationale*,VIII, *Annexes*, respectively 114–17 and 118–21.

the *Ancien Régime* or the current departments which, in his view, were equally arbitrary, the organisers had adopted the term 'region' as used by the geographers. According to them France was divided in various regions – which could each be further subdivided into smaller areas (*pays*) – in which the interaction between the natural environment and the population over the centuries had resulted in different types of life. Although presumably based on objective facts, the map occasioned heated debate. Some regions were accepted by the delegates without much discussion, whereas others were seriously contested. When no easy agreement could be reached Hiriart, who presided over the meeting, sent those concerned to a separate room in order to reach a definite arrangement. In this way ten more regions were added to the map although the organisers presented them as subdivisions of the original regions. For practical and organisational reasons, most regions were eventually composed of clusters of neighbouring departments which, whenever possible, were baptised with the names of ancient provinces.[25]

But what about Algeria? This was a fair question posed by one of the participants as, contrary to other colonies, Algeria was seen as an integral part of France and divided into three departments. This issue had been debated within the Regionalism Commission as well, and the answer had been to place Algeria, Tunis and Morocco on the other bank of the Seine, whereas Corsica was located on the tip of the Île des Cygnes, a small island in the river, which now symbolised the Mediterranean Sea. Finally, however, it was decided to place all French colonies, including Algeria, on the Île des Cygnes, where only the Pont de Passy separated them from Corsica (figure 31). Some delegates also proposed to construct the pavilions in permanent materials, which would give a more authentic appearance and would make it possible to keep the Centre open after the exhibition as a kind of permanent representation of the regions in Paris. However, as the chosen terrain belonged to the railroad company, this was not possible.[26]

The reclassification of the regions also caused some practical problems, especially with the architectural contest that had been organised in a great hurry in order to allow the jury, which met on the margins of the conference, to take a rapid decision. Thus some regions were left without

[25] 'Rapport général de M. Léandre Vaillat' in: Labbé, *Exposition Internationale*, VIII, *Annexes* 107–14 and Hurtt, 'Rivalry and Representation' 208–17.
[26] Hurtt, 'Rivalry and Representation' 203–4 and 215–16 and 'Discours de M. Letrosne' 107.

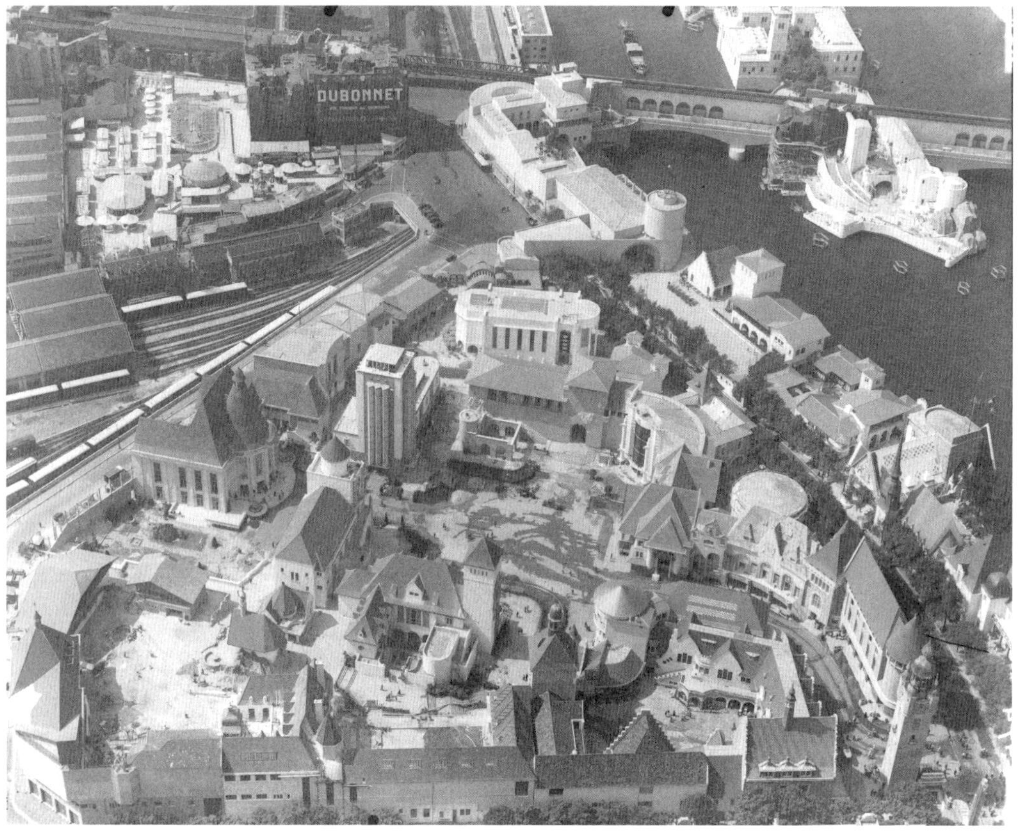

31 View of the Centre régional from the Eiffel Tower, Paris, 1937. On the upper right is the Île des Cygnes, with the pavilion of Algeria on one side of the Passy bridge, and Corsica on the other. The maritime provinces are located along the Seine and the mountainous regions are on the opposite site, in the lower left corner.

a winner and consequently had to organise new local contests, which significantly delayed the construction process (figure 32).[27]

Other changes would further influence and delay the Regional Centre. France was not the only country that saw the exhibition as a means of combating the effects of the economic crisis by stimulating international demand for its own products. Many governments hoped that their participation in Paris would have positive economic effects, while at the same time it would encourage feelings of national pride by showing their

[27] Ibid., 187–90 and 221–5. See for the results of the contest also: A. Louvet, 'Les Concours pour l'Exposition de 1937 (Programme nº 11): Le Centre régional', *L'Architecture* (1935) 213–27 and Léandre Vaillat, 'Un Centre régional: Pour l'exposition de 1937', *L'Illustration* (20 April 1935) 467–72.

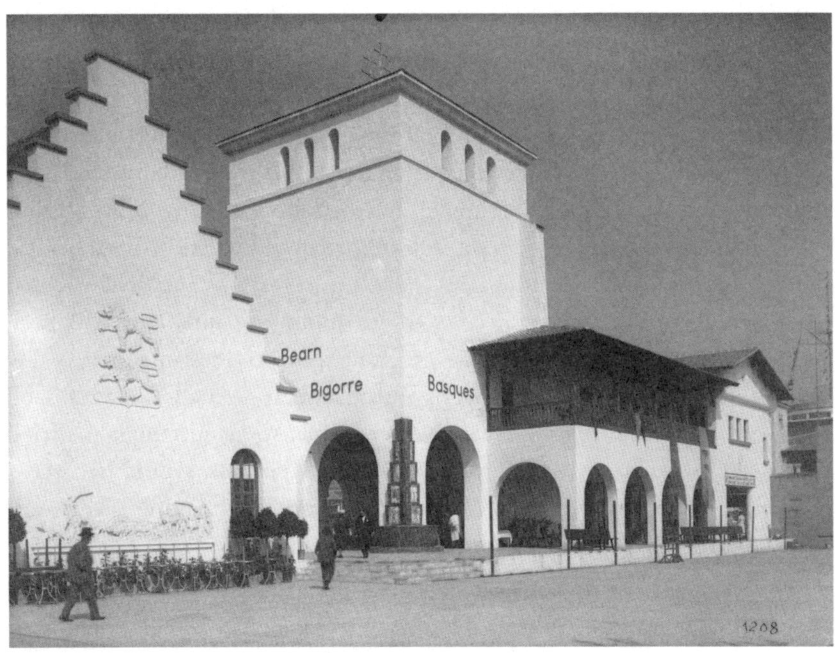

32 Pavilion of the Basque Country, Béarn and Bigorre, Centre régional, Paris, 1937. The three areas that formed the Pyrénées Atlantiques could not agree on the architectural design. Their pavilion therefore consisted of three connected buildings.

achievements in a conspicuous building. As the response from abroad exceeded expectations and countries like Germany and the Soviet Union requested large lots for their imposing pavilions, the exhibition terrains had to be expanded several times. As a result, France also had to step up its own efforts and participation in order to keep up with its foreign competitors. Thus, at the start of 1936, in order to increase the French presence at the exposition, various public services and ministries were allowed to participate with their own exhibits. The exhibition eventually became a full-scale international exhibition, almost comparable to the enormous World's Fair of 1900. However, this did not favour the Regional Centre as it was not extended, nor did it receive additional subsidies.[28]

The victory of the Popular Front in the elections of May 1936 would bring new changes that further diminished the importance of the Regional Centre. The Popular Front was an electoral coalition between left-wing Radicals, Socialists and Communists that had been hatched in the aftermath of the events in February 1934, and which ended the long-lasting enmity between Socialists and Communists in order to prevent a further advance of international fascism. The electoral triumph aroused hopes for

[28] Ibid., 242–58, Labbé, *Exposition Internationale*, I 46–83 and François Pinchon, 'La conception et l'organisation de l'exposition' 39–41.

a left-wing revolution among many of its supporters. Even before the new government – led for the first time by a Socialist prime minister, Léon Blum – assumed power, strikes began to paralyse the economy as workers were eager to cash in on 'their' victory by obtaining higher wages, the forty-hour week, two weeks of paid holidays and the recognition of the right to strike. The new government awarded most of their demands, but the strikes had created important delays in the construction activities for the exhibition. Moreover, the new social measures substantially increased the wage costs and indirectly also led to mounting inflation. Although the government tried to accelerate construction activities in the next few months, strikes and slowdowns over political and economic issues continued to plague the exhibition while, at the same time, some entrepreneurs tried to hinder its progress as they feared that the exposition would become a showpiece of the Popular Front. As a consequence most pavilions were not finished until one or several months after the inauguration of the exposition on 24 May 1937.[29]

Although the Blum administration did not introduce major changes in the exhibition plans, it clearly put its own accent on the project. Thus, it could influence the content and outlook of most of the recently admitted State pavilions. Moreover, the *Union des artistes modernes*, which until then had been excluded as internationalist, was allowed to construct its own pavilion, as was the *Confédération Générale du Travail* (General Confederation of Labour), the recently unified socialist and communist trade union. The Prime Minister himself also took the initiative to add two pavilions dedicated to peace and work, and a major retrospective of masterpieces of French art, which should also include the so-called minor arts. He further intervened with the organisers in favour of two avant-garde projects that had been excluded until then: Le Corbusier's Pavillon des Temps Nouveaux and an abstract mural by Sonia and Robert Delaunay. The intention of Labbé to exclude modernist art and architecture from the official French pavilions was thus effectively frustrated. The government, as part of its goal to democratise access to culture, also took measures to make the exhibition more attractive and affordable to lower-class visitors by establishing a half-price day, offering reduced train fares from the provinces and providing cheap accommodation for youth groups.[30] The Regional Centre in turn

---

[29] Eugen Weber, *The Hollow Years: France in the 1930s* (London 1995) 169–73, Labbé, *Exposition Internationale*, I 67–83 and Peer, *France on Display* 3140.
[30] Peer, *France on Display* 33–9 and 99–135, Hurtt, 'Rivalry and Representation' 156–64, Pascal Ory, 'Le Front Populaire et l'Exposition', in: Bertrand Lemoine ed., *Cinquantenaire de l'Exposition Internationale des Arts et des Techniques dans la Vie Moderne* (Paris 1987) 30–6

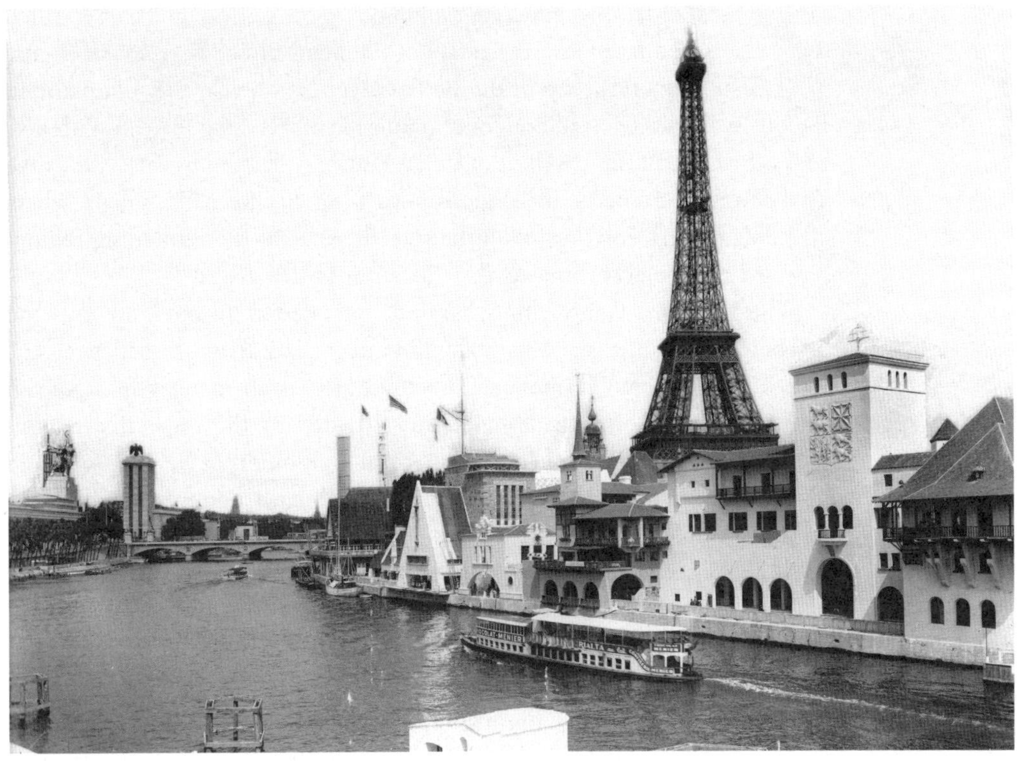

33 View of the *Centre régional* from the Seine, International Exhibition, Paris, 1937. From left to right there are Normandy, Brittany, Poitou, Guyenne-Gascoigne and the pavilion of the Basque Country, Béarn and Bigorre (now from the opposite side, compared to figure 32). In the background on the left are the pavilions of the Soviet Union and Nazi Germany, behind Normandy is the United States and on the right, the Eiffel Tower.

received no special favours and whereas at the start in 1934 it was meant to be the central showcase of the country, occupying 5 of the 30 ha foreseen, in the end it would only take up 5 out of 100 ha, and was almost ignored by the government.

Nevertheless, the Regional Centre was largely built as planned. Emile Maigrot (1880–1961), the architect who co-ordinated the construction of the Centre, described it in detail in *L'Architecture*, asserting that it was a living synthesis of all French regions. The location of the Centre at a former coal depository had caused some difficulties, but could also be used to differentiate the various parts. Thus the maritime provinces were located in

and Pascal Ory, *La Belle Illusion: Culture et politique sous le signe du Front populaire 1935–1938* (Paris 1994) 280–8.

geographical order on a concrete capping over the railway line to Versailles. They also had a façade on the quays of the Seine about 10 m lower (figure 33). Corsica lay on the tip of the Île des Cygnes, whereas the mountainous regions were placed at the opposite corner on an elevated plateau with fake rocks. In front of the pavilion of Île de France – defined by Maigrot as the vital centre of France – the regions with a big city formed a square where all kinds of performances could be staged, whereas the remaining regions received a place according to their location on the map.[31]

The Regional Centre, thus, was not intended as an open-air museum of copied buildings made by a few architects and artists as had been the case of the Pueblo Español in Barcelona, nor as an incoherent amalgam of regional pavilions, all designed and directed by the respective regions themselves, such as at the Ibero-American Exhibition of Seville. It should be a unified whole, with a modernised regionalist design for which the selected architects of each of the regions would be responsible. The organisation consequently was not completely centralised as in Barcelona, nor completely decentralised as in Seville. It was a mixture of both, which required much negotiation and could even lead to disagreement and frustration.

The Regionalism Commission was responsible for the general programme, the architectural contests and the general co-ordination, and had to approve the regional contributions. However, they were closely supervised by the general commissioner and they depended on the government for the budget. However, only at the end of 1935 was it known how much money was available for the project. The various regional committees were to organise and co-ordinate the contributions from their respective regions. They furthermore had to find financial resources, as the government paid only part of the costs. The regional committees also had to negotiate with the various professional associations, tourist offices and chambers of commerce and agriculture, whereas at the same time they had to consult their departmental committees.[32]

Conflicts arose on all levels, and at certain points the Regionalism Commission even threatened Labbé and the government to hand in its resignation, whereas various regional committees did the same to the

---

[31] Émile Maigrot, 'Le Centre regional à l'Exposition de 1937', *L'Architecture* (February 1937) 57–69. See for an analysis of the various pavilions: Deborah D. Hurtt, 'Simulating France, Seducing the World: The Regional Center at the 1937 Paris Exposition' in: D. Medina Lasansky and Brian McLaren eds., *Architecture and Tourism: Perception, Performance and Place* (Oxford and New York 2004) 147–65.
[32] Labbé, *Exposition Internationale*, I 223–33, Hurtt, 'Rivalry and Representation' 242–50.

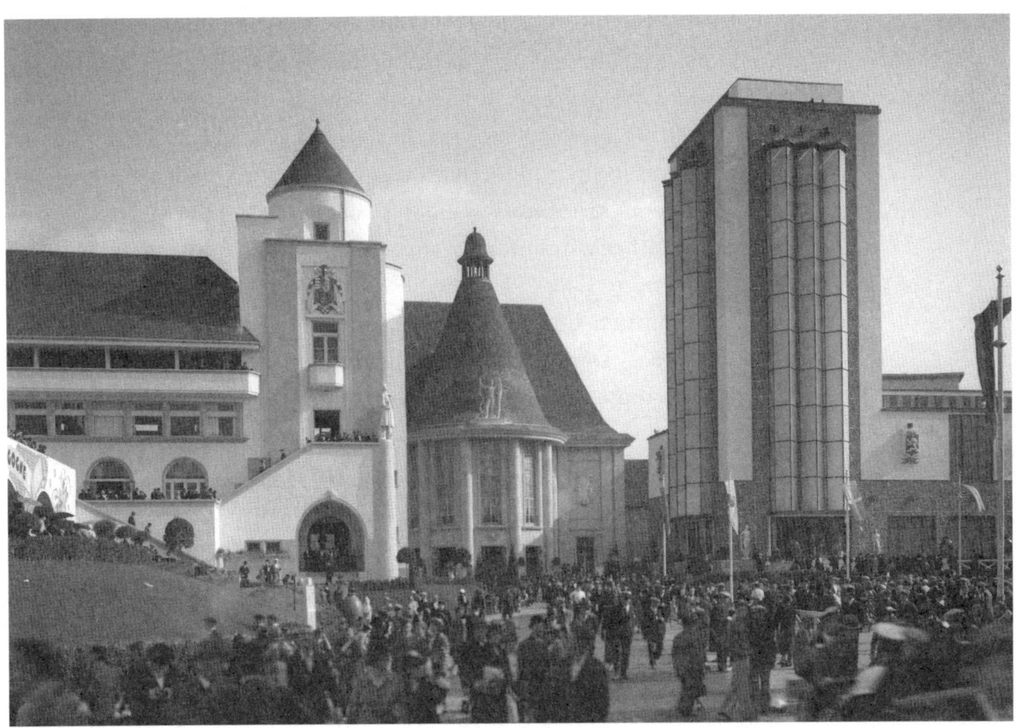

34 View of the Grand Place of the Centre régional with, from left to right, Lorraine, Île de France and the too modern pavilion of the Lyonnais, Paris, 1937.

Parisian organisers. This sometimes even endangered the whole project, or the participation of a specific region. Thus the Alsatian committee resigned at the end of 1936 after Labbé approved a commercial project, which consisted in the construction of a picturesque Alsatian village for the exposition's amusement park. The members of the committee argued that it would give an inaccurate and pejorative image of the region and would pull away artisans from the region's pavilion in the Regional Centre. Only after Old Alsace was renamed Old France, vernacular constructions copied from other regions were added and artisans were prohibited from participating in the venture, did the Alsatian committee resume its activities. Nobody could imagine a Regional Centre with only the recently reconquered Alsace missing.[33]

Most conflicts between regional committees and the Parisian organisers arose over the way the regions would actually be represented at the Regional Centre. Thus the designs for the Languedoc and the Lyonnais pavilions were rejected by the central organisers as too modern (figure 34). The committee from the Lyonnais, however, defended the choice of its jury

[33] Hurtt, 'Rivalry and Representation' 242–317, especially 302–14.

as it saw the region, which comprised only the department of the Rhône, as essentially modern and urban. One of its members further argued that the region did not have a proper vernacular style. So the best way to express its identity was by giving a modern image of Lyon and its surroundings. In the end, accordingly, a modern rectangular pavilion with a flat roof and a tower with geometrical bow windows was built.[34]

In contrast, other committees resisted the requirement that the regional style should be up to date. Thus members from the committee of region 6 bis, which comprised the Bourbonnais, Nivernais and Berry, complained that the directives from Paris forced them to betray the spirit of their region, whereas representatives from Normandy lamented the ban on wood panels, which they considered a characteristic feature of their regional architecture.[35]

Just as the architects were controlled by Paris, so were the artisans. All contributions had to be approved by the Regionalism Commission's artisan committee. But first every region had to select its own craftsmen. This proved to be extremely difficult for some regions. Thus the president of the Roussillon committee stated that he had trouble finding any local artisans at all. Similar complaints could be heard from the Marne and Lyon.[36] However, when artisans were found, the Parisian organisers were often disappointed by the quality of their work. Many products were mediocre, lacked regional character or were 'slavish copies of old styles'. They thus required updated designs made by artists that could serve as models for the artisans. However, almost all of the 500 models made by provincial artists were rejected by the artisan committee, which consisted among others of Charles-Brun and Georges-Henri Rivière. Instead it provided some 200 patterns, produced by Parisian artists who originated from the provinces, for items such as a 'Breton chest', chairs from the Limousin, 'Burgundy clogs' and a 'milk pot from Bresse'. As French national prestige was at stake quality was more important than regional autonomy.[37]

Although most authors interpret these quarrels as a serious conflict of interests between a powerful, centralist Parisian administration that

---

[34] Ibid., 289–98, Peer, *France on Display* 80–2 and Elise Marie Moentmann, 'The Search for French Identity in the Regions: National versus Local Visions of France in the 1930s', *French History* XVII (2003) 307–27, especially 323–4.

[35] Moentmann, 'The Search for French Identity' 325–6. See for similar negotiations also: Philip Whalen, 'Burgundian Regionalism and French Republican Commercial Culture at the 1937 Paris International Exposition', *Cultural Analysis* 6 (2007) 31–69 and Le Couédic, *Les Architectes et l'idée bretonne* 656–741.

[36] Ibid., 319–20.

[37] Peer, *France on Display* 88–93.

constantly overruled the subordinate regional committees,[38] I would argue that the main source of discord was the wish of the organisers to construct not a mere collection of regional pavilions but a convincing Regional Centre, which furthermore had to be a worthy representation of France that could compete with the contributions of other nations. Although all but two members of the Regionalism Commission resided and worked in Paris, most of them originated from the provinces and were dedicated to the cause of regionalism and administrative decentralisation, and the same applied to general commissioner Labbé. The experience of previous exhibitions, both in France and elsewhere (Seville), had made apparent that without clear guidelines and a unified organisation committee the Regional Centre would become an incoherent whole, as was also shown by the conflicting demands of, for example, the Lyonnais and Normandy. By delegating a great part of the organisation to the regions instead of taking the reins firmly in its own hands, as had been done in Barcelona, the Regional Commission chose a more difficult and in fact more democratic solution, as it preferred to bring into practice its regionalist ideals.

More important for the final result was the lack of enthusiasm and support from the new Popular Front government. It did not hinder the realisation of the Regional Centre, but it did not give it special attention or an increased budget either. The Socialists and Communists in particular preferred other strategies to reach the inhabitants than the decentralised and maybe somewhat paternalistic way advocated by most regionalists. Instead of reinforcing regional identities and having people participate in regional associations and corporations, they preferred to mobilise the masses in national unions, syndicates and youth organisations. Although they also tried to stimulate national unity, they explicitly directed themselves to the lower classes and not to the regions. In their policy towards the countryside they consequently preferred to address themselves to the class of farmers rather than to the regions, as became manifest in their strong support for the *Centre rural* (Rural Centre).

The Rural Centre showed that the leaders of the Popular Front had a more positive attitude towards modernity and technological advances than most regionalists. The Rural Centre had been initiated in January 1936 by the ministry of Agriculture in close co-operation with the national professional agricultural societies, and thus functioned in a similar corporatist way as a great part of the rest of the exhibition. However,

---

38 Hurtt, 'Rivalry and Representation' 250–314, Peer, *France on Display* 84–98 and Moentmann, 'The Search for French Identity'.

from June 1936 the socialist minister of Agriculture, Georges Monnet, was in charge and he decided that the Ministry would fully fund the highly modern model village, conveying an image of rural progress, modern comfort and well-being, with machinery, fully equipped houses and six co-operatives. Nevertheless, the modern constructions of the Rural Centre were cloaked in traditional forms, such as steep tile roofs, evoking a generic French rural style that belonged to no region in particular. In order to show that modernisation would not uproot the countryside, all kinds of regionalist activities, such as folklore festivals organised by Charles-Brun, traditional artisans at work and women dressed in provincial costume, should enliven the Rural Centre. The town hall accordingly housed the village museum of Romenay-en-Bresse, set-up by Rivière.[39] Thus, whereas in the Regional Centre international modernity had to be reconciled with regional traditions, in the Rural Centre regional traditions merely functioned as a picturesque adornment to make modernity acceptable to a presumably traditional public of farmers.

Meanwhile the international situation had deteriorated. In 1935 Fascist Italy had invaded Abyssinia, despite fierce protests from France, England and most other European countries. In March 1936 Hitler's troops occupied the demilitarised Rhineland, thus openly violating the Versailles Treaty. And both Hitler and Mussolini openly interfered in the Spanish Civil War by massively supporting General Franco who fought against the democratically elected Popular Front government. Not even the Non-Intervention Pact, which they signed, stopped them. This Pact had been an initiative of the Blum administration in order to avoid a new international war, but many supporters of the French Popular Front felt they were betraying their Spanish comrades. The situation in France did not progress, either. The policy of the Popular Front government polarised public opinion in France and the high hopes of many of its voters were dashed as the inflation undermined their rise in income. The economic situation did not improve and on 21 June 1937, less than a month after the opening of the exposition, Blum resigned. His cabinet was replaced by a more moderate left-wing government led by Chautemps.

Understandably, in official declarations in May 1937 most leading members of the government emphasised that the message of the exhibition was a message of peace. Thus Paul Bastid, the Radical Socialist minister of

---

[39]   Peer, *France on Display* 99–135.

Commerce who was responsible for the exhibition, declared that the fraternal collaboration of all social classes of France and their hospitality would certainly stimulate the détente between the fifty participating countries. He thus concluded his intervention: 'Peace in the interior between the social classes, peace in the exterior between the nations of good will, that's what the meaning of the Exposition of 1937 should be.'[40]

Whereas the members of the government pleaded for peace and social harmony without referring specifically to the original goals of the exposition, this was not true for the general commissioner and his deputy. Both underlined the importance of the exhibition for France and defended its initial programme. Paul Léon, for example, repeated that the exhibition was intended to show the quality and artistic inventiveness of French producers. He even argued that France should better focus on high-quality products as it could not compete with the abundance of cheap labour in Asia, nor with the standardised and mechanised production of America. Edmond Labbé still maintained that the exhibition showed the defeat of modernist architecture, whereas the Regional Centre symbolised 'the union of all Frenchmen'. Implicitly he seemed to consider it as a peaceful reply to the more aggressive pavilions of the Soviet Union and Nazi Germany as in his final report he wrote that to foreign visitors the Regional Centre showed 'a united, strong, hard working and confident France'.[41] France, he seemed to suggest, made clear that unity could be combined with diversity, and that this was a better solution than to impose unity from above as was done by these totalitarian States.

Maigrot, the architect of the Regional Centre, even seemed to criticise the Popular Front. In a short article in the official magazine of the exposition, he used the term *faisceau* to describe how all French regions would be assembled around the Île de France. In a polarised atmosphere in which strikes and obstruction threatened the timely completion of almost all pavilions, he hoped that the varied artisanal products of regional France would carry the memory of a 'diverse, kind and attractive France, of a France attached to work'. He implicitly seemed to compare the peacefulness of the countryside to the current state of class hatred, which especially hindered his work in Paris. According to the architect

<hr>

40 Paul Bastid, 'Appel à la fraternité française', *Exposition Paris 1937 Arts et techniques dans la vie moderne: Magazine officiel édité par le Commissariat Général* 12 (May 1937). See also Yvon Delbos, 'L'exposition: Message de Paix!', *Exposition Paris 1937*, 12 (May 1937).
41 Paul Léon, 'Le Goût est pour les français le plus fructueux des commerces', *Exposition Paris 1937*, 12 (May 1937), Edmond Labbé, 'Les Leçons de l'Exposition de 1937', *Exposition Paris 1937*, 12 (May 1937) and Labbé, *Exposition Internationale*, VIII, *Annexes* xxxi.

the regions responded to the 'necessities of the hour' by their 'daily work without accusations and hate'. Thanks to 'the mostly anonymous effort of all' it will be 'the soul of France and its hundred faces that shimmer in the Regional Centre'.[42]

In the architectural press there was less talk about fraternity and détente. Most of the twenty prominent architects, planners and critics who participated in an inquiry in *L'Architecture d'Aujourd'hui* regretted the positioning of the exhibition in the centre of Paris and asserted that it would have been preferable for it to have been planned more in advance and situated on the outskirts of the city. This way a new, logically planned park or neighbourhood could have remained at the conclusion of the exhibition. Most also criticised the many changes in government, the delays caused by strikes, budgetary confusions and the lack of energetic guidance – some remembered nostalgically how Field Marshal Hubert Lyautey had uniformly organised the Colonial Exhibition of 1931.[43]

The Regional Centre, nonetheless, was extensively reviewed in the press. Conservative critics generally praised it, whereas those in favour of modern solutions fundamentally criticised its basic assumptions. Only five days after the official opening of the exposition, *L'Illustration* published an extensive review of the Centre, although two more months would pass before it was open to the public. As a result most of the illustrations were engravings or paintings. The reviewer, who gave no hint that the Centre was still a construction site, recapitulated the main aims of the organisers and gave a short survey of the pavilions.[44] More detailed and equally descriptive articles, most of them positive reviews of individual pavilions, appeared in *Construction Moderne*. Thus, Jean Favier stated that Edmond Labbé had rendered a great service to French architecture and to regionalism by showing that a sensitive interpretation of the past and tradition was still possible, whereas his colleague Georges Braive congratulated Maigrot for having united the particular styles of all regions in a 'harmonious ensemble'.[45]

The extensive review of the Regional Centre in *L'Architecture*, which since 1926 was the journal of the three main architectural associations, was

<hr>

42 E. Maigrot, 'Que doit être le Centre régional', *Exposition Paris 1937*, 10 (February 1937).

43 'La Leçon de l'Exposition de 1937: Enquête de l'Architecture d'aujourd'hui', *L'Architecture d'Aujourd'hui* (August 1937) 3–12.

44 Raymond Lecuyer, 'Le Centre régional', *L'Illustration* (29 May 1937).

45 Jean Favier, 'Le Centre régional à l'exposition de 1937', *La Construction Moderne* (2 January 1938) 186 and Georges Braive, 'Adieu au Centre régional et à l'Exposition', *La Construction Moderne* (8 May 1938) 408–9.

written by Waldemar George. During the 1920s this Polish-born critic had actively supported the cause of modern art and architecture, but in the early 1930s he had started to revise his sympathies in favour of Italian-style fascism and a more traditionalist aesthetic position. In his review he staunchly defended the regionalist principles. He believed that the particular art and architecture of each French region had suffered because of political centralisation and the rise of modern industry. The 'herd instinct, the social levelling, and the attraction of the cities' have replaced traditional buildings, roofs and furniture with impersonal and exchangeable modern alternatives. A standardised and uniform country would, according to the critic, lose not only its charm, but also its vigour and its vital élan. As a result it was necessary to reinforce the self-consciousness of the inhabitants of the provinces and stimulate their profound sense of identity. The Regional Centre, where architects had recovered the laws of a forgotten language, thus was a first step towards national salvation.[46]

Marcel Genermont, the president of the Provincial Association of French Architects, was more critical. In an article in *L'Architecture d'Aujourd'hui*, a journal favourable to modernist architecture, he criticised the exhibition for its outdated conception and for lacking ambition. Instead of young audacious men, the organisers were ministers or aged public servants with old-fashioned ideas about exhibitions. With the new highways, fast trains and airplanes it would have been possible to organise a truly national exposition, a 'French season' with, apart from a Parisian fair, a great number of activities and exhibits in all the main provincial cities. Now the Regional Centre was the only serious attempt to also encompass the provinces in this national enterprise. Nonetheless, it would have been better if the Centre had been constructed in real materials so that at the end of the exhibition it could have functioned as a permanent exhibition of the artistic and economic wealth of the provinces, a place where provincials could unite and a unique attraction for tourists.[47]

Other critics even totally rejected the whole concept of combining regional traditions and modern techniques. Thus, Jean Gallotti, the critic of *Art et Décoration*, found the Regional Centre a complete failure. Although the author did not beforehand discard the possibility of fruitfully combining regionalism and modernity, he fundamentally criticised the final result. The regionalist character should be conveyed particularly by the proper

[46] Waldemar George, 'Le Centre Régional', *L'Architecture* (15 October 1937) 317–32, especially 317–18 and 332.
[47] Marcel Genermont, 'L'Exposition que nous aurions pu faire…', *L'Architecture d'Aujourd'hui* (September 1937) 77.

forms of each province, which implied that those forms were selected that were characteristic for one region only. This meant that one should at least return to the middle of the nineteenth century in the countryside and in the cities sometimes even to the Middle Ages. Instead of the great masterpieces of the past, such as Gabriel's Bourse of Bordeaux, inspiration should be found in original house types of Gascony. And in the countryside of Normandy one does not retain the ordinary nineteenth-century houses that are to be encountered in every village, but the isolated farmstead or gentry house with half-timbered walls, which was a pure survival from the Middle Ages. Thus more than continuing a tradition, this meant 'turning back, searching for a lost past'. The Regional Centre consequently was not a success, as instead of a 'spontaneous modernity' the visitor would only encounter retrospective reproductions or artificial interpretations, whereas the juxtaposition of different provincial styles had resulted in an incoherent and theatrical whole.[48]

Neither did Maurice Barret, the reviewer from *L'Architecture d'Aujourd'hui* believe in the mystique of the *Volksgeist* and he consequently unmasked the pavilions of the Regional Centre as artificial and nostalgic reinventions. They provided a picturesque ensemble for tourists, but were of no interest for the advance of architecture or the applied arts. Barret asserted that the whole exposition was badly co-ordinated and not very future oriented, and he consequently characterised it as a 'charming and fantastic funfair'. Although he dedicated ample space to the Regional Centre, he agreed with Gallotti that it did not form a unity and that most pavilions were stereotypical pastiches. These pavilions, he maintained, wanted to 'express the inexpressible, namely *an essentially human geography*, expressing a state of culture and a perfect adaptation of man to the material world'. For the public, however, it only 'expressed the picturesque: the picturesque of open air spectacles, dances, plays, the picturesque of displays where craft products are exposed, the picturesque of cafés and restaurants where regionalist gastronomy is expressed'. He therefore concluded that it created a 'kind of humming of the picturesque totally oriented towards the past'.[49]

Summarising, we can say that the Regional Centre had mixed results. From the start it had some serious rivals. In 1933 Monzie and Perret launched a well-orchestrated, but finally frustrated campaign to appropriate

[48] Jean Gallotti, 'Le Centre régional', *Art et Décoration* (1937) 11, 355–60.
[49] Maurice Barret, 'Exposition internationale de Paris 1937', *L'Architecture d'Aujourd'hui* (August 1937) 108–14, especially 109.

the project and construct a kind of open-air museum with copied buildings from all French regions within a more monumental exhibition ground, whereas the Popular Front wholeheartedly endorsed the more modern and generic Rural Centre. Nonetheless, the Centre received widespread support from both moderately conservative and progressive circles, and was probably seen as a means to overcome the deep rifts in French society. General commissioner Labbé, assisted by dedicated regionalists such as Léon, Letrosne and Charles-Brun, thus decided to give the Regional Centre a pivotal role in the exhibition and in this way convert it into a true national enterprise. He involved all kind of national professional organisations, regional bodies and associations in its organisation, whereas every region was given the responsibility for its own pavilion. Although the Parisian organisers were highly concerned about the unity and quality of the final result, in fact this step demonstrated a serious intent to realise a very broad regional participation and thus further the cause of administrative decentralisation. Finally, with over 30 million visitors the exhibition was a great success with the public and this certainly also applied to the Regional Centre.

Labbé, however, was more ambitious. He did not only want to favour regional decentralisation, but also to actively stimulate the revival of artistic and architectural regionalism by trying to modernise it. This aim was, however, doomed to failure. Before 1914 keen observers had already remarked that there was a fundamental difference between a vernacular and a regionalist construction. A vernacular building was made by applying familiar construction techniques to local building materials. A contemporary architect, on the contrary, was aware of an almost infinite number of forms and traditions and, in order to build in a regionalist style he consciously had to select a regional model and the appropriate local materials. Nevertheless, he could still design an organic whole by respecting the proper characteristics of each material and sincerely applying local traditions. However, by applying cheaper modern materials such as concrete and steel to traditional forms the architect fundamentally contradicted the basic principles of regionalism and would only produce a fake, picturesque façade with no relation to the internal structure. This way they precisely would do what the nineteenth-century historicist architects had done and which had been fiercely denounced by earlier advocates of architectural regionalism.

Furthermore, as Gallotti has argued, regional styles were defined by selecting those traditional constructions that did not exist elsewhere. In more modern terms, we could call this with Hobsbawm a clear example of 'invention of tradition'. This was not a problem for regionalists and nationalists, who wanted to stimulate a more pronounced regional and national consciousness, nor did it impede a profitable use of this type of architecture for commercial and touristic purposes. However, it would not produce a convincing modern architectural style that could be applied to a wide variety of buildings. Nonetheless, another and less ambitious option was also hinted at in Gallotti's review: one could also try to formulate a more generic and simplified regionalist style based on the ordinary houses encountered almost everywhere. This seemed to have been the recipe at the Rural Centre and would also be the preferred solution at some German exhibitions.

9

Munich and Düsseldorf

The picturesque regionalism that could be found in Seville and Paris was almost absent in post-war German exhibitions, whereas regional diversity even seemed to be anathema. Nonetheless, in the 1930s two major national exhibitions, in Munich and Düsseldorf, showed model settlements in a more simplified, generic regionalist style. And in contrast to Spain and France, the exhibitions were not organised by representatives of an older generation – many of whom were convinced regionalists, but by considerably younger architects who adhered to the Nazi ideology.

Somewhat surprisingly, no official world's fairs were held in Germany until the year 2000. In the 1880s and 1890s the Association of Berlin Merchants and Manufacturers had proposed to stage a major international exhibition in Berlin, however, the government did not want to take the financial responsibility. And when in 1892 France announced another international exhibition for 1900 all plans were cancelled. Instead the Berlin association organised a specialised, but still huge Industrial Exhibition in 1896.[1] Unlike France, the German government apparently preferred to spend money and effort in setting up an extensive welfare system than in organising prestigious events such as a Universal Exposition. However, various national exhibitions on a grand scale were held, as were lot of specialised fairs, many of which were international in scope.

The German Empire also participated in many international exhibitions with a proper pavilion and picturesque vernacular and regionalist elements in the decades before the First World War. Like most other countries Germany used historicist or eclectic styles for its national pavilions. Remarkably most pavilions were inspired by civic constructions such as town halls and bourgeois houses and showed no references to Prussia.

---

[1] Winfried Kretschmer, *Geschichte der Weltausstellungen* (Frankfurt and New York 1999) 140–1 and Holger Möller, *Das deutsche Messe- und Ausstellungswesen: Standortstruktur und räumliche Entwicklung seit dem 19. Jahrhundert* (Trier 1989) 99.

Thus, Johannes Radke (1853–1938) designed an eclectic pavilion, broadly modelled on a South-German town hall, with typical German elements and motifs from different sixteenth- and seventeenth-century buildings for both the World's Fair in Chicago in 1893 and the Parisian exhibition of 1900. Apart from some minor half-timbered façades there were no vernacular references.[2] In Chicago, however, the Empire also participated with a German village that consisted of thirty-six mainly vernacular constructions. This had been a private initiative and the village was located at the amusement centre along the Midway Plaisance. The village contained copies of a castle, a town hall and four typical farm houses from different parts of the country.[3]

At the 1910 World's Fair in Brussels, Germany was even represented by a more or less regionalist pavilion designed by Emanuel von Seidl (1856–1919), who specialised in South-German country houses. He designed a picturesque German pavilion and restaurant with gables, mansard roofs and smooth, almost completely unadorned walls, whereas Peter Behrens and Bruno Paul, both prominent members of the Werkbund, were responsible for the exhibition halls. These low, horizontal buildings with tiled roofs together with the pavilion resembled an updated South-German farm with huge barns. Consequently it differed greatly from the rather conventional neo-Baroque exhibition palaces and the historicist pavilions of the other participating nations.[4] However, at none of these exhibitions was there an official representation of the various German regions.

After defeat in the First World War, the fall of the Empire and the arrival of the Weimar Republic, the architectural panorama seems to have changed drastically. More than in almost any other European country modernist architecture rapidly rose to prominence and its supporters started to dominate the pages of the architectural press. As early as 1919 Walter Gropius opened the famous Bauhaus, an innovating art school that almost immediately became a laboratory for avant-garde art and architecture. When in 1924 the severe post-war economic crisis had passed, modernist architects also began to receive official assignments from various national, regional and municipal authorities, mainly thanks to the support of progressive liberal and socialist politicians and officials.

---

[2] Paul Sigel, *Exponiert: Deutsche Pavillons auf Weltausstellungen* (Berlin 2000) 32–60.

[3] Martin Wörner, *Vergnügen und Belehren: Volkskultur auf den Weltausstellungen* (Münster 1999) 72–8 and Bjarne Stoklund, 'How the Peasant House became a National Symbol: A Chapter in the History of Museums and Nation-Building', *Ethnologia Europaea* XXIX (1999) 5–18, especially 15–16.

[4] Sigel, *Exponiert* 62–85.

A new tax for house owners – introduced after the hyperflation of 1923 had made most properties essentially mortgage-free – provided money for cheap loans to building societies and this was mostly spent on social housing. Although in some regions and cities neo-vernacular houses in picturesque neighbourhoods continued to be built, many authorities and building societies preferred cheap, mass-produced apartments. In 1927 the national government even supported the trend towards industrial efficiency by establishing a federal agency that had to subsidise experiments with new, economic building methods. Frankfurt and Berlin would take the lead in adopting modernism, and although in general most apartment buildings were still constructed in more traditional styles, some other cities would soon follow their example.[5]

Thus, it was not a complete surprise when in the summer of 1928 Ludwig Mies van der Rohe, a promising representative of the new architectural avant-garde, was asked to design the German pavilion at the International Exhibition in Barcelona. As Germany did not participate in the 1925 Parisian international exhibition, Mies' modernist masterpiece would be the only pavilion that represented the Weimar Republic. Mies, however, was not appointed by progressive circles that generally supported modernist architecture, but by Georg von Schnitzler, a member of the board of I.G. Farben, Germany's major chemical company. He had been named general commissioner for the German section by a conservative coalition government led by the catholic Wilhelm Marx. As time was running short Mies, who at the time also was a vice-president of the Werkbund, was given complete freedom to design the pavilion. Apparently even conservative officials and politicians preferred to represent Germany as a modern and functional country. His pavilion, with its flat roof on thin metal posts, huge glass panels and free-standing walls, was an exercise in the aesthetic possibilities of the new construction techniques and would become one of the hallmarks of modern architecture.[6]

However, Barcelona was far away. More influential was the Werkbund exposition *Die Wohnung* (The Dwelling) that Mies van der Rohe organised in 1927 and which was a good example of the many smaller and more

[5] Barbara Miller Lane, *Architecture and Politics in Germany, 1918–1945* (Cambridge 1968) 87–125, Barbara Miller Lane, 'Die Moderne und die Politik in Deutschland zwischen 1919 und 1945' in: Vittorio Magnago Lampugnani and Romana Schneider eds., *Moderne Architektur in Deutschland 1900 bis 1950: Expressionismus und Neue Sachlichkeit* (Stuttgart 1994) 225–50 and Joachim Petsch, *Baukunst und Stadtplanung im Dritten Reich* (Munich and Vienna 1976) 32–56.
[6] Sigel, *Exponiert* 102–27. Von Schnitzler would later become a member of the NSDAP and a close collaborator of the Nazi government.

specialised exhibitions and fairs that were regularly organised in various German towns. The initiative for this exposition was taken by the Stuttgart chapter of the German Werkbund that by then was almost entirely dominated by representatives of the modern tendencies. It was led by the Heilbronn-born Peter Bruckmann, vice-president of the Werkbund, who in 1918, together with Friedrich Neumann and Theodor Heuss, had been a founding member of the progressive liberal Deutsche Demokratische Partei. Bruckmann proposed Mies as the artistic director of the exhibition. The Weissenhof settlement, which was the site of the exposition, would house twenty-one buildings by sixteen selected modern architects, among whom were Behrens, Poelzig, Gropius, Taut, Mies himself, Le Corbusier and the Dutch functionalist Oud. They also had to design the interiors and furniture. Most of these architects would also become a member of the *Ring*, an association of modernist architects led by Mies. The apartment buildings and detached and terraced houses, all with flat roofs, were a showcase of modern architecture and design and proved to be a huge success with about half a million visitors.[7]

Nonetheless, as would happen in France some years later, modern architecture began to be fiercely criticised. From about 1926 conservative architects and critics began to launch a frontal attack. In 1928, presided over by the painter, critic and architect Paul Schultze-Naumburg, the former architectural commentator of *Der Kunstwart*, they even formed a group called the *Block*. Among its members were Paul Bonatz (1877–1956), Paul Schmitthenner and German Bestelmeyer (1874–1942). In a short manifesto they asserted that they did not reject the use of new materials and techniques, but that this should not mean that the character of the German people and the particulars of the natural environment could be ignored.[8] The arguments in general were similar to those used in France. Some critics, for example, stated that standardised construction would increase the unemployment figures and that flat roofs did not suit the German climate and mores. Uniform and machine-made houses would uproot the inhabitants, lead to degeneration and impede people from feeling at home. And whereas in France this type of architecture often was rejected as foreign or 'German', German critics preferred adjectives such

---

[7] Karin Kirsch, 'Die Weißenhofsiedlung: Ein internationales Manifest' in: Vittorio Magnago Lampugnani and Romana Schneider eds., *Moderne Architektur in Deutschland 1900 bis 1950: Expressionismus und Neue Sachlichkeit* (Stuttgart 1994) 205–24 and Richard Pommer and Christian F. Otto, *Weissenhof 1927 and the Modern Movement in Architecture* (Chicago 1991).

[8] Norbert Borrmann, *Paul Schultze-Naumburg: Maler, Publizist, Architekt 1869–1949* (Essen 1989) 182.

as 'nomadic', 'oriental', or 'bolshevist'. Schultze-Naumburg even began to apply the recent racial theories of his friend Hans Günther to prove that the rise of modernist architecture was a result of the racial decline of the German people.[9]

Around 1929 these arguments also began to be used by the conservative press and some right-wing politicians. However, only Hitler's Nationalsozialistische Deutsche Arbeiterpartei (NSDAP) would launch a full-scale campaign against modern architecture. This was mainly done after some influential Nazis adopted Schultze-Naumburg's racially based rejection of modern art and architecture. In 1929 Schultze-Naumburg became a member of the *Kampfbund für deutsche Kultur* (Fighting League for German Culture) – which had been founded shortly earlier by Alfred Rosenberg, the main Nazi ideologue – whereas in 1930 he would become a member of the NSDAP. In April that year Schultze-Naumburg was appointed director of the Art Academy in Weimar – which until its move to Dessau in 1925 had housed the Bauhaus – by Walter Frick, the new NSDAP minister of the Interior of Thuringia. He immediately removed paintings by Kandinsky, Klee and Schmidt-Rottluff and discharged almost all of the teachers as, according to him, they were still too much attached to the ideals of Gropius. After the coalition government, of which Frick was a member, fell in 1931 Schultze-Naumburg's contract was left to run out. However, his architectural ideas were then widely disseminated by both the *Kampfbund* and the party press, such as Rosenberg's *Völkischer Beobachter* (People's Observer). Hitler and other Nazi bosses even honoured him with a visit at his home and in 1932 he became a member of the Reichstag for the NSDAP. Although modern architecture had often been positively reviewed in the Nazi press, it became a favourite target from then on. It was considered a symbol of the Weimar Republic's 'cultural bolshevism', which seriously threatened the health and well-being of the German people.[10]

Many conservative and regionalist architects hoped that after the Nazi take-over they would receive commissions from the new regime and that, with the help of Rosenberg, they would be able to control architectural matters. During the summer of 1933 some of their most prominent enemies had already been removed from their posts, the Bauhaus was closed and the Society of German Architects and the Werkbund were taken over by loyal Nazi professionals. The last two organisations were integrated into the *Kampfbund für deutsche Architekten und Ingenieure* (Fighting League for

[9] Lane, *Architecture and Politics* 133–45.
[10] Ibid., 143–67 and Borrmann, *Schultze-Naumburg* 183–95.

German Architects and Engineers), which was a branch of Rosenberg's Fighting League for German Culture. However, it was not Rosenberg who came to control cultural life but Joseph Goebbels who, in the autumn of 1933, established the *Reichskulturkammer* (Reich Culture Chamber) as a branch of his Propaganda Ministry. Soon thereafter the entire *Kampfbund* became a subsection of *Kraft durch Freude* (Strength through Joy), the leisure organisation of the German Labour Front and consequently lost almost all its significance. All artists, writers, architects, actors, journalists and musicians on the other hand were obliged to become a member of the *Kulturkammer* to be able to practise their profession. Whereas the purpose of Rosenberg was to disqualify architects on aesthetic principles, Goebbels' *Kulturkammer* limited itself mainly to excluding Jews. Although prominent modernist architects were not selected for major commissions, the same was true for most of the *Block* architects and by 1935 even Schultze-Naumburg had become irrelevant.[11]

Hitler himself clearly preferred a modernised neo-classicist style – first the work of Paul Ludwig Troost (1878–1934), then of the young Albert Speer (1905–81) – for his own megalomaniac projects. These should express the unity and power of the German nation. Thus, for the World's Fair in Paris Speer designed a monumental German pavilion. Nazi Germany thus gave no room to regionalism in its main representative buildings, nor did it show the regional variety of the Reich as France had with the Regional Centre. Regional variety was only hinted at in a very minimal way in the interior of Speer's pavilion of 1937. In the huge stained glass at the rear wall of the pavilion the German eagle with the swastika hovered over the emblems of the seventeen principal German cities.[12] A similar version of downplayed regional diversity could be seen at the Olympic Village that was constructed for the 1936 Olympic Games of Berlin. The village, in a rural setting outside the capital, was constructed broadly in the shape of a map of the Third Reich, with the refectory representing Berlin. The 140 one-storey barracks for the almost 4,000 athletes were named, according to their place in the village, after the main German cities. However, these buildings were all identical.[13] Hence, on both occasions the nation was not symbolised as an ensemble of regions, each with its own characteristics, but as a unified country in which cities were the main reference points. In this way both the Weimar Republic and the Third Reich more or less

---

11   Ibid., 169–84 and Borrmann, *Schultze-Naumburg* 198–200.
12   Sigel, *Exponiert* 163.
13   Judith Holmes, *Olympiad 1936: Blaze of Glory for Hitler's Reich* (New York 1971) 70–80.

radicalised the trend that could already be discerned before 1914 to avoid the development of clearly delimited and strong regional identities.

However, regionalism was not absent from the Third Reich. Many regionalist architects even tried to profit from the regime change. Thus, already in 1927 Schmitthenner, a professor of architecture in Stuttgart and member of the *Block*, had tried to organise an exposition that was intended as an answer to the Weissenhof show of Mies van der Rohe. This exhibition was to take place at the Kochenhof settlement in Stuttgart. However, as he did not succeed the Werkbund developed plans to organise another exhibition at the Kochenhof, dedicated to modern houses built in timber to help combat the current crisis of the German wood industry. Nonetheless, in March 1933, less than two months after the rise of Hitler, Schmitthenner – who that year would become a member of the NSDAP – succeeded in taking over the German Wood for Housing Construction and Dwellings' Exhibition. He invited other, traditionalist architects and apart from the obvious use of timber he prescribed a saddle roof for all constructions. The exhibition was opened to the public that same summer.[14]

Munich 1934

Less improvised was the *Deutsche Siedlungsausstellung* (German Settlement Exhibition) in Munich. It consisted mainly of a model development in Ramersdorf on the outskirts of the city which, after being used as an exposition, should be handed over to the buyers of the individual dwellings. Already in 1930 Guido Harbers (1897–1977), a young architect working in the building department of the city administration, had proposed the construction of a model settlement with small single-family homes. His proposal was declined, mainly for financial reasons. However, after the Nazis had taken over the Munich town hall, Harbers took advantage of the situation and, in May 1933, successfully resubmitted his proposal. Harbers was in a good position to have his project adopted. In 1925 he had become the brother-in-law of Hermann Esser, a fiercely anti-Semitic collaborator of the *Völkischer Beobachter* and a close collaborator of Hitler in the early years of the NSDAP. And in 1930, shortly after the economic crisis had reached Germany, the architect decided to join the party. Consequently, when his superior was forced to retire in March 1933, Harbers succeeded him as head of the municipal building department.[15] Nonetheless, judging

14 Stefanie Plarre, *Die Kochenhofsiedlung – Das Gegenmodell zur Weißenhofsiedlung: Paul Schmitthenners Siedlungsprojekt in Stuttgart von 1927 bis 1933* (Stuttgart 2001).
15 Ursula Henn, *Die Mustersiedlung Ramersdorf in München: Ein Siedlungskonzept zwischen*

from his writings and exhibition plans, he was more someone who took advantage of the moment to realise his professional ambitions than a fanatical, ideologically driven Nazi.

Harbers also maintained good contacts within the professional world, as in 1927 he had become editor and in 1930 editor in chief of *Der Baumeister* (The Master Builder), an architectural monthly published by Callwey. In the next few years Callwey would also publish three illustrated books by Harbers on small single-family homes in which he defended a moderate regionalism. In these books he advocated the use of local building materials and traditions. He also pleaded for taking into account the environment, although he himself took a European perspective distinguishing between its northern and southern parts and areas close to the sea and other more continental regions. He did not propagate backward-looking copies, but rather preferred simple, cheap constructions and even showed a few examples with a modernist flat roof.[16]

Harbers was aware of the continuing delicate economic situation and consequently took care to present his project as a viable and attractive option. He thus shrewdly defined Ramersdorf as a 'small suburban settlement' in order to benefit from a 1931 law of the conservative Brüning government that promoted rural homesteads for the unemployed by tax exemptions and cheap loans. To lower the costs the unemployed should help build their own house, which should have a considerable subsistence garden where the inhabitants could also keep some livestock. This measure was meant to diminish the concentration of the dissatisfied masses in big cities by resettling them in suburban or rural areas. Gottfried Feder, one of the Nazis from the first hour who became head of the Fighting League for Architects in 1932, would continue this anti-urban policy after his appointment in the spring of 1934 as Reich settlement commissioner. Rooting the degenerated population of the metropolis in the soil of the homeland once again would, according to him, 'strengthen the race'. However, within a year Feder was discharged and consequently Nazi Germany would, mainly for financial reasons, return to the policy of the Weimar Republic by focusing on terraced houses and apartment buildings in the suburbs of the main cities. Although Harbers asserted in his proposal that the Germans were 'gifted for colonisation' and that for lack of possibilities abroad the country should direct its efforts to the interior colonisation, he in fact did not want to construct a rural settlement with homesteads for the unemployed, but a

Tradition und Moderne (Munich 1987) 91–120.
[16] Henn, *Mustersiedlung Ramersdorf* 120–8 and Guido Harbers, *Das Kleinhaus, seine Konstruktion und Einrichtung* (2nd edn., Munich 1932) 6–8 and 26.

comfortable neighbourhood for the skilled worker and the middle class. Hence, most plots were smaller than the minimum of 600 m² foreseen in the law, and the majority of the houses by far exceeded the budget of the urban poor.[17]

Harbers, who was the author of the very lengthy, but anonymous review in *Der Baumeister*, further maintained that the goal of the exhibition was to help realise the 'innermost wish' of the Führer to 'give back to the German people the joy of living'. The German Settlement Exhibition, according to the project submitted in May, should show that a modest single-family home in a tranquil neighbourhood that guaranteed freedom of movement to both parents and children would be a good and attractive option for the broad middle strata of the population. As the event would also support the goals of the new regime to improve the economy and provide jobs, the new municipal government decided to seize the opportunity and approved the project.[18]

The exhibition consisted of four parts, the model settlement in Ramersdorf, a small art exhibition, a garden show on adjacent terrain and an exhibition of plans and interior decoration at the Munich exhibition grounds. The settlement would contain 192 single-family homes with a garden, of which 152 would be free-standing. The houses were intended for families with at least three children and would have a living area of 60, 80, 100 or 120 m². After a contest in the summer of 1933 thirty-four different house types by seventeen Munich architects were selected. Harbers himself had made the plan of the settlement in which he respected the existing trees (figure 35). He also stipulated that the constructions should be cheap and economical in use. Modernist flat roofs were implicitly proscribed as the roof should follow native traditions, whereas local customary materials should be applied; the use of timber should however be avoided.[19]

As the houses had to be cheap they were done in a more generic regionalist style and in many ways resembled the functionalist designs of modernist architects. All houses were rectangular without recesses and had a simple saddle roof without eaves. The walls of houses were all uniformly plastered in white and contained almost no decoration (figure 36). As a result, the flat facades of these cubic forms were interrupted only by

---

[17] Ibid., 42–51, 141–8 and 203–5, 'Die Deutsche Siedlungsausstellung in München: Die Mustersiedlung Ramersdorf', *Zentralblatt der Bauverwaltung* (19 September 1934) 549–57, especially 551, Lane, *Architecture and Politics* 175 and 205–11 and Anna Teut, *Architektur im Dritten Reich 1933–1945* (Frankfurt am Main 1967) 251–3.

[18] Ibid., 146–54 and 343 and 'Die Siedlung München-Ramersdorf', *Der Baumeister* (September 1934) 289–319.

[19] Ibid., 163–9, 243–7, 273 and 330–9.

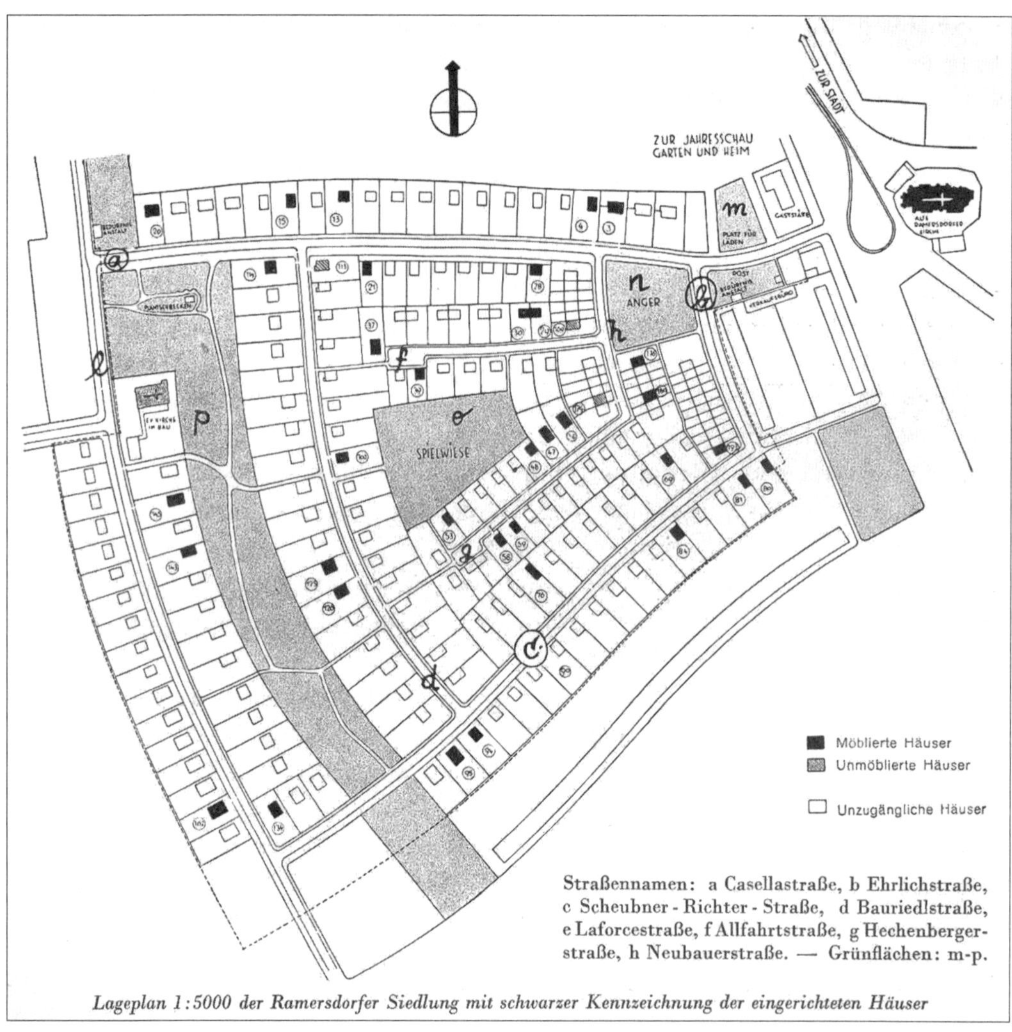

Lageplan 1:5000 der Ramersdorfer Siedlung mit schwarzer Kennzeichnung der eingerichteten Häuser

35 Plan of Ramersdorf, Munich, 1934.

windows and doors. Regionalist elements, apart from the tiled roofs and the shutters, were not very prominent. Although the settlement was not laid out like a village or garden city, with winding streets and a central square with public buildings, most roads had a slight curve to avoid a monotonous streetscape. The houses were carefully oriented and most had a sheltered terrace.[20]

According to the quite factual review in the *Zentrallblat der Bauverwaltung*, edited by the Prussian Finance Ministry, Harbers had expressed the hope that the 'glimmer of homeland [*Heimat*], typical for the old German small

20 Ibid., 237–79.

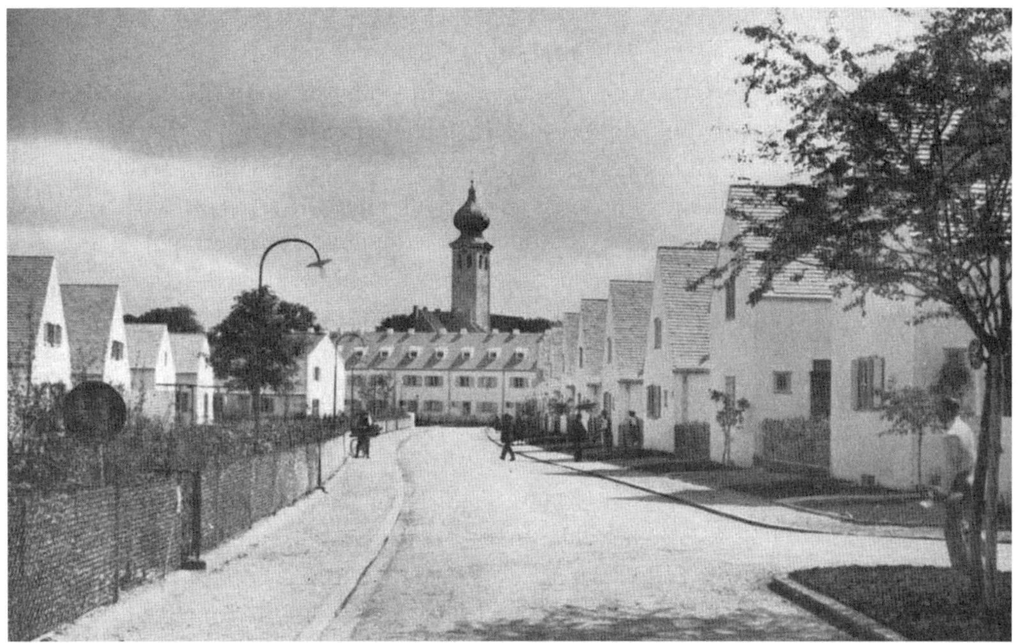

36 Hechenbergerstrasse (now Krottenmühlestrasse), Ramersdorf, Munich, 1934. Harbers deliberately oriented the street towards the baroque tower of the ancient village church of Ramersdorf, while he located the main garden of each house on its south side.

town' would also hover over the roofs, commons, streets and playgrounds of this settlement. Ursula Henn, in her study of Ramersdorf, also asserts that these simple, gabled houses without eaves, balconies and timber could be seen as typical of Northern Upper Bavaria. Nonetheless, in his own writings Harbers made no reference to any regional specificity. In his review of the exhibition he gave details of all individual houses, while focusing mainly on the dimensions, the distribution of the rooms and the size of the mortgage.[21] Even the interiors that could be seen in the exhibition halls and some of the houses were quite modern and functional without being futuristic. As the show was arranged according to the parts of the day, exhibiting interiors for the morning, the afternoon and the evening, there was no place for regional singularities. And whereas two decades earlier architects like Riemerschmid would also use the vernacular

[21]   Ibid., 276–7 and 'Die Deutsche Siedlungsausstellung in München' 556. See for Harbers: 'Die Siedlung München-Ramersdorf' 289–319 and 'Weitere Typen von Einfamilienhäusern in der Deutschen Siedlungsausstellung München 1934', *Der Baumeister* (October 1934) 337–57 and Guido Harbers, 'Randbemerkungen zur "Deutschen Siedlungsausstellung München 1934"', *Die Kunst* (August 1934) 284–92.

in the interiors of country houses, now even a farmer's room was equipped with simple, functional furniture.[22]

Harbers received the support of both the municipal and Bavarian authorities, among them Hermann Esser, who had become Bavarian Minister of Economy. On the national level Harbers received some backing, although many of those who supported his project were secondary figures, and some would soon lose the Darwinian struggle for power within the bureaucratic chaos that characterised the Nazi regime. This was especially the case with Feder who in December would be dismissed as Reich settlement commissioner by Hjalmar Schacht, the new Minister of Economy. In July 1934, however, Feder, who was very critical of the excrescences of capitalism, still organised a national dwelling conference in Munich. He was assisted by Wilhelm Ludovici, a close collaborator of Hitler's deputy Rudolf Hess, who in March 1934 was appointed head of the homestead office within Robert Ley's German Labour Front, and he also became Feder's deputy at the Ministry of Economy. On this occasion Feder expressed the hope that in the near future new small towns would change the face of Germany and convert its inhabitants into 'happy and cheerful people, rescued from all miserable housing and economic distress'. Although he clearly preferred new rural settlements, he declared Ramersdorf to be a 'pioneering' project. The participants of the meeting visited both the exhibition halls and the Ramersdorf settlement.[23]

Nonetheless, it seems that the principal party leaders were not really interested in the German Settlement Exhibition. Thus, the construction activities had to be halted because an already awarded national loan was delayed for several months. Harbers did his best to court Hitler and other high-ranking Nazis. He thus named the streets of the settlement after the 'martyrs' of the Beer Hall Putsch, the Nazis' first failed attempt to seize power in 1923. He tried to make Hitler the patron of the exhibition and even thought of calling his project the 'Adolf Hitler Settlement'. However, none of the leading party bosses was present at the various official ceremonies, although it had to be admitted that the delayed inauguration

---

[22] 'Einige "Wohnelemente" aus Halle II der Deutschen Siedlungs Ausstellung München 1934', *Der Baumeister* (November 1934) 369–91, especially 391 and Herbert Hoffmann, 'Erster Bericht über die Deutsche Siedlungsausstellung München 1934', *Moderne Bauformen* (July 1934) 405–8, especially 407.

[23] Henn, *Mustersiedlung Ramersdorf* 184–98. Henn failed to notice Feder's conference. See: 'Die Münchener Reichswohnungskonferenz', *Bauen, Siedeln, Wohnen* (25 July 1934) 199–200. See also: Dan P. Silverman, *Hitler's Economy: Nazi Work Creation Programs, 1933–1936* (Cambridge 1998) 28–47 and 103–4 and Ronald Smelser, *Robert Ley: Hitler's Labor Front Leader* (Oxford, New York and Hamburg 1988) 199–201.

of the settlement on 30 June coincided with the Night of the Long Knives, when Hitler violently crushed a presumed conspiracy among the leaders of the SA, the Nazis' paramilitary organisation. Apparently, Hitler and his main collaborators gave little priority to Harbers' project of raising the standards of German housing culture. Harbers even thought that the indifferent attitude of the national party bosses negatively influenced the number of visitors, which would only reach about 300,000. And although most of the houses were sold almost immediately, eventually the financial results of the exhibition proved to be a disaster.[24]

The division within the party ranks was also visible in the press. In general, the exhibition received considerable attention from the architectural press, especially from Harbers' own *Der Baumeister*. Most reviews, as was often the case in these professional journals, were quite factual and neutral in tone. However, a few magazines were more critical, although they obviously had to remain within certain limits as during the spring and summer of 1933 the architectural journals either were taken over by the Nazis or had to conform to the ideas of the new regime. Thus, by 1934 no German magazine openly dared to defend the Bauhaus ideals.[25]

The aging Theodor Fischer wrote a positive review of the Ramersdorf exposition in *Die Bauzeitung*. He described the settlement of his former pupil as a good middle course between the too individualistic neighbourhoods of former times and the more recent, unrealistic 'drawing-board inventions'. By overcoming both the picturesque regionalism of the early decades of the twentieth century and the uniform modernism of the 1920s, Harbers had tried to develop a good house for the ordinary people while taking into account their real needs.[26]

Bauen, Siedeln, Wohnen (Constructing, Settling, Living) a journal edited by the German Labour Front (the Nazi organisation that had replaced the trade unions) was also very positive about the German Settlement Exhibition. According to the author, the exposed interiors gave a good impression of the 'new spirit of the age', whereas the settlement was skilfully integrated in the landscape. He even concluded that the exhibition presented a programme for a new and fruitful housing and settlement policy. He seemed to emphasise more than other reviewers the regionalist aspect of

---

24 Henn, *Mustersiedlung Ramersdorf* 179–236. The final deficit amounted to over 1 million Reichsmark, which was slightly more than 20 per cent of the overall costs.

25 Lane, *Architecture and Politics* 169–82. See also: Karl Arndt, 'Die Münchener Architekturszene 1933/1934 als ästhetisch-politisches Konfliktfeld' in: Martin Broszat, Elke Fröhlich and Anton Grossmann eds., *Bayern in der NS-Zeit* III, *Herrschaft und Gesellschaft im Konflikt* Teil B (Munich 1981) 443–513.

26 Theodor Fischer, 'Ramersdorf', *Die Bauzeitung* (25 September 1934) 329–30.

Harbers' project when he maintained that Ramersdorf, with its 'charming houses, its green commons and the winding paths passing through woods and bushes' immediately provoked a 'homely feeling (*Heimatgefühl*)'. He also asserted that according to Harbers one of the fundamental principles of the exhibition would be its 'German style'.[27]

Nonetheless, the exhibition was also openly criticised by reviewers who more or less identified with the National Socialist cause. They probably also made clear why Harbers' project was not seen as a real priority by most Nazi leaders. *Bauwelt*, a journal that until some years earlier had supported modernist architecture, for example, published a review by Otto Völkers, in which the author stated that the exposition stood at the 'start of a new movement' and therefore should be valued positively. However, he also detected a series of 'youthful errors', which consisted mainly in a lack of artisanal skills. Völkers also mildly criticised the introductory exhibits on the history of settlements, which were largely based on Harbers' books on single-family homes, for showing too many foreign examples, whereas the part on 'eternal forms' should better concentrate on the subtle differences in the shape of houses between the various nations, instead of showing the 'superficial similarities'. The author further complained that the old and thoroughly German mode of timber framing was almost entirely absent from the exhibition. In contrast to the Weissenhof Settlement, which had been a hardly digestible mixture of good and bad innovations to which no one remained indifferent, the German Settlement Exhibition was merely stimulating, showing a lot of not completely new, but interesting things. Nevertheless, he doubted that the municipal government should subsidise comfortable houses for the upper middle-class.[28]

More critical remarks could be found in *Deutsche Bauhütte*, the only architectural journal that, since the late 1920s, had persisted in its denunciation of the modernist style. It used the occasion to continue its critique of Bauhaus by publishing a detailed and technical review by Fritz Kress, the director of a carpentry school, who mainly focused on the mistakes made in the construction of tresses and staircases. The lack of the traditional eaves would also cause serious humidity problems. He explained these errors as the inexperience of the young architects that had designed some of the model houses. They were no longer accustomed to building

---

27 Dr Roland Schupp, 'Die Deutsche Siedlungsausstellung München 1934 – Eine Bau- und Raumkünstlerisch Zielweisende Tat', *Bauen, Siedeln, Wohnen* (25 July 1934) 200–3.
28 Otto Völkers, 'Zur Deutschen Siedlungsausstellung in München 1934', *Bauwelt* (27 September 1934) 1–6. The same article, with exactly the same title and illustrations was also published in *Monatshefte für Baukunst und Städtebau* (1934) 509–14.

half-timbered or timbered houses and had been misled by the 'propaganda for the test architecture' of the 'Marxist architects'.[29]

Another author in the same journal maintained that the Nazi revolution should also have consequences in the architectural domain. First it should undo the influence of modernist architects as their work threatened to debase the German being. It was due to them that the German people 'forgot the laws of nature and climate, landscape and national character'. The insolent acts of 'foreign elements that mercilessly forced their stamp on the area' had uprooted both man and the landscape. However, according to the critic, Ramersdorf did not constitute a solution as the houses were too similar. The unity of the equal saddle roofs, which was reminiscent of the old imposed democratic egalitarianism, 'had an unfruitful effect on the place and the area'. A third author also deplored that the organisers had failed to really apply the principles of the new regime. Some of the interiors shown in the exhibition halls, such as a conservatory, a music room or a tearoom, clearly belonged to the old 'capitalist, liberal camp'. He even asked: For whom should we build? And he also gave the answer: For the 23 million members of the German Labour Front and for the 8 million members of the SA. Consequently, the spacious single family houses propagated by Harbers did not constitute a solution for the majority of Hitler's faithful followers.[30]

Although some regionalist arguments were present both in the ideas of Harbers and many of the reviews, Harbers seemed more interested in improving the living conditions of his fellow countrymen, providing them with comfortable homes in an attractive setting. Regionalism was no longer the leading ideology. It had become a kind of accepted trend from which one could freely pick some elements, while there was no need any longer to adopt the whole. The urgent need to build in an efficient and cheap way probably was the main cause for the decline of regionalism, and this trend had been reinforced by the rise of modernism. And despite the fierce nationalism of the Nazis and their admiration for traditional rural values they did not advocate a complete return to the regionalist principles, be it in architecture or in other areas. Their stress on national

[29] Fritz Kress, 'Kritische Berichte von der Deutschen Siedlungsausstellung in München: Lehren des Holzbaues', *Deutsche Bauhütte* (20 June 1934) 154–8. This article was also published in a summarised form after the article of Völkers in both *Bauwelt* and *Monatshefte für Baukunst und Städtebau*.

[30] P. Rössler, 'Kritische Berichte von der Deutschen Siedlungsausstellung in München', *Deutsche Bauhütte* (20 June 1934) 151–2 and C.R.V., 'Kritische Berichte von der Deutschen Siedlungsausstellung in München: Nachdenkliche Betrachtung mit Bildern', *Deutsche Bauhütte* (20 June 1934) 152–3.

unity even seemed to leave less space for recognising local and regional differences. Thus, no critic or organiser used the word 'Bavarian', 'local', or 'regional' to characterise a part of the exhibition, which seemed to embody more an abstracted, generic regionalism. Putting the regional variety of the country in the spotlight, as had been done in the Parisian Regional Centre, seemed to be no option. In the model settlement of a later, more ambitious exhibition, however, regionalism nonetheless seemed to play a more influential role.

Düsseldorf 1937

The *Schaffendes Volk* (which could be translated as Creating or Toiling People) exhibition in Düsseldorf, for which the initiative was taken in 1934, was more wholeheartedly backed by the new regime than Harbers' model settlement and would, with nearly 7 million visitors, be the biggest exposition of the Nazi era.[31] The exhibition, which was open between May and October 1937, was organised by the town of Düsseldorf and was, like the German Settlement Exhibition, mainly a local affair. It was promoted by ambitious Nazis who had risen to leading positions in the wake of Hitler's take-over and had a double origin as it combined a local exhibition tradition with a Werkbund project.

Already in 1926 the Werkbund leadership had accepted a proposal to stage a major exhibition called 'Die neue Zeit' (The New Era) to show the results of the new, more peaceful and progressive epoch that had started after 1918. The exhibition was to have been held in Cologne in 1931. However, because of the difficult economic situation after the crash of 1929 the event had to be postponed. Nevertheless, after the Nazis came to power the idea was revived by Carl Christoph Lörcher (1884–1966), a member of Rosenberg's *Kampfbund* who, following the Führer principle that was then being copied in all domains, became the new indisputable leader of the Werkbund.[32]

At the same time, leading Düsseldorf Nazis were eager to show that also on a local level the new regime was capable of executing ambitious projects. They first focused their attention on the already existing Schlageter monument, which commemorated the death of Albert Leo Schlageter. He had been a fiercely nationalist member of the right-wing Freikorps who,

---

[31] Möller, *Das deutsche Messe- und Ausstellungswesen* 137.

[32] Stefanie Schäfers, *Vom Werkbund zum Vierjahresplan: Die Ausstellung 'Schaffendes Volk',
Düsseldorf 1937* (Düsseldorf 2001) 61–8. See for the Werkbund: Joan Campbell, *The German
Werkbund: The Politics of Reform in the Applied Arts* (Princeton 1978) 243–88.

after the occupation of the Ruhr by French and Belgian troops in 1923, had committed acts of sabotage. After he had blown up a railway bridge he was executed by the French. German nationalists consequently made him into a martyr and in 1931 inaugurated a monument with a 31 m-high cross on the heath near Düsseldorf where he had been executed. Nazi officials now wanted to transform the monument into a huge assembly space for the German people. Early in 1934 the town organised a contest for the design of a new monumental shrine for this 'first soldier of the Third Reich', containing an amphitheatre for about 100,000 people, a sports arena for 50,000 and a parade ground for 300.000, which probably even functioned as a source of inspiration for the Nazi party rally grounds in Nuremberg, as its architect Albert Speer was one of the members of the jury. A park and new settlements should further connect the area with the town. On the same jury, Lörcher and the architect Peter Grund (1892–1966), the recently appointed director of the local Art Academy, came up with the plan to organise a major Werkbund exhibition in Düsseldorf. The new municipal administration fully supported the plan as it wanted to seize with both hands the chance to continue the long-standing local tradition of exhibitions.[33]

The exhibition was to combine a model garden city with a garden show and an exposition of art and craft products. In fact the exhibition would be a kind of 'new era in the new Reich' show. Initially planned for 1935, the exhibition was soon postponed to 1937. With its emphasis on daily life, it was intended to be a kind of supplement to Speer's German pavilion in Paris where the highlights of German production could be seen in a monumental setting. The organisers further hoped to attract visitors from the relatively nearby French World's Fair.[34]

However, two measures would cause a substantial change of course. The first was the appointment in 1935, at the intercession of Walther Funk, State Secretary at the Propaganda Ministry, of Ernst Maiwald as head manager of the exhibition. Maiwald worked at the international department of the German exhibition office and in 1929 had been responsible for the German contribution to the International Exhibition in Barcelona as Schnitzler's deputy. He thus brought along experience and good contacts with the industrial world. The Werkbund – which in the meantime had become almost irrelevant – was the main victim of this move and lost its already

---

[33] Schäfers, *Vom Werkbund zum Vierjahresplan* 68–70 and 116–25. See also Kurt Düwell, 'Regionalismus und Nationalsozialismus am Beispiel des Rheinlands', *Rheinische Vierteljahresblätter* 59 (1995) 194–210.
[34] Ibid., 68–82.

diminished influence on the exposition. Thus the stress on artisanal products was replaced by a stronger participation of German industry and a new stress on raw materials, which the Third Reich needed for its rearmament schemes. The second change was introduced by Hitler's announcement, in October 1936, of the Four-Year Plan to speed up economic preparation for war. This had to be done mainly by a new emphasis on autarky and the production of synthetic materials to substitute the raw materials that Germany so badly lacked. Hermann Göring, who was the patron of the exhibition, was put in charge of the execution of the plan. As the exhibition already coincided with many parts of the new economic programme, the organisers shortly afterwards proclaimed that the *Schaffendes Volk: Große Reichsausstellung Düsseldorf-Schlageterstadt 1937* (Creating People: Great Exhibition of the Reich Düsseldorf–Schlagetertown) would show the ideals, achievements and future projects of the Four-Year Plan.[35] In this way, they succeeded in positioning the exhibition more prominently to the public, while at the same time increasing its ideological content.

Although the organisers constantly sought the approval of Berlin, the main decisions were taken on a local level. One of the measures was to locate the exhibition in the north of the town between the Rhine, the future Schlageter forum and the old exhibition terrains from the Gesolei, a major exposition on health care, social welfare and sports which, in 1926, had been a huge success with more than 7 million visitors. The Schlageter forum had not progressed much since the contest of 1934 as the national party leadership showed little enthusiasm to provide funds for the monumental constructions. However, Peter Grund, who was responsible for both the lay-out of the exhibition and the forum, decided to lead the main axis of the exhibition to the monument. Similar to Puig i Cadafalch's monumental avenue at the foot of the Montjuïc and Perret's rejected project for the International Exhibition of Paris, Grund designed a monumental and partly symmetrical lay-out. However, instead of directing the axis from the Schlageter monument to the Rhine the German architect chose to connect it with the classicist façade of the new Art Academy, which because of the First World War had remained unfinished and was incorporated into the exhibition ground. This meant that the banks of the Rhine and its spectacular vista were not really used and that the overall plan was poorly organised – as, for example, the main model settlement was hidden behind the exhibition halls (figure 37).[36]

[35] Ibid., 83–8 and 97–9.
[36] Ibid., 111–46.

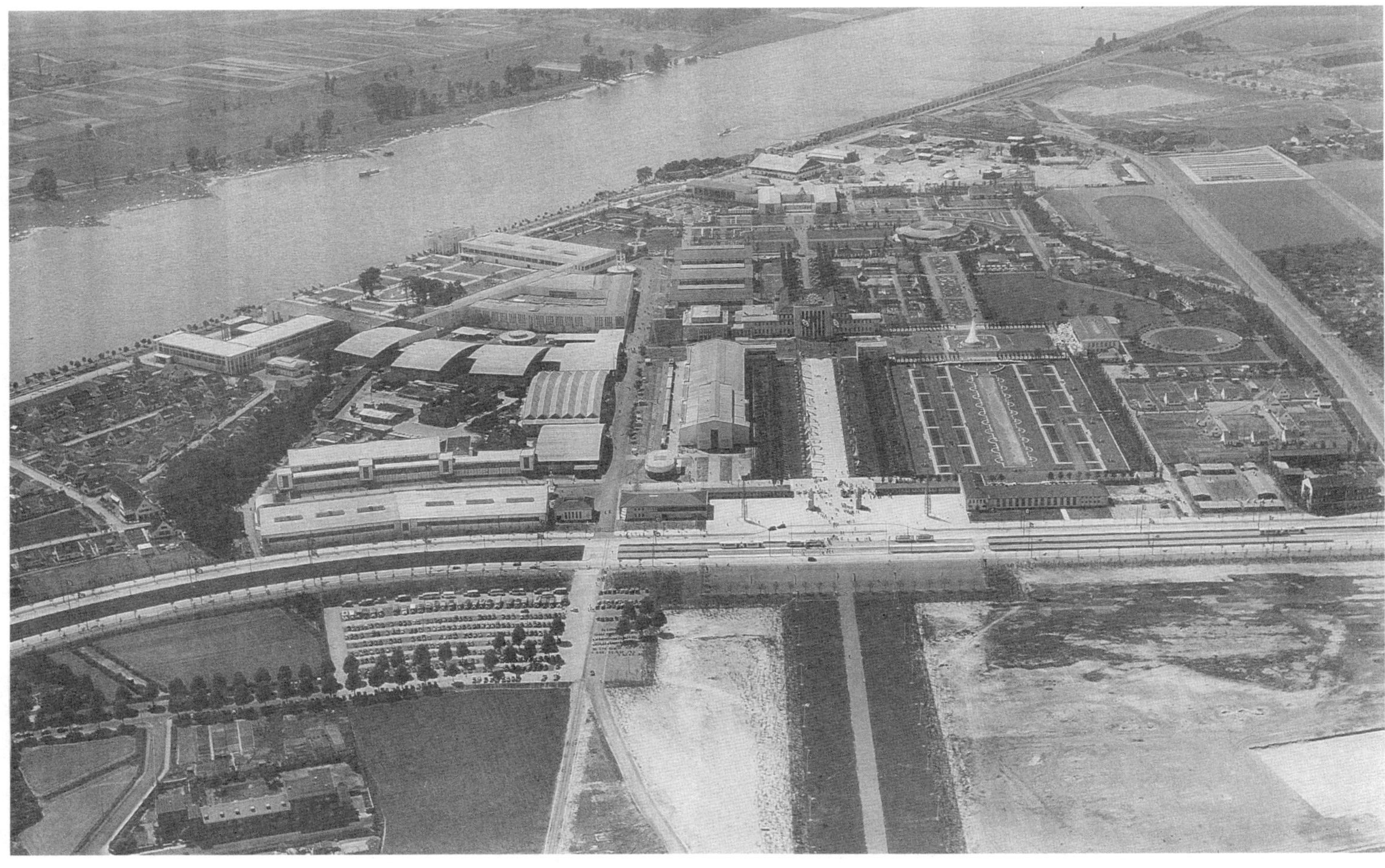

37 Aerial view of the exhibition ground of the *Schaffendes Volk* Exhibition, Düsseldorf, 1937. The central axis led from the Schlageter Forum, which is not on the photo, to the transformed building of the Art Academy. On the far left is the Schlageter Settlement, and the much smaller Gustloff Settlement is on the right. The funfair was located in a separate area, and can be seen in the upper part of the picture.

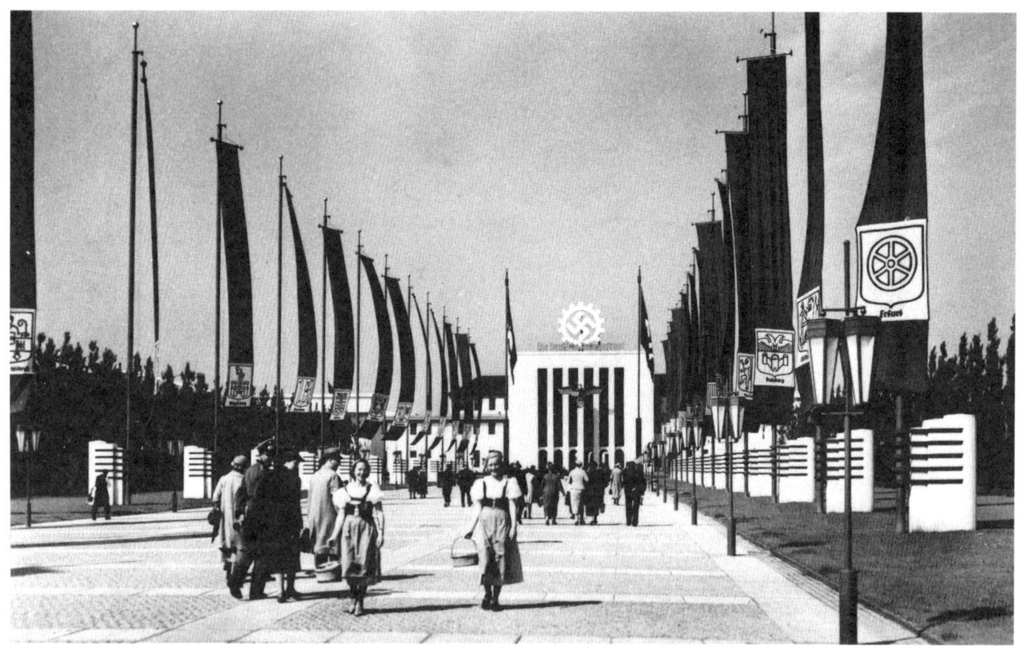

38 Main axis of the *Schaffendes Volk* Exhibition with the fake façade of the new Art Academy. In the foreground are two women in traditional costume with lottery tickets.

The monumental layout with three parallel axes also required similar buildings, and as the massive new Art Academy, which should function as the powerful termination of the main axis, was built of brick it received a fake austere classicist façade, topped with the swastika of the German Labour Front (figure 38). This monumentality was also reflected in the geometrical garden show, which was laid out mainly along the large rectangular water basin with fountains that formed the water axis. Surprisingly, most exhibition halls were done in a sober functionalist style. These were temporary constructions and as according to the Four-Year Plan Germany should economise in its usage of materials, most of these constructions could be re-used elsewhere. Thus, many of the Bauhaus ideals, which had been condemned by Schultze-Naumburg and leading Nazis like Rosenberg, were now openly applied in these utilitarian buildings.[37] Modernist principles, thanks to the new emphasis on industrial production, even seemed to gain the upper hand.

A more picturesque regionalism was also present at the exhibition, although in a subordinate role. Thus, in a corner of the garden show, a model

[37] Ibid., 165–83 and 216–33. The use of functionalism for utilitarian constructions was not an exception, see also: Winfried Nerdinger, 'Bauhaus-Architekten im "Dritten Reich"', in: Winfried Nerdinger ed., *Bauhaus-Moderne im Nationalsozialismus: Zwischen Anbiederung und Verfolgung* (Munich 1993) 153–79.

forestry from the Lüneburg Heath in Lower Saxony with half-timbered walls and a hipped roof could be found. Some secondary buildings, such as a Hitler Youth Hostel, were built in a sober style inspired by vernacular buildings from the Lower-Rhine. Regionalism, however, was most visibly present in the folkloric costume of the young women who sold the lottery tickets, and in the restaurants, which mostly specialised in regional fare and thus were clearly recognisable from the outside. There were privately run establishments of varying sizes from Upper Bavaria, Franconia, Hamburg and Lower Saxony, whereas the area around Düsseldorf supplied taverns or cafés from the Bergisches Land, the Lower Rhine, the Mosel and the Harz. Most of these restaurants, like the enormous Upper Bavarian Beer Hall, were located at the peripheral but very popular funfair. Only at the central axis was the whole of Germany symbolically united under two huge Nazi flags, as a double row of thirty-six banners represented the main cities of the Reich.[38] Thus, in spite of the anti-urban ideas of some Nazi ideologues, the Nazis preferred to depict national unity – as they had done in Speer's pavilion in Paris and at the Olympic village in Berlin – as a homogeneous assembly of cities and not as a composition of different regions each with their own personality.

However, the exhibition was much more a unified whole than the accumulation of highly different elements and pavilions in a park-like setting that characterised the Parisian World's Fair. In Düsseldorf the different parts were more closely knit together by the architectural control of Grund, who had to approve the designs of all constructions and, more importantly, Maiwald's coherent programme. This in fact incorporated a central element of the regionalist ideology as its theme was the interaction of the German people with its surroundings, although the attention shifted from the harmonious interaction between man and nature that had existed in the past to the need of a more forceful human intervention in the present and future. The centrepiece of the exhibition was the raw materials display which was introduced in the first hall. Here the public could see how the main materials – coal, minerals, earth, stone and timber – were transformed into products. This theme was further elaborated in most of the other halls, where different branches of industry showed how they processed these materials. This was not a lifeless show as all the machines exhibited were in full operation. Another hall, dedicated to the German *Lebensraum* (living space), displayed the possibilities and limitations of Germany's natural conditions and resources, making it plain that the country had to exploit its

---

[38] Ibid, 164–5, 175–9 and 183.

resources more systematically and invent substitutes for those raw materials it lacked. The settlements, in turn, showed how the toiling German people could be housed, more in harmony with the environment and in better conditions, in both new suburbs and in settlements that were needed to colonise existing uncultivated areas. Finally, the garden exposition was to provide inspiration for recreational areas such as parks and gardens, while showing the love of the German people for nature.[39]

Although the exhibition proved to be a success, some major problems were hidden behind the façade. Many local Nazi leaders were implicated in a blackmail scandal that surfaced shortly before the exhibition and which led to the dismissal of mayor Wagenführ in April 1937. The fact that many of them, such as Gauleiter Florian and head architect Grund, also acquired a nice plot in the model settlement on very favourable terms, led to further rumours among the population. Moreover, some of the statues, commissioned by Grund, were removed during the exhibition for lack of quality, and Edwin Scharff even got into trouble because of his sculptures. He was asked by Grund to produce two statues of a man holding a horse, but because of financial and technical problems the statues were not finished in time which, because of their prominent position at the main entrance of the exhibition led to an embarrassing situation. Photographs of one of the unfinished statues even turned up at the notorious Degenerate Art Exhibit, which opened that same summer in Munich. This in fact finished off Scharff's career. In July that same year Grund was also discharged – probably for acting high-handedly and for his implication in these scandals – both as head architect of the exhibition and as director of the Art Academy. Finally, the exhibition ended with a significant deficit of almost 3 million Reichsmark. Nonetheless, these problems did not seriously affect the exhibition as they did not pass the strict censorship of the press.[40]

The biggest model settlement, located between the city, the river and the rest of the exhibition ground, was meant as a central part of the exposition and was named after Schlageter. Although at the start the streets were to receive the names of German colonial politicians, finally it was decided to follow the example of Ramersdorf, dedicating them to the martyrs of the Beer Hall Putsch. Soon, however, the settlement lost its prominent place. Initially it was hoped to build a settlement of

---

[39] E.W. Maiwald, '"Schaffendes Volk": Programm und Erfolg' and Ernst Walther, 'Der deutsche Lebensraum' in: Ernst W. Maiwald ed., *Reichsausstellung 'Schaffendes Volk' Düsseldorf 1937: Ein Bericht* (Düsseldorf 1939), I, respectively 31–40 and 63–77.
[40] Schäfers, *Vom Werkbund zum Vierjahresplan* 193–9, 213–16 and 308–12.

up to 150 free-standing houses in which all principal social groups and professions would form a harmonious community. But as the houses cost around 12,000, 20,000 and 30,000 Reichsmark, this in fact meant that even more than in Ramersdorf the poorest classes were excluded. Because of budgetary restraints and the changed focus finally it was decided to limit the amount of dwellings to eighty-four, and only eight model houses would be built by the town. The future inhabitants were made responsible for the construction and financing of the remaining houses, although the local savings bank could provide a mortgage on favourable conditions. They should take up residence in their new homes before the start of the exhibition. Nevertheless, the architects chosen by the future owners had to be approved by the organising committee, while they should follow the guidelines drawn up by Grund, who also chose the architects of the model houses and designed the overall lay-out.[41]

A small overview in one of the halls on the history of Düsseldorf, compiled by the municipality, in a way explained the main goals of the Schlageterstadt, which in great part was based on regionalist arguments. It showed how the 'rootedness of the houses, crafts and families in the soil' had given the inhabitants of the medieval town a true homeland (*Heimat*). Although the 'age of liberalism' – which referred to the preceding decades – had produced a few splendid avenues and squares, in general it had led to speculation, overpopulation and inorganic growth of the town. The uprooted masses in particular were housed in inhuman circumstances, where all bonds with nature were lost and class struggle poisoned social life. Fortunately, according to one of the authors of the official report of the exhibition, in 1933 a new era had set in. A clear rearrangement of workplaces, living quarters and recreation areas should lead to true communities within the town, where all fellow Germans through a 'proper home, a small garden or a park again acquires an interest in the native soil'. The individualism of the former period, which had produced incoherent villa colonies and slums, had been replaced by a new sense of community that should, as in the old German small towns, result in harmonious and functional settlements.[42]

Grund, who had been the architect of the first concrete church of Germany but also designed more traditional houses, adhered more openly to the principles of regionalism than Harbers had done in Ramersdorf. Grund, for example, declared that with the Schlagetertown he wanted to avoid

---

41 Ibid., 92–5 and 261–71 and 279–80.
42 Walther, 'Der deutsche Lebensraum' and Arnold Emundts, 'Die Schlageterstadt' in: Maiwald ed., *Reichsausstellung 'Schaffendes Volk'*, I, respectively 71–3 and 95–6.

the 'monotony and schematism' of most post-war developments. Instead he proposed to look for inspiration to old towns and villages, which were adjusted to the local landscape and culture and which consisted of unified, organically constructed communities with a clear centre. This meant that he tried to accommodate the streets and squares to the 'vastness of the landscape of the Lower Rhine', use local materials and find inspiration in the 'traditional construction culture' of the area.[43] Nonetheless, Grund, like other German architects before him, made sure that his ideals could not be interpreted as a claim for political decentralisation. Thus, although he referred to a particular region, the area from Düsseldorf down the Rhine to the Dutch border known as the Lower Rhine, this was not a very clearly delimitated region and it had never constituted a political entity. Thus his references to the Lower Rhine could not be misunderstood as an implicit plea for more regional autonomy.[44]

The head architect showed his regionalist inspiration in the lay-out which contained a large meadow that, like a traditional village green, formed the heart of the settlement. Grund further proscribed two-storey and semi-detached houses, whereas all constructions should have brick, whitewashed walls, which according to him had been customary in both Düsseldorf and the surrounding Lower Rhine countryside. They should also have a typical saddle roof with an inclination of 40–45 degrees, covered with grey Rhenian tiles (figure 39). Big windows and doors should connect the interiors with the gardens, and whenever possible existing trees were integrated in the lay-out. The gardens of the model houses, which were fully furnished and open to visitors during the exhibition, were designed by Alwin Seifert, the assistant of Fritz Todt responsible for embedding the new Autobahns in the surrounding landscape. He produced simple gardens with only native plants and trees and a direct entrance from the living quarters. However, Grund's main tool to give the whole settlement a unified outlook was a 1.20 m-high whitewashed brick wall that connected all premises and separated the front gardens from the street.[45]

43 Peter Grund, 'Düsseldorf Schlageterstadt', *Moderne Bauformen* (1937) 341–2. The article, in a slightly different version, also appeared as 'Die Gestaltung der Schlageterstadt', *Baugilde* (1937) 597–8 and as 'Die Gestaltung der Schlageterstadt', *Deutsche Bauzeitung* (June 1937) 75–81.
44 The only political unit that almost coincided with the Lower Rhine was the Prussian province Jülich, Kleve, Berg which was an assembly of smaller principalities. In 1815 it had become a new province of Prussia – including also Cologne – but already in 1822 it was incorporated in the much bigger Rhine Province.
45 Grund, 'Die Gestaltung der Schlageterstadt' 597–8, Emundts, 'Die Schlageterstadt' 95–9 and Schäfers, *Vom Werkbund zum Vierjahresplan* 264–76 and 295–8. The organisation also strongly advised that every house should have a proper air-raid shelter.

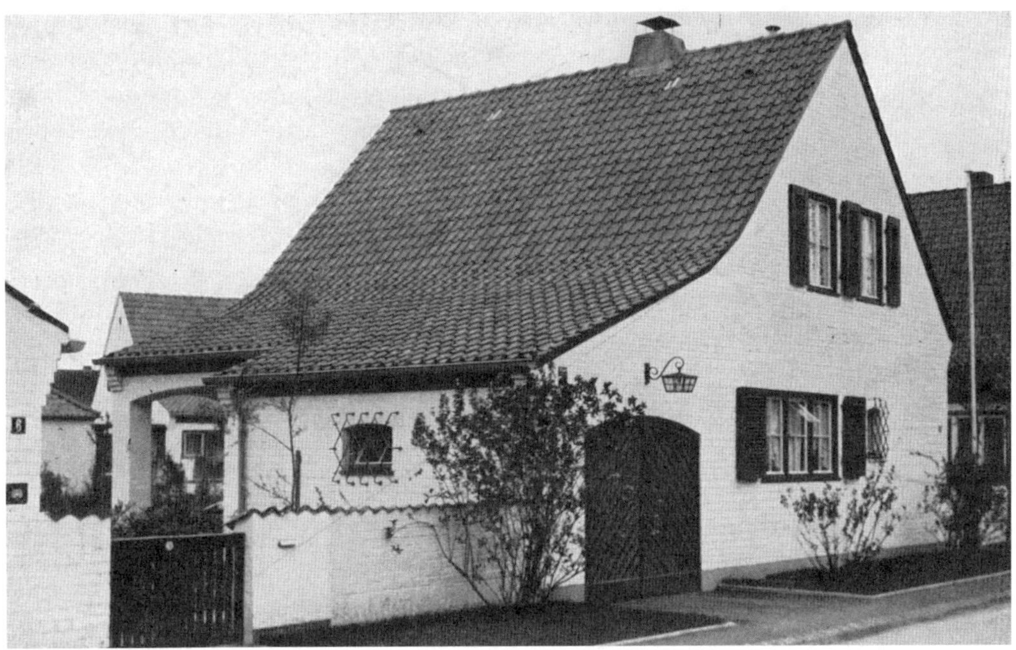

39 House at the Scheubner-Richter-Strasse (now Robert-Bernardis-Strasse), Schlageter Settlement, Düsseldorf, 1937. This house, constructed by Helmut Nicolaus Schröder, was among the smallest in the settlement, although it contained a garage, a covered terrace and a substantial garden.

The same principles were also applied to the small homestead settlement at the other end of the exhibition ground, in a corner of the garden show. As land prices in Düsseldorf were high it was decided to keep the houses and gardens relatively small in order not to exceed the budget of a worker's family. And as the town had to finance and prepare the land only a tiny settlement with thirteen houses and a settlers' school was constructed. The settlement, named after another Nazi martyr Wilhelm Gustloff who, as a leader of the Swiss branch of the NSDAP, had been shot in 1936 by a Jewish student, looked even more like a village than the middle-class Schlageterstadt. The thirteen free-standing houses with their 800–1,000 m² gardens – which was slightly under the minimum that in 1936 had been established as the norm for this kind of homestead – were assembled around a village green that functioned as common pasture land for small animals, a playground for children and a meeting place for the community (figure 40). The Lower Rhine construction materials, saddle roof and the low whitewashed brick wall that connected the houses were identical to the bigger settlement. Only the living quarters were significantly smaller (48–65 m²), whereas the homesteads all had a small stable and a kitchen garden.[46]

---

[46] L. Schmalhorst, 'Die Wilhelm-Gustloff-Siedlung' in: Maiwald ed., *Reichsausstellung 'Schaffendes Volk'*, I 101–4, *Reichsausstellung Schaffendes Volk Düsseldorf 1937 Mai-Oktober* (Düsseldorf 1937) 119–24 and Schäfers, *Vom Werkbund zum Vierjahresplan* 249–60.

271

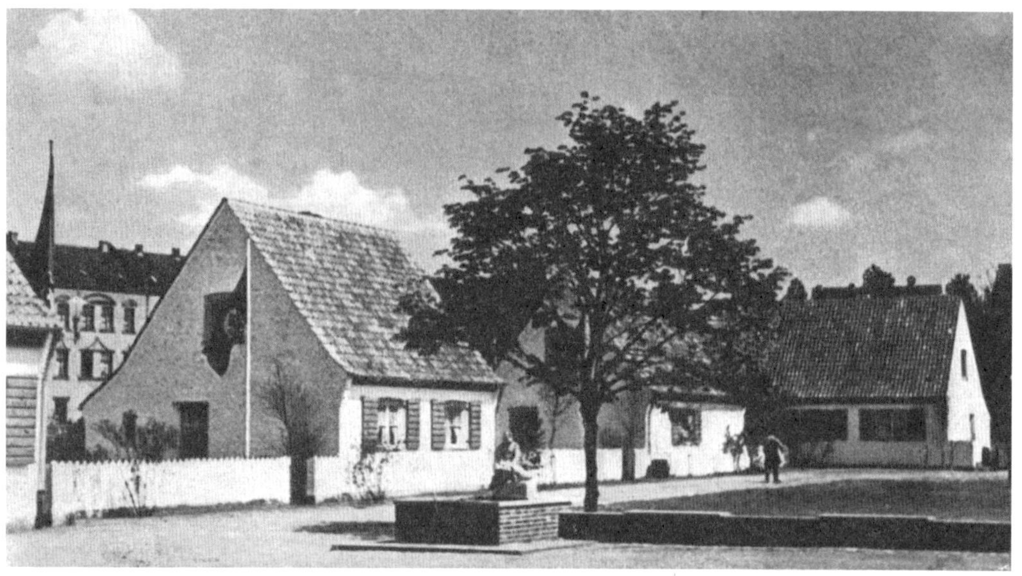

40 Village green with three homesteads at the Wilhelm Gustloff Settlement, Düsseldorf, 1937.

The catalogue of the exhibition stated that for the maintenance of social peace it was essential to provide homes for the working population. As a result the Third Reich had decided to construct 100,000 homesteads a year to combat the housing shortage. However, it was not easy to design a cheap and healthy house for a large family with an efficient layout. The model houses of the Gustloff settlement were to provide inspiration for future building schemes. A further issue of concern was the selection of the settlers. The houses were no longer built for the unemployed, as had been the case in the early 1930s, but for capable, hard-working and 'racially valuable' workers. As most of them originated from the cities, they should be taught how to work the land and keep small animals. The houses were meant for families in which the man was the wage-earner, while the wives would be mainly responsible for the garden and the animals.[47]

Looking at the model settlements it seemed that regionalism had again triumphed, although not in the picturesque manner as in Seville or Paris, but toned down in a sober and more uniform way. This impression could also be obtained from the catalogue, where the description of the Gustloff Settlement ended with a quote from a recently deceased Gauleiter:

47 Schmalhorst, 'Wilhelm-Gustloff-Siedlung', I 101–4, *Reichsausstellung Schaffendes Volk* 119–20 and Schäfers, *Vom Werkbund zum Vierjahresplan* 258–60. See for the change in the settlement policy also: Ute Peltz-Dreckmann, *Nationalsozialistischer Siedlungsbau: Versuch einer Analyse der die Siedlungspolitik bestimmenden Faktoren am Beispiel des Nationalsozialismus* (Munich 1978) 134, 137–40.

'The march of national socialism is the way to the homeland' (*Heimat*).[48] However, this proved to be a false impression, as the main priority of Hitler's policy was not to provide a comfortable and peaceful home in spacious green neighbourhoods for all Germans. The improvement of the living conditions was clearly subordinate to Hitler's programme of preparing the country for war, and as a result the share of spending on housing in the total State budget sharply diminished.[49] Although one could argue that the settlements in a regionalist style only served propaganda purposes and had to convince the population of future prosperity, it seems clear that many lower-level Nazis and local collaborators such as Grund and Harbers sincerely believed that the regime would focus on raising the standards of living and improve housing conditions. Hitler's true intentions, nonetheless, could be intuited in the hall dedicated to the German *Lebensraum*.

At the entrance of the *Lebensraum* exhibit the organiser, the city planner Gustav Langen, still paid tribute to regionalism by showing how, during the last ten centuries, 'our fathers' had struggled to create the 'homeland' by using the country's natural resources and producing all kind of artisanal objects. Consequently, the German nature, landscape and monuments had to be actively preserved. However, in the rest of the hall he made clear that Germany's natural resources were too limited for its present and future needs. Thus, too intensive cultivation had diminished the ground's fertility. Drastic measures, such as the development of the Lüneburg Heath and other marshes and moorlands, could change this alarming situation and provide work for hundreds of thousands of new settlers. The structural lack of water for the needs of the German people, livestock, industry and agriculture also required vigorous intervention on a grand scale. Wind protection measures should further influence the climate in a positive way. However, not only did the German nature and its resources have to be restructured, it was also necessary to reallocate the population, the industry and the infrastructure in a more logical way. As some areas were too densely populated a resettlement of part of the population and industry to the countryside was highly recommendable. Reviewing the German living space in this way, and taking into consideration the lack of raw materials, which was the leitmotiv of the Four-Year Plan, there were two possible solutions. The first was a more systematic protection and exploitation of existing resources, which also included the resettlement of part of the

---

48   *Reichsausstellung Schaffendes Volk* 124.
49   Peltz-Dreckmann, *Nationalsozialistischer Siedlungsbau* 144, 168–73 and 188–9.

population to the countryside and especially to newly cultivated areas; secondly, a comparison of the map of the German population density with a similar map of the world made it clear that, according to the author of the official report on the exhibition, Germany could 'claim the right to develop other almost uninhabited spaces'.[50]

Although the exhibition in fact only elaborated the first option, it is obvious that Hitler preferred the second: the country needed more living space, which for lack of colonies had to be found in Eastern Europe. Both solutions were fundamentally contrary to the regionalist ideals. The first entailed a large-scale intervention in nature and huge resettlement programmes, which were contrary to a supposed longstanding, harmonious interaction between man and nature; the second meant war. During subsequent years Hitler also made clear that a slow adaptation of nature, inspired by tradition, was not to his liking. Instead he preferred natural and social engineering on a scale never seen before. Thus already before the war he started a vast 'euthanasia' campaign directed against disabled people, with tens of thousands of victims. The war in the East led to ethnic cleansing on an unprecedented scale. A 'perfect' way to increase the *Lebensraum* of the ethnically pure German people was the reclaiming of swamps in occupied Poland and Ukraine, where thousands of Jews and other 'racially unfit' were worked to death in order to provide future German settlers with badly needed new land. That his social engineering in fact meant racial engineering was made clear in the extermination camps, where millions of Jews were gassed to death.[51]

The emphasis on race also makes clear why regionalism was disregarded by the leading Nazis. Racial factors were more important than historical traditions and environmental influences. As a result it was not very urgent to root people in the soil, reconnect them with tradition and house them in cottages in their native region. Like the Breton architect Bouillé, who thought that a Celt would remain a Celt wherever he was 'exiled', to Hitler it did not matter where a German lived, as a consequence it was no problem

---

[50]   Walther, 'Der deutsche Lebensraum' 63–77. The same arguments could be found in the article by Gustav Langen, the city planner who, as leader of the German Archive for Settlement Issues, had organised the exhibit: Gustav Langen, 'Die Halle "Deutscher Lebensraum" auf der Ausstellung "Schaffendes Volk", Düsseldorf 1937', *Zentralblatt der Bauverwaltung* (12 May 1937) 473–4.

[51]   See for example Götz Aly, *'Endlösung': Völkerverschiebung und der Mord an den europäischen Juden* (Frankfurt am Main 1995), Thomas M. Lekan, *Imagining the Nation in Nature: Landscape Preservation and German Identity 1885–1945* (Cambridge 2004) 153–252 and David Blackbourn, *The Conquest of Water: Water, Landscape and the Making of Modern Germany* (London 2006) 239–96.

to him to move people as if they were cattle. Homestead settlements in a generic regionalist style would be perfect to rapidly reroot 'ethnically pure' Germans in the newly conquered areas in Eastern Europe and thus enormously expand the fatherland. Regions and regional identities, as a result, lost their interest in the face of Hitler's all-encompassing racial determinism.

How, then, did the press judge the role of regionalism? As could be expected with an exhibition that received full support from Berlin and was visited by many leading Nazis, most reviews were very positive and recommended a trip to Düsseldorf. A substantial number of the critics limited themselves to giving a brief, approving description of the different elements of the exhibition. For instance, Wernher Witthaus, in a rather superficial review in the *Zentralblatt der Bauverwaltung*, praised the 'healthy guidelines' for the architects of the Schlageterstadt, the lay-out of the exhibition and the unity with the surrounding landscape. More ideologically charged was the positive comment in the *Deutsche Bauhütte*, the journal that in 1934 had harshly criticised the Ramersdorf settlement for not complying with the new ideals of the Third Reich. The Düsseldorf exhibition, according to the anonymous author, distanced itself totally from the prevailing liberalistic tone of former exhibitions with their 'gilded cartouche architecture' and unhealthy competition as it bore testimony to the new guided economy that served the State and its Four-Year Plan.[52]

Nonetheless, negative remarks could also be found in the specialised press, although obviously nobody dared to criticise the more political aspects of the exhibition. Thus Ingo Beucker (1906–90), a young architect who had studied with Schmitthenner in Stuttgart, criticised the lack of unity between the various parts of the exhibition in his review in *Baugilde*. This was somewhat surprising as he had been commissioned by Grund to design one of the model houses in the Schlagetertown. Nevertheless, as he had been one of the winners of the architectural contest of the Schlageter Forum, he clearly had his own ideas about the lay-out of the exhibition ground. He also explained that some deficiencies were due to organisational problems. Hence, the existing sewage treatment plant, which lay between the settlement and the halls, could not be removed, and a planned Führer Tower, intended to function as a focal point of the exhibition, was not

52 Witthaus, 'Reichsausstellung "Schaffendes Volk" in Düsseldorf: Die Städtebauliche Ausrichtung', *Zentralblatt der Bauverwaltung* (4 August 1937) 791–4 and 'Von der Reichsausstellung "Schaffendes Volk" in Düsseldorf', *Deutsche Bauhütte* (1937) 220–1.

built.[53] Another critic, most probably the young architect Alfons Leitl, similarly criticised the lack of logical transitions between the various parts of the exhibition and the lay-out of the main square next to the river, where a huge fountain and a small pavilion almost impeded the view to the Rhine from the terrace of the restaurant. He praised the settlements as the short winding streets, the identically inclined roofs and other common elements had resulted in a pleasant unified whole. Nevertheless, he was not convinced by most individual houses as the architects had used too much unnecessary, pretty details, such as traditional keystones, glass bars and rounded arches.[54]

In their comments, some reviewers clearly put their own spin on events. Notwithstanding the fact that the focus of the exhibition had moved to the Four-Year Plan and the industrial exhibits in the halls, some still underlined the more regionalist elements. This was fully understandable for the architect Winfried Wendland (1903–98), a close collaborator of Lörcher at the Werkbund who, in February 1936, announced the initial plan of the exhibition in *Baugilde*. At that stage he still thought that a great show of arts and crafts would form one of the main attractions of the exhibition. Regionalism in his view would have a prominent place in this exhibit as every region or province (*Gau*) should provide a typical arts or crafts workshop. Guido Harbers who, in his *Der Baumeister*, dedicated only a few pages to the exhibition, again used some broadly regionalist arguments. In his short notice he mentioned that at the exhibition one could see the constant high quality of German production and its 'variety according to the characteristics of the tribes'. He further argued that in the garden show 'technique and culture, human diligence and nature interpenetrate and complement each other'.[55]

Emil Fahrenkamp (1885–1966), the well-known, moderately modernist architect of the halls at the main square, on the contrary, defended functionalist principles in his own article on the exhibition. These aesthetic preferences were no obstacle for him to become the successor of Grund

<hr>

53 Ingo Beucker, 'Ausstellung "Schaffendes Volk", Düsseldorf 1937', *Baugilde* (15 June 1937) 589–91. See also: Schäfers, *Vom Werkbund zum Vierjahresplan*, 122, 300 and 407.
54 Ll., 'Schaffendes Volk: Die Düsseldorfer Ausstellung', *Monatshefte für Baukunst und Städtebau* (1937) 205–6 and Ll, 'Die Wohnsiedlung des schaffenden Volkes', *Monatshefte für Baukunst und Städtebau* (1937) 233–4. Both articles were also published in *Bauwelt*, respectively (3 June 1937) 1–2 and (1 July 1937) 1–2.
55 Winfried Wendland, '"Schaffendes Volk": Große Deutsche Ausstellung 1937 Düsseldorf-Schlageterstadt', *Baugilde* (15 February 1936) 129 and Guido Harbers, 'Aus den Ausstellungen "Schaffendes Volk" Düsseldorf 1937 und Jahresschau "Garten und Heim" Dresden 1937', *Der Baumeister* (September 1937) 279.

as director of the local Art Academy that same year.[56] Other authors also stressed more modernist aspects. Thus, Hans Weingarten asserted in *Die Bauzeitung* that also the German construction industry had to do its part by applying more synthetic materials. He further was very enthusiastic about the 18 m overhanging reinforced concrete slab that protected the pavilion of the Slag Cement Association. Nonetheless, he also praised the 'homely farmhouse style' of the model settlement, as its inhabitants were reconnected with the soil, and in a way 'the town is given back to the landscape'. In another article in the same magazine the houses were – similar to the program of the Regional Centre in Paris – presented as a renovated, up-to-date regionalism. Thus both the individual houses and the settlement fitted perfectly in the Lower Rhine landscape, whereas the architects had used new materials to design light and airy rooms. According to the anonymous author this type of 'neue Bauen' – which was the generally accepted German name for architectural modernism – provided an excellent solution to the problems of the 'national-socialist community housing'. Nonetheless, it seemed that community feelings were most needed among the workers, as in another notice on the Gustloff Settlement, the author maintained that the village green was a meeting place where the concept of 'national community' should become a reality, and even added: 'Particularly the homestead settler should know that he too is only a link in the chain of our community life.'[57]

Even *Bauen, Siedeln, Wohnen* who in 1934 had stressed the regionalist aspect of the Ramersdorf settlement, now put more emphasis on modern aspects and the use of new materials. It also mentioned that one model house was electrically fully equipped, whereas another functioned with gas. Although it also underscored the need to provide the worker with a healthy and pleasant home that fitted well into the surrounding landscape, it presented the settler who had to develop new land for the fatherland as a 'front-line soldier of the battle for production'.[58]

The vital question of how to combine modernity with tradition – or, better still, when to apply modern solutions and when regionalist recipes – was answered in an anonymous review in *Bauwelt*. The author first

[56]   Emil Fahrenkamp, 'Ausstellungsbauten', *Moderne Bauformen* (1937) 338–40.

[57]   Hans Weingarten, 'Reichsausstellung "Schaffendes Volk", Düsseldorf: Vierjahresplan bringt neue Aufgaben – neues Bauen, Siedeln und Wohnen!', 'Ein Stadtteil ausstellungsmässig gesehen' and 'Eine Heimstättensiedlung auf der Ausstellung "Schaffendes Volk"', *Die Bauzeitung* (10 May 1937), respectively 189–93, 194–6 and 198–9.

[58]   'Die Schlageterstadt – Ein neuer Stadtteil Düsseldorfs' and 'Reichsausstellung "Schaffendes Volk" in Düsseldorf', *Bauen, Siedeln, Wohnen* (1 June 1937), respectively 279–83 and 276–8.

stressed the need to further experiment with new construction materials. The exhibition halls and pavilions in particular were a perfect field for innovation and at the Düsseldorf exhibition the significant traits of the future could already be discerned: unpretentious, simple and straight forms almost without decoration and strong horizontal lines. Nonetheless, the author also acknowledged that when building a house one should not only follow rational principles, but also serve the needs of the soul. As a result it would not be wise to replace the old familiar forms with new technical and economically efficient ones. Sentimental values, after all, were only shaped during longer periods of time. Therefore it was perfectly logical to take old towns and villages as a model for the new settlement, as Grund had done. Very suggestive and sentimental also were some of the structures at the fun fair, by which he probably referred to the Bavarian beer hall.[59]

In fact, the critic perfectly indicated that, as the exhibition had made clear, the use of a regionalist style was only justified in two domains. First as a sober, generic regionalism applied to free-standing and terraced houses in new suburbs, where the houses were loosely modelled on simple vernacular houses which were not largely typical of one region only. Whereas before 1914 picturesque villas with irregular plans, complicated roofs, bow-windows and dormers had set the tone, now rectangular forms, straight walls and simple inclined roofs were preferred. The house should be cheap and efficient but nonetheless provide a pleasant and comfortable home by the stress on its cosiness and its closeness to nature and local traditions.

The other domain in which regionalism was still viable was in the commercial and tourist sector, of which exhibition pavilions also could form a part. In general regionalist references in this field were more exuberant. They now had to embody either a specific region by selecting its most idiosyncratic elements, or provide a more general image of tradition, artisanship and authenticity.

In both cases, however, regionalism was justified for non-architectural reasons. Thus the attempts, in both France and in Germany, to revive and modernise regionalism as a relevant architectural current had, in fact, failed. It was no longer an innovative tendency, but just a recipe that could be attached to any structure as all other styles from the past. In fact, it was its own principles of authenticity, constructive honesty and the need to profit from the specific characteristics of each material that impeded the use of concrete and steel. One could openly show the new materials but use

---

59 'Schaffendes Volk: Erster Eindruck von der Düsseldorfer Ausstellung', *Bauwelt* (13 May 1937) 420–2.

traditional forms that had been developed for other materials, or hide them in a traditional wrapping. In both cases, however, the proper ideals were betrayed. And for reasons of efficiency and economy it became increasingly illogical to reject the use of the new techniques and materials.

At the same time it has become clear that the Nazis attempted to appropriate regionalism for its own purposes. First they adopted the rejection of functionalism by traditional architects like Schultze-Naumburg. It even seems that a considerable faction of high Nazi officials sincerely supported most of the regionalist ideals. This seemed to have been the case for Rosenberg, Feder, Ludovici and Wendland, and partly also for other leading Nazis such as Ley and the minister of Agriculture, Walther Darré, a close friend of Schulze-Naumburg. However, most of them were soon relegated to less influential positions, while others seemed to have lost their interest in regionalism when they understood that Hitler's priorities lay elsewhere. The rearmament programme, the preparations for war, the quest for *Lebensraum*, the dominance of racial issues, and especially the highly interventionist attitude to both the natural environment and to human beings was incompatible with the regionalist ideal of a varied society that was the product of the harmonious and organic interrelationship between man and nature.

Conclusion

International exhibitions were nationalist ventures par excellence. They should show the greatness of the proper nation and in the 1920s and 1930s regionalism received a prominent place at major expositions in all the countries under review. Strikingly, however, the nationalist tone was determined in the first place by the presence or lack of a colonial empire. Thus, although France had difficulties in keeping up with other leading nations in some fields, its enormous colonial empire still guaranteed its status as great power and this was an important source of national pride. This became manifest in the huge International Colonial Exhibition of 1931 which even received slightly more visitors than the considerably bigger World's Fair of 1937. And in 1937 the colonies were prominently presented as an organic extension of the motherland, embodied by the Regional Centre. In Spain and Germany, however, the situation was different, which could be noted in their less confident attitude.

Spain had lost its last main remaining colonies in 1898 and subsequently directed its efforts to reinforcing the bonds with the former American colonies in a kind of commonwealth of Spanish-speaking countries. This had been the main rationale behind the Ibero-American Exhibition in Seville, which included pavilions of the former American colonies and even of the rather modest remaining African possessions. Nonetheless, this could not redeem the loss of the once immense empire; and the awareness of the fundamental weakness of Spain's international position led to a broadly felt insecurity. For example, this was reflected in the exaggerated and aggrieved nationalistic remarks of various critics; some even asserted, referring to the exhibition ground in Seville, that 'nothing similar was ever made in the world'.

In Germany, many were also under the spell of the colonialist logic, and this was particularly true for most Nazis. As latecomer Germany had lost its rather modest colonial empire with the Versailles Treaty, a sense of frustration was widely felt. The Nazis even felt claustrophobically restricted in a too limited territory, which according to them even threatened the vital power of the nation. Following the traditional channels of emigration, the solution could best be found in the east. This was also clearly visible at the exhibition in Düsseldorf with its stress on *Lebensraum* and homesteads for future settlers. And it was probably for failing to address these issues in Ramersdorf, where Harbers had paid only lip service to the need of inner colonisation, that the German Settlement Exhibition was largely ignored by the party leadership.

Regionalism, at least for the various exhibitions, received the support of most parties along the political spectrum. From Nazis, right-wing nationalists and conservatives to liberals, moderate and progressive republicans and socialists, all major interwar political currents seemed in favour of regionalism. More difficult to ascertain is the ideological content that was contributed to regionalism by the various architects, organisers and politicians.

In Spain, regionalist architecture was embraced in different fashions and for different reasons. The organisers of the Barcelona World's Fair did not see this current as a serious option and merely chose to construct a kind of open-air museum with vernacular copies from all Spanish regions. For most local politicians this seemed to imply that they saw a modern and cosmopolitan Catalonia as being connected to the admirable Spanish heritage. In Seville, ruled by a small bipartisan oligarchy, regionalism became the official style of the entire exhibition. This time it seemed that its use was meant to give the workers and lower-middle classes a dignified place in both the local community and the nation by stressing the value of artisanal quality production, whereas at the same time, by stimulating feelings of regional and national identification, it should induce the masses to accept the existing political system and its local representatives. This could be interpreted as an undemocratic attempt to stimulate a deferential attitude towards the existing authorities, but as the activities of González Álvarez made clear, this could also be explained as a sincere endeavour to convert the city's inhabitants into conscientious citizens. Primo de Rivera appropriated both exhibitions for his own goals, although only when in 1925 he decided that his regime had to mobilise the active support of the population did he secure a rapid completion of the preparations. Any hints at political regionalism were proscribed, but the dictator happily embraced harmless expressions of cultural regionalism, which perfectly accorded with his own mainly paternalistic political and social views.

The Parisian World's Fair of 1937, which had been conceived just before the end of the exhibitions of Barcelona and Seville, showed a different kind of regionalism. The organisers wanted to modernise regionalist architecture by using contemporary materials and techniques while respecting regional traditions and natural circumstances, whereas at the same time they hoped to re-animate the crafts by improving their standards. These attempts, at least in the architectural field, were not very convincing as regionalism could not live up to its own principles. Also the decentralised organisation of the Regional Centre was not a great success as most pavilions could only be inaugurated when the exhibition had been open to the public for several months. Some critics even longed for a more authoritarian strong hand. Nonetheless, the delays were not so much caused by a weak organisation as by strikes and a lagging interest among the new Popular Front government, whose priorities lay elsewhere. One could even maintain that by making every region responsible for its proper representation, although within a clearly supervised unified framework, the organisers chose to bring into practice the ideal of regional decentralisation, thus offering channels for a broad nationwide participation.

Whereas regional variety was respected and even highlighted as the essence of a unified fatherland in Spain and France, this was not the case in Germany. However, here municipal and regional autonomy traditionally was much stronger than in the heavily centralised political systems of France and Spain. Probably the trauma of the long history of a divided and marginalised Germany did not allow regionalism to closely identify with a particular existing or former political unit as happened in France and Spain. Thus in Munich one could refer to an Upper Bavarian style, whereas in Düsseldorf the organisers even openly spoke of a Lower Rhine tradition. However, both loosely defined areas were parts of larger political entities such as Bavaria and the Prussian Rhine Province. Moreover, at

German exhibitions instead of a more picturesque regionalism that clearly stressed the particular characteristics of one specific region, the organisers preferred a generic regionalism that referred to the countryside in a much more general sense. The Nazis seemed even less inclined to show Germany's regional variety. When they decided to represent the various geographical parts of the country in a representative building or complex, they chose to depict the country as an abstracted and uniform assembly of towns. However, especially in the early years, Nazi Germany was not a monolithic whole. Feder and some other high-ranking Nazis apparently hoped to transform Germany into a rural utopia of traditional small towns and villages. By reconnecting the German nation to the soil and its native traditions, regionalism could function as a weapon against the dehumanisation of capitalism and the degenerated life in the big metropolis. Others, like Harbers and Grund, preferred to create peaceful middle-class havens by using a more generic regionalism to construct comfortable and cosy homes in a pleasant green neighbourhood. Hitler, on the other hand, did not show much interest in regionalism as he was obsessed with the creation of a racially pure, extended German Empire, in which regional differences seemed irrelevant. Regionalism was clearly subordinate to his quest for *Lebensraum*, and seemed only useful for giving the population the prospect of a peaceful home in the future in order to better resist the hardships of the coming war.

Thus, the exhibitions also showed the limitations of regionalism. Its most fervent supporters belonged to the moderate progressive and conservative political establishment, whereas the Catalan elites, the French Popular Front government and the Nazis were less enthusiastic. The first preferred to give Barcelona a modern and cosmopolitan outlook in order to reinforce a proper Catalan sense of identity. The left-wing politicians of the Popular Front, in turn, were not very interested in regional differences and tried to mobilise the lower classes through their own organisations, which were divided along ideological and not along regional lines. And from the opposite side of the political spectrum, the same in fact was true for the Nazis, although for Hitler race seemed the decisive factor.

The exhibitions in Barcelona, Seville, Paris, Munich and Düsseldorf confirmed the decline of regionalist architecture as a convincing and innovative architectural current that had already become clear in the aftermath of the First World War. The reconstitution of the devastated areas was not done, as had been planned optimistically during that war, in a neo-vernacular style with local materials and in harmony with the surrounding nature. The magnitude of the enterprise, the difficult economic situation and the urgency to provide many people with a decent home within the shortest possible period made it necessary to use new materials and techniques and build in a more efficient, almost industrial way. The subsequent rise and success of a more functional ethos relegated regionalist architecture to a secondary position. Although regionalist buildings continued to be designed and constructed, in fact regionalism only had a meaningful heritage in two areas: tourism and suburban housing. This was also evident at the analysed exhibitions. Thus regionalism could profitably be applied in spectacular picturesque exhibition buildings – of which many of the pavilions of the Regional Centre and particularly González Álvarez's masterpiece at the Plaza de España were a good example – that had to attract visitors. The model settlements in Munich and Düsseldorf, on the other hand, showed a more watered-down regionalism that in the first instance was meant to make the inhabitants feel at home, by intimately connecting them to the *Heimat*, which was the German term that perfectly embodied this more generic regionalism.

As we have seen, regionalism was absorbed, purged, disarmed and finally perverted by the Nazis. Many regionalists happily collaborated with the new regime, but most soon became irrelevant. Vichy France, which in fact also made regionalism part of its ideology, largely followed the same steps. As a result after 1945 the memory of regionalism had become tainted by its association with fascism. The renewed rise of modernism furthermore enormously raised the status of the earlier avant-gardes. As a result the regionalist ideology was for several decades condemned to a historiographical limbo, and this was also true for regionalist architecture. Both were now seen as backward-looking movements that were mere obstacles on the road of progress and as a consequence they were almost completely disregarded by all kind of scholars; when they received some attention, it was generally used to condemn them as precursors of fascism. However, as we have seen, this is an extremely biased interpretation.

Conclusion

Regionalism was an international phenomenon. Its ideology, arguments, rhetoric and values were almost identical in Germany, France and Spain, and its rise, heyday and demise showed great similarities and parallels. In this regard, it also resembled the careers of its most important representatives. The culture of regionalism, thus, was fundamentally the work of one generation, born between about 1860 and 1875.

The regionalist ideology was quite simple. A regional culture – like its national counterpart – was the product of a specific *Volksgeist*, which was the result of the interaction between man and his natural environment over the ages, as embodied in tradition. Moreover, regionalists, like the new nationalists, urged that contemporary painters, artists, architects, writers and musicians should also conform to the particular *Volksgeist* of a region in order to produce 'good' art.

In the case of painting this meant that an artist should preferably try to explicate the particular *Volksgeist* of a certain area in his work. This could best be done – as the regionalist painters treated in this book did – by showing the organic interaction of man and nature in a specific area. However, by depicting typical landscapes, buildings or people, a painter could also contribute his bit – although in a less ambitious manner – towards a better interpretation of the 'soul' of a particular region. One could even imagine that by painting the uprooted life of the workers in industrial areas, or the decadent life of the cosmopolitan upper classes in the big metropolis, an artist could also further the cause of regionalism by showing the ill fate of those who had lost contact with their 'roots'. The regionalist ideology thus mainly influenced the subject of the painting: showing a synthesis of regional life, the 'spirit' of a specific region. However, indirectly it also had an impact on stylistic issues. The populist character of regionalism meant that a painting should be comprehensible to ordinary people. The stress on authenticity, nonetheless, impeded a return to the slick and theatrical style of academic art, whereas the painterly innovations of the impressionists could be used to produce lively images and snapshots of regional life. Nevertheless technical virtuosity should not occupy centre stage, nor should a painter merely show an aspect of visual reality. By making technique subordinate to the topic and art to ideology, regionalist painting was rapidly swept away by the rise of the avant-garde. Around 1905 it had already lost its main innovative impetus, and after the First World War it became almost completely irrelevant, in both the art market and in artistic debates. However, this did not mean that regionalist and nationalist arguments disappeared as they continued to play an important role in the artistic discussions in the 1920s and 1930s.

Regionalism had a greater impact on architecture, although it started slightly later than in painting. According to the regionalist ideology constructions, and particularly houses, should be adapted to the local *Volksgeist*, which in practice meant that local construction materials should be used together with forms and techniques that were traditionally used in a specific area. Architects should not slavishly copy vernacular examples, but creatively use local traditions and materials to design up-to-date buildings that perfectly suited the needs of the users while fitting harmoniously into the environment. In the early years of the twentieth century, when regionalism became a favourite style for the construction of country houses and villas, various striking forms, elements and materials from a number of typical vernacular buildings were combined to construct attractive ensembles, in which the multiform spaces – mostly under a huge inclined roof – formed a unified, organic whole. Later on, particularly in new garden cities and social housing developments, a more generic regionalism also became popular. The favoured sources of inspiration were no longer the most conspicuous buildings from a particular region which could not be found anywhere else, but a more generic regionalist type: a simple, rectangular house, with an inclined tiled roof, eventually with shutters or other clearly recognisable traditional elements, and a garden.

As with painting, regionalism's emphasis on authenticity and tradition hampered the successful adaptation of regionalist architecture to the new circumstances of the interwar period. This was the case especially with the upcoming techniques based on steel and concrete which were not connected to any area or local tradition in particular. A regionalist house in concrete, steel and glass was a contradiction in terms. The difficult economic situation in the post-war years and after 1929, moreover, made it urgent to build dwellings in an effective and cheap way with efficient (and thus modern) materials, prefabricated elements and industrial techniques.

By using natural materials that had become more expensive and labour-intensive artisanal techniques, regionalism in its most picturesque variant simply priced itself out of the market. As a result, after about 1920 regionalist architecture – like regionalist painting slightly before – was not any longer a very relevant current in the architectural debates, although in practice it continued to play an important role. For non-architectural reasons, a watered down version of regionalism remained especially popular in the field of social housing, exhibitions and tourism, as it could give people a sense of home, reinforce regional and national identities, or provide a convenient – and often commercially successful – image of authenticity and tradition to restaurants, hotels and producers of artisanal products. In social housing this meant the rise of a more generic regionalism that was produced in a cheap and standardised form. For tourism and at exhibitions, on the contrary, an excessive and generally artificial or even fake regionalism became popular to attract the attention of potential visitors.

At the various major exhibitions in the 1920s and 1930s, regionalism was therefore not used primarily because it was seen as a vigorous and relevant cultural tendency, but mainly because it was considered politically useful. Nonetheless, the forms it took varied remarkably. At the Barcelona World's Fair of 1929 the Spanish village embodied the vernacular and artisanal heritage of Spain as a complement to the treasures of high art that were shown at the National Palace just above it. At the Ibero-American Exhibition of Seville in the same year almost all pavilions were constructed in a somewhat eclectic regionalist style. It was assumed that regionalism would strengthen both the local and national character of Seville, attract tourists and stimulate the local artisanal industries. At the same time it would encourage the population to identify with both the city and the nation and indirectly also with the existing political system and its leading elite. The Parisian World's Fair of 1937, and especially the Regional Centre, were meant to show the regional variety of France and the intimate and indissoluble relation between the regions and the fatherland. The decentralised organisation aimed to further encourage the participation of people from the provinces and stimulate artisanal production all over the country. In Nazi Germany, on the contrary, a regionalism that underlined the idiosyncratic character of a specific region had only a very peripheral role at exhibitions. Thus, at the *Schaffendes Volk* exhibition in Düsseldorf in 1937 a picturesque regionalism was merely applied to sell lottery tickets, regional dishes and drinks. On the other hand, both in Düsseldorf and at the 1934 German Settlement Exhibition in Munich, a more generic regionalism applied to housing was on display. Simple but comfortable houses with an inclined, tiled roof, shutters and a garden in a pleasant green environment were designed to give the 'racially pure' inhabitants a sense of home and (re)connect them to the German soil.

However, the different political usages of regionalism and the different forms it could take should not be understood as different (national) currents within the regionalist ideology. The arguments, values and rhetoric used in the various domains and countries were generally very similar if not identical. However, regionalism could be expressed in different forms and for different uses. As a consequence, it is not regionalism itself that has to be explained from a national context, which is what many scholars have done, but it is the preference for a specific form of regionalism or its dominant presence in a specific field, which should be explained within a national or local background, or with reference to the decisions of individual artists, architects, organisers or politicians.

Let us first turn to what regionalist painting, architecture and pavilions can tell us about regionalism in general. A striking common element in regionalist painting was that its main representatives and advocates had a clear preference for certain regions, such as Brittany in France, the coastal areas in Germany and Castile in Spain. From reviews by sympathetic critics we can deduce that these regions were regarded as largely untouched by foreign influence and international modernity; here the vestiges of an original, even pre-Roman, civilisation could be found. In fact, the regionalist painters focused on those areas where supposedly some of the ingredients of the original national *Volksgeist* could still be found. According to some critics, these original elements could be helpful to combat the current decadence and regenerate the country as it was widely felt that a national identity crisis could be overcome by a wholesale reorientation towards the nation's presumed true collective personality. This means that regionalist painting was closely connected with the nation-building activities of a new exalted nationalism, as promoted by Langbehn, Barrès, Ganivet and others. The perspective of these painters (and critics) was essentially national, which in part was understandable because they produced their work essentially for a national and even an international market. However, almost none of the painters, or the authors who defended their work, had close contacts with a particular regional movement, and most artists were not even born or raised in the region they preferred to depict. Although nationalist in intention, their paintings clearly (re-)defined the identities of many picturesque regions, and they also contributed strongly to the new appreciation of the traditional popular culture of the provinces and its incorporation into the national heritage.

In the case of architecture, regionalism seemed less attached to the centre and to the new exalted or *völkisch* nationalism. Regionalist architects moreover clearly preferred other regions than the painters as they had to build where there was sufficient demand. Thus in France, where they depended mostly on commissions for second homes, it was not remote Brittany that attracted most architects but Normandy and other parts of the Atlantic coast that were within easy reach of Paris. The ancient, half-timbered manor houses of the Norman countryside, moreover, provided a highly picturesque model for new villas in a characteristic regional style, whereas granite, which was considered the typical construction material of Brittany, seemed less suitable for designing a charming and cheerful house at the beach. However, because their constructions were not hidden in museums or private dwellings, they played a more prominent role than painters in the process of (re-)defining the new regional identities by selecting those buildings, architectural forms, materials and landscapes which they deemed most typical for a particular region, or most suited to (re-)root its inhabitants.

Nonetheless, it has to be admitted that many architects and clients were not completely orthodox and did not only use vernacular elements from the region where a house was constructed, when applying the regionalist recipe. However, like the painters, the great majority of regionalist architects did not maintain close contacts with a particular regional movement, and many did not just specialise in one regional style. Moreover, strong regional movements, especially those that propagated myths of resistance and demanded more political autonomy, as was the case in the Basque Country and Brittany, in general opposed regionalist architecture. The picturesque and rural image these architects gave of their region apparently did not suit their wish to be taken seriously as a self-confident partner *vis-à-vis* the capital. This was most obvious in Catalonia where prominent architects as Domènech and Puig i Cadafalch played a leading role in the Catalan movement and where most architects preferred to use highly modern and cosmopolitan styles in which vernacular elements merely had a decorative role.

Thus as with painting, regionalist architecture was not produced as a result of a 'revolt of the provinces', and the regional identities it constructed were generally seen as aspects of a common, underlying national unity. In fact, the work of the architects was more practical and less didactic than that of the painters. However, by (re)connecting the people to local traditions and nature and making them feel at home, their activities could also be seen as forming part of the nation-building process. According to most critics, for example, the neo-vernacular houses in the garden cities and new suburbs for the middle and lower classes aimed to give their inhabitants a homely feeling and reconcile them with their social and natural environment. Indirectly this also implied the strengthening of their bonds with the existing political system, which had helped them to acquire a comfortable house in a pleasant neighbourhood. Thus, it was assumed that a greater regional awareness would also increase identification with the nation.

The exhibitions seemed more connected with the local level. Nonetheless, the initiative, which mostly came from the authorities and social elites of provincial capitals, was only taken when regionalism had already become a mainstream movement. Paris, of course, was not a provincial city, but even here the first proposals were formulated by deputies and senators from outside the capital, while officials and politicians from the provinces played an important role in its realisation. But again the fundamental unity of the nation was put first. This was most clearly visible in Seville and Paris where all the regions of the nation were assembled with a proper pavilion in a unified whole. In Munich and Düsseldorf the nationalist message was paramount as well – which in Nazi Germany was self-evident – as the generic regionalism of the model settlements could with minor modifications be applied anywhere in the country and even in areas that still had to be conquered. In Barcelona even leaders of the regional movement understood that in order to compete in the international arena and get the necessary subsidies from Madrid, Catalonia could not present itself alone. It was thought that Catalan industry and modernity should be accompanied by Spanish art and traditions. Consequently, even those who were not eager to give elements of a presumably primitive culture of the countryside a prominent place in their collective self-image, found a useful role for regionalism in stressing the fundamental (historical) unity of the whole nation.

Therefore, in none of the cases that were studied was regionalism applied with the explicit or implicit intention of defining an idiosyncratic identity of a particular region for its own sake. Regionalism, in brief, seemed to be almost incompatible with regional movements with a clear political programme directed towards more autonomy, or even independence. For these movements regionalism was not a very attractive option, as its image of a tranquil, harmonious and docile regional community did not suit their ideals. This was not the case, as became clear in France, with more moderate pleas for decentralisation, which were in fact meant to strengthen the organic unity of the country by combating the supposed stifling centralisation that hampered the free development of a substantial part of the nation's forces. How, then, should we label movements such as in Catalonia, the Basque Country and somewhat more belatedly in Brittany that pleaded for political autonomy and attracted a fairly massive support? Should we call them (peripheral) nationalisms, as many of their followers nowadays do? Or should we see them as unsuccessful national movements, as Miroslav Hroch has characterised the comparable Flemish movement in his path-breaking *Social Preconditions of National Revival in Europe*? Nevertheless, their development and ideology showed many similarities with other regional movements, although at a certain stage (in Catalonia and the Basque Country around 1900, in Brittany about two decades later) instead of subordinating a proper regional identity to a greater national community they began to put them on the same level, and in some cases even to reverse the hierarchy.

Regionalism, at least in France, Germany and Spain, was meant to reinforce the national unity within the existing nation-state and strengthen the national awareness of the population by providing it with local roots. It was meant as an integrative force, not by pointing to outsiders, foreigners, enemies and all kind of external threats, but by stressing more positive aspects such as harmony, solidarity and unity in diversity. This study thus confirms the findings of recent studies on specific regional movements. Nevertheless, as most scholars focus on one region or one regional movement and mainly use regional sources, they implicitly and often even explicitly assert that regionalism should be seen as a growing self-awareness and confidence, thus as an 'awakening of the regions'. Although my research is based primarily on artists, architects and magazines that addressed themselves to a national public, the conclusion that regionalism was principally a transnational phenomenon that was more connected with the main cultural centres of each country than with the provinces seems justified. Regionalism emerged primarily as a response of innovative national intellectual elites to new, international artistic, cultural and political trends and not among reformist elites from provincial towns.

Today scholars are in agreement about the implicit nationalist content of regionalism, but there is less clarity on its political background. As we have seen regionalism was embraced and supported by a broad spectrum of political parties and ideological currents. Although it has been difficult to assemble many clear indications of the exact political affinities of many of its advocates and the explicit political aims of many regionalist expressions, it is still possible to draw some conclusions. Regionalism was not endorsed by those old-fashioned liberals and conservatives who still held on to the traditional nineteenth-century society in which the suffrage was restricted and the notables self-evidently constituted the political and cultural elite. The same was true for those who wholeheartedly embraced modernity or who fiercely rejected existing society. Revolutionary socialists and anarchists seemed to have rejected regionalism from the start as sentimental bourgeois nostalgia, which was meant to mislead the working classes and avoid social revolution. In the prosperous second half of the 1920s, many progressive democrats also preferred modernism to regionalism. One could further assert that around 1936 – although their interpretations of modernity diverged enormously – both the French Socialists and the Nazis, even if they seemed predisposed to support regionalism, in practice gave priority to their own projects to modernise society.

Within the remaining broad political mainstream, at least until 1914 or maybe even until the direct aftermath of the First World War, the group that promoted regionalism most actively seemed to have come from the ranks of the reformist social-liberals. In France many of those who adhered to Léon Bourgeois' *Solidarisme* and activists of the Musée Social were among the main advocates of regionalism and especially part of the garden city movement. The same was true in Germany, where this role was taken up most clearly by a social-liberal circle around Friedrich Naumann. The political preferences of the main Spanish regionalists were possibly more diverse, although it seems very probable that most Spanish advocates of the garden city also adhered to the main principles of social-liberalism. Other groups that supported regionalism, such as socially concerned conservatives, social Catholics and social-democrats, similarly rejected the outdated laissez-faire liberalism of the late nineteenth century.

As a result, we can conclude that regionalism belonged to a very specific phase in European history: the transition from the nineteenth-century society led by notables to a modern mass society, which took place between the end of the nineteenth century and the 1930s. Regionalism could be seen as a somewhat paternalistic attempt to integrate the new voters into the existing political system by intensifying and extending the nation-building process. In order to socialise the masses, the proponents of regionalism consciously broadened the national identity which they thought the lower strata should adopt, by including regional folk culture and local traditions into their own artistic productions. In this way they tried to define more clearly recognisable regional identities, which could help the lower strata of the population to identify with the more abstract nation, while at the same time giving them a more dignified place within the national community by admitting the products of rural popular culture to the heritage of the nation.

This has particularly become clear in the case of Hamburg and Seville. Both cities were governed by small oligarchies that effectively resisted a more thorough democratisation of local political life. In both port cities regionalism became the more or less official architectural style, while the workers of these cities were still seen as politically immature. Before giving them their share of power, they should first be socialised into responsible citizens who would be fully aware of the worth of both the local and national heritage, which every right-minded inhabitant would wholeheartedly defend.

Regionalism thus functioned best in a society where the traditional deference towards the authorities and elites still existed. This also explains why it rapidly declined after the First World War. The mass-slaughter of the war, the extension and growing effectiveness of the suffrage and the successful rebellion of the Russian workers and their apparent rise to power in the Russian Revolution made the deferential attitude of the lower classes towards the traditional elites increasingly obsolete all over Europe. Moreover, although many of its elements and arguments continued to exist or were revived, in fact regionalism as a coherent ideology rapidly disintegrated after the end of *Belle Époque*. As a consequence, at least until 1914, regionalism was not a reactionary movement that nostalgically looked back to an idealised past, but was essentially a modern – although somewhat patronising – movement that tried to formulate an answer to the fundamental problems of its age.

Like nationalism in the Romantic era, regionalism was presented as a new but neutral interpretation of reality, based on the recent findings of science, such as geography, biology, history and ethnography. Thus it was considered completely natural and logical to adhere to its principles. While at the same time leaving out the more polemical aspects of the new, exalted nationalism, such as xenophobia and anti-Semitism, regionalism was presented as a neutral middle-ground to which every right-minded citizen could adhere. One could even argue that in times of crises or political polarisation, regionalism was used by relatively moderate political currents to overcome deep rifts within society and draw away electoral support from more radical groups. Thus, apart from a line of defence against revolutionary socialism, regionalism could also be employed to disarm more radical, xenophobic nationalists.

After looking at the common elements of the culture of regionalism, we now have to focus on the more superficial national differences. Germany was unmistakably more dynamic and innovative than France and Spain.

This was especially true for regionalist architecture as the German market for new constructions was much bigger. From the end of the nineteenth century, urbanisation and industrialisation proceeded much faster in the German Empire, and consequently housing was much more of an issue there. Moreover, perhaps in reaction to the greater strength of the socialist movement, German politicians seemed more prepared than their French colleagues to actively combat the miserable living conditions of the working classes by grand-scale social housing projects. Thus, architects inspired by regionalism found a huge field, first in designing villas and country houses and later on also in garden cities and social housing. The clear connections between regionalist architecture and a more general reformist attitude, such as a new appreciation of the natural environment and artisanal traditions, a more natural and healthy lifestyle, pedagogical reform and a genuine preoccupation with the 'social question', showed that a modern, reform-minded (upper) middle class was stronger in numbers and had much more impact in Germany than in France and Spain.

As a consequence, the regionalist message in Germany was translated into practical results, especially in social housing. The need to construct as many comfortable homes as possible led to the development of a simplified and more generic regionalism that could easily be applied to cheap workers' cottages. Efforts were directed towards reconnecting the workers to a presumably healthier semi-rural environment and inducing them to adopt a more dignified lifestyle, largely modelled after an idealised image of the conduct of the modest and traditional middle classes of the countryside and small towns with their clearly defined gender roles. In France and Spain, on the contrary, few garden cities and cheap housing developments were built, and these were generally not, as in Germany, mixed neighbourhoods but small workers' colonies.

Regionalism, nonetheless, seemed more apt for the Spanish case, where power was monopolised by a relatively limited group of notables. Although this system, based on electoral fraud and clientelism, started to show cracks in big cities such as Barcelona and Bilbao, it continued to function until the coup of Primo de Rivera in 1923; and an effective democracy only came into being in 1931 with the Second Republic. Thus, although since 1890 all adult males could vote, in practice the political influence of the lower classes was very limited. The dominant role of regionalist painting and the longevity of regionalist architecture, which on a more theoretical level should try to convert the largely illiterate workers and peasants into responsible citizens, confirmed that Spain was an ideal seed bed for regionalist culture.

France, with a better functioning democracy than Spain and a weaker workers' movement than Germany, was situated in between the two and regionalism therefore seemed to be a somewhat more superficial phenomenon there. Regionalist painting was only one of the many new trends around the turn of the century. Regionalist architecture had most impact in seaside resorts and other touristic areas, although it was also applied to garden cities and social housing. But as the 'social question', compared to Germany, was seen as less urgent, not much was done to improve the living conditions of the workers. Moreover, when, in the 1930s regionalism was revived to strengthen national unity, it failed to prevent the rise to power of the Popular Front in 1936. However, one could also argue that the acceptance of the existing democratic system by the new government meant that in fact the lower classes had been successfully integrated into the Third Republic, although it is not clear to what extent regionalism had contributed to this integration.

Another difference between the three countries could be found in the way regional identities were defined. Contrary to what happened in Spain and France, regions were only loosely defined by German regionalist painters, architects and those who defended their work. The regions to which they referred could be very small, such as a ridge of hills, or very big, such as northern Germany. In many reviews a regionalist house was not even related to a specific region but only to its immediate surroundings. One could argue that natural differences within Germany were probably less clear and obvious than in France and Spain. However, regional identities in France and Spain were not so much related to different geographical or climatic zones as to historical territories, such as Brittany, Normandy, Castile and Andalusia. These were no longer effective political or administrative units as they had been replaced, respectively in 1790 and 1833, by uniform and generally smaller departments or provinces. The bigger, traditional regions thus had lost their function. Nonetheless, they seemed a good potential counterweight to the capital, where according to many regionalists too much power was concentrated; decentralisation in their eyes would strengthen the nation. Power and administrative functions, however, should not be conferred on artificial and arbitrary units such as the departments, but on natural regions with a long history and presumably a strong collective personality.

In Germany, where cities, provinces and the various States within the Empire and the Weimar Republic had considerable autonomy, regionalism was not connected to a plea for devolution. Probably to avoid any association with the former despised *Kleinstaaterei* – the division of Germany in many small principalities – regionalists generally did not wish to reinforce the identity of actually existing States or provinces, nor did they wish to represent the country as an ensemble of different regions. Thus, the more generic and vague term *Heimat* perfectly suited their purposes, as it could refer simultaneously to the familiar, local, regional and national sphere. Nonetheless, it seems that this more generic regionalism was also present in other countries with less centralised political systems, such as England, the Netherlands and the Scandinavian countries – where it generally also underlined national unity – and as a consequence was not a particular German feature.

In France, cultural regionalism was closely connected to attempts to decentralise the existing political system. Regionalism thus was equated with the emancipation of the provinces and the opening of new channels for political participation. In Spain, in turn, it was not so much a general reform of the strongly centralised administration that was a recurrent point on the political agenda, but the plea for autonomy by particularly Catalonia and the Basque Country. The regional movements in these areas thus were not typical of regionalism, but constituted clear exceptions, more so when one takes into account that in French Catalonia and in Valencia, where large parts of the population spoke Catalan dialects, and in the French Basque Country, these claims were not made. Thus, the existence of a proper language and a different ethnic or historical background cannot sufficiently explain this divergence from the more general pattern. It seems that the presence of a big modern town – like Barcelona and Bilbao that were the indisputable centres of, respectively, the Catalan and Basque movements – which did not have French counterparts, constituted an indispensible precondition. Furthermore, after the defeat in the war of 1898, Spain was a weak and unattractive nation-state that could not offer its citizens in a sufficient way – compared to France and other West European states – an efficient and professional administration, possibilities for political participation, a good educational system, the beginnings of a social welfare system, or military victories and opportunities in a considerable colonial empire. Especially in a period when more and more small European 'nations' got their own state, independence or at least 'home rule' became a viable option for the two most modern regions of the country. In order to avoid the possible 'disintegration' of Spain, regionalists elsewhere in the country put more emphasis on the indissoluble unity of the nation than their counterparts in France and Germany, where this was not much of an issue.

We have already seen that regionalism should be understood essentially as a new phase in the nation-building process. But what more can regionalism tell us about nationalism and the construction of territorial identities in general? There has been much debate on the question whether national identities were invented or whether they were generally built upon earlier ethnic identities. Most regional identities that we have seen in this study were not invented from scratch. Generally they were explicitly constructed with the help of historical memories and existing images and stereotypes. However, by adopting rural low culture as a source of identification, the existing vague regional identities were in fact almost completely transformed. The multiform existing rural habits, traditions and artisanal products of former times were redefined into more clearly delineated, modern regional cultures. Self-evident and unconscious customs from the countryside – which often were peculiar to a specific social group – were recreated into the self-conscious collective identity of a whole region. Moreover, as with national identities, in general those elements that were shared with other areas were not deemed characteristic, whereas buildings, habits, traditions, garments, crafts and landscapes that were seen as unique – although they often were rather odd or rare – had a much better chance to be selected as a quintessential element of a particular region's identity. Furthermore, the selected elements should also have positive connotations – thus artisanal and rural trades were only chosen when they were almost disappearing and were no longer immediately associated with hard work and suffering, but with tradition, closeness to nature and authenticity.

Regionalism consequently was the product of an urban, middle-class society that projected its own romanticised image upon the countryside. The creation of regional identities was thus mainly done from the outside, by modern, cosmopolitan urban professionals. It were not the modest farmers and artisans themselves who decided to adopt a new identity, but it was projected on to them, often to their own surprise, by modern intellectuals and professionals from both their own region, such as Mistral, and from elsewhere, like Rostand. This process of regional identity construction (as with national identities) was executed by selecting, appropriating and inventing, a recipe that was applied everywhere. The result, however, also depended upon the specific circumstances, although in the end it was those that formulated the new identity, and the public that had to accept it, who determined which particular aspects were included and which elements were forgotten, overlooked or rejected.

Another issue that has attracted much discussion is the apparent difference between a political or civic, and a more cultural or ethnic, nationalism. Recently most scholars have agreed that in most cases both variants, or aspects, were present and this was also the case with regionalism. Regionalism, like the exalted nationalism that rose to prominence at the same time, was particularly occupied with defining collective identities. This was mainly done by cultural means. In this way, it closely resembled cultural nationalism as it underlined the importance of common traditions and habits, and of a shared past, language and culture. Although regionalists, at least in the sources consulted for this study, generally did not openly ask for imperialist expansion, nor reject foreigners and outsiders – and in this they differed from the more exalted new nationalists – by defining regional identities, they implicitly excluded those who did not share the common heritage from the regional community and formulated a collective identity to which all original inhabitants should adhere. Nevertheless, this did not mean, as most painters and architects themselves proved, that one had to be born in a region to be part of the true regional community; however, a sustained effort was needed to adapt oneself to a region's mores.

Nonetheless, elements of civic nationalism were not completely absent. Although regionalism was not directly concerned with civic rights, which were arranged by the national government and parliament, in some ways it could also be seen as a – maybe somewhat paternalistic – democratic and emancipatory movement, as it proposed to give the inhabitants of the countryside a dignified place in the national community, and included their traditions and popular culture in the country's patrimony. It often, as in the case of the Regional Centre, also encouraged regional participation.

On the other hand, one could also interpret regionalism negatively as a swindle invented by the upper classes, or used by dictators, to deceive the lower classes and to remain in power. In any case, regardless of the value one would like to attach to their activities, regionalists were highly concerned with the way the lower classes would exert their civic rights. They sincerely hoped that the new voters would behave as 'good' citizens; that is, as worthy members of both the national and regional community. It even seems that political concerns were more important than cultural ones. Thus ethnic and linguistic borders, such as in Brittany, the Basque Country, or French Flanders, were not particularly addressed or even downplayed by regionalist painters, architects and in regionalist pavilions as most regionalists wanted to integrate all inhabitants of the countryside, regardless of language, ethnicity, class and religion into the national community.

Consequently regionalists were especially preoccupied with those in the countryside and the towns who were not very aware of their national identity and civic duties, or those who seemed to prefer the international solidarity of the workers. Maybe, one could add that they even addressed those who put the community of believers (those loyal to a foreign power, such as the Pope in Rome) above the nation, or those cosmopolitan intellectuals who adhered to a vague internationalism. Nonetheless, it seems clear that most regionalists were principally concerned with the integration of the uprooted rural and urban working classes into the national community, and that out of fear for a proletarian revolution, they supplied the national identity with local roots. Thus, in fact regionalism was also closely connected to political nationalism, although this time, it was not the recognition, formulation and extent of the civic rights that were at stake, but the way they were used. Reinforcing regional identities was in fact a way to induce the lower classes to assimilate decent middle-class manners, disguised in a local garb.

Regionalism, however, was not only a phase in the nation-building process and as such a cultural ideology with huge political implications, but also a new cultural form that had an enormous impact on both the existing high culture and the rising avant-garde. Regionalism was one of the major innovating artistic trends in Europe in the decades after 1890 and regionalist arguments were omnipresent in all kind of cultural debates. Whereas during the Romantic era culture had been nationalised, regionalism now resulted in a redefinition of culture in regional terms. One could possibly even maintain that it was the dominant cultural movement during the first decade of the twentieth century. This becomes especially clear if we look at the various avant-garde movements that gradually displaced regionalist art and architecture from the public scene. The avant-garde – although many of its members for shorter or longer periods adopted some of the regionalist arguments and motifs – in the end defined itself in large measure in response to regionalism (or were defined in such a way by later propagandists). Thus regionalist culture functioned as an almost forgotten trigger for the development of new innovative cultural movements. Its importance, therefore, not only lies in the art works, buildings and writings it produced, but also in its indispensable role in the genesis of modern art and architecture. Without a proper understanding of regionalism we therefore get a very incomplete picture of the cultural developments of the first decades of the twentieth century and an extremely biased image of the rise of the avant-garde and the subsequent triumph of artistic modernism. Moreover, the heritage of regionalism is still visible in many areas: in tourism, in housing, in the preservation of ancient buildings, in nature conservation, in uncountable local and regional museums, and in a great number of regional associations. During the last few years, in times of increased globalisation, we even see a growing appreciation of regional folk culture in architecture, furniture, music, and food, and we even witness a renewed interest in the first Golden Age of the culture of regionalism.

Bibliography

Primary sources

PERIODICAL LITERATURE
ABC
El año artístico
L'Architecte
L'Architecture
L'Architecture d'Aujourd'hui
L'Architecture Moderne
Arquitectura
Arquitectura y Construcción
L'Art Décoratif
Arte Español
Art et Décoration
L'Art et les Artistes
Les Arts
Bauen, Siedeln, Wohnen
Baugilde
Der Baumeister
Die Baupolitik
Bauwelt
Die Bauzeitung
Blanco y Negro
La Construcción Moderna
La Construction Moderne
Dekorative Kunst
Deutsche Bauhütte
Deutsche Bauzeitung
Deutsche Kunst und Dekoration
La Esfera
*Exposition Paris 1937 Arts et techniques dans la vie moderne: Magazine officiel édité par le
    Commissariat Général*
El Flamenco: Semanario anti-flamenquista
La Gazette des Beaux-Arts
Die Graphische Künste
Heraldo de Madrid
Hermes
L'Illustration

El Imparcial
Die Kunst
Kunst für Alle
Kunstwart
La Lectura
Mercure de France
Mirador
Moderne Bauformen
Monatshefte für Baukunst und Städtebau
Museum
La Nación
Pequeñas monografías de arte
Pequeñas Monografías: Revista mensual
Revista del Cuerpo de Arquitectos Municipales de España
Revue bleue
La Revue de l'Art Ancien et Moderne
Revue de Paris
Der Städtebau
The Studio
Le Temps
La Vie à la Campagne
La Vie Urbaine
Wasmuths Monatshefte für Baukunst
Westermanns Illustrierte Deutsche Monatshefte
Zeitschrift für bildende Kunst
Zentralblatt der Bauverwaltung

CONTEMPORARY PRINTED SOURCES

Agache, Alfred, Marcel Auburtin and Edouard Redont, *Comment reconstruire nos cités détruites: Notions d'urbanisme s'appliquant aux villes, bourgs et villages* (Paris 1915).

Bantzer, Carl, *Hessens Land und Leute in der deutschen Malerei: Mit Kunstchronik von Willingshausen. Erweiterter Sonderdruck aus Hessenland* (Marburg 1933–35).

Barrès, Maurice, *Les Déracinés* (Paris 1897).

Barrès, Maurice, *Scènes et doctrines du nationalisme* (Paris 1902).

Bartels, Adolf, *Heimatkunst: Ein Wort zur Verständigung* (Munich and Leipzig 1904).

Colas, Louis, *L'Habitation basque: De l'art regional en France* (Paris 1926).

Deibel, Freidrich, *Ludwig Dettmann* (Bielefeld and Leipzig, s.a. [1910]).

Denis, Maurice, *Théories (1890–1910): Du symbolisme et de Gauguin vers un nouvel ordre classique* (Paris 1920).

Encina, Juan de la, *La trama del arte vasco* (Bilbao 1919).

Ganivet, Ángel, *Granada la Bella* (1896).

Ganivet, Ángel, *Idearium español* (Madrid 1897).

Harbers, Guido, *Das Kleinhaus, seine Konstruktion und Einrichtung* (2nd edn., Munich 1932).

Howard, Ebenezer, *Garden Cities of Tomorrow* (London 1902).

Labbé, Edmond, *Exposition Internationale des Arts et Techniques: Paris 1937. Rapport Générale* (Paris 1938) 11 vols.

Langbehn, Julius, *Rembrandt als Erzieher: Von einem Deutschen* (Leipzig 1890).

Maiwald, Ernst W. ed., *Reichsausstellung 'Schaffendes Volk' Düsseldorf 1937: Ein Bericht* (Düsseldorf 1939) 2 vols.

Muthesius, Hermann, *Stilarchitektur und Baukunst: Wandlungen der Architektur und der gewerblichen Künste im 19. Jahrhundert und ihr heutiger Standpunkt* (2nd rev. edn., Mülheim-Ruhr 1903).

Muthesius, Hermann, *Das englische Haus: Entwicklung, Bedingungen, Anlage, Aufbau, Einrichtung und Innenraum* (1904, 2nd edn., Berlin 1908).

Reichsausstellung Schaffendes Volk Düsseldorf 1937 Mai-Oktober (Düsseldorf 1937).

Rilke, Rainer Maria, *Worpswede: Fritz Mackensen, Otto Modersohn, Fritz Overbeck, Hans am Ende, Heinrich Vogeler* (2nd edn., Bielefeld and Leipzig 1905).

Schmidt, Karl Eugen, *Französische Malerei des 19. Jahrhunderts* (Leipzig 1903).

Vaillat, Léandre, *La Cité renaissante* (Paris 1918).

Vinnen, Carl ed., *Ein Protest deutscher Künstler* (Jena 1911).

Secondary sources

Abram, Joseph, 'Perret et l'exposition' in: Bertrand Lemoine ed., *Cinquantenaire de l'Exposition Internationale des Arts et des Techniques dans la Vie Moderne* (Paris 1987) 66–72.

Aly, Götz, *'Endlösung': Völkerverschiebung und der Mord an den europäischen Juden* (Frankfurt am Main 1995).

Anderson, Benedict, *Imagined Communities: Reflections on the Origin and Spread of Nationalism* (1983, revised edn., London and New York 1991).

Applegate, Celia, 'A Europe of Regions: Reflections on the Historiography of Sub-National Places in Modern Times', *American Historical Review* (1999) 1157–83.

Applegate, Celia, *A Nation of Provincials: The German Idea of Heimat* (Berkeley 1990).

Archilés, Ferran and Manuel Martí, 'Ethnicity, Region and Nation: Valencian Identity and the Spanish Nation-State', *Ethnic and Racial Studies* (2001) 779–97.

Arndt, Karl, 'Die Münchener Architekturszene 1933/1934 als ästhetisch-politisches Konfliktfeld' in: Martin Broszat, Elke Fröhlich and Anton Grossmann eds., *Bayern in der NS-Zeit* III *Herrschaft und Gesellschaft im Konflikt* Teil B (Munich 1981) 443–513.

Arozamena, Jesús María de, *Ignacio Zuloaga: El pintor, el hombre* (San Sebastian 1970).

Bantzer, Andreas ed., *Carl Bantzer: Ein Leben in Briefen. Briefe – Berichte – Werksverzeichnis* (2nd edn., Willingshausen 1998).

Basurto, Nieves, *Leonardo Rucabado y la arquitectura montañes* (Madrid 1986).

Baudouï, Rémi, 'La Cité-jardin française entre mythes et réalités' in: Paulette Girard and Bruno Fayolle Lusac eds., *Cités, cités-jardins: une histoire européene. Actes du colloque de Toulouse des 18 et 19 novembre 1993* (Toulouse 1996) 88–100.

Bausinger, Hermann, 'Heimat in einer offenen Gesellschaft: Begriffsgeschichte als Problemgeschichte' in: Will Cremer and Ansgar Klein eds., *Heimat, Analysen, Themen, Perspektiven* (Bielefeld 1990) 76–91.

Baycroft, Timothy, *Culture, Identity and Nationalism: French Flanders in the Nineteenth and Twentieth Century* (Woodbridge 2004).

Baycroft, Timothy and Mark Hewitson eds., *What is a Nation? Europe 1789–1914* (Oxford 2006).

Bell, David A., *The Cult of the Nation in France: Inventing Nationalism, 1680–1800* (Cambridge and London 2001).

Ben-Ami, Shlomo, *Fascism from Above: The Dictatorship of Primo de Rivera in Spain 1923–1930* (Oxford 1983).

Bergdoll, Barry, *European Architecture 1750–1890* (Oxford and New York 2000).

Bergmann, Klaus, *Agrarromantik und Großstadtfeindlichkeit* (Meisenheim am Glan 1970).

Bernal Muñoz, Luis, *La mirada del 98: Arte y literatura en la Edad de Plata* (Madrid 1998).

Bertho-Lavenir, Catherine, 'L'Idée régionaliste: naissance et développement' in: François Loyer and Bernard Toulier eds., *Le Régionalisme, architecture et identité* (Paris 2001) 28–48.

Blackbourn, David, *The Conquest of Water: Water, Landscape and the Making of Modern Germany* (London 2006).

Boa, Elizabeth and Rachel Palfreyman, *Heimat: A German Dream. Regional Loyalties and National Identity in German Culture, 1890–1990* (Oxford 2000).

Boime, Albert, *The Academy and French Painting in the Nineteenth Century* (London 1971).

Borrmann, Norbert, *Paul Schultze-Naumburg: 1869–1949, Maler, Publizist, Architekt. Vom Kulturreformer der Jahrhundertwende zum Kulturpolitiker im Dritten Reich: ein Lebens und Zeitdokument* (Essen 1989).

Braojos Garrido, Alfonso, *Alfonso XIII y la Exposición Iberoamericana de Sevilla de 1929* (Seville 1992).

Brinkmann, Sören, *Der Stolz der Provinzen, Regionalbewußtein und Nationalstaatsbau im Spanien des 19. Jahrhunderts* (Frankfurt 2005).

Buder, Stanley, *Visionaries and Planners: The Garden City Movement and the Modern Community* (Oxford and New York 1990).

Bullock, Nicholas and James Read, *The Movement for Housing Reform in Germany and France 1840–1914* (Cambridge 1985).

Bushart, Magdalena, *Der Geist der Gotik und die expressionistische Kunst: Kunstgeschichte und Kunsttheorie 1911–1912* (Munich 1990).

Cabo, Miguel and Fernando Molina, 'The Long and Winding Road of Nationalization: Eugen Weber's Peasants into Frenchmen in Modern European History (1976–2006)', *European History Quarterly* (2009) 264–86.

Calvo Serraller, Francisco, *Paisajes de luz y muerte: La pintura española del 98* (Barcelona 1998).

Campbell, Joan, *The German Werkbund: The Politics of Reform in the Applied Arts* (Princeton 1978).

Canizaro, Vincent B. ed., *Architectural Regionalism: Collected Writings on Place, Identity, Modernity, and Tradition* (New York 2007).

Cariou, André, *Charles Cottet et la Bretagne* (Raillé 1988).

Cariou, André, *Lucien Simon* (Paris 2002).

Carl Bantzer 1857–1941: Foto/Zeichnung/Gemälde. Synthetischer Realismus (Marburg 1977).

Castañer, Esteban, 'Catalogne: à la recherche d'une architecture nationaliste' in: François Loyer and Bernard Toulier eds., *Le Régionalisme, architecture et identité* (Paris 2001) 208–20.

Castrillo Romón, María, 'Les lois des habitations à bon marché et la construction des colonies résidentielle en Espagne' in: Paulette Girard and Bruno Fayolle Lussac eds., *Cités, cités-jardins: Une histoire européenne* (Talence 1996) 161–9.

Castrillo Romón, María, *Reformismo, vivienda y ciudad: Orígenes y desarrollo del debate en España 1850–1920* (Valladolid 2001).

Chanet, Jean-François, *L'École républicaine et les petites patries* (Paris 1996).

Clout, Hugh, *After the Ruins: Restoring the Countryside of Northern France after the Great War* (Exeter 1996).

Clout, Hugh, 'The Great Reconstruction of Towns and Cities in France 1918–1935', *Planning Perspectives* (2005) 1–34.

Collet, Isabelle, 'Le Monde rural aux expositions universelles de 1900 et 1937' in: *Muséologie et ethnologie* (Paris 1987) 100–40.

Confino, Alon, 'The Nation as a Local Metaphor: Heimat, National Memory and the German Empire, 1871–1918', *History and Memory* (1993) 42–86.

Confino, Alon, *The Nation as a Local Metaphor: Württemberg, Imperial Germany, and National Memory, 1871–1918* (Chapel Hill 1997).

Confino, Alon, *Germany as a Culture of Remembrance: Promises and Limits of Writing History* (Chapel Hill 2006).

Couédic, Daniel le, *Les Architectes et l'idée bretonne 1904–1945: D'un renouveau des arts à la renaissance d'une identité* (Saint-Brieuc 1995).

Cruz Seoane, María and María Dolores Sáiz, *Historia del periodismo en España 3: El siglo XX: 1898–1936* (Madrid 1996).

Cusack, Tricia, 'Bourgeois Leisure on the Seine: Impressionism, Forgetting and National Identity in the French Third Republic', *National Identities* (2007) 163–82.

Delouche, Denise, *Peintres de la Bretagne: Découverte d'une province* (Paris 1977).

Ditt, Karl, 'Die deutsche Heimatbewegung 1871–1945' in: Will Cremer and Ansgar Klein eds., *Heimat: Analysen, Themen, Perspektiven* (Bielefeld 1990) 135–55.

Ditt, Karl, '"Mit Westfalengruß und Heil Hitler": Die Westfälische Heimatbewegung 1918–1945' in: Edeltraud Klueting ed., *Antimodernismus und Reform: Zur Geschichte der deutschen Heimatbewegung* (Darmstadt 1991) 191–215

Ditt, Karl, 'Konservative Kulturvorstellungen und Kulturpolitik vom Kaiserreich bis zum Dritten Reich', *Neue Politische Literatur*, XLI (1996) 230–60.

Ditt, Karl, 'The Idea of German Cultural Regions in the Third Reich: The Work of Franz Petri', *Journal of Historical Geography* 27 (2001) 241–58.

Ditt, Karl, 'Der Wandel historischer Raumbegriffe im 20. Jahrhundert und das Beispiel Westfalen', *Geographische Zeitschrift* 93 (2005) 45–61.

Dorman, Robert L., *Revolt of the Provinces: The Regionalist Movement in America, 1920–1945* (Chapel Hill 1993).

Drexler A. ed., *The Architecture of the École des Beaux-Arts* (New York 1977).

Düwell, Kurt, 'Regionalismus und Nationalsozialismus am Beispiel des Rheinlands', *Rheinische Vierteljahresblätter* 59 (1995) 194–210.

Faure, Christian, *Le projet culturel de Vichy* (Paris 1989).

Fidel, Enrique, 'La Ciudad jardín madrileña: colonias del Ensanche' in: http://urbancidades.wordpress.com/2007/09/29/la-ciudad-jardin-madrilena.

Flacke, Monika ed., *Mythen der Nationen: Ein europäisches Panorama* (Berlin 1998).

Fontbona, Francesc and Francesc Miralles, *Del modernisme al noucentisme 1888–1917*, Vol. VII, Història de l'art català (Barcelona 1985).

Forcadell Álvarez, Carlos and María Cruz Romeo Mateo eds., *Provincia y nación: Los territorios del liberalismo* (Saragossa 2006).

Ford, Caroline, *Creating the Nation in Provincial France: Religion and Political Identity in Brittany* (Princeton 1993).

Forrier, Michel, *Petite Histoire d'Arnaga* (Pau 2006).

Fradera, Josep M., 'La política liberal y el descubrimiento de una identidad distinctiva en Cataluña (1835–1865)', *Hispania* (2000) 673–702.

Frank, Harmut, 'Heimatschutz und typologisches Entwerfen: Modernisierung und Tradition beim Wiederaufbau von Ostpreußen 1915–1927' in: Vittorio Lampugnani and Romana Schneider eds., *Moderne Architektur in Deutschland 1900 bis 1950: Reform und Tradition* (Stuttgart 1992) 105–33.

Frank, Hartmut ed., *Fritz Schumacher: Reformkultur und Moderne* (Stuttgart 1994).

Friedeburg, Robert von, *Ländliche Gesellschaft und Obrigkeit: Gemeindeprotest und politische Mobilisierung im 18. und 19. Jahrhundert* (Göttingen 1997).

Fullaonda, D., *Manuel María Smith Ibarra, arquitecto 1879–1956* (Madrid 1980).

Gaudin, Jean-Pierre, 'The French Garden City' in: Stephan V. Ward ed., *The Garden City: Past, Present and Future* (London 1992) 52–69.

Gellner, Ernest *Nations and Nationalism* (Ithaca 1983).

Genet-Delacroix, Marie-Claude, *Art et État sous la IIIe République: Le système des Beaux-Arts 1870–1940* (Paris 1992).

Gerson, Stéphane, *The Pride of Place: Local Memories and Political Culture in Nineteenth-Century France* (Ithaca and London 2003).

Golan, Romy, *Modernity and Nostalgia: Art and Politics in France between the Wars* (New Haven and London 1995).

González de Durana, Javier, *Ideologías artísticas en el País Vasco de 1900: Arte y política en los orígenes de la modernidad* (Bilbao 1992).

Grandas, M. Carmen, *L'Exposició Internacional de Barcelona de 1929* (Barcelona 1988).

Granja, José Luis de la, *El siglo de Euskadi: El nacionalismo vasco en la España del siglo XX* (Madrid 2003).

Granja, José Luis de la, Justo Beramendi and Pere Anguera, *La España de los nacionalismos y las autonomías* (Madrid 2003).

Green, Abigail, *Fatherlands: State-Building and Nationhood in Nineteenth-Century Germany* (Cambridge 2001).

Green, Abigail, 'The Federal Alternative? A New View of Modern German History', *Historical Journal* (2003) 187–202.

Grislain, Jean-Étienne, 'Simplicité et distinction', *Monuments historiques* 144 (April–May 1986) 57–63.

Guéné, Hélène and François Loyer, *L'église, l'état et les architectes: Rennes 1870–1940* (Paris 1995).

Guerrand, Roger-Henri and Christine Moissinac, *Henri Sellier, urbaniste et réformateur social* (Paris 2005).

Guy, Kolleen M., *When Champagne became French: Wine and the making of National Identity* (Baltimore 2007).

Hall, Peter, *Cities of Tomorrow: An Intellectual History of Urban Planning and Design in the Twentieth Century* (3rd edn., Oxford 2002).

Hamm, Ulrike and Bernd Küster, *Fritz Mackensen 1866–1953* (Lilienthal 1990).

Hartmann, Kristiana, *Deutsche Gartenstadtbewegung: Kulturpolitik und Gesellschaftreform* (Munich 1976).

Hartung, Werner, *Konservative Zivilisationskritik und regionale Identität am Beispiel der niedersächsischen Heimatbewegung 1895 bis 1919* (Hanover 1991).

Henn, Ursula, *Die Mustersiedlung Ramersdorf in München: Ein Siedlungskonzept zwischen Tradition und Moderne* (Munich 1987).

Henry, Delphine, *Chemin vert: L'oeuvre d'éducation populaire dans une cité jardin emblématique, Reims 1919–1939* (Reims 2002).

Herbert, James D., *Fauve Painting: The Making of Cultural Politics* (New Haven and London 1992).

Herbert, James D., *Paris 1937: Worlds on Exhibition* (Ithaca 1998).

Hermann Muthesius, 1861–1927 (Berlin 1977).

Hernando, Javier, *Arquitectura en España, 1770–1900* (Madrid 1989).

Hipp, Hermann, 'Fritz Schumachers Hamburg: Die reformierte Großstadt', in: Vittorio Lampugnani and Romana Schneider eds., *Moderne Architektur in Deutschland 1900 bis 1950: Reform und Tradition* (Stuttgart 1992) 151–85.

Hobsbawm, Eric, 'Mass-Producing Traditions: Europe, 1870–1914' in: Eric Hobsbawm and Terence Ranger eds., *The Invention of Tradition* (Cambridge 1983) 263–309.

Hobsbawm, Eric, *Nations and Nationalism since 1780: Programme, Myth, Reality* (Cambridge 1990).

Hobsbawm, Eric and Terence Ranger eds., *The Invention of Tradition* (Cambridge 1983).

Hofer, Sigrid, *Reformarchitektur 1900–1918: Deutsche Baukünstler auf der Suche nach dem nationalen Stil* (Stuttgart 2005).

Holmes, Judith, *Olympiad 1936: Blaze of Glory for Hitler's Reich* (New York 1971).

Horne, Janet R., *A Social Laboratory for Modern France: The Musée Social and the Rise of the Welfare State* (Durham and London 2002).

Howard, Jeremy, *Art Nouveau: International and National Styles in Europe* (Manchester 1996).

Hroch, Miroslav, *Social Preconditions of National Revival in Europe: A Comparative Analysis of the Social Composition of Patriotic Groups among the Smaller European Nations* (1985; New York 2000).

Hurtt, Deborah D., 'Simulating France, Seducing the World: The Regional Center at the 1937 Paris Exposition' in: D. Medina Lasansky and Brian McLaren eds.,

Architecture and Tourism: Perception, Performance and Place (Oxford and New York 2004) 147–65.

Hurtt, Deborah Dawson, 'Rivalry and Representation: Regionalist Architecture and the Road to the 1937 Paris Exposition' (PhD dissertation, University of Virginia, 2005).

Ignacio Zuloaga, 1870–1945 (Bilbao 1990).

Isac, Ángel, *Eclecticismo y pensamiento arquitectónico en España: Discursos, revistas, congresos 1846–1919* (Granada 1987).

Jenkins, Jennifer, *Provincial Modernity: Local Culture and Liberal Politics in Fin-de-Siècle Hamburg* (Ithaca 2003).

Jensen, Robert, *Marketing Modernism in Fin-de-Siècle Europe* (Princeton 1994).

Jiménez Burillo, Pablo ed., *Joaquín Sorolla (1863–1923)* (Madrid 1995).

Jonas, Stéphane, 'Les Jardins d'Ungemach à Strasbourg: Une cité-jardin d'origine nataliste (1923–1950)' in: Paulette Girard and Bruno Fayolle Lusac eds., *Cités, cités-jardins: une histoire européene. Actes du colloque de Toulouse des 18 et 19 novembre 1993* (Toulouse 1996) 65–87.

Kirsch, Karin, 'Die Weißenhofsiedlung: Ein internationales Manifest' in: Vittorio Magnago Lampugnani and Romana Schneider eds., *Moderne Architektur in Deutschland 1900 bis 1950: Expressionismus und Neue Sachlichkeit* (Stuttgart 1994) 205–24.

Koshar, Rudy, *Germany's Transient Pasts. Preservation and National Memory in the Twentieth Century* (Chapel Hill 1998).

Kretschmer, Winfried, *Geschichte der Weltausstellungen* (Frankfurt and New York 1999).

Kühne, Thomas, 'Die Region als Konstrukt: Regionalgeschichte als Kulturgeschichte' in: James Retallack ed., *Sachsen in Deutschland: Politik, Kultur und Gesellschaft 1830–1918* (Bielefeld 2000), 253–64.

Kunz, Georg, *Verortete Geschichte: Regionales Geschichtsbewusstsein in den deutschen Historischen Vereinen des 19. Jahrhunderts* (Göttingen 2000).

Küster, Bernd, *Carl Bantzer* (Marburg 1993).

Küster, Bernd and Jürgen Wittstock, *Carl Bantzer: Aufbruch und Tradition* (Frankfurt am Main 2002).

Lafuente Ferrari, Enrique, *La vida y el arte de Ignacio Zuloaga* (3rd edn., Barcelona 1990).

Lampugnani, Vittorio and Romana Schneider eds., *Moderne Architektur in Deutschland 1900 bis 1950: Reform und Tradition* (Stuttgart 1992).

Lane, Barbara Miller, *Architecture and Politics in Germany, 1918–1945* (Cambridge 1968).

Lane, Barbara Miller, 'Die Moderne und die Politik in Deutschland zwischen 1919 und 1945' in: Vittorio Magnago Lampugnani and Romana Schneider eds., *Moderne Architektur in Deutschland 1900 bis 1950: Expressionismus und Neue Sachlichkeit* (Stuttgart 1994) 225–50.

Lane, Barbara Miller, *National Romanticism and Modern Architecture in Germany and the Scandinavian Countries* (Cambridge 2000).

Lasserre, Claude, 'Le Néo-basque: Une autre face de la modernité (1920–1940)', *Monuments Historiques* (October–November 1986) 65–73.

Leerssen, Joep, *National Thought in Europe: A Cultural History* (Amsterdam 2006).

Lekan, Thomas M., *Imagining the Nation in Nature: Landscape Preservation and German Identity, 1885–1945* (Cambridge 2004).

Lixfeld, Hannjost, *Folklore and Fascism: The Reich Institute for German Volkskunde* (Bloomington 1994).

Lloyd, Sue, *The Man Who Was Cyrano: A Life of Edmond Rostand, Creator of Cyrano de Bergerac* (Bloomington 2002).

Lowenthal, David, *The Past is a Foreign Country* (Cambridge 1985).

Loyer, François, *Histoire de l'architecture française de la Révolution à nos jours* (Paris 1999).

Loyer, François and Bernard Toulier eds., *Le Régionalisme, architecture et identité* (Paris 2001).

Lübbren, Nina, *Rural Artists' Colonies in Europe 1870–1910* (Manchester 2001).

Maciuika, John V., *Before the Bauhaus: Architecture, Politics and the German State, 1890–1920* (Cambridge 2005).

Magri, Susanna and Christian Topalov, 'De la cité-jardin à la ville rationalisée: Un tournant du projet réformateur, 1905–1925. Etude comparative France, Grande-Bretagne, Italie, Etats-Unis', *Revue française de sociologie* (1987) 417–51.

Marfany, Joan-Lluis, *La cultura del catalanisme en els seus inicis* (Barcelona 1995).

Marlais, Michael, *Conservative Echoes in Fin-de-Siècle Parisian Art Criticism* (University Park 1992).

Marrey, Bernard, *Louis Bonnier 1856–1946* (Liège 1988).

Martin, Jean-Clément, 'La construction culturelle d'une région, la Vendée' in: Heinz-Gerhard Haupt, Michael Müller and Stuart Woolf eds., *Regional and National Identities in Europe in the XIXth and XXth Centuries* (The Hague 1998) 437–65.

Mauron, Claude, *Frédéric Mistral* (Paris 1993).

McCully, Marilyn, *Els Quatre Gats: Art in Barcelona around 1900* (Princeton 1978).

McWilliam, Neil, 'Le Paysan au salon: Critique d'art et construction d'une classe sous le Second Empire' in: Jean-Paul Bouillon ed., *La critique d'art en France 1850–1900* (Saint-Etienne 1989) 81–95.

Meacham, Stanish, *Regaining Paradise: Englishness and the Early Garden City Movement* (New Haven 1999).

Mendelson, Jordana, *Documenting Spain: Artists, Exhibition Culture, and the Modern Nation, 1929–1939* (University Park 2005).

Meyer, Edina, *Paul Mebes: Miethausbau in Berlin 1906–1938* (Berlin 1972).

Mihail, Benoît, *Une Flandre à la française: L'identité régionale à l'épreuve du modèle républicain* (Saintes 2006).

Moch, Leslie, *The Pariahs of Yesterday: Bretons in Paris* (forthcoming).

Moentmann, Elise Marie, 'The Search for French Identity in the Regions: National versus Local Visions of France in the 1930s', *French History* XVII (2003) 307–27.

Molina Aparicio, Fernando, 'Modernidad e identidad nacional: El nacionalismo español del siglo XIX y su historiografía', *Historia Social* (2005) 147–72.

Möller, Holger, *Das deutsche Messe- und Ausstellungswesen: Standortstruktur und räumliche Entwicklung seit dem 19. Jahrhundert* (Trier 1989).

Müller, Jutta, *Otto H. Engel: Ein Künstlerleben um 1900 zwischen Berlin und Schleswig-Holstein* (Flensburg 1990).

Muller, Priscilla E. and Marcus B. Burke, *Sorolla: The Hispanic Society* (New York 2004).

Navascués Palacio, Pedro, 'Regionaliso y arquitectura en España (1900–1930)', *Arquitectura & Vivienda* 3 (1985) 28–36.

Navascués Palacio, Pedro, 'Nacionalismo, regionalismo y arquitectura' in: Idem, *Arquitectura española (1808–1914)* Summa Artis XXXV** (Madrid 1993) 668–707.

Nerdinger, Winfried, 'Bauhaus-Architekten im "Dritten Reich"', in: Winfried Nerdinger ed., *Bauhaus-Moderne im Nationalsozialismus: Zwischen Anbiederung und Verfolgung* (Munich 1993) 153–79.

Núñez, Xosé-Manoel, 'The Region as Essence of the Fatherland: Regionalist Variants of Spanish Nationalism (1840–1936)', *European History Quarterly* (2001) 483–518.

Núñez Seixas, Xosé M., 'De impuras naciones: Historiografía reciente y cuestión nacional en España', *Alcores* (2007) 211–39.

Núñez, Xosé-Manoel and Maiken Umbach, 'Hijacked Heimats: National Appropriations of Local and Regional Identities in Germany and Spain, 1930–1945', *European Review of History* XV (2008) 295–316.

Núñez, X. M., 'Überlegungen zum Problem der territorialen Identitäten: Provinz, Region und Nation im Spanien des 19. und 20. Jahrhunderts' in: Sven-Oliver Müller, Jörg Requate und Charlotte Tacke eds., *Unterwegs in Europa: Beiträge zu einer pluralen europäischen Geschichte* (Frankfurt am Main and New York 2008) 115–36.

Núñez Seixas, Xosé M. ed., *Ayer*, 64, *La construcción de la identidad regional en Europa y España (siglos XIX and XX)* (2006).

Oberkrone, Willi, *Volksgeschichte: Methodische Innovation und völkische Ideologisierung in der deutschen Geschichtswissenschaft, 1918–1945* (Göttingen 1993).

Olsen, Donald J., *The City as a Work of Art: London, Paris, Vienna* (New Haven and London 1986).

Orton, Fred and Griselda Pollock, 'Les Données bretonnantes: La Prairie de répresentation', *Art History*, 3 (1980) 314–45.

Ory, Pascal, 'Le Front Populaire et l'Exposition', in: Bertrand Lemoine ed., *Cinquantenaire de l'Exposition Internationale des Arts et des Techniques dans la Vie Moderne* (Paris 1987) 30–6.

Ory, Pascal, *La Belle Illusion: Culture et politique sous le signe du Front populaire 1935–1938* (Paris 1994).

Pabón, Jesús, *Cambó 1876–1918* (Barcelona 1952).

Paliza Monduate, Maite, *Manuel María de Smith Ibarra: Arquitecto* (Bilbao 1990).

Paret, Peter, *The Berlin Secession: Modernism and its Enemies in Imperial Germany* (Cambridge 1980).

Parsons, Christopher and Neil McWilliam, '"Le Paysan de Paris": Alfred Sensier and the Myth of Rural France', *Oxford Art Journal* (1983) 37–58.

Paul, Barbara, *Hugo von Tschudi und die moderne französische Kunst im deutschen Kaiserreich* (Mainz 1993).

Peer, Shanny, *France on Display: Peasants, Provincials, and Folklore in the 1937 Paris World's Fair* (New York 1998).

Peltz-Dreckmann, Ute, *Nationalsozialistischer Siedlungsbau: Versuch einer Analyse der die Siedlungspolitik bestimmenden Faktoren am Beispiel des Nationalsozialismus* (Munich 1978).

Pese, Claus ed., *Künstlerkolonien in Europa: Im Zeichen der Ebene und des Himmels* (Nuremberg 2001).

Petillon, Chantal and Didier Terrier, 'Une Corporation cheminote: Le travail et les hommes à la Compagnie de chemins de fer du Nord (1832–1937)', in: www.commission-historique59.com/bulletins/avril2005.html.

Petsch, Joachim, *Baukunst und Stadtplanung im Dritten Reich* (Munich and Vienna 1976).

Pike, Frederick B., *Hispanismo, 1898–1936: Spanish Conservatives and Liberals and their Relations with Spanish-America* (Notre Dame 1971).

Pinchon, Jean-François, 'La Conception et l'organisation de l'exposition' in: Bertrand Lemoine ed., *Cinquantenaire de l'Exposition Internationale des Arts et des Techniques dans la Vie Moderne* (Paris 1987) 36–43.

Plarre, Stefanie, *Die Kochenhofsiedlung – Das Gegenmodell zur Weißenhofsiedlung: Paul Schmitthenners Siedlungsprojekt in Stuttgart von 1927 bis 1933* (Stuttgart 2001).

Pommer, Richard and Christian F. Otto, *Weissenhof 1927 and the Modern Movement in Architecture* (Chicago 1991).

Power, Anne, *Hovels to High Rise: State Housing in Europe since 1850* (London and New York 1993).

Radkau, Joachim, *Das Zeitalter der Nervosität: Deutschland zwischen Bismarck und Hitler* (Darmstadt 1998).

Rebérioux, Madeleine, 'L'Exposition de 1937 et le contexte politique des années trente' in: Bertrand Lemoine ed., *Cinquantenaire de l'Exposition Internationale des Arts et des Techniques dans la Vie Moderne* (Paris 1987) 26–30.

Rennhofer, Maria, *Kunstzeitschriften der Jahrhundertwende in Deutschland und Österreich 1895–1914* (Vienna and Munich 1987).

Reyero, Carlos and Mireia Freixa, *Pintura y escultura en España (1800–1910)* (Madrid 1999).

Riquer, Borja de, 'La débil nacionalización española en el siglo XIX', *Historia Social* 20 (1994) 97–114.

Robb, Graham, *The Discovery of France: Historical Geography from the Revolution to the First World War* (New York and London 2007).

Rocamora, Juan Antonio, 'Un nacionalismo fracasado: el Iberismo', *Espacio, Tiempo y Forma*, V *Historia Contemporánea* (1989) 2, 29–56.

Rodríguez Bernal, Eduardo, *La Exposición Ibero-Americana de Sevilla de 1929 a través de la prensa local: Su génesis y primeras manifestaciones (1905–1914)* (Seville 1981).

Rodríguez Bernal, Eduardo, *Historia de la Exposición Ibero-Americana de Sevilla de 1929* (Seville 1994).

Rodríguez Llera, Ramón, 'Rucabado en Santander', *Arquitectos*, 57 (June 1982) 32–50.

Rollins, William H., *A Greener Vision of Home: Cultural Politics and Environmental Reform in the German Heimatschutz Movement 1904–1918* (Ann Arbor 1997).

Sahlins, Peter, *Boundaries: The Making of France and Spain in the Pyrenees* (Berkeley 1989).

Sánchez Gómez, Luis Ángel, 'África en Sevilla: La Exhibición colonial de la Exposición Iberoamericana de 1929', *Hispania* (2006) 1,045–82.

Santvoort, Linda van, Jan de Maeyer and Tom Verschaffel eds., *Sources of Regionalism in the Nineteenth Century: Art, Architecture and Literature* (Leuven 2008).

Schäfers, Stefanie, *Vom Werkbund zum Vierjahresplan: Die Ausstellung 'Schaffendes Volk', Düsseldorf 1937* (Düsseldorf 2001).

Scharfte, Martin, 'Hessisches Abendmahl: Exkurs zu Wissenschaft und Vergewisserung in volkskundlichem und folkloristischem Tableau', *Hessische Blätter für Volks- und Kulturforschung* (1990) 9–46.

Schollmeier, Axel, *Gartenstädte in Deutschland: Ihre Geschichte, Städtebaulicher Entwicklung und Architektur zu Beginn des 20. Jahrhunderts* (Münster 1990).

Schubert, Dirk ed., *Die Gartenstadtidee zwischen reaktionärer Ideologie und pragmatischer Umsetzung: Theodor Fritschs völkische Version der Gartenstadt* (Dortmund 2004).

Schwartz, Frederic J., *The Werkbund: Design Theory and Mass Culture before the First World War* (New Haven 1996).

Sigel, Paul, *Exponiert: Deutsche Pavillons auf Weltausstellungen* (Berlin 2000).

Silver, Kenneth E., *Esprit de Corps: The Art of the Parisian Avant-Garde and the First World War, 1914–1925* (Princeton and London 1989).

Silverman, Dan P., *Hitler's Economy: Nazi Work Creation Programs, 1933–1936* (Cambridge 1998).

Smelser, Ronald, *Robert Ley: Hitler's Labor Front Leader* (Oxford, New York, Hamburg 1988).

Smith, Anthony D., *The Ethnic Origins of Nations* (Oxford 1986).

Smith, Anthony D., *Nationalism and Modernism: A Critical Survey of Recent Theories of Nations and Nationalism* (London and New York 1998).

Smith, Timothy B., 'The Plight of the Able-Bodied Poor and Unemployed in Urban France, 1880–1914', *European History Quarterly* (2000) 147–84.

Solà-Morales, Ignasi de, *La Exposición Internacional de Barcelona 1914–1929: Arquitectura y Ciudad* (Barcelona 1985).

Speitkamp, Winfried, *Die Verwaltung der Geschichte: Denkmalpflege und Staat in Deutschland 1871–1933* (Göttingen 1996).

Sternhell, Zeev, *Maurice Barrès et le nationalisme français* (Paris 1972).

Stern, Fritz, *The Politics of Cultural Despair: A Study in the Rise of the Germanic Ideology* (Berkeley 1961).

Stoklund, Bjarne, 'The Role of International Exhibitions in the Construction of National Cultures in the 19th Century', *Ethnologia Europaea* XXIV (1994) 35–45.

Stoklund, Bjarne, 'How the Peasant House Became a National Symbol: A Chapter in the History of Museums and Nation-Building', *Ethnologia Europaea* XXIX (1999) 5–18.

Storm, Eric, *La perspectiva del progreso: Pensamiento político en la España del cambio de siglo (1890–1914)* (Madrid 2001).

Storm, Eric, 'Regionalism in History, 1890–1945: The Cultural Approach', *European History Quarterly* (2003) 251–65.

Storm, Eric, 'The Problems of the Spanish Nation-Building Process around 1900', *National Identities* (2004) 143–57.

Storm, Eric, 'Painting Regional Identities: Nationalism in the Arts, France, Germany and Spain, 1890–1914', *European History Quarterly* 557–82 (2009).

Suárez-Cortina, Manuel, *Casonas, hidalgos y linajes: La invención de la tradición cántabra* (Santander 1994).

Sutcliffe, Anthony, *Towards the Planned City: Germany, Britain, the United States and France 1870–1914* (New York 1981).

Sutcliffe, Anthony, 'Le Contexte urbanistique de l'oeuvre d'Henri Sellier: La transcription du modèle anglais de la cité-jardin' in: Katherine Burlen ed., *La Banlieue oasis: Henri Sellier et les cités-jardins, 1900–1940* (Saint-Denis 1987) 67–80.

Sutcliffe, Anthony, *Paris: An Architectural History* (New Haven and London 1993).

Tacke, Charlotte, 'National Symbols in France and Germany in the Nineteenth Century' in: Heinz-Gerhard Haupt, Michael Müller and Stuart Woolf eds., *Regional and National Identities in Europe in the XIXth and XXth Centuries* (The Hague 1998) 411–36.

Terán, Fernando de, *Historia del urbanismo en España III Siglos XIX y XX* (Madrid 1999).

Teut, Anna, *Architektur im Dritten Reich 1933–1945* (Frankfurt am Main 1967).

Ther, Philipp and Holm Sundhausen eds., *Regionale Bewegungen und Regionalismen in europäischen Zwischenräumen seit der Mitte des 19. Jahrhunderts* (Marburg 2003).

Thiesse, Anne-Marie, *Écrire la France. Le Mouvement littéraire régionaliste de langue française entre la Belle Epoque et la Libération* (Paris 1991).

Thiesse, Anne-Marie, *Ils apprenait la France: L'Exaltation des regions dans le discourse patriotique* (Paris 1997).

Thiesse, Anne-Marie, *La Création des identités nationales: Europe XVIIIe–XXe siècle* (Paris 1999).

Thomas, Greg M., 'The Topographical Aesthetic in French Tourism and Landscape' (2002) in http://19th-artworldwide.org/spring_02/articles/thom.html.

Thomson, Richard ed., *Framing France: The Representation of Landscape in France, 1870–1914* (Manchester and New York 1998).

Topalov, Christian 'Les "Réformateurs" et leurs reseaux: Enjeux d'un objet de recherche' in: Idem ed., *Laboratoires du nouveau siècle: La nébuleuse réformatrice et ses réseaux en France, 1880–1914* (Paris 1999) 11–61.

Toulier, Bernard, 'L'Assimilation du régionalisme dans l'architecture balnéaire', in: François Loyer and Bernard Toulier eds., *Le Régionalisme, architecture et identité* (Paris 2001) 96–110.

Tournoux, Marie-Noël, *Deauville: Les Styles normands: Itinéraires du patrimoine* (Deauville 1999).

Trillo de Leyva, Manuel, *La Exposición Iberoamericana: La transformación urbana de Sevilla* (Seville 1980).

Troy, Nancy J., *Modernism and the Decorative Arts in France: Art Nouveau to Le Corbusier* (New Haven and London 1991).

Tusell, Javier, *Arte, historia y política en España (1890–1939)* (Madrid 1999).

Udovicki, Danilo, 'Projets et concours', in: Bertrand Lemoine ed., *Cinquantenaire de l'Exposition Internationale des Arts et des Techniques dans la Vie Moderne* (Paris 1987) 44–66.

Umbach, Maiken, 'A Tale of Second Cities: Autonomy, Culture, and the Law in Hamburg and Barcelona in the Late Nineteenth Century', *American Historical Review* 110 (2005) 659–92.

Umbach, Maiken, 'Nation and Region: Regionalism in Modern European Nation-States' in: Timothy Baycroft and Mark Hewitson eds., *What is a Nation? Europe 1789–1914* (Oxford 2006) 63–81.

Urrutia, Ángel, *Arquitectura española del siglo XX* (Madrid 1997).

Varela, Javier, 'El mito de Castilla en la generación del 98', *Claves de la Razón Práctica* (December 1996) 10–18.

Vigato, Jean-Claude, *L'Architecture régionaliste. France 1890–1950* (Paris 1994).

Vigato, Jean Claude, 'La Cité-jardin et l'architecture régionaliste' in: Paulette Girard and Bruno Fayolle Lusac eds., *Cités, cités-jardins: Une histoire européene. Actes du colloque de Toulouse des 18 et 19 novembre 1993* (Toulouse 1996) 115–26.

Villar Movellán, Alberto, *La arquitectura del regionalismo en Sevilla (1900–1936)* (Seville 1975).

Villar Movellán, Alberto, 'Tres aspectos del historicismo regionalista: ética, libertad y clientela' in: José Joaquín Yarza Luaces and Francesca Español Bertrán eds., *Ve Congrés espanyol d'història de l'art* (Barcelona 1987) 199–204.

Weber, Eugen, *Peasants into Frenchmen: The Modernization of Rural France* (Stanford 1976).

Weber, Eugen, *The Hollow Years: France in the 1930s* (London 1995).

Weichlein, Siegfried, *Nation und Region: Integrationsprozesse im Bismarckreich* (Düsseldorf 2004).

Wesemael, Pieter van, *Architecture of Instruction and Delight: A Socio-Historical Analysis of World Exhibitions as a Didactic Phenomenon (1798–1851–1970)* (Rotterdam 2001).

Whalen, Philip, 'Burgundian Regionalism and French Republican Commercial Culture at the 1937 Paris International Exposition', *Cultural Analysis* 6 (2007) 31–69.

Wilson, Jeffrey K., 'Imagining a Homeland: Constructing Heimat in the German East, 1871–1914', *National Identities* (2007) 331–49.

Wörner, Martin, *Vergnügen und Belehren: Volkskultur auf den Weltausstellungen 1850–1900* (Münster 1999).

Wright, Julian, *The Regionalist Movement in France 1890–1914: Jean Charles-Brun and French Political Thought* (Oxford 2003).

Zimmer, Oliver, *Nationalism in Europe, 1890–1940* (Basingstoke and New York 2003).